THE HUB OF THE HIGHLANDS

The Book of Inverness and District

The Hub
of the Highlands

The Book of Inverness and District

*The Centenary Volume
of
Inverness Field Club
1875 - 1975*

Jointly published by the Inverness Field Club and
James Thin, The Mercat Press, Edinburgh

First published June, 1975, by
Inverness Field Club and Paul Harris
Reprinted 1990 by Inverness Field Club and
James Thin, The Mercat Press,
53-59 South Bridge, Edinburgh

ISBN 0 901824 93 3

Printed in Great Britain by Billing & Sons Ltd., Worcester

CONTENTS

LATER HISTORY

THE MODERN SCENE

LIST OF ILLUSTRATIONS

FOREWORD

Lord Cameron

It is a privilege to be permitted to write a brief foreword to this fascinating and timely volume, fascinating in its variety of Topic and the skill and learning brought to bear upon them, and timely in a period when the tide of industrial development is so rapidly rising and, in so doing, threatening to engulf so much of the structure and traditions of this Highland society. Even a glance at the table of contents is enough to testify to the breadth and depth of the studies which are here brought together.

This, the Centenary book of the Inverness Field Club, is a work which not only reflects the greatest credit on the Club for its conception and preparation, but represents a real and valuable contribution to the literature of the Highlands.

From the ordering of the hills and framing of the earth to the material problems of transport, trade and industry today and the impact of their solution on the history and economy of the region, it is all here, and not least the stormy history of this critically important area of Scotland. The story of St. Columba's confrontation with King Brude, the long internecine struggle of the Mormaers of Moray, with their Shakespearean overtones in the history of Macbeth, as told in Professor Barrow's authoritative exposition, as well as the more familiar tales of Jacobite risings and intrigues give the history itself a peculiar glamour, a history of the gradual emergence from violence and feud into a world of more sober and peaceful development. The story is unfolded with meticulous care and loving detail. But this is not merely a work of historical research.

Today Inverness and its surrounding district stand on the threshold of changes which will inevitably and radically alter much that is historic, valuable and familiar. It is hard to determine what price, in destruction or damage, must or should be paid for the material prosperity which these changes offer and are expected to bring, if not already bringing. To do so at least requires understanding of what is at stake and what are the real values which have to be balanced. The enterprise and care which have brought this volume to birth have rendered a great public service in recording, fairly and accurately, what are those assets which Nature and Man have created and provided, and in directing attention to the losses, often irreparable, which their heedless destruction or casting away could so easily cause.

I would earnestly commend this admirable work to all for whom the history and prosperity of this ancient and vital district of the Highlands is of concern, and counsel them to keep it, not on the higher shelves of their libraries, but at their elbows — a constant reminder that, as we are the heirs and beneficiaries of countless generations of Highlanders, so too are we all trustees of that heritage for their and our posterity.

INTRODUCTION

To commemorate the foundation one hundred years ago of the Inverness Scientific Society and Field Club, the Council of the Club present to the public this compilation of essays and articles. The volume is neither a complete guide nor a textbook, but aspires to stimulate interest in the countryside around the Highland Capital and arouse enthusiasm for the preservation of those works of our forefathers' dedicated craftmanship that still remain. The Council hope that it will be considered a fitting memorial to all those who, during the last century, enjoyed the companionship of kindred spirits in the study and appreciation of the countryside, and gratefully acknowledge their debt to all who played a part in the production of the book. Especially they thank the Honourable Lord Cameron for his elegant Foreword.

JAMES BRUCE,
President, Inverness Field Club,
1972-1975.

INTRODUCTION TO 1990 REPRINT

This is a reprint of *The Hub of the Highlands, the Book of Inverness and District*, the Centenary Volume of the Inverness Field Club. It first appeared in 1975 to mark that event, and has been out of print for some time. *The Hub*, as it is widely known, was written by thirty-two different authors, some of whom have since died, therefore it was thought that the contents of the chapters should not be changed, although the pace of discovery and change of opinion is so fast now that some would doubtless have been written differently had they come out new in 1990 instead of 1975.

The improved A9 road from the south, bringing not only the everyday supplies to the town, but also thousands of tourists during the lengthening season, the completion of the Kessock Bridge in 1982, the new Friars' Bridge over the river Ness in 1987 and the interior relief road that joins the two bridges avoiding the centre of Inverness, have made the Royal Burgh even more of a Hub than it was when this book was written. The development of the yards that build the rigs and modules for the oil wells in the North Sea and their associated housing have also affected the traffic in, through and round the burgh. The passengers at Dalcross Airport increase yearly and the Harbour is kept busy with supplies to the town, principally of oil, and the export of timber from the maturing forests in the hinterland. The railway north was struck when the Ness Bridge fell in seconds in February, 1989, but the new bridge is now complete and during the difficult year the passengers and goods were transported by road to Dingwall and continued their journeys from there.

Since 1975 the Inverness Field Club has published a number of books, *The Middle Ages in the Highlands*, and *The Seventeenth Century in the Highlands* being the collected papers given in 1980 and 1985. Others are *Old Inverness in Pictures* and *An Inverness Miscellany No. 1* and *No. 2*, as well as *The Glen Urquhart Story*. The 'Catchment Area' of the *Hub* was, in theory, at any rate, that part of the county of Inverness that the Founding Fathers could reasonably hope to reach in their Excursions. The basic maps were assumed to have a dotted line round them so that more distant places could be mentioned.

A Hub is the centre of a wide circle and this book can carry the reader from the geological complexities of the Great Glen Fault to the first regular British internal air mail, which flew from Inverness and to the frontispiece, which was taken by a passing satellite.

GEOFFREY GILL,
President, Inverness Field Club, 1990.

LORAINE MACLEAN OF DOCHGARROCH,
President, Inverness Field Club, 1984-1987.
Editor.

ACKNOWLEDGMENTS

Editors of such a collection as this have the pleasant duty to thank all those who have given so largely of their time and knowledge to make the book. This they do now, and they hope that all the contributors will accept their thanks. Their names are in the Table of Contents, but it should be mentioned here that the maps and the dust cover are the work of Edward Meldrum, and that he and William Glashan have also drawn the sketches which appear through the book at the end of chapters.

The Editors do not claim any wide knowledge and therefore must say that the opinions expressed by the learned authors are those of the writers of the articles. The time that must elapse between the writing and the reading of the book may even have outdated some of the views, so quickly do things change.

Our thanks are due as well to those who have supported us financially. First come the Members, who have been most generous in their loans and gifts. Then come the Town and County Councils of Inverness, the Inverness and Loch Ness Tourist Association, the University of Aberdeen and Trust Houses (Forte) Ltd. The Marc Fitch Fund made us a handsome grant, as did the Scottish Malt Distillers. We have also been greatly helped by the Highlands and Islands Development Board.

Having thus acknowledged the members and friends of the Club of the 1970's, their predecessors who have kept it alive for one hundred years must be remembered, too. In 1875, Mr William Jolly was the first President and some words from his first address to the Club will bear repeating. "Many good men are deterred from joining any Scientific Society by the idea that great erudition, much scientific knowledge and elaborate papers are asked for and are necessary to constitute efficient membership. Our objects, as a local association, are very much less ambitious and much more human and sensible. We are all learners."

Mr Jolly and his friends were fired by Professor Young's Ettles Lecture in November, 1875, and made an expedition to the Abriachan quarries in "a persistent rainfall, with a shroud of mist enveloping the valley and a steady depression of the barometer." Despite this damp outing, they enjoyed themselves so much that they at once took the Town Hall and formed the Inverness Scientific Society and Field Club. To them "Science" meant "Knowledge", but today its meaning is so much more limited that in 1973 the title was officially changed to the Inverness Field Club, which had been its accepted name for some time.

Over the first fifty years nine volumes of Transactions were published, recording the talks given, sometimes several short ones in an evening, and the expeditions to interesting places, but rising costs seem to have checked publication in the 1920s. The Transactions are constantly used by researchers into the wide range of subjects covered. The Public Library and the Museum are largely the result of the encouragement of the Club, which used to meet there yearly to inspect the latest gifts and loans. In 1971, following the very successful "Dark Ages Week" in 1970, a small book was published, "The Dark Ages in the Highlands," which contained most of the lectures given at that time and this, too, is well thought of.

From the original Rules, which were reviewed in 1973 and found to need scarcely any alteration, the Club is for "Study and Investigation and specially to Explore the District." "Members may be of either sex" and there were to be "readings of papers" from October to April and "Excursions during the summer months." Though the Club has had its ups and downs, these pursuits still continue, with coloured slides instead of the Magic Lantern and horse-power instead of horses. Though much has changed, so much remains from 1875 that Mr Jolly may be allowed to speak again.

"There exists amongst all an eager pursuit of certain aims in wealth, rank and social position, (but) the pursuit of mere power and pelf makes us narrow-souled, low-toned money seekers . . . This tendency it is our duty, our pleasure and our interest to endeavour to counteract . . . Science flows through our time like a wide and clean-flowing river . . . There is even a superabundance of objects of interest to which excursions can be made, even in our own neighbourhood. What we recommend is *recreative* science . . . The employment of our leisure moments, which we are to use for higher ends, in pursuits which will make us better business men, better parents and better citizens."

With Mr Jolly's ideals still before us as we move into

the Field Club's second century, we offer this book as an introduction to further visits to the "objects of interest" and as an attempt to explain to our fellow members and to those with an interest in these parts some of the many pieces that have come together over the centuries to make Inverness and District truly *The Hub of the Highlands*.

Editor: Loraine Maclean of Dochgarroch.

Editorial Committee: Alan Lawson, Edward Meldrum, Katharine Stewart.

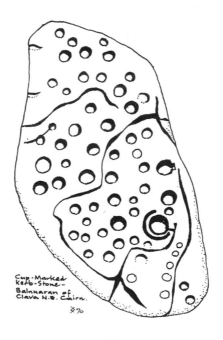

Cup-Marked
Kerb-Stone —
Balnuaran of
Clava N.E. Cairn.

THE NATURAL BACKGROUND

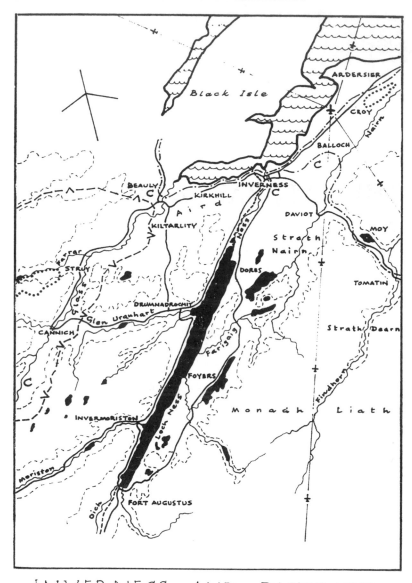

INVERNESS AND DISTRICT
DISTRIBUTION MAP 1

Road · ⌒   Rail · ⌐·⌐·   Canal ·⌐⌐⌐   Air ·⌐·⌐+·⌐·
305 M/1000 Ft Contour ·⌐⌐⌐·   National Park (proposed) · ⌐⌐∧⌐
Site of Special Scientific Interest · ·⌐·⌐·   Conservation Area · C

SCALE · 8 ... 5 ... 0 ... 5 ... 10 ... 15 KM
5 ... 0 ... 5 ... 10 MILES

LOOK TO THE ROCKS

GEOFFREY GILL

A book such as this must necessarily begin with Geology, for even a limited understanding of this science helps to explain every article that follows. The landscape that varies with every turn of the road, the stones that have been used in the buildings, the flowers and the style of agriculture, the lines of communication, the recent discovery of oil off-shore, all are related to the distant, but still continuing, geological history of this area. Unfortunately, Geology is a science that has its own jargon, and, though this article has been written as simply as possible, technical words are unavoidable, and so a glossary has been given at the end.

The dominant features of the landscape surrounding the Inner Moray Firth are considered principally to be the result of water erosion during the last 60-100 million years and of recent glacial action, but some of its broader features are due to the nature of the underlying rocks and the structural events which have effected them. Large tracts of country to the West of Inverness have been carved from highly metamorphosed sediments, which for the most part are thought to belong to the Pre-Cambrian Moine series. Except for small outcrops of Upper Jurassic sandstones and fossiliferous limestones and shales at Ethie in the Black Isle, the observable overlying sedimentary rocks belong entirely to the Middle and Upper Divisions of the Devonian Old Red Sandstone series.

In a region of considerable complexity, no component has had a greater impact on the erosional and sedimentary history than the north-east/south-west structural weakness associated with the Great Glen Fault and its continuation parallel to the south-east coastline of the Black Isle. This weakness, according to some recent statements, may have been in existence from Pre-Cambrian times.[1]

The Moine rocks vary rapidly in their appearance from place to place. Some are thinly laminated and flaggy, but more frequently they possess a contrasting, coarsely crystalline banded texture which is hard and resistant to erosion. Usually they consist almost entirely of muscovite and quartz, but hornblende may be an important additional mineral, and garnet may be abundant locally. Near Inverness they form the hilly ground on either side of the Moniack Burn, and also the broken country between the Upper Nairn and Loch Duntelchaig. The sea cliffs at Rosemarkie and the Cromarty Sutors reveal their eastern extent. Essentially they are the latest development of a mixed, well-sorted pile of sands and clays which, according to recent measurements near Carn Chuinneag, Ross-shire, are over 50,000 feet (15,545 m.) thick.[2] At every point where they are exposed, there is clear evidence that these rocks have been subjected to intense and repeated deforming earth movements. Small and large-scale folds are widespread and are, nearly everywhere, accompanied by well-developed textural features, of which schistosity and various types of linear structure are the most notable.

In those parts of the Highlands which have been mapped in detail, up to four such deformations have been discovered[3], but only two or three have been identified in the present area, where it is considered that the rocks underwent the most intense alterations during the last of these events. At this time the enormous crustal pressures created sufficient heat to cause localised melting and widespread re-crystallation of these ancient sediments. Always there is the clear imprint of increased temperature and the apparent mineralogical simplicity of the Moinian rocks belies a long and complicated metamorphic history.

Before the last decade, careful mapping and rock analyses had enabled workers on Highland geology to solve some of the many problems associated with Moinian stratigraphy. The advent of modern geochemical and physical techniques, however, have heralded significant advances and new interpretations[4]. Foremost among such developments has been the discovery of how to determine the age of whole rock and individual crystal by radiometric assay. As most Highland crystalline rocks are too much altered for any fossils they may contain to be preserved in a recognisable form, geologists had to await the arrival of these isotope dating methods before even a tentative regional chronology of Moinian events could be made. Within the last few years, following detailed geophysical surveys of our ocean floors, new theories, based on current ideas of continental drift, ocean floor spreading[5] and plate tectonics, have been advanced for the development of the mountain-building episodes responsible for the deformation of the Moinian sediments. A growing volume of evidence gives support to the suggestion that these deposits may not have been built up during a single phase of sedimentation, and that the metamorphic and structural events span a greater length of time than formerly was supposed. Certain distinctions based on chemical and structural analyses have been made between the Moines of the West Highlands and those further to the east, and an increasing number of isotopic dates from the former area, which give the whole rock and crystal ages of the order of 740-820 million years, suggest that these western sediments underwent a period of deformation at that time. If the laboratory data have been correctly interpreted, these dates imply that a significant part of the Moinian succession must be older than 800 million years, and that the lowest division, at least, was subject to a Pre-Cambrian deformation approximately 700 million years ago, before the laying down of the Upper Moine sediments[6] which probably occur in the Inverness area.

In 1969, following the rapid advances in global tectonics, J. F. Dewey[7] suggested that approximately 500 million years ago, in Lower Ordovician times, a consuming plate margin and an associated oceanic trough developed on the northern edge of the present-day Southern Uplands of Scotland. The Inverness area was then part of the continental slope of a proto-Atlantic ocean, which had been receiving Moinian sediments from a northerly source since Pre-Cambrian times. A hundred million years of ocean closure and crustal compression along the margin of the consuming plate, terminating in Lower Old Red Sandstone times, led to the upheaval and folding of the sediments — a sequence which follows the traditional chronology of Caledonian events. The term "proto-Atlantic ocean" is often used to describe this ancient ocean on account of the remarkable correspondence in the alignment of the Caledonian mountain structures and the present-day mid-Atlantic ridge.[8]

This theory has recently been questioned[9] and it is suggested now that, instead of representing a long, passive phase of sedimentation, followed by a short mountain-building period, the Moine rocks reflect three distinct episodes of mountain-building activity, two of which may pre-date Caledonian times. During a long period of earth's history, erosional debris was annealed to the northern continental area as a consuming plate margin moved away from the continental nucleus (Fig. 1). This theory depends, not only on isotope dates, but also on the correct identification of certain rock assemblages within the Moine series, which may be the altered sediments and lavas of a type usually associated with earthquake-prone, deep marine troughs of more recent times. In the Inverness area, attention has been

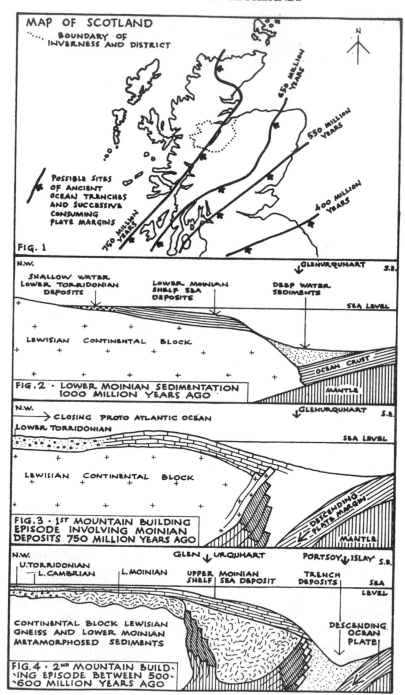

MAP OF SCOTLAND

BOUNDARY OF INVERNESS AND DISTRICT

POSSIBLE SITES OF ANCIENT OCEAN TRENCHES AND SUCCESSIVE CONSUMING PLATE MARGINS

650 MILLION YEARS

550 MILLION YEARS

400 MILLION YEARS

750 MILLION YEARS

FIG. 1

N.W.   GLENURQUHART   S.E.

SHALLOW WATER LOWER TORRIDONIAN DEPOSITS

LOWER MOINIAN SHELF SEA DEPOSITS

DEEP WATER SEDIMENTS

SEA LEVEL

LEWISIAN CONTINENTAL BLOCK

OCEAN CRUST

MANTLE

FIG. 2 · LOWER MOINIAN SEDIMENTATION 1000 MILLION YEARS AGO

N.W.   GLENURQUHART   S.E.

CLOSING PROTO ATLANTIC OCEAN

LOWER TORRIDONIAN

SEA LEVEL

LEWISIAN CONTINENTAL BLOCK

DESCENDING PLATE MARGIN

MANTLE

FIG. 3 · 1ST MOUNTAIN BUILDING EPISODE INVOLVING MOINIAN DEPOSITS 750 MILLION YEARS AGO

N.W.   GLEN URQUHART   PORTSOY ISLAY   S.E.

U.TORRIDONIAN L.CAMBRIAN

L. MOINIAN

UPPER MOINIAN SHELF SEA DEPOSIT

TRENCH DEPOSITS

SEA LEVEL

CONTINENTAL BLOCK LEWISIAN GNEISS AND LOWER MOINIAN METAMORPHOSED SEDIMENTS

DESCENDING OCEAN PLATE

FIG. 4 · 2ND MOUNTAIN BUILDING EPISODE BETWEEN 500-600 MILLION YEARS AGO drawn to certain crystalline rocks which outcrop to the west of the Great Glen, between Nigg and Glen Urquhart. The occurrence of slices of hornblende-rich rock in Easter Ross, serpentines and peridotites near Loch Gorm, garnet-bearing gneiss at Rosemarkie, and crystalline limestones at Rebeg and Glen Urquhart could indicate the position, some 1,000 million years ago, of an ocean plate margin[10] (Fig. 2). If this is so, a deep water trench of an ancient ocean basin may have followed the approximate path of the Great Glen Fault from Easter Ross to Ardgour in Northern Argyll, while, somewhere to the north-west, an old Lewisian land mass provided sediments for the adjacent Lower Moinian shelf seas. The closure of this ocean and the thrusting at the plate margin, some 750 million years ago, folded and uplifted these sediments, adding new land to the continental region (Fig. 3). So ended the first episode.

The second is thought to have begun about 50 million years later, with the development of an ocean plate margin to the south of the new continental area, along a line through what is now Portsoy, Glen Lui and Islay. Continental erosion of the Lewisian basement rocks and the metamorphosed deposits of the earlier episode now provided sediments for the Upper Moinian shelf seas which covered the site of the Great Glen trough (Fig 4). It ended in Upper Pre-Cambrian-Lower Cambrian times, when crustal compression associated with the descending plate margin folded and metamorphosed these sediments, and the accompanying volcanic activity produced such features as the epidiorite sills which today form tiny discontinuous outcrops between Abriachan and Farley.

The third episode began about 550 million years ago, in mid-Cambrian times, with the re-birth of the proto-Atlantic ocean and the development of a consuming plate margin to the north of the present-day Southern Uplands. The concluding earth movements, about 500 million years ago, in Lower Ordovician times, resulted in a deformation and metamorphic episode which overprinted the earlier events which had affected the Moinian rocks. Later still, some 400 million years ago, in Lower Devonian times, further mountain-building activity produced the granite masses of Foyers, Abriachan and Moy, the pegmatite veins of Erchless and Farley, and the dykes of dark minette at Easter Croachail in Strathglass. By then, the consuming plate margin lay to the south of the Southern Uplands.

Neither of these theories can be definitive statements, as supporting field evidence is limited and difficult to evaluate;

also the concept of plate tectonics, while gaining increased support by earth scientists, is by no means universally accepted. The theories should, however, serve to illuminate part of the Dark Ages in Highland geology.

The presence of such minerals as andalusite and silliminite in the envelope of the heat-altered rocks surrounding the Foyers granitic complex, indicates that this intrusive body was emplaced at a depth of about four miles within the Moinian cover, suggesting that by Lower Old Red Sandstone times, the Inner Moray Firth must have been an upland area of considerable elevation. By Middle Old Red Sandstone times, however, the surface had been worn down to the upper levels of the intrusion, as large blocks of the constituent granite material can be found in the overlying sediments deposited at this time. In what is relatively a short space of geological time of about 20 million years, over 20,000 feet (6095 m.) of Moinian schists were stripped from the Foyers uplands[11].

The coarse breccias and conglomerates which occur at the base of the Middle Old Red Sandstone succession, form conspicuous features of the landscape today. The examples to be seen at Tor Achilty, Aigas and Meall nan Caorach form the western limits of the series, and fine roadside sections occur further to the east at Clachnaharry, where the conglomeratic beds of Craig Phadrig and Ord Hill are breached by the Kessock Narrows.

It is clear from the way in which they are dispersed in fans fringing the high ground of metamorphic rocks, and from the rapid lateral variations in the lower beds that, at least during the earlier periods of deposition, the Inner Moray Firth formed a basin in which the strata accumulated. The individual contacts of the Moine and Middle Old Red Sandstone sediments in north-east Scotland have been analysed by Godard[12], who has shown that the ancient basement rocks often plunge steeply under the sandstone at gradients often greater than 40°. Such an irregular plane of unconformity suggests the rapid internment of the existing landscape. An example of this buried landscape is clearly exhibited at Carn Dearg, two miles southwest of Foyers, where a hill of Moine schists is flanked on three sides by basal breccias dipping outwards from the hill. Careful mapping by Stevenson[13] has recently demonstrated that at Foyers, Middle Old Red Sandstone sediments probably originated in an alluvial fan environment on the edge of a fault-bounded mountain area to the south-east, and that a continuous piedmont deposit of grits, sandstones and shales formed at the foot of a scarp in an intermontane basin, which was part of a series of such features along the line of the present Great Glen. In all probability, the basal breccias were formed from talus spreads on the mountain sides. There is evidence from Foyers which suggests that the screes were re-worked by violent spates, as their channels are deeply cut through the earlier layers of debris and the basement rocks. Also, the presence of fresh feldspar crystals in the piedmont grits, with mud-cracks and rain-prints in the shales, indicate that the climate was subject to periods of drought. Examples of these rain-prints and silt-filled mud-cracks can be seen in the green shales exposed in the small roadside quarry at Castle Kitchie, about two miles north-east of Inverfarigaig.

Although it is difficult to make comparisons with present day landscapes, the nature of the Foyers uplands in Middle Old Red Sandstone times appears to be very similar to the fault-bounded Death Valley of California, with its fringing bajadas, arroyos and desert pavements[15].

Gradually, as the old land surface was buried, so pro-gressively higher horizons of the Middle Old Red Sandstone succession overlapped on to the crystalline rocks. This is par-ticularly well shown at Clava, near Culloden Moor. The outlier of Old Red Sandstone deposits in the Findhorn gorge at Shenachie clearly indicates a more widespread burial of the eastern Highland landscape than is indicated by the present Middle Old Red Sandstone outcrop. A slow crustal down-warping of the Moray Firth area enabled the several thousand feet of sandstones and shales to accumulate, which today forms the land between the Beauly and Dornoch Firths and to the south-east of Inverness between Foyers and Nairn.

Over the years, the limestone bands and nodules occurring in the Middle Old Red Sandstone succession have attracted considerable attention. Ever since the day when Hugh Miller found his "effigy of a creature," the fossil fish, which tend to occur in these nodules, have been the source of much scientific interest. These ancient fish faunas of the Inner Moray Firth are very similar to those occurring in the classic Middle Old Red Sandstone flagstone exposures at Achanaras in Caithness. Fish remains and fragmentary land plants have been obtained from the north-west shore of Lochan an Eoin Ruadha, near Loch Ashie, and from Clava Bridge, but details of the exact sites where they were found are hard to get, and many of the specimens were collected long ago. Over the years, the most productive sites appear to have been at Ethie and at the old limestone quarries at Lethen, near Nairn.

The Middle Old Red Sandstone series underwent a period

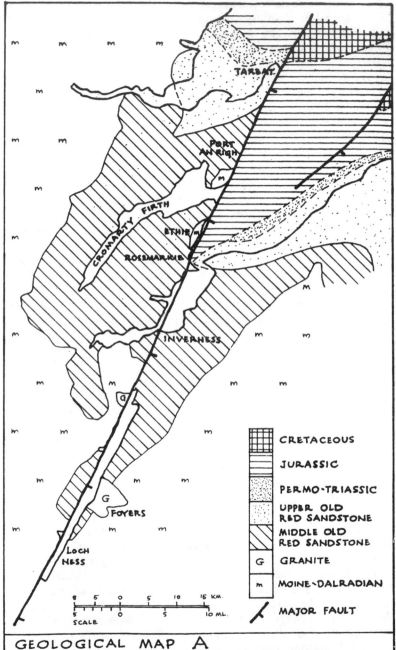

TARBAT

PORT AN RIGH

CROMARTY FIRTH

ETHIE

ROSEMARKIE

INVERNESS

G

G

FOYERS

LOCH NESS

CRETACEOUS

JURASSIC

PERMO-TRIASSIC

UPPER OLD
RED SANDSTONE

MIDDLE OLD
RED SANDSTONE

G   GRANITE

m   MOINE-DALRADIAN

MAJOR FAULT

5 5 0 5 10 15 KM.
5   0   5   10 ML.
SCALE

GEOLOGICAL MAP A
PRESENT DAY DISTRIBUTION OF ROCK TYPES IN THE
INNER MORAY FIRTH AREA

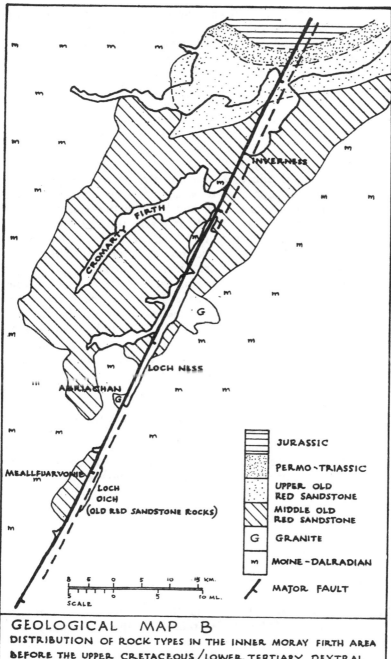

GEOLOGICAL MAP B
DISTRIBUTION OF ROCK TYPES IN THE INNER MORAY FIRTH AREA
BEFORE THE UPPER CRETACEOUS/LOWER TERTIARY DEXTRAL
MOVEMENT ALONG THE GREAT GLEN FAULT

of gentle warping and erosion before the deposition of Upper Old Red Sandstone sediments. Today, rocks of this age outcrop between Tain and Tarbet Ness, and extend eastwards from Ardersier, but for the most part they are buried by material carried by Pleistocene ice and glacial meltwater streams. Where they are exposed in river sections and small quarries, the rocks indicate, through the presence of ripple marks, sun cracks and other sedimentary structures, a landscape of low mountains and flat plains subject to periods of desert-like conditions[16].

The deep trench-like hollow of the Great Glen has long attracted attention by virtue of its great length, straightness and topographical effect. Unfortunately, its true magnitude is not always readily appreciated because of recent glacial infilling and submergence at its eastern end beneath the waters of Loch Ness and the Inner Moray Firth. It marks the trace of a major fault system of great antiquity which, within historical times, formed one of the principal seismic lines in the British Isles. Between 1768 and 1906, more than 56 earthquakes occurred along this line, mostly centred in the Inverness area[17]. None, however, has been recorded since 1934. At the surface, the fault system is marked by a zone of crushed, sheared and finely powdered rocks between $1\frac{1}{2}$ and $2\frac{1}{2}$ miles (2.4 - 4 km.) wide[18], and in addition it appears to separate areas of distinct structural style and rocks of different ages and metamorphic characteristics. Historically, the first reference to the Great Glen Fault was made to Members of the Geological Society by Sir Roderick Murchison and Sir Archibald Geikie in 1861[19], when they stated that the "fracture is more extensive than any other in the country." About 50 years later, in 1914, J. Horne and L. W. Hinxman[20], reporting the results of their survey work in the Inverness and Beauly area, described the features as a normal fault, which had allowed the land to the east to subside some 6,000 feet (1830 m.) to that on the opposite side of the fault.

In 1946, however, Kennedy[21] made the revolutionary suggestion that the Great Glen Fault, far from being the product of vertical displacement, was, in fact, the result of a large-scale lateral movement of many miles in Pre-Upper Carboniferous times, whereby the land to the east had moved 65 miles north-eastwards relative to that on the opposite side of the Fault Plane. He pointed to such indirect evidence as the straightness of the fault trace, and the abnormally wide shatter-belt, both features characteristic of transcurrent faults in other parts of the world. More specifically, he tried to show that certain structures which occur on either side of the fault had a common origin and had been intersected and displaced by the fault. In particular, he drew attention to the apparently close similarity between the Foyers and Strontian granitic intrusions, and their relationship to the adjacent metamorphic rocks. This suggestion has been questioned[22], although it has also been argued that these granitic masses have a common origin and that the differences which have been demonstrated are due to the fact that more of the component granites have been eroded from the Strontian complex than at Foyers, as a result of vertical movements along the Fault[23].

The resurgence of interest in the Fault system during the last few years stems from a more detailed geological knowledge of the area and from the developments in ocean floor tectonics. There appears to be agreement on the transcurrent nature of the fracture, although minor vertical movements are now known to have taken place[24]. There is, however, considerable diversity of opinion on the timing and direction of the movement.

In 1969, Holgate[25], in a detailed account of the structure, pointed out that, if the land lying to the east of the Fault were moved approximately 18 miles (30 km.) south-westwards, the continuous nature of the outcrops of the Old Red Sandstone series and the Moray Firth Mesozoic sediments at Ethie, Port an Righ and Brora would be restored (Map B). Also the massive Middle Old Red Sandstone conglomerates at Foyers, which are quite different lithologically from the rocks thought to be of similar age at Mealfourvonie, would then match very well with the conglomerates between Clachnaharry and Kessock. Several faults associated with the Great Glen system can be seen between Inverfarigaig and Foyers, cutting the Moinian, Middle Old Red Sandstone and granite rocks of the Foyers intrusion. As the granites are known to be Lower Old Red Sandstone in age, the faulting must have occurred after their emplacement. In addition, the metamorphic rocks appear to have undergone far greater crushing than the sedimentary deposits, giving support to the suggestion that the first great movement along the fault took place before Middle Old Red Sandstone times, and was probably associated with the later episodes of the Caledonian mountain-building activity. Following a study of the Tertiary dyke swarms of Loch Linnhe and Lismore, the central igneous complex of Mull, and the Great Glen drainage system, Holgate concluded that the 18 mile dextral movement must have taken place between 50-60 million years ago, in Lower Eocene times. If the Foyers / Strontian intrusions have a common origin, and Holgate's Eocene movements did occur, the earlier sinistral displacements must have been approximately 83 miles (133 km.) Supporting evidence for large-scale sinistral movements has recently been provided. Following detailed petrological and X-ray analysis of over 240 gneissose rock specimens collected from a wide area of metamorphic rocks on either side of the Great Glen Fault, J. A. Winchester has been able to redefine the pattern of regional metamorphism within the Moinian outcrops. The current disposition of the major elements of this pattern suggest that such movements must have been in the region of 100 miles (160 km.)[26].

Commenting on the history of the Fault, Garson and Plant[27] have questioned the need for a Lower Old Red Sandstone sinistral movement. They argue that the well-known physical differences between the Foyers/Strontian granites preclude a common origin, and the distribution of certain metamorphic rock types near Foyers match equally well with those in Caithness as with those near Strontian. They maintain that the present position of all the rocks of Pre-Lower Devonian age intersected by the Great Glen Fault can be explained adequately by a 55-60 mile (88-96 km.) dextral movement after the emplacement of the Caledonian granites. Later, after the deposition of the younger sedimentary rocks of the Moray Firth area, there occurred a further displacement of some 20 miles (32 km.) in the same direction during Upper Cretaceous times.

Such widely varied statements patently indicate a dearth of definite facts about the nature and origin of this fault system. Although it is thought that the present Atlantic ocean came into existence relatively recently, in Upper Jurassic times[28], it may be rather premature to consider the Great Glen fracture to be part of a global structure extending from Spitzbergen to the Maritime Provinces of Canada[29]. If the present-day rate of movement along the transcurrent San Andreas Fault of California is maintained, Los Angeles will become, in about 50 million years, the twin town of San Francisco. On such a time scale, it is not too far-reaching to suggest that lateral shifts of several score miles could have occurred along the Great Glen Fault, and that, in former times, the geological foundations of Inverness may well have lain adjacent to the site of modern Corpach in Lochaber, or Wick in Caithness. A recent series of lectures held in Inverness was entitled "The Unstable Earth," and in this short article an attempt has been made to show both the instability and the durability of our area. Most of what has been shown here can only be as yet theory, possibility, surmise. any one of which may be over-turned by future discoveries.

GLOSSARY

BRECCIA — A rock composed of a consolidated mass of angular fragments.

CONGLOMERATE — A rock consisting of a consolidated mass of well-rounded pebbles set in a finer matrix.

DEXTRAL — When the observer views the Fault, plane motion on the distant side will be towards the right.

EPIDIORITE — A name given to metamorphosed basic igneous rock. During the alteration process, hornblende usually replaces augite.

GNEISS — A metamorphic rock, frequently with a mineral composition resembling that of granite, but the constituents are arranged in bands or folia.

GRANITE — A coarsely grained igneous rock, consisting essentially of quartz, orthoclase feldspar, muscovite and/or biotite.

MINETTE — A dark alkali-rich igneous rock, exhibiting large crystals of biotite and augite in a ground mass of alkali feldspar.

OCEAN FLOOR SPREADING — Where two crustal plates drift apart, fissuring allows the upwelling of the basaltic material which is annealed to the plate edges. As such fissures occur in the middle of the ocean floor, the continents embedded in the plate slowly separate.

PERIDOTITE — An igneous rock consisting largely of olivine with some pyroxene. The rock is entirely devoid of feldspar.

PLATE TECTONICS — The notion that the earth's crust consists of plates that are created at one edge and destroyed at the other. They float in the mantle, describing a circular path on the sphere of the earth.

SERPENTINITES — These rocks mainly consist of the mineral serpentine.

SINISTRAL — When the observer views the Fault, plane motion on the distant side will be towards the left.

TRANSCURRENT FAULT — A horizontal shearing movement in a near vertical plane, due to compressive stress. The terms tear or wrench are often used to describe this type of fault.

UNCONFORMITY — A fundamental break between two phases of deposition.

WARP — The gentle flexing of the crustal rocks of the earth.

REFERENCES

1. Garson, M. S., & Plant, J., *Nature Physical Sc.* Vol. 242, 1973.
2. Shepherd, J., *Scot. Journal Geol.* Vol 9, 1973.
3. Johnson (ed.), *The British Caledonides,* Oliver & Boyd, Edinburgh, 1963.
4. Giletti, B. J., Moorbath, S., and Lambert, R. St. John, *Q.J.G.S.* Vol. CXVIII.
5. Dietz, R. S., *Nature* Vol. 190, 1961.
6. Dunning, F. W., *Scot. Journal Geol.* Vol. 8, 1972.
7. Dewey, J. F., *Nature* Vol. 222, April 1969.
8. Wilson, J. T., *Nature* Vol. 211, 1966.
9. Garson, M. S., & Plant, J., *Nature Physical Sc.* Vol 242, 1973.
10. Garson, M. S., & Plant, J., *Nature Physical Sc.* Vol 242, 1973.
11. Marston, R. J., *Q.J.G.S.* Vol 126, 1971.
12. Godard, A., *Recherches de Geomorphologie en Ecosse du Nord-Ouest,* Paris, 1965.
13. Stevenson, D., *Scot. Journal Geol.* Vol 8(2), 1972.
14. Stevenson, D., *Scot. Journal Geol.* Vol 8(2), 1972.
15. Van Engeln, *Geomorphology,* Macmillan, New York, 1949.
16. Johnstone, G. S., "The Grampian Highlands," *Brit. Reg. Geol.,* 1966.
17. Ahmad, M. U., *Nature,* January, 1967.
18. Garson, M. S., & Plant, J., *Nature Physical Sc.* Vol 240, 1972.
19. Murchison, R.I., & Geikie, A., *Q.J.G.S.* Vol 17, 1861.
20. Horne, J., & Hinxman, L. W., *Mem. Geol. Serv.,* 1914.
21. Kennedy, W. Q., *Q.J.G.S.* Vol 102, 1946.
22. Munro, M., *Scot. Journal Geol.* Vol 1, p. 152, 1965.
23. Marston, R. J., *Nature* Vol 214, April 1967.
24. McQuillan, R., & Binns, P. E., *Nature Physical Sc.* Vol 241, 1973.
25. Holgate, N., *Scot. Journal Geol.* Vol 5(2), 1969.
26. Winchester, J. A., *Nature Physical Sc.* Vol 246, 1973.
27. Garson, M. S., & Plant, J., *Nature Physical Sc.* Vol 240, 1972.
28. Funnell, B. M., & Smith, A. Gilbert, *Nature* Vol 219, 1968.
29. Wilson, J. T., *Nature* Vol 195, 1962.

GEOMORPHIC EVOLUTION

JOHN SMITH

The area under consideration comprises the easterly flowing straths of the Farrar, Affric and Cannich, which together feed the Beauly system, the Ness drainage basin centred on Loch Ness, and parts of the central Nairn and Findhorn Valleys. These valley systems drain a dissected plateau of Moine rock series, and pass into the Moray Firth coastlands, which are floored by Old Red Sandstone rocks. The western boundary of the Old Red Sandstone series consists of basal conglomerates and breccias forming a rim of tabular hills, in contrast to the more subdued country of the Moine series. Faulting has created lines of structural weakness which have acted as major factors influencing drainage evolution. The most notable of these are the Great Glen and Strath Glass faults which have been subsequently exploited by weathering and glacial processes to create major valleys which cut across the generally easterly trending component of drainage.

Although influenced by the downwarped basin of the Moray Firth, the drainage network carries remnants of the original consequent river pattern of the Scottish Highlands[4]. The reconstructed Cenomanian drainage pattern is clearly visible in the upper parts of Affric, Farrar and Glen Urquhart. The major fault-lines, with their relatively wide fracture zones, have captured previously easterly flowing streams and diverted them northwards. Glen Affric, for example, is clearly part of a major stream which at one time flowed due east through Glen Urquhart, while the upper Findhorn originally flowed into the Nairn through the Moy depression before being diverted into the Shenachie gorge. Dating of these events is problematic, but glacial meltwaters have clearly assisted in the cutting of the Findhorn gorge. Although the original surface on which the streams were initiated have disappeared, the stages in downcutting are visible in the form of upland erosion surfaces.

The preglacial pattern of relief and drainage has been remodelled by the events of the Pleistocene period, during which ice-sheets overdeepened existing valley systems and formed the unconsolidated deposits which today form the soil resources within the area. The great interest of past members of the

C

Inverness Field Club in the events of glaciation is reflected by the articles in the Transactions which deal with it. Their observations form the basis for the description of glacial events which follows.

No evidence exists within the area of the maximal dimensions of the Pleistocene icesheets. The extensive peat cover on the high interfluves, together with the sheets of frost-shattered debris on the tops, especially around the Monar basin, conceals erratic carry. The relative homogeneity of the countryrock and the lack of detailed geological mapping are additional factors limiting the tracing of the horizontal or vertical distribution of erratics. Evidence elsewhere in the Highlands of Scotland, however, indicates a maximal thickness of ice some 4,000 to 5,000 feet (1220-1525m) above sea level sloping eastwards from around the present watershed[8]. The distinctive Inchbae augengneiss has been traced both east and west of the present watershed, indicating oscillations of the position of the iceshed[2], and the eastern component of the erratic carry extends on to the Black Isle and coastal Moray. A predominantly easterly flow is also indicated by the numerous striae recorded south and east of Inverness[10]. The eastern boundary of the Old Red Sandstone outcrop along the Great Glen can also be used to trace easterly carry of boulders towards Strath Nairn.

A north-easterly component of ice flow had been recognised through the carry of Strath Errick granites, indicating that the Great Glen functioned as a major axis of ice flow, but that the flow was diverted eastwards into the Moray Firth coastland by ice from central Ross-shire. Striae near the western watersheds of the Fannich and Affric systems indicate a westerly flow of ice across the watershed at one time, in sympathy with the westerly carry of Inchbae erratics through the Dirie Mor towards Loch Broom. Iceshed migration, possibly as a result of the climatic role played by the North Atlantic sea, must have assisted in the pattern of watershed breaching evident in Upper Glen Affric, creating a system of low passes through to the west coast of the mainland[5].

Striae and Rannoch granite carry north-eastwards down the Spey valley suggest another major ice dispersal centre in the South-West Grampians deflected eastwards in lower Strath Nairn by the powerful stream from the interior of Ross. A movement of ice from beyond the coastline to the land is indicated by the controversial Clava deposit in lower Strath Nairn[7]. The deposit, which was studied in great detail by a committee of British Association experts in 1893, consists of blue shell-rich clay sandwiched between till and gravel, both of which contain high proportions of Old Red Sandstone material. Within the clay occurred Jurassic derived material and a low proportion of Old Red Sandstone material, indicating erratic carry from the north at a time predating the north-easterly ice movement described above. The Clava shell bed is most likely to be a total erratic, subsequently covered by materials deposited by the most recent major glaciation. The nearest known locality for Jurassic material outcrop is at Ethie on the eastern Black Isle coast.

During the period of maximum glaciation, ice seems to have moved freely from one valley system to the next. Ice-worn cols indicate a movement westward from the Loch Monar basin into Strath Carron, and eastwards into the head of Glen Orrin, in both cases in excess of 2,000 feet (608 m) above sea level. Caorann Mor, Glen Licht and Glen Gaorsaic are excellent examples of ice-breached cols leading west and south from the head of Glen Affric. Considerable overdeepening of pre-existing valleys also occurred, notably Loch Ness, Loch Affric and Loch Monar. These, together with many others, occupy rock basins of glacial origin. Striae also indicate that there was ice movement from Glen Cannich in an east-northeastwards direction, and from Glen Strath Farrar into Glen Cannich.

Additional rock basins occur below great thicknesses of glacial and marine deposits. A three hundred foot bore in the Ness valley in 1893 passed through fluvioglacial deposits without reaching bedrock, indicating that the Loch Ness basin continues through to the Beauly Firth. The numerous corries etched into the inland straths were created at the onset of glaciation in the vicinity of the snowline. As the ice surfaces built up, they were overwhelmed by the icesheet, but were re-occupied by glaciers and functioned as ice sources in the late-glacial period.

The pattern of deglaciation has been responsible for the major depositional landforms within the area. As many of these occur near the present coastline, to understand their origin fully, it is important to note that during maximum glaciation, world sea level fell to almost 300 feet (90 m) below present sea level. The weight of land ice was sufficient to depress the regional crust by a figure of several hundred feet. Melting of world ice bodies, beginning some 18,000 years ago, progressively raised sea level, while regional ice loads were shed, resulting in a slow but consistent recovery of depressed crust. Melting of the Scottish ice sheet through downcasting, progressively exposed sections of coastline on which shorelines could be cut, but it is likely that a considerable amount of crustal recovery had taken place before land was exposed on which shorelines could be cut. Older shorelines now lie buried beneath the Moray Firth. The more recent story of crustal adjustment and sea level rise is recorded through the altitude and distribution of raised shorelines, which indicate changing land-sea relationships, i.e., the position of the shoreline.

Deglaciaton in this area took the form of substantial periods of retreat, punctuated by periods when the ice margin was stabilised or, on occasion, pushed forward over territory previously vacated. At such periods, substantial ice-contact deposits accumulated around its margin. These largely water-laid deposits of sand and gravel take the form of ridges, terraces and irregular mounds according to the exact conditions of their formation either within, around, or on top of the ice. In several cases, the sand and gravel was deposited from the ice into the sea. In general, the sand and gravel deposits occur within valley bottoms where the main volume of glacial meltwater was funnelled. The depositional materials are frequently associated with meltwater channels which appear in the landscape as dry valleys, often with no relationship to existing drainage networks. Good examples of meltwater channels occur in the High Wood, Culloden Forest, along the northern flanks of Glen Affric, and the Slochd Mor which carries the A9 trunk road south towards Tomatin. The erosive power of meltwater is testified by the impressive gorges at Foyers and Inverfarigaig.

Sinuous ice contact esker ridges occur in conjunction with kettleholes and kame terraces in the Ness narrows between Dochgarroch and Inverness, culminating in the 200 foot (60 m) esker of Tomnahurich and Torvean, which dominates the city of Inverness. Successive downcasting of the ice left the kame terrace sequence on the north side of Strath Nairn beside Clava. In the Ness valley, these fluvioglacial features rest on the boulder clay. The Flemington esker system runs eastwards for eight miles (12 km.) from Culaird past Loch Flemington to Meikle Kildrummie, and takes the form of a complex pattern of braided ridges, a mirror-image of the sub-glacial streams which constructed them in tunnels under the ice. Large quantities of sand and gravel were built out from the ice into high sea levels, in delta forms, at Muir of Ord, Lovat Bridge and the lower end of Glen Urquhart. The various terrace remnants surviving represent the stages in downcutting as land-sea relationships changed. As the icesheet downwasted and retreated further, deposition of meltwater forms extended up-valley, but only in Strath Nairn are the ice-contact fluvioglacial forms repeated on the scale found in the lower valleys. Most of the upland parts of the area testify rather to the erosive power of ice. Signs of excessive downcasting occur, however, in the form of marginal meltwater channels, kame terraces and ablation blocks, suggesting a prolonged period of retreat and virtual ice stagnation. Glen Glasha, a high side valley of Glen Affric, contains a small esker system orientated across valley, which dams up Loch an Sguid. Its cross valley pattern suggests a sub-glacial origin.

Important stadial positions of the ice margin can be recognised at Fortrose-Ardersier, where largely water-laid deposits have been re-modelled through a succession of changing sea levels into cuspate forelands. Sections in the old sea cliff behind Ardersier reveal a sandy deposit with extensive folding and faulting of the beds. Its appearance is very reminiscent of rucked-up marine silts and sands, and it is significant that Jamieson recorded finding blue clay with marine shells there in 1884[1]. Westwards, important deglaciation stages have been recognised at Garve, lower Glen Urquhart and at the entrance to the Beauly gorge system. The last three stages were probably contemporaneous and coincidental with a sea level some 90 feet (30 m) above the present shoreline. At this period, the sea penetrated into Loch Ness and high shorelines were cut in favourable sites along the shores of the Loch. There followed a long period of extensive ice melting, with a small ice-re-advance evidenced by small end-moraines sitting in the high corries of the interior, particularly those facing north. Examples of this can be seen in Coire Lapaich and Coire Coulavie on the northern side of Glen Affric. The precise dating of these events must await absolute dating through peat and pollen analysis, but they may well be correlated with the dated end-moraine at Loch a' Gharbhrian in Ross[3].

The position of the shoreline at any time within the last twelve thousand years has been governed by the interplay of eustatic and isostatic forces. According to which force was dominant, the position of the shoreline rose or fell. There resulted a succession of regressions and transgressions evidenced by shore marks cut into the glacial deposits. The oldest raised shorelines were formed during the late-glacial period, about twelve thousand years ago, when material from the ice margins poured into the sea in the form of deltas as seen at Muir of Ord, Lovat Bridge and, on a smaller scale, at Drumnadrochit, Invermoriston, Foyers and Inverfarigaig. These have subsequently been raised to their present position over 100 feet (32 m) above sea level. This shoreline can be traced as a discontinuous feature cutting the moraine at Ardersier, and into the Beauly Firth, Munlochy Bay and Loch Ness. The ice-contact deposits within the Ness narrows were slightly modified by this high sea level, but the shoreline has been identified at several sites, especially where the sea lapped around the margins of kettleholes.

A particularly well-marked shoreline occurs at Dores, where the long fetch of the loch and the prevailing winds favoured shoreline formation. In general, the steep sides of Loch Ness have not permitted the survival, or indeed the formation of shorelines except where side-valleys fed in large quantities of material.

Following on this late-glacial transgression, land recovery outpaced world sea level rise, and the late-glacial beach was raised, and the shoreline correspondingly regressed. As the weight of ice during glacial maximum was unequally distributed over the area, the highest shoreline is very gently tilted, a result of unequal depression, and subsequent recovery. The tilt is so small that it can only be detected by accurate levelling. The period of shoreline regression was followed by a second major transgression (approximate date 6000 B.P. [Before present]) when the old sea cliffs which margin the southern shore of the Beauly Firth were created. The A9 road between Inverness and Beauly runs at its base between Bunchrew and Berryfield. The rise in sea level clearly provide a large amount of material for shoreline regulation, and the strandplain of the Carse of Delnies, and the other "carse" lands around Beauly, were formed during this period. It is notable that the post-glacial beach is not represented within Loch Ness. The completion of land recovery took the shoreline to its present position and the present shorelines were constructed. The deltaic formation of the Longman and the strandplain and spit complexes at Whiteness Head, together with the sedimentation of the Beauly Firth, are thus relatively recent phenomena.

The post-glacial period was characterised by a marked amelioration of climate with the spread of a dense vegetation cover, following the virtual cessation of periglacial activities. Frost action became confined to the high summits, and the gradual build-up of peat on inter-fluves and in basins followed. The valley slopes over-steepened by the passage of ice, adjusted themselves to the new climatic conditions, and many valley floors, as in Strath Glass, were strongly alluviated by river deposition, masking glacially-originated basins.

BIBLIOGRAPHY

1. Horne, J., "The geology of Nairnshire," *Trans. Inver. Sc. Soc.* III, 47-51, 1884.
2. Horne, J., "The ice-shed in the North-West Highlands," *Trans. Inver. Sc. Soc.*, IV, 212-213, 1892.
3. Kirk, W., & Godwin, H., "A late-glacial site at Loch Droma, Ross and Cromarty," *Trans. Roy. Soc. Edinb.* 65, 225-249, 1963.
4. Linton, D. L., "Problems of Scottish scenery," *Scott. Geog. Mag.* 67, 65-85, 1951.
5. Linton, D. L., "Watershed breaching by ice in Scotland," *Trans. Inst. Brit. Geogr.* 15, 1-15, 1951.
6. Peach, B. N., et al, "The geology of Ben Wyvis, Cairn Chuinneag, Inchbae and the surrounding country," *Mem. Geol. Surv.*, 1912.
7. Report of Committee of British Association, "The Clava Shell Bed," *Trans. Inver. Sc. Soc.* IV, 300-339, 1894.
8. Sissons, J. B., *The evolution of Scotland's Scenery*, Edinburgh, 1967.
9. Small, A., & Smith, J. S., "The Strathpeffer and Inverness Area," *British Landscapes Through Maps* 13, 1-25, 1971.
10. Wallace, T. D., "Glacial evidence in the Moray Firth," *Trans. Inver. Sc. Soc.* VI, 145-160, 1901.

SOME LOCAL BOTANY

MARGARET BARRON and GWEN BUSH

Shimmer of sea, gently sloping patchwork of arable fields, rolling moorlands leading the eye to the higher hills — such a vista can be seen from many vantage points near Inverness. The picture is softened by the clumps and woods of deciduous trees whose presence usually rims the watercourses large and small. In other directions, the darker, more angular blocks of conifers spread over the hillsides, and here and there can be seen the glimmer of loch or the sparkle of a river. Thus, while the district cannot compare with the well-known areas of great botanical interest, the very diversity of habitat revealed in this view ensures that the flora within ten miles of Inverness consists of many different species and plant associations, ranging from the Eel-grass of the tidal mudflats to the arctic-alpine Purple Saxifrage.

The geology of the area is treated elsewhere, but, in brief, one can say that the parent rocks are mainly either the Devonian conglomerates and sandstones, or the more acid Moine schists to the west and southwest, though glacial drift overlies much of the Inverness district. There are one or two small outcrops of limestone, and here and there other rocks outcrop whose base-rich status can be divined from the more interesting vegetation around them.

Inverness enjoys a genial climate, and is comparatively mild in winter, but a considerable difference can be noticed even a few hundred feet up, and spring comes to the lowland areas a week or two earlier than to the uplands of 500 to 700 ft. (150 to 215 m.) Near the coast, the annual rainfall is seldom greater than 25 ins. (62.5 cm.), but this figure increases further inland in the hills. In such a varied district as this, differing altitude and exposure can provide a series of local climates.

All these factors influence the type of vegetation and so, for the purpose of describing the plants, it is best to divide the area into different habitats. These are, the sea coast, woodlands, moorland and hill, and wetlands. On the ground, of course, these divisions are seldom clear-cut, but can overlap and merge into each other.

SEA COAST

From Beauly to Nairn the coastline is low-lying and without cliffs, and much of the shore consists of extensive mud-flats. The first plants to catch the eye on this muddy foreshore are likely to be the erect, succulent stems of Glasswort *(Salicornia spp)*, as that favourite food of wintering duck, Eel-grass *(Zostera spp)*, is usually at lower tidal level, and anyway not so conspicuous. Glasswort is found not only on the mud, but also on the more sandy patches which occur occasionally. Areas of saltmarsh are not extensive in the district, usually fringing sheltered bays in the firth, and there are to be seen such typical saltmarsh plants as Sea Plantain *(Plantago maritima)*, Sea Arrow-grass *(Triglochin maritima)*, Sea Aster *(Aster tripolium)* and the well-known Thrift or Sea Pink *(Armeria maritima)*. Scurvy-grass *(Cochlearia officinalis)* and the charming little Sea Milkwort *(Glaux maritima)* which, lacking petals, has instead a clover-coloured calyx, are also to be found. Here and there, usually in the more brackish marshes, beds of Reeds *(Phragmites communis)* stand out, and associated with them are likely to be Mud Rush *(Juncus gerardii)*, and the Sea Club-rush *(Scirpus maritimus)*, with its distinctive stout triangular stem and deep green leaves.

The most attractive stretch of coast is undoubtedly that at Whiteness, part in Nairnshire and part in Inverness-shire. Salt marsh, sand dune and shingle spit are all represented and a very varied flora results. On the shingle can still be found a few patches of the Northern Shore-wort or Oyster Plant *(Mertensia maritima)* with its gentian-blue flowers and decumbent fleshy blue grey leaves, reputedly tasting like oysters! Unfortunately this handsome plant seems to be decreasing everywhere. Sea Rocket *(Cakile maritima)* and Sea Sandwort *(Honkenya peploides)* grow on the sand with, behind them, the sand fixing grasses, Marram *(Ammophila arenaria)*, Sand Couch-grass *(Agropyron junceiforme)* and, near the point, Lyme-grass *(Elymus arenarius)*. The shorter turf is a carpet of flowers, from the dainty Purging Flax *(Linum catharticum)* and Knotted Pearlwort *(Sagina nodosa)*, with its clusters of little linear leaves, to the massed colours of the acid-yellow Wall-pepper *(Sedum acre)*, the purple Thyme *(Thymus drucei)* and the golden Birdsfoot-trefoil *(Lotus corniculatus)*. Lovage *(Ligusticum scoticum)*, a shiny-leaved umbellifer more often associated with rocky coasts in Scotland and the north of England, has been found there, as has another umbellifer, which is rather uncommon in the north, Bur Chervil *(Anthriscus caucalis)*. That unusual little fern, the Moonwort *(Botrichium lunaria)* can sometimes be discovered, as can plants of the Lesser Butterfly Orchid (*Platanthera bifolia*).

At present, the area adjacent to Whiteness has been invaded by industry connected with North Sea Oil, and access is restricted. There are also plans for reclaiming part of Longman Bay, immediately east of Inverness, and it remains to be seen what effect these two schemes will have on the coastal habitat and its associated communities.

LOWLAND

The lowland area forms a coastal strip varying in width from approximately three miles to less than half a mile, and also extending some miles up the Ness valley, Strathnairn and Strathglass and it is farmed fairly extensively. Round Loch Ness the hills rise so steeply from the waterside that there is virtually no lowland beside it, except for small areas at Foyers, Drumnadrochit, Invermoriston and Fort Augustus. Over the centuries all the British countryside, save for the tops of the highest hills, has been altered in varying degree by man and his multifarious activities, but in this section we look at those parts which are most directly influenced by man at the present day; e.g. arable land, urban districts and roadsides.

The weeds of arable land are not now as conspicuous as they used to be. More rigorous specifications for the purity of agricultural seed combined with modern spraying techniques have eliminated most of the showy weeds from our cornfields, but root-fields usually still offer a selection of weeds, though here, too, suitable pre-emergent sprays have been developed and their use is increasing. The tall, mealy-leaved Fat Hen (*Chenopodium album*) is often conspicuous, and Red Shank (*Polygonum persicaria*) and the blue-flowered Bugloss (*Anchusa arvensis*) can be seen in the drills; and one northern botanist was delighted to find the unusual scarlet-petalled Pheasant's Eye (*Adonis annua*) in a beet field in 1971. It is in the disturbed ground at the verges of recently completed road-works that one more often sees nowadays such plants as Corn Marigold (*Chrysanthemum segetum*), Ox-eye Daisy (*Chrysanthemum leucanthemum*), Long-headed Poppy (*Papaver dubium*) and even Charlock (*Sinapis arvensis*). The Hemp-nettle (*Galeopsis tetrahit*) and species of Fumitory (*Fumaria spp*) also flourish there and Field Pennycress (*Thlaspi arvense*) is occasionally seen. Pineapple Weed (*Matricaria matricarioides*) is an abundant and increasing weed, found especially in gateways and on well-trodden paths and tracks. First recorded in Britain in 1871, it was in 1913 that the first known sight of it in the Inverness district, in the vicinity of the station, was reported to the Inverness Field Club.

The hedges, railway and roadsides are, as elsewhere, important habitats for plants. In Inverness-shire we are fortunate that chemical herbicides are not applied to the roadsides and, even passing along in a car, one cannot fail to be impressed by the seasonal displays of colour — the blue of Wild Hyacinth *(Endymion non-scriptus)* with the white of Greater Stitchwort *(Stellaria holostea)*, the rich yellow of Birdsfoot-trefoil *(Lotus corniculatus)*, the striking blue-purple of Tufted Vetch *(Vicia cracca)*, often associated with the yellow Lady's Bedstraw *(Galium verum)*, and then the well-known Bluebell *(Campanula rotundifolia)*. Umbellifers are common by hedges and roads, from the early-flowering Cow Parsley *(Anthriscus sylvestris)* and Sweet Cicely *(Myrrhis odorata)* to the later Hogweed *(Heracleum sphondylium)* and Upright Hedge-parsley *(Torilis japonica)*. The Giant Hogweed *(Heracleum mantegazzianum)*, which can grow to a height of 10 ft. (3 m.) or more, is found in several localities, a particularly fine stand of the plant occurs near Milton of Allanfearn. Much less common, and known in only one or two places in the district, is Master-wort *(Peucedanum ostruthium)*.

A favourite walk with both visitors and Invernessians is that through the Ness Islands, but these are now so tidy, with tarmac on the paths, that wild flowers are not obvious, those present being usually near backwaters and away from the paths. The strong-scelling Ramsons *(Allium ursinum)* is found and also Winter Heliotrope *(Petasites fragrans)*, which can be seen in flower as early as January. It is interesting too, that a small colony of Northern Bedstraw *(Galium boreale)* persists in the Islands, for a plant from that locality is preserved in the herbarium of Dr Hugh Clark, in the Inverness museum. Dr Clark's collecting was largely carried out in the years 1854-55. Beside another pedestrian way, Few-flowered Leek *(Allium paradoxum)* is well established and each spring it is good to see it still flourishing.

Railway embankments are frequently the sites of interesting plants, and the stretch of line from Bunchrew to Kirkhill provides quite a variety. Striking clumps of the yellow-flowered Tansy *(Chrysanthemum vulgare)* catch the eye at Phopachy Bridge and the large leaves of Butterbur *(Petasites hybridus)* can be seen in profusion near Lentran, while three different species of Toadflax have been noticed — the Common *(Linaria vulgaris)*, the Pale *(L. repens)* and, on one occasion, the Small *(Chaenorhinum minus)*. East of Inverness, near Stratton, Weld or Dyer's Rocket *(Reseda luteola)* and the Sweet Violet *(Viola odorata)* are found. Weld can also be seen beside the canal, near the "sandy braes" of Torvean, and on the canal banks grow Wall Lettuce *(Mycelis muralis)* and Jack-by-the-Hedge *(Alliaria petiolata).* When the canal was constructed, Whin *(Ulex europaeus)* was planted on the banks to help to stabilise them. In the late spring and early summer, the sheer intensity of the yellow of Whin in bloom can be quite overwhelming, and around Inverness there are many places where it can be seen to advantage besides the canal banks — the Leachkin, by the Dores road, Culloden Moor and many others. The Broom *(Sarothamnus scoparius)* adds its quota to the golden glow.

WOODLANDS

Plantations of conifers are numerous in our area, but their density and uniformity of age and consequent shade lead to a virtual absence of ground flora beneath the trees. By paths and ditches, however, such plants as Wood-sorrel *(Oxalis acetosella),* Common Speedwell *(Veronica officinalis)* and Bugle *(Ajuga reptans)* can be seen, with the grasses Yorkshire Fog *(Holcus lunatus)* and Common Bent *(Agrostis tenuis),* and such ferns as Male Fern *(Dryopteris filix-mas,)* Broad Buckler-fern *(D. dilata)* and the very common Hard-fern *(Blechnum spicant).* Where the forest roads have been constructed, Sand Spurrey *(Spergularia rubra)* and Wall Lettuce *(Mycelis muralis)* have been found, presumably introduced with the road metal.

Much more attractive are the older, more open pine-woods. Here, though the number of species may not be great, a distinctive northern flora appears. Through widespread Ling *(Calluna vulgaris),* Blaeberry *(Vaccinium myrtillus)* and mosses, grow, in season, the delightful starry-flowered Chickweed Wintergreen *(Trientalis europaea),* species of Wintergreen *(Pyrola spp)* and the many whitish spikes of Creeping Lady's Tresses *(Goodyera repens).* Rowan *(Sorbus aucuparia),* singly or in small groups, occurs quite frequently. These woods are not native, though so much a part of the Highland scene. In that fascinating book, "The Native Pinewoods of Scotland," by Steven and Carlisle, the surviving remnants of the once extensive Caledonian forest are listed and defined. Only one of the groupings comes within this area, that of Strathglass, subdivided into the woods of Glen Strathfarrar, Glen Affric, Glen Cannich and Guisachan with Cougie. In these woods, the plant communities are very similar to those mentioned above.

Our most widespread tree is the Birch *(Betula spp)* and it can be a graceful, well-grown tree, or smaller and shrubbier as it colonises felled areas or abandoned grassland, with drainage now imperfect. It is in the latter situation that one can some-times find the uncommon Coral-root Orchid *(Corallorhiza trifida)*, a plant with no true foliage leaves, and its flowers a dingy yellow. Both Birch *(Betula pubescens)* and Silver Birch *(B. pendula)* are found in the district and in their shelter there is usually a well-developed undergrowth where the Wood Anemone *(Anemone nemorosa)*, Common Violet *(Viola riviniana)* and Common Cow-wheat *(Melampyrum pratense)* are frequent, as well as many ferns and mosses.

In the late 18th and in the 19th century, many estate owners made quite extensive plantings of hardwoods, and to this day we can enjoy those of Common Oak *(Quercus robur)* and Beech *(Fagus sylvatica)*. The beechwods with their close canopy allow little else to grow, but are in themselves things of great beauty, whether in fresh spring green or in tawny autumn splendour. The oakwoods, on the other hand, provide us with a great variety of herbs from early spring onwards. Wood Anemone, Wood Sorrel and Dog's Mercury *(Mercurialis peren-nis)* are all common, and there one can occasionally find Sanicle *(Sanicula europaea)*, Bird's-nest Orchid *(Neottia nidus-avis)* and Early Purple Orchid *(Orchis mascula)*. That attractive grass, the Slender False-broom *(Brachypodium sylvaticum)*, with its wide yellow-green leaves, can usually be seen. In this district, the Sessile Oak *(Quercus petraea)* is relatively uncommon.

Reelig Glen, now laid out by the Forestry Commission as one of their Forest Walks, is well worth a visit. In addition to the many fine exotic trees there, the plant growth in the glen is luxuriant and much richer than that of the average northern wood. Wood Vetch *(Vicia sylvatica)*, both Golden Saxifrages *(Chrysosplenium alternifolium* and *C. oppositifolium)*, the sweet-scented Woodruff *(Galium odoratum)*, the Melancholy Thistle *(Cirsium heterophyllum)* and the Twayblade *(Listera ovata)* all grow there, as do more than a dozen different species of fern. The glen is also rich in mosses, liverworts, lichens and fungi, to be seen on rocks and on the ground, on living trees and on old stumps and bits of rotting wood — a paradise for the specialist in these difficult families.

An autumn expedition to gather Hazel nuts *(Corylus avel-lana)* was an annual event in childhood days, and Loch Ness-side south of Dores, Glenurquhart, Strathglass and Nairnside all have goodly numbers of this attractive shrub. In spring there is usually a fine show of Primroses *(Primula vulgaris)* in these copses and Wild Strawberry *(Fragaria vesca)* and the Early Purple Orchid occur, as do both Hairy Woodrush *(Luzula pilosa)* and Greater Woodrush *(L. sylvatica)*. Later in the year Yellow

Pimpernel *(Lysiamachia nemorum)* and Figwort *(Scrophularia nodosa)* with its disagreeable smell, are to be found.

By rivers, streams and lochsides, we frequently come across small woods of Alder *(Alnus glutinosa)* and there the yellow-flowered Marsh Hawk's-beard *(Crepis paludosa)* often grows beside the bright blue of Water Forget-me-not *(Myosotis scorpioides)*. At Urquhart Bay, on Loch Ness, there is a quite extensive Alder swamp and, in "The Vegetation of Scotland," ed. J. H. Burnett, there is a pair of photographs, one taken in 1905 and the other in 1960, which shows just how this has developed over the years.

We must mention the Bird-Cherry *(Prunus padus)*, for in early summer the hedgerows of Strathglass and Glen Urquhart are white with the blossoms of this showy tree.

MOORLAND AND HILL

The impact of colour is most noticeable on the hills and moors, with the reddish shades of Bell-heather *(Erica cinerea)* in July, followed by great sweeps of purple as the Ling *(Calluna vulgaris)* comes into flower in August. By far the largest part of our area lies between 500 and 2500 ft. (150 m. and 760 m.) above sea level, and heather moors are extensive where this land is level or gently sloping and there is a thin layer of peaty soil. It is only heather that the motorist sees as he speeds along, but a walk over Drumashie Moor, for instance will soon show that it is not "just heather," and closer inspection reveals a number of attractive plants. In early summer, the gleam of yellow may indicate the presence of Petty Whin *(Genista anglica)*, and the crimson of Bitter Vetch *(Lathyrus montanus)* and the deep blue of Common Violet *(Viola riviniana)* can be seen. Much less conspicuous is the Lesser Twayblade *(Listera cordata)* with its pair of rather heart-shaped leaves and slender spike of brownish flowers — one of our smallest orchids. A little later, one may come across the Intermediate Wintergreen *(Pyrola media)* with its pink-tinged flowers, and also the deep-rose-coloured Fragrant Orchid *(Gymnadenia conopsea)* and the widespread Moorland Spotted Orchid *(Dactylorchis maculata ssp. ericetorum)*. Long branches of Stag's-horn Clubmoss *(Lycopodium clavatum)* may be seen creeping over the ground, but the fertile branches bearing the cones are erect, an attractive sight. Blaeberry, Cowberry *(Vaccinium vitis-idaea)* and Bearberry *(Arctostaphylos uva-ursi)* are fairly common, the last forming a dense mat with its dark green leaves, while silvery panicles of Wavy Hair-grass *(Deschampsia flexuosa)* glisten and catch the eye.

The Stratherrick hills are not high, but some interesting plants reward the diligent searcher. In March, often with snow not far away, the beautiful flowers of Purple Saxifrage *(Saxifraga oppositifolia)* make their appearance on damp friable rock, harbingers of another year of botanising in the hills. The bright stars of Yellow Mountain Saxifrage *(S. azoides)* appear later in trickling gullies and wet flushes, and Mossy Saxifrage *(S. hypnoides)* grows on rocky ledges nearby. Both these saxifrages can be seen by the roadside near Aigas, in Strathglass, with much less effort! In the same area of Stratherrick, one rocky buttress displays four species of spleenwort, Green Spleenwort *(Asplenium viride)*, Maidenhair Spleenwort *(A. trichomanes)*, Black Spleenwort *(A. adiantum-nigrum)* and Wall-Rue *(A. ruta-muraria);* Hairy Rock-cress *(Arabis hirsuta)* and Stone Bramble *(Rubus saxatilis)* are found there, too.

In the crevices of the cliffs and in large scree, where soil can collect and be enriched by minerals leached by rain from the hills above, trees, mainly Birch and Rowan, take root. In these situations they are safe from grazing sheep and deer. At the foot of such slopes, the ground is constantly damp and there is a thick carpet of mosses under the scrub Birch, and lichens frequently cover the trunks and branches of the trees.

Extensive spreads of Bracken *(Pteridium aquilinum)* are not common in the area, but where they do occur they are usually on better land that has been allowed to deteriorate.

Prominent in any view along Loch Ness, Mealfuarvonie, the last outlier of the Old Red Sandstone, provides a quite extensive range of species. On grassy slopes, both Greater and Lesser Butterfly Orchids *(Platanthera chlorantha* and *P. bifolia)* occur and also the greenish-flowered Frog Orchid *(Coeloglossum viride)*. The long ridge of the hill is floristically poor, with Heather, Cotton-grass *(Eriophorum vaginatum* and *E. angustifolium)*, Deer-grass *(Tricophorum cespitosum)* and spreads of Cloudberry *(Rubus chamaemorus)*. The steeper rocks and gullies have more variety and in the spring they may be draped with curtains of Purple Saxifrage, while later other montane species can be seen, including Alpine Cinquefoil *(Potentilla crantzii)*, Alpine Saussurea *(Saussurea alpina)*, Scottish Asphodel *(Tofieldia pusilla)* and the Holly Fern *(Polystichum lonchitis)*.

Only in the West of this area do the hills rise to over 3000 ft. (914 m.), where the fine ridges of Glen Affric and Glen Cannich support further mountain plants. Above the frosted slopes the hills are golden-brown in autumn with the Deer-grass, but higher up, where the vegetation is shorter and sparser, the tiny Least Willow *(Salix herbacea)* can be found, and in spring on gravel or rock, pink cushions of Moss Campion *(Silene acaulis)* and spreading mats of Trailing Azalea *(Loiseleuria procumbens).* Associated with the damp edges of late snow patches are Dwarf Cudweed *(Gnaphalium supinum)* and Sibbaldia *(Sibbaldia procumbens).* Other flowers of the hills are Alpine Meadow-Rue *(Thalictrum alpinum),* Starwort Mouse-ear Chickweed *(Cerastium cerastoides)* and, on damp ledges, Mountain Sorrel *(Oxyria dignya).* The Stiff Sedge *(Carex bigelowii)* and the Spiked Woodrush *(Luzula spicata)* are usual plants of the higher hills, but the rare Highland Cudweed *(Gnaphalium norvegicum)* is also to be found here.

WETLANDS

The division between moorland and bog is seldom clearcut. On the drier moors, Ling and Bell-heather predominate, but, where drainage is poorer, there will be many scattered plants of Cross-leaved Heath *(Erica tetralix)* and the single-headed Hare's-tail *(Eriophorum vaginatum)* and, in the wetter places, increasing amounts of Common Cotton-grass, so that the ground looks white with its nodding silky tassels. Sphagnum mosses take over where the ground is permanently waterlogged and may form an almost complete cover, with the yellow Bog Asphodel *(Narthecium ossifragum)* growing through it in July and August. In this sort of situation there are often patches of Bog Myrtle *(Myrica gale)* which is so memorably fragrant when the leaves are wet or crushed.

Most of our Highland lochs receive acid drainage and are not rich in plant species. Typically, they show a zone of Shoreweed *(Littorella uniflora)* and Water Lobelia *(Lobelia dortmanna)* in the coarse sands in the shallows, with Quill-wort *(Isoetes lacustris)* and Water Horsetail *(Equisetum fluviatile)* beyond. Only the delicate lilac flowers of the Lobelia and the stems of the Horsetail show above the water. Sometimes an accumulation of organic debris occurs near an inflowing stream and produces a vegetation composed of hummocks of Sphagnum mosses set in a system of little pools and channels. There one finds the Bog Pondweed *(Potamogeton polygonifolius),* sedges such as the Slender Sedge *(Carex lasiocarpa),* Mud Sedge *(C. limosa)* and Common Sedge *(C. nigra)* and sometimes the fine, grass-like Floating Scirpus *(Eleogiton fluitans).* Bladderwort *(Utricularis spp),* inconspicuous when not flowering, bears small under-water bladders which trap minute aquatic animals. Our two other insectivorous plants, Butterwort *(Pinguicula vulgaris)* and Sundew *(Drosera spp)* are also usually present in such an association. Much more rarely, one may come across the Bog

Orchid *(Hammarbya paludosa);* less than 4 ins. (10 cm.) high and with a spike of tiny yellowish-green flowers, smaller than those of any other British orchid, it merges into the background of sphagnum.

Lochan na Curra, on Drumashie Moor, shows a fine succession of vegetation. Its east end is stony and bare of plants. To the west, Broad-leaved Pondweed *(Potamogeton natans)* and rafts of the White Water Lily *(Nymphaea alba)* merge into the growth of Bogbean *(Menyanthes trifoliata),* which has feathery pink and white flowers. Stands of the Bottle Sedge *(Carex rostrata)* follow, and then the Bog Myrtle and the Slender Sedge take over. As the sedges become fewer, Heather comes in, and finally there is an area of scrub Birch.

Long and narrow, with its stony shores falling steeply to the depths and greatly affected by wave action, Loch Ness has a poor acquatic flora. Urquhart Bay is one of the few places with water-edge vegetation, and it contains the Alder swamp mentioned previously. On the shores from Aldourie southwards, however, much Sea Campion *(Silene maritima),* Intermediate Enchanter's Nightshade *(Circaea intermedia)* and Herb Robert *(Geranium robertianum)* can be seen on the shingle. With its bright pink flowers and its leaves often quite red, the Herb Robert is a colourful sight. The Common Enchanter's Nightshade *(Circaea lutetiana)* grows under the scrub immediately above the shore.

In its upper reaches the Nairn is an uninteresting river, though the Farigaig, not far distant, has some most attractive stretches. By waterfall and rocky banks, the colourful Wood Cranesbill *(Geranium sylvaticum)* and Golden-rod *(Solidago virgaurea)* can be seen, as well as many ferns and mosses. The creamy-barked Aspen *(Populus tremula)* grows there, surely one of the few plants sometimes heard before it is seen, for its leaves tremble in the slightest air current. Nearby, in late summer, one can occasionally find Grass of Parnassus *(Parnassus palustris)* — a beautiful plant with its single flower heads of delicately veined white petals, but not, of course, a grass.

The Falls of Foyers are an attraction in themselves, but further interest is added to a visit by even a casual glance at the vegetation there. Massed round the head of the falls are banks of the fleshy-leaved Rose-root *(Sedum rosea),* one of that group of plants which can be found both on high mountain ledges and on the sea cliffs. Yellow Mountain Saxifrage *(Saxifraga azoides),* Mossy Saxifrage *(S. hypnoides)* and Golden Saxifrage *(Chrysosplenium oppositifolia)* are all present, while, on one occasion, the eye was caught by a beautiful Early Purple

D

Orchid *(Orchis macula)* growing out of a fallen tree trunk by the path. A few miles away, the old bridge at Whitebridge is a colourful sight in early summer, clad in Fairy Foxglove *(Erinus alpinus)*.

On the flat floor of Strathglass, there are pools and marshes and little muddy backwaters left in the old river meanders. There one can find the delicate Marsh Speedwell *(Veronica scutellata)* and the Marsh Willowherb *(Epilobium palustre)*, Marsh Cinque-foil *(Potentilla palustris)*, Red-rattle *(Pedicularis palustris)* and the single-stemmed Common Spike-rush *(Eleocharis palustris)*. Uncommon in the district, Skull-cap *(Scutellaria galericulata)* grows in the shade of the Alders there, as does the Remote Sedge *(Carex remota)*. In June, the vivid blue Lupins *(Lupinus noot-katensis)* are a splendid sight on the shingle and little islands of the rivers Glass and Beauly. This Lupin is shorter and stubbier than the garden varieties. On the river shingle, and also on damp rocks by rivers and on wet gravel in ditches, grows the New Zealand Willow-herb *(Epilobium pedunculare)* which is a tiny prostrate plant, unlike all the other Willow-herbs, except that the seeds have the characteristic long silky hairs attached to them.

The streams and rivers flow through all types of habitat, from their sources in the wet flushes of the higher hills, down through moors, pastures, farmland and villages, and because of their shelter, moisture, shade and higher mineral content, they frequently carry a wider range of species than their surroundings. Because they are not sprayed with herbicides, nor ploughed, nor overgrazed, they are often a refuge for plants, and beside, and under, bridges a fine mixture of roadside, rock and marsh plants can co-exist.

The burns tumbling down to join the River Enrick in Glen Urquhart are a good example of these rich habitats, and well worth exploring. The rocky gorges provide a range of many ferns; Lady Fern *(Athyrium filix-femina)*, Male Fern *(Dryopteris filix-mas)*, Hard Shield-fern *(Polystichum aculeatum)* and the beautiful Oak Fern *(Thelypteris dryopteris)* and Beech Fern *(T. phegopteris)* among them. On the more open reaches, marshy stretches by the streams offer a wealth of colourful flowers. The gold of Marsh Marigold *(Caltha palustris)* and the striking yellow Globe Flower *(Trollius europaeus)* show there, and also Ragged Robin *(Lychnis flos-cuculi)* and the creamy plumes of Meadowsweet *(Filipendula ulmaria)*. The rich purple of Northern Fen Orchid *(Dactylorchis purpurella)* can sometimes be seen, and, later on, blue Devil's-bit Scabious *(Succisa pratensis)*, and the off-white Sneezewort *(Achillea ptarmica)*. The handsome heads of Melancholy Thistle *(Cirsium heterophyllum)* are a frequent sight in Glen Urquhart, by the roadside as well as by the streams and river.

It is hoped that this brief account of some of the plants of north-east Inverness-shire will provide some incentive to explore more widely and to look more closely at the flowers about in this district. But when you find them, may we ask you to make sure that they are still left to delight those who come along after you?

In this Centenary Celebration of the Inverness Field Club, we thought it appropriate to look at some of the records and lists of plants made over the years.

Very little has been published concerning the botany solely of the Inverness area, and prior to the 19th century, records were few and fragmentary. The first edition of "Anderson's Guide to the Highlands" (1834), gave lists of plants for various localities in the north and west, and Alexander Murray's "Northern Flora" (1836) contained a few references to Inverness-shire. Similarly, the Reverend Dr Gordon, of Birnie, in his "Collectanea to the Flora of Moray" (1845), listed material from this district as his territory was the old Province of Moray.

The New Statistical Account of 1845 is little help. About a dozen flowers and various shrubs and trees were mentioned for the parish of Urquhart and Glenmoriston, a few more for Ardersier, and approximately fifty for Inverness, though many of these were outwith the parish boundary. Eight other parishes in the area had either no botany section at all, or one which referred only to trees and plantings and, literally, one or two flowers. The minister of Kilmorack stated baldly, "There is nothing very peculiar in the flora of this parish," and then named a few trees and the White Water Lily! Only the Reverend C. Fraser, of Kiltarlity, had anything like a comprehensive list, over two hundred plants, though unfortunately no localities are given.

In 1868, Peter Anderson produced a "Guide to Inverness and its Neighbourhood," and this contained an appendix on local plants by P. J. Anderson. Then came the Field Club. In his first address, Dr Aitken, a founder member, hoped that the club would attempt to draw up an exhaustive catalogue of the flora of the Inverness district. When the first volume of the Transactions appeared in 1885, it did contain a plant list. Compiled by Dr Aitken, with the assistance of several Field Club members and other botanists, it included plants found on Field Club excursions, and thus ranged beyond the county to such places as the Culbin Sands and the Black Isle. Over 520 species were listed and it was hoped that further contributions would increase this number. The second volume had another list, this time of the flowering plants in the parish of Croy, by the minister, the Reverend Thomas Fraser. Although he named over 320 species, no indication of their situations was given.

A few years later, John Don, then a teacher at the Burgh Technical and Art School and previously at Raining's School, produced a booklet entitled "Flowering Plants of Inverness-Shire and Some Parts of Adjoining Counties." We have seen only Part I, containing the dicotyledons, but in the introduction Don promised further instalments, one classifying the monocotyledons, and others with ferns, mosses, fungi and algae to follow. So far as is known, however, these were never published. The longest list yet appeared in 1905, when Dr Gordon A. Lang's "List of Flowers and Ferns of Inverness and District" was printed. He referred to over 650 species and varieties, and in many cases gave some indication of the locality, such as "Canal banks", or "Muirtown".

Reading through these old catalogues, one is struck as much by the continuity of some species as by the disappearance of others. The destruction of suitable habitats by drainage, differing agricultural practices and building, for instance, has led to some species vanishing from their old stations, but others can be still seen in the very places in which they were observed so long ago.

Since Dr Lang's time, no further plant list of the district has appeared, though articles and papers in various periodicals have dealt with individual localities.

Between 1954 and 1960, however, members of the Botanical Society of the British Isles carried out a nationwide programme of field work, which culminated in the publication of "The Atlas of the British Flora" in 1962. This contains a comprehensive series of maps illustrating the distribution of the plants of Great Britain and Ireland, based on the 10 km. square of the Ordnance Survey National Grid. Approximately 3,500 squares required to be mapped. More recently, the Committee for the Study of the Scottish Flora decided to undertake an Inverness-shire Survey. Accordingly, 1970 saw the start of a five year period of field recording in the county, the recording unit in this case being the 5 km. quadrat.

So perhaps that hope for an exhaustive catalogue of the flora, expressed so long ago by Dr Aitken, will be nearer fulfilment as the Field Club celebrates its centenary.

The nomenclature used throughout is that adopted in the "Flora of the British Isles", by A. R. Clapham, T. G. Tutin and E. F. Warburg (2nd edition, 1962).

The writers are indebted to the "News and Notes" quarterly leaflet of the Inverness Botany Group and to their fellow members of that club.

Wood Anemone   ⨯ 75
(Anemone nemorosa)

WILD ANIMALS OF INVERNESS AND DISTRICT

ANDREW CURRIE

Other authors have written about the plants and the birds of Inverness and district; I therefore propose to discuss the vertebrate fauna, other than birds (including mammals, amphibians, reptiles and fish) and to say something about the invertebrate fauna.

The range of habitat from coast to hill land, with woodland, moorland, river valley and farmland in between, present a fine variety from which the species can each select their niche, and around Inverness we are fortunate in possessing a fauna which has wide appeal. True, some of the creatures which favour warmer conditions are missing, being confined to the southern parts of the British Isles; on the other hand, our wilderness areas allow us to enjoy many species, such as Red Deer, Pine Marten and Wild Cat, which are missing from the more built-up regions. All those who live on the land take note of our larger animals, but, alas, there is much less information available on the small mammals, such as the mice and voles, and the nocturnal bats, which require the special attention of the expert. Similarly, amphibians such as the three sorts of newt are difficult to identify, and records are therefore scarce. In interpreting the accounts which follow for each species, the reader should bear in mind this imbalance of available information.

With regard to the invertebrate fauna, this chapter makes no attempt at completeness. An account is given of the sort of range of animals to be expected in freshwater and coastal habitats, and some reference is made to the better known invertebrates, the butterflies and bees for example. Proper assessment of invertebrates is a matter for the expert, and few such studies have been carried out near Inverness. Perhaps what is mentioned will whet the appetite of some budding local naturalist.

Hedgehog, *Erinaceus europaeus.* — This familiar animal is

The Mammals

present throughout the agricultural and wooded areas of the Inverness district. It frequents fields, hedgerows and roadsides, as well as gardens and parks. The Hedgehog is seldom seen above 400 ft. (120 m.) and does not normally occur on heather. Numbers seem to be decreasing and the animal is often killed on roads.

Mole, *Talpa europaea.* — Few people see the Mole itself, but mole-hills are an accepted feature of the countryside. Moles are plentiful throughout the Inverness area, and occur in almost every habitat other than dense woodland. They are regularly present up to 1500 ft. (457 m.) and have been noted at the summit of Sgurr na Lapaich (3773 ft., 1145 m.).

Common Shrew, *Sorex araneus.* — There is difficulty in identifying the two species of shrew, but this is the one commonly encountered. Available records show that it is indeed common throughout the Inverness district, ascending to the highest hills in summer, if there is adequate cover.

Pygmy Shrew, *Sorex minutus.* — This is the smallest Scottish mammal, distinguishable from the Common Shrew by the smaller size and the relatively long tail. It appears to be ubiquitous, though less common than the Common Shrew in woodland. Otherwise, it is present in all types of habitat, often at great heights.

Water Shrew, *Neomys fodiens.* — Though numerous in the Highlands, this animal is scarce near Inverness. It is restricted to low ground near streams, and has been seen in such places as Culbin and the mouth of the Alness River.

Daubenton's Bat, *Myotis daubentoni.* — Few people can identify bats, and the less common ones go unnoticed. Daubenton's Bat is local in distribution in Scotland, and probably occurs near Inverness. It has been reported flying low over the Beauly Firth, a habitat which is characteristic.

Pipistrelle Bat, *Pipistrellus pipistrellus.* — This smallest of the bats is also the most common, occurring all round Inverness and district. The species may be losing ground, probably because of the clearing of old buildings in town and country, and also because of the increased use of insecticides. There is real cause for concern regarding the survival of the bats.

Long-eared Bat, *Plecotus auritus.* — This animal reaches its most northerly limits near Inverness, and it is frequently seen nearby. It is probably overlooked by most people.

Rabbit, *Oryctolagus cuniculus.* — The Rabbit is present everywhere, except on high ground, and is a major pest to farmers and foresters. Myxomatosis, which struck in 1954 in

Scotland, took a toll of 90% of the population. Despite the fact that the disease still circulates, killing out local populations, Rabbits have recovered markedly and are again becoming a nuisance. The disease caused repercussions among populations of other land mammals and birds of prey. Carnivorous animals which fed on rabbits were affected, particularly Fox, Wild Cat, Pine Marten, Stoat and Weasel.

Brown Hare, *Lepus europaeus*. — This animal is plentiful on any open ground up to just over 1000 ft. (300 m.), and is shot regularly, obtaining high prices in the European market. Hares appear to decrease to the south-west, and are very scarce, if not absent, around Fort Augustus. Keepers suggest that the Brown Hare does not mix with the Rabbit, and that populations increased after the elimination of Rabbits by myxomatosis.

Mountain Hare, *Lepus timidus*. — The Mountain or Blue Hare is an animal of high inland moorland, usually over 1000 ft. (300 m.), though it occasionally comes close to the firths. Distribution is not uniform, and there are periodic fluctuations in numbers. Fifty years ago, the Mountain Hare was common, but a decline was noted from the 1930s, especially west of the Caledonian Canal. To the east of Inverness, evidence of a decline is less conclusive. At present, numbers are small west of Inverness, but to the south there are concentrations in the Tomatin, Coignafearn, Daviot area. The greatest numbers are undoubtedly to the east, in the counties of Moray and Nairn, and Banff, where populations reach as high as 51-75 animals to 1000 acres (Hewson, 1954).

Red Squirrel, *Sciurus vulgaris*. — The Red Squirrel is present in suitable woods throughout the Inverness area, showing a preference for coniferous woods. It is also present in deciduous woods, especially Hazel, but is absent from Birch. These preferences largely dictate the distribution. During the 18th century, Red Squirrels came almost to extinction, surviving only in the denser forests of Inverness. Lady Lovat reintroduced them at Beaufort Castle in 1844, and this and other introductions provide the basis of present populations, particularly those in the Black Isle, Nairn and Inverness north of the Caledonian Canal. The original native squirrel *(S. vulgaris* ssp. *leucourus)* is still present around the Aviemore, Carrbridge and Grantown-on-Spey region. In mature animals of this native race, the tail bleaches to a creamy white during the summer. The general impression in Easter Ross and West Inverness is of a slight increase in squirrels and a more marked increase in East Inverness and Nairn.

Bank Vole, *Clethrionomys glareolus*. — This creature of deciduous woodland, scrub and bracken occurs where there is suitable cover and ascends to over 2000 ft. (610 m.). From available records it is much less common and widespread than the Short-tailed Vole, and is perhaps absent from many areas, though common in others.

Short-tailed Vole, *Microtus agrestis*. — The mice and voles are under-recorded, since trapping is the only way to achieve positive identification, and little is done near Inverness. The Field or Short-tailed Vole is better known, however, because of the damage it causes to grass and young trees. The animal is present where there is low cover including grassland, plantations, marginal land and marshes, and ascends to high hills. "Vole plagues" have devastated pastures in the south, but the Highlands have escaped these. The Field Vole is the prey of Kestrel, Short-eared Owl, Fox and Stoat, and fluctuations in numbers affect the predator species profoundly. Near Nairn there was a "plague" twenty years ago, and the animal is widely distributed and common in Inverness and district.

Water Vole, *Arvicola amphibius*. — The Water Vole is a very attractive mammal, living by burns up to about 2000 ft. (610 m.). It is very local near Inverness and is never present in large numbers. Most records are from low land near the Moray Firth, though some are present further up the glens, including Glen Mazeran and Glen Affric.

Wood Mouse, *Apodemus sylvaticus*. — Known also as the Long-tailed Field Mouse, this small mammal lives in drier woodland and scrub, sometimes extending upwards to quite high land. It is much scarcer than the Short-tailed Vole. It is probably widespread, but there are very few positive records.

House Mouse, *Mus musculus*. — Despite the name, this mouse lives in open fields and hedges as well as close to buildings, and tends to move in during the winter. In towns, they live in buildings all the time. This animal is present throughout the Inverness district.

Brown Rat, *Rattus norvegicus*.—This most hated of animals reached the country during the early 18th century, and now has a distribution closely related to man and his buildings. Farms and waste places attract Brown Rats, which are present everywhere.

Common Porpoise, *Phocaena phocoena*. — The Porpoise is the most common Scottish member of the whale family and has a wide distribution through coastal seas and estuaries. They have long been known in the Kessock to Chanonry waters, often being seen by passengers on the ferry. Schools of three to ten are usual, but larger numbers are present around the entrance to the Cromarty Firth.

Fox, *Vulpes vulpes.*—A great deal more factual information is available about carnivorous mammals than about the mice and voles, mainly because they are larger and more readily seen, and because of their flesh-eating habits. The Fox is a nocturnal animal, inhabiting a wide range of territory from low ground to high ground. As a predator of lambs, poultry and game, it is in turn preyed upon by shepherds and gamekeepers. Foxes are present throughout the area, though there has been perhaps some decrease on the higher ground, according to some keepers. During recent years, there has been a spread to the coasts of Moray and Nairn and also on to the Black Isle. Hewson and Kolb (1973) identify this spread as having occurred since 1960 and attribute it not to change in land use, but rather to food availability. This observation concurs with reports by keepers and naturalists who have pointed out the predator/prey relationship between the Fox and the Rabbit. The myxomatosis epidemic, altering, as it did, Rabbit populations, has had a corresponding effect upon the Fox. The Fox also eats small mammals, birds and beetles.

Pine Marten, *Martes martes.* — The Pine Marten is really a woodland animal living on the ground among conifers, but it also frequents rocky ground where trees are scarce. The animal reached very low numbers, but Lockie (1964) has reported a considerable spread between 1946 and 1960, based upon Forestry Commission records. This western animal originally found the Caledonian Canal a barrier to its spread, but by the 1960s it had been reported from a number of forests south of the Canal. At present, Pine Martens are present in small numbers over a wide area round Inverness, though seldom close to the coast. North and west of the Canal, there are many more animals, though there is a wide local variation and the species is nowhere numerous. It is absent from the Black Isle. The wandering habits of the animal must be taken into account, and on the fringes of distribution, records are of stragglers. One may perhaps expect an increase in the future in woodlands around Inverness and district.

Stoat, *Mustela erminea.* — The Weasel and Stoat occupy much the same range and are present wherever there are voles, mice and rabbits. The Stoat, or Ermine, is probably commoner than the Weasel and is present through a wide range of local habitats from farming land and woodland, even on to some moorland. The Stoat prefers Rabbits as food, and the abundance or otherwise of Rabbits has an effect on Stoat numbers. Myxomatosis caused considerable decreases. In the absence of Rabbits, small mammals are eaten. Quite wide population fluctuations are to be expected.

Weasel, *Mustela nivalis.* — Preferring the smaller mammals as food, the Weasel has never been so much affected by myxomatotsis as its close relation. Neither do Weasels show so much fluctuation in numbers as does the Stoat. Weasels are more often seen on arable land, though they are also present in most forest areas. They are widespread, though not numerous.

Mink, *Mustela vison.* — The Mink is a fur producing animal, raised in captivity and fetching good prices. They escape from time to time and are so widespread nationally as to be a serious pest. In the area around Inverness, a quick and efficient trapping programme organised, until recently, by the Department of Agriculture for Scotland, has prevented the species from becoming established.

Badger, *Meles meles.* — The Badger is a great favourite with most people and, while there is occasional persecution, it is generally allowed the freedom of the woods and hillsides. There is evidence that it has increased in numbers near Inverness and indeed throughout the Highlands during the past thirty years (Darling and Boyd 1964). The Badger does not occur everywhere, however, and the distribution is controlled by the fact that the Badger prefers sandy or gravelly banks in which to dig, but avoids peaty areas. In general, the animal is present in the area of river and woodland, but avoids coastal flatlands and the moorlands. Badgers also live in cairns, and this has been noted in Strathglass, for example. Further south, the Spey Valley has some of the largest Badger populations in Scotland. A recent Act of Parliament gives legal protection to the animal, preventing anyone other than the owner or occupier of land from killing them, except under licence.

Otter, *Lutra lutra.* — Otters are animals which are commonly present, but seldom seen. They move considerable distances between rivers and the sea or loch, often by well-known and traditional routes. Population density is never high, and one Otter to six miles of stream has been suggested as a normal number. Otters are numerous in both Ross and Cromarty and Inverness (Stephens 1957) and are known from the Rivers Conon, Beauly, Nairn and Findhorn, as well as inland at Loch Ness and the glens. They take a lot of fish, but are only trapped when they affect fish farms. They are useful in killing eels.

Wild Cat, *Felis silvestris.* — The Wild Cat is a nocturnal creature distinguished from the domestic tabby by the greater size and more robust build, and by the blunt, bushy black tip to the banded tail. The animal likes tree cover for hunting and inhabits the rocks and trees of glens and also drier hill drains and burns. There has been an increase in numbers between 1961 and 1972, and Jenkins (1962) describes them as widely distributed over hill ground, particularly in Inverness. There have also been increases in Moray and Nairn. Reports from some areas suggest that the Wild Cat has spread since myxomatosis and has replaced the Fox on moorland. While the evidence is neither uniform nor clear, there is no doubt that myxomatosis has once again affected the ecology of the species. The spread of forest may also have helped the spread of Wild Cat. Cats are widely trapped by keepers who regard them as vermin, feeding as they do on Rabbits, Hares, small mammals and Red Grouse.

Common Seal, *Phoca vitulina.* — This is an important animal in firths and estuaries. Unfortunately, owing to the difficulty of separating the two species, there is some confusion as to the numbers of Common Seal and Grey Seal. Mammal Society maps (1971) show the Common Seal as by far the most frequent, whereas some local people say that Greys are the more common. Rae (1968) says that of 65 seals killed in the Moray Firth, 43 were Greys and 22 were Common. Whatever the species, there is no doubt that there are many seals on this coast. The Common Seal is present in the three firths of the Moray Basin, but uncommon on the open coast. The preference for sheltered water is marked. Up to 100 may be seen sunning themselves on the sand banks of the Beauly Firth, and the young are born there. They also go up the Beauly River. Breeding has also been recorded in Munlochy Bay. They have been reported feeding on Salmon at river mouths and on Herring and Sprats in Findhorn Bay.

Grey Seal, *Halichoerus grypus.* — Despite the name, colour is not a reliable means of identification. The female Grey Seal has a straight nose and the male a "roman" nose, whereas the Common Seal has a more dog-like nose, concave. When seen full-face, the nostrils are different, those of the Grey being almost parallel, while those of the Common form a "V" shape, almost touching below. Mammal Society maps (1971) show the clear preference of the Grey Seal for open coastlines, nevertheless there has been noted more recently an extension of range into areas once associated with the Common Seal, in the Dornoch Firth, for example. This accords with evidence of increased stocks. Grey Seals concentrate around fishing vessels in the Moray Firth, and are present, and a nuisance, along the Moray and Nairn coasts and at Ardersier. Excursions into the Beauly Firth appear to coincide with runs of fish, and there are records of Grey Seals a couple of miles up the Beauly River. Breeding takes place on islands off the north and west coast. Fish remains are found in about 90% of stomachs, and fish of the salmon family in about 30% of stomachs, (Rae, 1968). The Conservation of Seals Act 1970 provides for the protection of both species, specifying prohibited methods of killing seals and providing for close seasons.

Fallow Deer, *Dama dama*. — Whitehead (1964) and Darling and Boyd (1964) describe Fallow Deer as still remaining in eastern parts of Ross and Cromarty, and from Loch Ness, in very small numbers. Hewson (1964) describes a decline since 1930 in the Spey Valley. Fallow were also once known in the Moy to Daviot area. There has been silence since these 1964 records, and one can only assume that Fallow Deer have become extinct in this area. This assumption is confirmed by the Deer Society records.

Sika Deer, *Cervus nippon*. — The Sika Deer is an introduction, brought into the country during the mid-19th century, and escaping from parks. The species was introduced to Loch Ness-side about 1900 (MacNally 1968) and frequents much the same habitat as the Roe Deer, where birch and hazel abound in a countryside of burns and lochs. It also ventures on to the open hill, but is seldom far from trees. There are two focal points of distribution, one based upon the south-east side of Loch Ness, and the other centred upon Achnasheen. MacNally (1970) says that there may be upwards of 300, all along the south-east side of Loch Ness in both private and state forests. Available records from the Achnasheen populations suggest numbers in excess of 150, but this may well be a low estimate. Sika are now extinct in the Black Isle.

Red Deer, *Cervus elaphus*. — The Red Deer is an animal of the open hillside and moorland, coming into the forest margins during the winter. Calves are born among the hills, usually during early June. Deer Society maps show this, the largest of our land mammals, to be present everywhere through the Highland mainland, save for quite wide gaps on eastern coastal zones. Much of Inverness and district comes into such a zone. There are no more than a few stragglers in Moray and Nairn. In Inverness, they are absent from the coastal areas, but increase inland, and Whithead (1964) has suggested that the County of Inverness supports one-third of Scottish Red Deer. They are also plentiful in Ross and Cromarty, though not now resident east of the Struie to Beauly Road. A wandering stag has been seen on the Black Isle, and this wandering habit will account for other sightings outwith the main habitat. Venison sells for high prices, especially in Western Europe. At the time of writing, the best cuts sell for £1 per pound, and an undressed animal will fetch 50p per pound. Deer stalking is important in the economy of the large estates. Deer farming has been studied, but not yet carried out commercially.

Roe Deer, *Capreolus capreolus.* — The Roe Deer frequent open woodlands and thickets, penetrating the deeper parts of the forest in winter. They are great wanderers, and the spread of afforestation has provided a succession of new habitats. Wherever there are trees, Roe Deer can be expected, and they also live in sheltered treeless ravines. The fawns are born in the shelter of woodlands. Roe Deer are widely distributed in Inverness and district, except on the higher treeless hills and moors. They are present in all Forestry Commission properties. The creature is very secretive, but may be seen at dusk grazing pastures adjacent to woods. The meat is in demand, and animals are at present fetching high prices, especially in Europe.

Wild Goat, *Capra hircus.* — Wild Goat occur in Asia Minor, but feral goats are present in remote parts of Scotland, especially in the Highlands. They are much more numerous in the west and their origin may go back several hundred years. Domestic goats also escape and revert to the wild very quickly, and the truly old stock interbreeds with more recent escapes. The main population of Wild Goat is that which roams within the great moorland area around the River Findhorn on either side of the A9 roadway. These animals are of a very old strain, and may be seen in small groups at such places as Moy and the Slochd. There may be up to forty animals between the Slochd and Nairn. Another area for Wild Goats is on the cliffs and slopes of Craigiehowe, Black Isle, but these are quite recent escapes from domestication. They number about thirty at present.

THE AMPHIBIANS

Common Frog, *Rana temporaria.* — The Frog is our commonest amphibian, frequenting small ponds and ditches for spawning, but otherwise spending most of its time on land. It is common and generally distributed throughout our area, both within the coastal belt and right up into the glens and hills. Frogs have been noted as high as 3400 ft. (1040 m.) in the Cairngorms (Darling and Boyd 1964). There is probably no district where the Frog does not occur, even though not in large numbers. A recent decline has been noted, and Cooke (1972) reports for this area a slight decrease in numbers between

1956 and 1965, and a moderate decrease between 1966 and 1970. Such decreases are related to loss of habitat for urbanisation and to deaths of adults on our roads. Frogs are also extensively used for teaching biology, and Frog spawn is regularly collected by children, a practice which nowadays ought to be discouraged.

Common Toad, *Bufo bufo.* — The Toad is present in such sites as ponds and ditches, preferring deepish water. Hibernation takes place on land, not necessarily close to water. It ascends to the lower moors, but the Toad does not frequent such high land as the Frog, though there is a record of tadpoles at 2000 ft. (610 m.). It is present all along the Moray coast, in Strathglass and and Lochluichart, but there are fewer noted further inland. Toads are less common than Frogs, and Cooke (1972) reports a moderate decrease from this area between 1961 and 1970. The reasons for the decrease are similar to those for the Frog, though the Toad is less likely to be used in schools or collected as spawn.

Smooth Newt, *Triturus vulgaris.* — The Smooth Newt is quite common in the north of Scotland. It is the least aquatic of the British newts, and seldom hibernates in water, preferring some damp place near a pond. Neither is it often present in hill areas.   This newt is reported from the area of Forres, Culbin and Miltonduff, but westwards there is a gap until one crosses to the west side of Loch Ness, with records from Drumnadrochit and Loch Achilty. The most northerly record is from Bonar Bridge. It must be remembered that newts are under-recorded, and their identity presents problems to some observers.

Crested Newt, *Triturus cristatus.* — This is the most aquatic of our newts, preferring deep ponds. It hibernates on land, usually. It is rare in northern Scotland, and is not a montane species. Old records exist from Abernethy and eastern Ross and Cromarty, but the only recent sighting is from Forres.

Palmate Newt, *Triturus helveticus.* — The Palmate Newt is much more of a montane creature, and is found in the hills as high as 2000 ft. (610 m.) It is the commonest of our newts, and appears to like any size of pond, and even brackish water. There are not many records from close to Inverness, but perhaps this is the problem of under-recording once more. There is an old record from near Forres, and a recent one from Elgin. To the south, there is a cluster of records from the Aviemore area. "Newts" are present in forests such as Ferness, Glen Mazeran and Affric, but though these are likely to be the present species, this is not confirmed. According to older accounts, the Palmate Newt was common in the Moray Basin.

THE REPTILES

Slow Worm, *Anguis fragilis.* — This is a lizard, not a snake, despite the appearance. It prefers drier places and is to be seen sunning itself on dry banks and slopes. It is common enough in the area, being found on both sides of Loch Ness, and through the Moray Firth lowlands. This elusive creature is probably more common than is realised.

Common Lizard, *Lacerta vivipara.* — This lizard chooses a range of habitats from hills to coastal dunes. It is widely spread around Inverness, with many records from both the coastal zone and reaching into the glens. They do not, however, occur in dense woodland, and they are restricted to the lower moorlands, seldom being seen above 1500 ft. (460 m.) in eastern Scotland.

Adder, *Vipera berus.* — Many people fear the Adder, our only poisonous snake, though it will only strike when cornered, and more often slips silently away when disturbed. It is widely distributed generally, preferring open moorland and hillside, and woodland fringes. It also occurs in marshy habitats, but shows a marked preference for sun-traps and dry banks. Around Inverness it is local, but may be abundant where it does occur. The Adder appears to be absent from a wide area between and southwards from Inverness and Nairn, but there are plenty of records further east, and to the west of Loch Ness. It is difficult to account for the absence of records from the huge moorland area south-east of Loch Ness.

THE AQUATIC FAUNA

Most of the lochs, rivers and burns of this area are poor in nutrients, and have a sparse aquatic invertebrate and fish fauna, with a rather limited range of species. Towards the north of Nairn, and particularly on the areas of coastal land, the lochs (Loch Loy, Loch Flemington, for example) are richer chemically, and these would be expected to have a more diverse and very much more abundant invertebrate fauna, and populations of faster-growing fish.

Fish

Relatively few species of freshwater fish occur this far north in Scotland. Brown Trout *(Salmo trutta* ssp. *fario)* and Eel *(Anguilla anguilla)* occur in virtually every loch or river, except those which periodically dry out, and some of the small very acid dubh lochans, while Salmon *(Salmo salar)* and Sea Trout *(Salmo trutta* ssp. *trutta)* occur in most of those with easy communication to the sea. Salmon are worth more in terms of hard cash than the other species, and form the basis, with Sea Trout, of a small commercial fishing industry, while these two, plus Brown Trout, are important as the basis of the traditional sport of angling, and, as such, are an important tourist attraction. The two common predatory fish, Pike *(Esox lucius)* and Perch *(Perca fluviatilis)* are both introduced species (no records exist of when they were brought to Scotland) and their distribution is much localised. Pike are fairly widespread in the lochs (including Loch Ness and Loch Ussie) and slow-flowing reaches of rivers, including the Beauly and the Conon systems. Perch, on the other hand, are recorded from some of the lochs in lower Strathconon only. Both species are considered vermin in this part of the country, and Pike, in particular, must have a significant adverse effect on the numbers of young Salmon and Sea Trout reaching the sea. The arctic salmonid fish, Char *(Salvelinus alpinus),* which is restricted to the northern parts of Britain, is found in a number of the deeper lochs, including Loch Ness, but is rarely taken by anglers. The North American species, Rainbow Trout *(Salmo gairdneri)* has been introduced into at least one loch in the area.

The smaller fish of the area include the Three-spined Stickleback *(Gasterosteus aculeatus),* the Ten-spined Stickleback *(Pungitius pungitius)* and the Minnow *(Phoxinus phoxinus).* Two lampreys also occur, the Sea Lamprey *(Petromyzon marinus)* and the River Lamprey *(Lampetra fluviatilis).* Unfortunately, the distribution of these fish is imperfectly known.

One fish which spends prolonged periods in fresh water in the lower stretches of the rivers, and in some of the lochs by the sea, is the Flounder *(Platichthys flesus).*

An estuarine vagrant which has been recorded from the Inner Moray Firth is the Sturgeon *(Acipenser sturio),* but this is rare.

Invertebrates

The invertebrates of the area are mainly those typical of oligotrophic conditions, particularly species associated with fast, stony rivers and wave-washed stony shores of lochs. Peat pool species are also well represented. Many Dragonflies *(Odonata)* are characteristic of the last type of habitat, and many of the commoner species, plus a few rare northern species, have been recorded from the Inverness area. Among the common species of the Sub-order *Zygoptera* (Damsel-flies) are the Common Blue Damsel-fly *(Ennalagma cyathigerum)* and the Large Red Damsel-fly *(Pyrrhosoma nymphula)* and, of the Sub-order *Anisoptera* (Hawker Dragon-fly), there are the black *Sympetrum danae* and *Libellula quadrimaculata,* which are found in, or flying round, most areas of still water. The rarities include the largest of the Dragon-flies, the Golden-ringed Dragon-fly *(Cordulegaster boltoni), Somatochlora arctica* and the slightly more widespread *Sympetrum nigrescens.*

Most of the common British species of Stonefly *(Plecoptera)* occur in the area, the "Needle-flies" *(leuctra* and *cannia* spp.) being very common in the burns where the adults are often abundant crawling over emergent stones. Species confined to the northern and "arctic" habitats include *Capnia atra* and *Protonemura monticola.* Mayflies *(Ephemeroptera)* are also fairly well represented, particularly by stream-dwelling *Baetidae* and *Ecdyonuridae,* and all three members of the restricted "arctic" family *Siphlonuridae* are present in high altitude lochs and burns. Caddis larvae *(Trichoptera)* are generally abundant in all but the fastest stretches of the rivers. A common species whose cases, which are square in cross section, often cover the tops of stones, is *Brachycentrus subnubilus,* and caseless net-spinning species, such as the *Polycentropus* and *Hydropsyche* spp. are often abundant beneath the stones both in rivers and on loch shores. The Water Beetles *(Coleoptera)* include some restricted northern species such as *Oreodytes borealis, Hygrotus novemlineatus* and the Whirligig Beetle *(Gryinus opacus),* the latter occurring in high altitude peat pools.

Molluscs *(Mollusca)* are not abundant in this region, except in the calcareous coastal areas, and even here relatively few species occur, compared with Britain further south. One species, the Pearl Mussel *(Margaritifera margaritifera)* is, however, abundant in the gravelly sections of the larger rivers.

THE COASTAL FAUNA

The coast of this part of Scotland may be divided roughly into two sections. The first of these includes the long tidal inlet of the Beauly/Inner Moray Firth. Within this, the Beauly Firth may be described as inner estuary, with low salinity, while the middle estuarine areas, including Longman Bay, Castle Stuart Bay and Munlochy Bay, have intermediate salinity. Outer estuarine areas, with high salinity, include the Bay of Ardersier and the inlet behind Whiteness Spit. The second section is the Outer Moray Firth, enclosed between Tarbat Ness and Burghead. This section, while not quite open coastline, is nevertheless open to the north-east gales, and quite exposed.

Fish.

Scottish coastal waters are rich feeding grounds for fish of commercial importance throughout the year. The most numerous and valuable of these occurring locally are Cod *(Gadus callarias)*, Whiting *(Gadus merlangus)* and Herring *(Clupea harengus)*, which are sometimes present in dense shoals in the Inner Moray Firth. Sprats *(Clupea sprattus)* also congregate in the estuaries, and large shoals enter the Beauly Firth, providing food for Goosander and other birds which follow the fish. Other fish (Rae 1967) present on our shores include Haddock *(Gadus aeglifinus)*, Dab *(Limanda limanda)*, Rough Dab *(Hippoglossoides platessoides)*, Lemon Sole *(Michrostomus kitt)*, Witch *(Glyptocephalus cynoglossus)*, Flounder (already mentioned under freshwater), Variegated Sole *(Microchirus variegatus)*, Grey Gurnard *(Trigla gurnardus)*, Pogge *(Agonus cataphractus)*, Dragonet *(Callionymus lyra)*, Butter-fish *(Pholis gunnelus)*, Yarrell's Blenny *(Chirolophis galerita)*, Fifteen-spined Stickleback *(Spinachia spinachia)*, Greater Pipe-fish *(Syngnathus acus)*, Skate *(Raja batis)* and Hag-fish *(Myxine glutinosa)*. Sand Eels *(Ammodytes* spp.) are a most important food species for Cod in the Moray Firth. The list is by no means complete.

Invertebrates

Over fifty species of worms, shellfish and crustaceans are present on the foreshore, and a list of the common species is given below. Those marked with an asterisk form an important component of the diet of wading birds.

Annelida (Worms) — *Arenicola marina* (Lugworm); *Fabrica sabella; *Nephyts hombergi* (Catworm); *Nereis diversicolor* (Ragworm); *Pygospio elegans; *Scoloplos armiger; Oligochaeta* sp. (Few-bristled Worm); *Peloscolex benedini.*

Mollusca (Shellfish) — *Cardium edule* (Common Cockle); *Hydrobia ulvae* (Laver Spire-shell); *Macoma balthica* (Baltic Tellin).

Crustacea (Crustaceans) — *Corophium volutator.*

Other interesting molluscs are present, including the Common Periwinkle *(Littorina littorea)*, Flat Periwinkle *(Littorina littoralis)* and the Rough Periwinkle *(Littorina saxatilis)*, Sand Gaper *(Mya arenaria)*, Common Mussel *(Mytilus edulis)*, *Retusa alba*, Cut-trough Shell *(Spisula subtruncata)*, Thin Tellin *(Tellina tenuis)* and Striped Venus *(Venus striatula)*. The Oyster *(Ostrea edulis)* is present, and there was once a fishery in the Moray Firth. They have since become scarce. Munlochy Bay seemed particularly suitable for the species, and an experimental laying of three-year-old Brittany oysters was made in the bay in June, 1957. The results were inconclusive. Other crustaceans present are the Shore Crab *(Carcinus maenas)*, the Shrimp *(Crangon vulgaris)* and Hermit Crab *(Eupagurus bernhardus)*. The following species of some interest may be added to the list. Norway Lobster *(Nephrops norvegicus)*, Common Lobster *(Homarus vulgaris)*, Squat Lobster *(Galathea squamifera)*, Prawn *(Pandalus* sp.) and Edible Crab *(Cancer pagurus)*, all crustaceans; Tower Shell *(Turritella communis)*, Common Squid *(Loligo forbesi)*, both mulluscs; and Sea Mouse *(Aphrodite aculeata)*, a marine bristle worm.

TERRESTRIAL INVERTEBRATES

Sources of informaton are so few, and so scattered, and local experts so rare, that it has not been possible to gather much information. I have relied on published work, mainly, and only those which are readily available. Insects only are discussed.

Lepidoptera (Butterflies and Moths). — The butterflies are attractive and of more general interest than most other insects. The following species are noted for the Inverness area: —

Erynnis tages, Dingy Skipper (rare); *Pieris brassicae,* Large White; *Pieris rapae,* Small White; *Pieris napi,* Green-veined White; *Anthocharis cardamines,* Orange Tip; *Callophrys rubi,* Green Hairstreak (rare); *Lycaena phlaeas,* Small Copper (rare); *Aricia artaxerxes,* Northern Brown Argus (rare); *Polyommatus icarus,* Common Blue; *Cupido minimus,* Small Blue (rare); *Aglais urticae,* Small Tortoiseshell; *Argynnis euphrosyne,* Pearl-bordered Fritillary (rare); *Argynnis aglaia,* Dark-green Fritillary; *Argynnis selene,* Small Pearl-bordered Fritillary; *Euphydryas aurinia,* Marsh Fritillary (very rare); *Pararge aegeria,* Speckled Wood (very rare); *Eumenis semele* Grayling (very rare); *Erebia aethiops,* Scotch Argus; *Moniola jurtina,* Meadow Brown; *Coenonympha pamphilus,* Small Heath; *Coenonympha tullia,* Large Heath.

These records are from the Provisional Atlas (Heath 1970).

Moths are perhaps less eye-catching than butterflies, though many are very attractive. The following are a few of the more abundant species: —

Trichiura crataegi, Pale Oak Eggar; *Lasiocampa quercus,* Oak Eggar; *Saturnia pavonia,* Emperor Moth; *Laothoe populi,* Poplar Hawk-moth; *Carura vinula,* Puss Moth; *Pheosia gnoma,* Lesser Swallow Prominent; *Arctia caja,* Garden Tiger; *Spilosoma lubricipeda,* White Ermine.

The serious student will find more records in the Provisional

Atlas (Heath and Skelton, 1973). Botanists will have noticed that the main plants associated with certain lepidoptera species are reflected in the Latin names listed above. Rothamsted Experimental Station have for some years now organised an Insect Survey, the results of which are published in Station Reports annually. Local centres from which data is available are Newton (Elgin) and Fort Augustus, as well as Ardross and Morangie to the north. Species of economic interest captured at light traps at these four centres include: —

Gortyna micacea, Rosy Rustic; *Cerapteryx graminis,* Antler Moth; *Erannis aurantaria,* Scarce Umber; *Apamea secalis,* Common Rustic; *Operophtera brumata,* Winter Moth.

There are many others which the student will find by referring to the sources quoted.

Hemiptera (Bugs). — The Rothamsted Insect Survey includes suction trapping of Aphids (green-flies etc.) and information of those of economic interest is published in Station Reports, annually.

Hymenoptera (Bees, Wasps, Ants etc.). — A preliminary Bumble Bee Atlas has been published by the Bee Research Association (1973). From this source, the following list of Bumble Bees for Inverness and District has been prepared: —

Bombus agrorum; Bombus hortorum; Bombus jonellus; Bombus lucorum; Bombus magnus; Bombus pratorum; Bombus terrestris; Psithyrus bohemicus.

Once more, the specialist is referred to the original source for more detailed information.

Collingwood (1961) has described the Ants of the Highlands, and notes the following species from the Inverness area: —

Leptothorax acervorum; Myrmica rubra; Myrmica ruginodis; Myrmica sulcinodis; Myrmica scabrinodis; Myrmica lobicornis; Myrmica sabuleti; Formica sanguinea; Formica exsecta; Formica lugubris; Formica aquilonia; Formica lemani; Lasius niger; Lasius flavus; Lasius umbratus.

The wood ants *(F. aquilonia and lugubris)* appear to be losing ground as a result of burning and clear felling. They are unlikely to return to areas from which they have been exterminated.

Siphonaptera (Fleas). — This group of species is of interest, since each is normally peculiar to one type of animal, although the Human Flea *(Pulex irritans)* also favours the Fox and Badger. The list below is based upon maps produced by the Biological Records Centre, and the host species is also given.

Ceratophyllus columbae, the Pigeon Flea (nests of *Columba livia); Ceratophyllus gallinae,* the Hen Flea (wide range of habitats); *Monopsyllus sciurorum,* the Red Squirrel Flea; *Megabothris rectangulatus; Malareus penicilliger,* most small mammals (esp. Bank Vole); *Peromyscopsylla spectabilis,* Bank Vole and Field Vole; *Leptopsylla segnis,* House Mouse Flea; *Ctenophthalmus nolilis,* Voles, Mice, Shrews and Rats; *Ctenophthalmus bisoctodentatus,* a Mole Flea; *Palaeopsylla minor,* a Common Mole Flea; *Hystrichopsylla talpae,* the Mole Flea (also Voles, Shrews and Field Mice); *Spilopsyllus cuniculi,* the Rabbit Flea; *Archaeopsylla erinacei,* the Hedgehog Flea; *Pulex irritans,* the Human Flea (often observed, but less often recorded!).

CONCLUSION

The paucity of information reflects the scattered nature of the sources, but it also serves to emphasise the urgent need for research work on our invertebrate fauna. If this limited account serves no other purpose, it may persuade some enthusiasts to take up specialist studies in some of the groups.

ACKNOWLEDGEMENTS

Most of the information in this account has come from the many people who have helped, and I acknowledge with thanks their contributions.

The Nature Conservancy have contributed through R. Britton in the section of aquatic fauna; R. N. Campbell on freshwater fish; V. P. W. Lowe on Red Squirrel; Miss S. Anderson (now with the Seals Research Unit) who carried out the invertebrate survey; J. Heath, who gave access to records from the Biological Records Centre and A. Macdonald with general mammal information. The Forestry Commission assisted in the persons of D. Elgy, A. Hinde, D. Ross, and A. Scott, who gave access to records. The Department of Agriculture and Fisheries for Scotland helped in the persons of J. Anderson on Mink and R. Hewson, who gave a preview of his joint paper on Foxes. The British Deer Society (Scotland) gave me access to their distribution maps. I would also like to acknowledge the advice given by Lovat Estates, Kyle and Glen (Highland Safaris), G. Gill, M. Harvie, D. Stewart and several keepers who have preferred to remain anonymous. Mrs I. L. B. Rose typed and edited the script. A more detailed account than is possible to include in this book has been deposited with the Inverness Field Club.

REFERENCES

Alford, D. U., *Preliminary Bumble Bee Atlas*, London Bee Research Association, 1973.

British Museum (Natural History), *List of British Vertebrates*, London, 1935.

Collingwood, C. A., "Ants in the Scottish Islands," *Scot. Nat.* 70, pp. 12-21, 1961.

Cooke, A. S., "Indication of Recent Changes in Status in the British Isles of the Frog *(Rana temporaria)* and the Toad *(Bufo bufo).*," *Jour. Zool.* 167, pp. 161-178, London, 1972.

Corbet, G. B., "Provisional Distribution Maps of British Mammals," *Mammal Review 1*, Nos. 4/5, 1971.

Darling, F. F., and Boyd, J. M., "The Highlands and Islands," *New Naturalist*, Collins, London, 1964.

Heath, J., "Provisional Atlas of the Insects of the British Isles. Part I. Lepidoptera Rhopalocera (Butterflies)," *N.E.R.C.*, Biological Records Centre, 1970.

Heath, J., and Skelton, M. J., "Provisional Atlas of the Insects of the British Isles. Part II. Lepidoptera (Moths — Part I)." *N.E.R.C.*, Biological Records Centre, 1973.

Hewson, R., "The Mountain Hare in Scotland in 1951." *Scot. Nat.* 66, pp. 70-88. 1954.

Hewson, R., "Fallow Deer in Banff and Moray," *Scot. Nat.* 71, pp. 90-94, 1964.

Hewson, R., and Kolb, H. H., "Changes in the Numbers and Distribution of Foxes *(Vulpes vulpes)* killed in Scotland from 1948-1970," *Jour. Zool.* 171, pp. 345-366, London, 1973.

Jenkins, D., "The present Status of the Wild Cat *(Felis silvestris)* in Scotland," *Scot. Nat.* 70, 126-138, 1962.

Lockie, J. D., "Distribution and Fluctuations of the Pine Marten *(Martes martes)* in Scotland," *Jour. Anim. Ecol.* 33, pp. 349-356, 1964.

MacNally, L., *Highland Year*, J. M. Dent & Sons Ltd., London, 1968.

MacNally, L., *Highland Deer Forest*, J. M. Dent & Sons Ltd., London, 1970.

Maitland, P. S., "Key to British Freshwater Fishes," *Freshwater Biological Association Scientific Publ. No. 27*, 1972.

Millar, R. H., "Scottish Oyster Investigations, 1946-1958," *Dept. of Agric. and Fisheries for Scotland Marine Research 1961* No. 3, H.M.S.O., Edinburgh, 1961.

Rae, B. B., "The food of Cod in the North Sea and on West of Scotland Grounds," *Dept. Agric. and Fisheries for Scotland Marine Research 1967* No. 1, H.M.S.O., Edinburgh, 1967.

Rae, B. B., "The Food of Seals in Scottish Waters," *Dept. of Agric. and Fisheries for Scotland Marine Research 1968* No. 2, H.M.S.O., Edinburgh, 1968.

Southern, H. M., *The Handbook of British Mammals*, The Mammal Society, Oxford, Blackwell, 1964.

Stephens, M. M., *The Natural History of the Otter*, Univ. Fed. Anim. Welfare, London, 1957.

Taylor, L. R., and French, R. A., "Rothamsted Insect Survey, *Rothamsted Experimental Station Reports, Part II*, 1970 et seq.

Taylor, R. H. R., *The Distribution of Reptiles and Amphibians in England, Wales, Scotland, Ireland and the Channel Islands*, (privately printed), 1963; also *Brit. J. Herpet 3*, pp. 95-115.

Whitehead, G. K., *The Deer of Great Britain and Ireland*, Routledge and Kegan Paul, London, 1964.

Wootton, A., *How to begin the study of entomology*, British Naturalists Association (n.d.).

WILD BIRDS ROUND INVERNESS

MAEVE RUSK

Inverness and its hinterland, stretching from the coast of the Inner Moray and the Beauly Firths south to the Monadhliaths and west to Cannich, have throughout the year a rich and varied bird population. From August, ducks such as mallard, teal and wigeon return to the firths after the breeding season. Shelduck cross the North Sea in order to moult, come back to Longman Bay in October and gradually move up the Beauly Firth from January in readiness for nesting. Winter flocks of red-breasted merganser occur. In recent years a large flock of goosander has been found in the middle of the Beauly Firth, remaining for only a few weeks from mid-December. Our wintering geese are mainly greylag. Pinkfoot pass through on spring and autumn passage. In the last twenty years, Canada geese have come in increasing numbers to moult in the Beauly Firth. There were about twenty to thirty in the early 1950s, but now there are several hundred, arriving in May and leaving late in August after the moult is completed. R. H. Dennis[1] has shown by ringing returns that they come from the Harrogate area. Mute swan numbers fluctuate, probably depending on feeding available elsewhere and in winter whooper swan visit the area. Several hundred wader, such as curlew, oystercatcher and redshank, with smaller numbers of dunlin, and bar-tailed godwit, winter on the Beauly Firth.

Near the mouth of the Caledonian Canal at Clachnaharry, tufted duck gather in hard weather when the inland lochs are frozen. Sometimes some scaup are found with them and, recently, goldeneye joined this flock. A few wader and gulls are often seen in the same area. Between the Canal mouth and the pier at South Kessock wigeon congregate offshore, and oystercatcher and curlew flocks are found in winter. Just inland, there are some brackish pools with mud around the edges, and it is here that a rarity, a citrine wagtail, was seen by R. H. Dennis[2] in the autumn of 1972 during a Scottish Ornithologists' Club excursion. At the mouth of the River Ness, off the sewage outflow, there is a winter flock of goldeneye which has gradually increased to over three hundred in 1972. Cormorant can be seen offshore, flying in long lines or small parties into the Beauly

Firth. At low water some sit out on the mud and shingle banks. Between the river mouth and Longman Point the seaweed-covered mud is a good feeding place for wader, mainly oystercatcher, lapwing, curlew and redshank, which are joined by flocks of golden plover for a few weeks in the autumn, and throughout the winter by turnstone.

East of Longman Point, the rubbish tip is a favourite feeding and roosting site for the large flock of herring gull, up to three thousand in winter. The greater black-backed gull with them number up to five hundred at times, and there are smaller numbers of black-headed gull and common gull. In late spring and summer, there are a few lesser black-backs. The occasional Iceland and glaucous gull joins the Longman or harbour flock in winter.

Land reclamation from the firth at Longman Bay has diminished the extent at the mud flats which form the winter feeding area for hundreds of duck and wader of many species, so that we are unlikely to see again the great flocks of wigeon numbering three thousand and of knot almost double that number. Smaller numbers of mallard, teal, wigeon and shellduck remain, together with flocks of oystercatcher, lapwing, ringed plover, curlew, bar-tailed godwit, redshank, knot and dunlin. Another, more insidious, threat to the feeding area, is the slow encroachment of sand, gradually replacing the mud, so that the invertebrate fauna becomes poorer. This is most noticeable north west of the mouth of the Mill Burn. Near the burn mouth sandwich and common tern come for a few weeks between the breeding season and their departure on migration. Further round the bay, the pintail flock wintering offshore number up to one hundred and forty, and are one of the largest concentrations of these species in the north of Scotland.

At Allanfearn the shore consists of shingle, and the duck and wader numbers become smaller still, until one reaches Alturlie Bay off Castle Stuart, where there are some concentrations of duck. The flatter shore between Ardersier and Fort George holds flocks of dunlin in winter. At the same season, black and red-throated diver may be seen flying past Fort George where the channel is narrow.

Further east, off Camp Sands, shelduck congregate, and the Carse of Ardersier used to be favoured by geese until the recent construction of the oil rig building site. It has also destroyed the sheltered inlet inside Whiteness Head, which supported many hundred duck and several thousand wader. There they used to have a relatively undisturbed feeding and roosting site. The shingle on the seaward side had a large breeding colony of tern, and the adjacent sand dunes had flocks of snow bunting in winter.

In spring and summer on farm land, corn bunting sing on fence posts and telegraph wires, and sky lark are common. In patches of whin one finds yellowhammer and linnet and an occasional stonechat. Pheasant are common, but partridge are very local in distribution. Rook and jackdaw feed in the fields and there are the usual hedgerow birds. The commonest raptor here is the kestrel. If there is adjacent woodland, some sparrowhawk are found as well as wood pigeon. The tawny owl is widely distributed, but the barn owl is scarce in most places. On rather higher ground there are oystercatcher and curlew, while lapwing are typical of marginal land. In autumn and winter the stubble fields provide food for winter flocks of chaffinch, yellowhammer, greenfinch, linnet and house sparrow. In some winters, they are joined by migrant brambling from Scandinavia.

The kind of birds found on a loch in this district depends on the feeding available and, to a certain extent, on shelter. Where a loch is situated on rich farm land, as is Loch Flemington, coot and moorhen abound. There are several pairs of little grebe and mallard and tufted duck are the most numerous among the duck in summer. There are also some mute swan. In wet areas near the edge of rivers and some lochs, there are reed bunting throughout the year, and the sedge warbler is a summer migrant. The grasshopper warbler is more often heard than seen, and is very local in distribution. If there are suitable islands on some of the inland lochs, common and black-headed gull form breeding colonies. Some of these lochs hold the main British breeding population of the Slavonian grebe, which is actually commoner in our area than the little grebe. Unfortunately this beautiful and uncommon bird has difficulty in hatching its eggs if it is subjected to too much disturbance. Tufted duck in summer, and a few goldeneye in winter share the same lochs.

In late April each year, pied wagtail move down Loch Ness and remain to breed beside the main road. They leave in autumn, and, apart from a few wintering on the banks of the river in Inverness, they are not seen until the following Spring.

Oystercatcher are common, and breed on the shingle of rivers well up to high moorland. Grey wagtail are more often on the middle stretches, and dipper there, and higher up. In summer, common sandpiper nest on the edges of lochs and rivers and, where there are marshy areas, also mallard, teal and a few wigeon.

In summer the commonest birds on the moors are meadow pipit, golden plover and red grouse, and wherever there are suitable rocky crevices or piles of stones for nest sites, one finds wheatear. Twite are fairly local. At somewhat lower levels, we often hear the cuckoo, in damper areas, the curlew, and in marshes, the drumming of the snipe. The short-eared owl is seen hunting when food is plentiful, but at other times it is uncommon. Where there are suitable cliffs or old trees, buzzard and kestrel are the commonest birds of prey. There are not very many golden eagle. In late summer the meadow pipit, wheatear and golden plover leave. In winter, the moors are almost deserted except for a few red grouse, but raven and especially hooded crow are well distributed in wilder country throughout the year.

We are fortunate in this part of Inverness-shire in having coniferous forests at all stages of growth, from the recently planted to the fully mature. As each grows up, it provides food, shelter and nesting sites for a wide variety if birds. In the early stages, when there is plenty of rough grass between the little trees, one finds meadow pipit, skylark, whinchat and willow warbler and the hunting kestrel. As the trees grow bigger, we find other birds, such as song thrush, blackbird, robin, hedge sparrow, wren, great, blue and coal tit, goldcrest, whitethroat, redpoll and chaffinch, the last named being the most common. Siskin are more often in older thinned forests and open scrub. Missel thrush are usual up in the glens or in higher woods. In mature coniferous woods with a plentiful cone crop, the Scottish crossbill feeds and breeds. Black grouse and capercaillie feed in the forests. Redstart nest in holes in trees in oak scrub. In our area, the song thrush is a partial migrant, leaving the glens in winter and returning in spring. In autumn and winter, flocks of migrant fieldfare and redwing feed on the berries of rowan, hawthorn and rose hips.

Inverness itself is not without its bird population. The Ness, flowing through the centre of the town, never freezes, so at all times of the year there are birds either on the river or its banks. The Ness Islands are always worth a visit, even in early January, when the dipper begins to sing from the rocks near-by. From autumn to spring, a few mallard and red-breasted merganser can often be seen, and sometimes a heron. Among the trees, great tit, blue tit and coal tit feed in winter flocks. The tree-creeper climbs the trunks of the older trees, and goldcrest feed and call from higher up. In winter there are siskin, too. In autumn, migrant redwing join the blackbirds, song thrushes and missel thrushes in stripping the berries. In spring the common sandpiper trills on the banks before passing upstream. In autumn and winter, redwing and field-fare feed on fields at the Bught, and oystercatchers are there at most seasons. In the town gardens there are blackbird, song thrush, robin, hedge sparrow, greenfinch, chaffinch, house sparrow, the three tits, great, blue and coal, and occasionally goldcrest. Starlings are resident, and their numbers are greatly increased in winter by migrants from the continent. They roost in various parts of Inverness and, in the last few years, are found on buildings, causing a clamour at dusk and inconvenience to pedestrians below. Herring-gull frequent roofs, and in the last few years have taken to nesting on them in small numbers. Another relatively new nesting species in the town is the collared dove. Swifts arrive in May and breed in Inverness. House martins are nesting in increasing numbers, but the sand martin colony on the canal bank died out when the nesting site became unusable. Of the crow family, we have both carrion and hooded crow, and hybrids, as well as jackdaws and small colonies of rook.

The commonest warbler is the willow warbler, where there is suitable scrub in waste ground, or even in the larger gardens. The occasional blackcap comes to bird tables in the winter. Sparrowhawk sometimes take their prey from gardens, and the tawny owl is heard at night. In some years even corncrake are heard around the burgh boundary, and one apparently bred in the disused garden at Eden Court in 1972, before the building of the theatre began. Cotoneasters grow well in Inverness, so waxwing, coming over the North Sea in irruption years, tend to stay a large part of the winter feeding on the berries, rather than merely passing through.

In this district, duck, geese and swans have been counted monthly on the coast for over twenty years on behalf of the Wildfowl Trust, and more recently, waders for the British Trust for Ornithology. In the years 1968-72 the area has been surveyed in 10 km. squares, on behalf of the latter, for an Atlas of breeding birds in Great Britain and Ireland, which is being compiled by Dr J. T. R. Sharrock. This will show their distribution compared with the rest of the country.

––––––––––

Records for the Inverness district are published in "Scottish Birds", the journal of the Scottish Ornithologists' Club. I am indebted to my fellow members of the Inverness Branch for bird records throughout the years, and in particular to M. I. Harvey.

REFERENCES

1. Dennis, R. H., "Capture of Moulting Canada Geese in the Beauly Firth," *Wildfowl Trust 15th Annual Report,* 1964.
2. Dennis, R. H., "Citrine Wagtail at Inverness," *Scottish Birds. The Journal of the Scottish Ornithologists' Club,* 7, p. 316, 1973.

Curlew
(Numenius Arquata)

ARCHAEOLOGY AND EARLY HISTORY

PREHISTORIC MONUMENTS

a. The Earlier Prehistoric Monuments

AUBREY BURL

After the Ice Ages, it was perhaps not until the 4th millenium B.C. that the environment around Inverness became attractive enough for Neolithic people to settle there. Once discovered, however, the area at the head of the Great Glen offered many advantages. Sheltered to the east and west by mountains, its soil fertile, its rainfall low in contrast to the heavy precipitation at the S.W. of the Glen, it must have appeared to the people who first came to it, an ideal area for settlement. And the Glen itself provided a simple route for the traveller from the south.

N.E. Ireland had been settled by stone-using farming communities during the mid-4th millennium. These people, whose economy may have depended on cattle-keeping, struggled to clear patches of land from the forest and, as they gradually came to control their surroundings, built great monuments in which rituals could be performed that included the use of human bones. Their light boats, made from cattle-hide stretched over light timber frames, crossed and re-crossed the waters of the Irish Sea, sometimes taking settlers to new parts, sometimes carrying prospectors searching for sources of stone suitable for their axes.

At some time, voyagers came to Loch Linnhe and sailed up it[1], an adventure in itself, because of the furious tidal race through the Corran Narrows. Once beyond that, the pleasant Lochy valley led N.E. towards the passable, but uninviting, shores of Loch Ness and then opened out into the wide, low-lying moors around Inverness. Here, on the easily worked sands and gravels of the gentle valley sides, the first farmers of the county settled.

Today one can see the remnants of their megalithic tombs, megalithic certainly, because they are constructed of large stones, tombs less certainly, because, although they contained human bones, their purpose may primarily have been more ritualistic than sepulchral. There are three probabilities. The first is that they are unlikely to be the handiwork of the very

F

earliest settlers, whose major concern would have been to clear the land and to establish homes. The second is that some of them, at least, are composite monuments of several different phases, much as cathedrals are compositions of successive architectural styles. Thirdly, their builders came to the area from the S.W. along the Great Glen, rather than from the east along the shores of the Moray Firth. Not only does the Glen provide an easy passage, but axes of porcellanite from Tievebulliagh mountain in N.E. Ireland have been found in N.E. Scotland[2], and many of the megalithic cairns are of forms compatible with others in S.W. Scotland[3]. Conversely, there is little evidence for influence from the east until a much later period.

The tombs are of the type known as passage-graves, monuments which consist of a passage built of large stones covered by slabs, leading to a central chamber which may be flat-topped or corbelled. Both passage and chamber were covered by a cairn, usually round, surrounded by kerb-stones. In the Inverness region, there are two major and a minor type of Neolithic tomb: representatives of the Orkney-Cromarty group, which possibly are the earliest here; long cairns, eastern in origin, few in number, and probably very late in the 3rd millennium B.C.; and the most spectacular of the Inverness megalithic monuments, the Clava cairns, which include both passage-graves and ring-cairns surrounded by stone circles.

1. *Orkney-Cromarty tombs.* In Inverness, these tombs are both badly ruined and on private land. Related monuments are widespread in northern Scotland from Easter Ross up to the Orkneys, the Inverness tombs being a small, outlying group of the tradition. The round cairns, originally about 30 foot (9.14 m.) in diameter, have long since been removed, revealing the remains of the rectangular or polygonal chamber in which the burials were placed, and the short, low passage along which the bodies or cremated bones were dragged. The entrances were almost invariably set between N.E. and S.E.

Rectangular chambers are common among the Neolithic peasant cultures of western Europe. Prototypes for the Inverness examples may be seen as early as the 4th millennium in Argyll, reaffirming the belief in the Great Glen route. These box-like chambers, sometimes subdivided in Inverness, have been seen as the stone equivalents of much earlier timber graves[4, 5], and may themselves possess extra features added by newcomers. This seems feasible at Kilcoy South[6] (ROS 24) [All references in round brackets are site-numbers related to detailed notes in the descriptive County gazeteers provided in Miss Henshall's magisterial works[7], particularly Volume I, 1963], where a single-

Beaker from Short Cist Burial.
Clunes, Kirkhill.

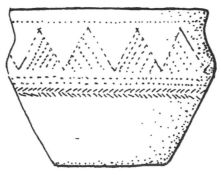

Food Vessel
from Cawdor

✳75

chamber and short passage later had a bigger chamber and passage conjoined to its entrance. Subsequently the second passage was further lengthened. The result is a complex monument, whose phases are difficult to disentangle and even more difficult to date.

Intermixing with the southern Scottish tradition of rectangular chambers is another of passage-graves containing small polygonal chambers, whose builders may ultimately have come from N.W. France, or even Iberia. In Easter Ross and Inverness-shire, monuments may be seen whose architecture combines both rectangular and polygonal chambers, hybrid forms that attest to a commingling of people and ideas. The development of small megalithic monuments with subdivided polygonal chambers and passages, marks the culmination of this process of integration and such tombs may have been built in the Inverness region down to the beginning of the 3rd millennium B.C.

Inside them are traces of ritual. In the chambers both inhumed and cremated bones of men, women and children have been found, as well as animal bones of considerable variety. It has been noticed that often there are only a few bones of each species, as though selection had taken place. Patches of charcoal sometimes occur on the chamber floors. There are infrequent scatters of white quartz pebbles. In the past, these relics have been considered contemporary with each other, so that the monuments have been interpreted as the sepulchral edifices of chiefs or priests, and their families, whose bones were placed in the mausolea over many generations by reverent followers. Any exceptional tomb in which no human bones were discovered was explained as a cenotaph, or as standing on acidic soil, which would have destroyed all organic material. Suspicions that such answers were incomplete have been increasing, especially since the excavation of the West Kennet barrow, Wiltshire, where, despite the abundance of human skeletal remains, there were few long bones and even fewer skulls. These must have been removed in antiquity. Much disturbance of bones in the chambers was observed, caused by people rummaging among them. "It is possible . . . to compose the ghoulish picture of a visitor to the barrow picking up a partly decomposed arm, detaching the humerus, and flinging the other bones in a dark corner. Similarly, the group of arthritic vertebrae found on the floor of the N.E. Chamber might have been picked up attached to a skull and then discarded."[8]

These megalithic "tombs" may in reality have been repositories for bones which were afterwards to be used in rituals whose nature we can only guess today. But, if the sites were periodically scavenged "and new cycles of burials were begun"[9], then it becomes all the more difficult to date them. The excavated artefacts are likely to belong only to the latest phases of the monument's use.

The majority of the Orkney-Cromarty tombs are to be found in the far north of Scotland. In Inverness-shire there are only five sites that belong to the group. Although their situation apparently impinges upon the territory of the Clava cairns, they usually occupy high ground, whereas most Clava sites are low-lying. Belladrum (INV 12) has a polygonal chamber. It is close to Kiltarlity and Belladrum North (INV 11), both Clava cairns. Leachkin (INV 38), also with a polygonal chamber once contained within a 70 foot (21.3 m.) cairn, stands on a high ridge; and Reelig (INV 46), the "Giant's Grave", survives as a misleadingly reconstructed stone setting, its cairn destroyed, terminating in a rectangular chamber. A flint, barbed-and-tanged arrowhead may have come from this site.

East of the Ness is Tomfat Plantation (INV 52), excavated recently[10]. This and Essich Moor (see below) are the only definite Orkney-Cromarty cairns on this side of the river in the area where Clava cairns are most numerous, suggesting that in general the two groups of cairn-builders remained apart, even though the Orkney-Cromarty preference for high-placed sites implies that they would not have been competing with the Clava people for territory.

2. *Long Cairns.* The construction of long mounds of earth or stones, sometimes incorporating chambers of wood or megaliths, is a phenomenon well-known in southern and eastern England in Neolithic times. Lately others have been recognised in Scotland, including that excavated at Dalladies, Kincardin-shire[11] and dated in its second phase to 3240 ± 105 B.C. Builders of these monuments, if they entered areas of earlier passage-graves, sometimes covered the small, round cairns beneath their own long mounds, perhaps to enhance the potency of their own site.

In Inverness there are only two known examples, a possible site at Glenbanchor (INV 33), at the very head of the Spey valley, 3 miles (4.83 km.) west of the most southerly Clava-type cairn at Altlarie (INV 3). It stands on the west bank of the Allt Fionndrigh and is an upstanding mound, 95 foot (28.9 m.) long, atypically aligned N.-S. The other is at Essich Moor (INV 31), on a narrow ridge along a high moor dividing the Nairn valley from Loch Ness. This is a splended example of a multi-phase hybrid monument, because the 380 foot (115.8 m.) long cairn, higher and wider at its S.S.W., conceals three single,

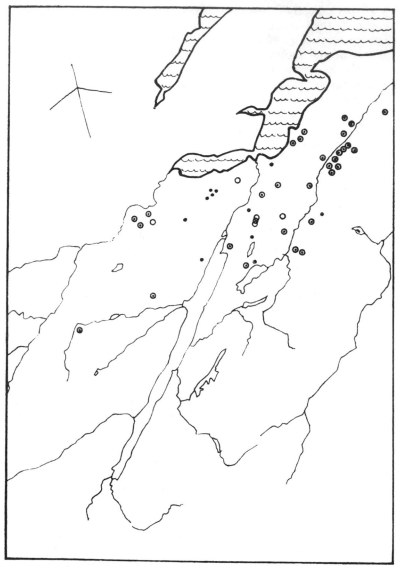

INVERNESS AND DISTRICT
DISTRIBUTION MAP 2

Clava Chambered Cairns   . ◉
Orkney/Cromarty Chambered Cairns . ○
Other Burial Cairns   . ●

SCALE .

rectangular chambers of the Orkney-Cromarty tradition, the two at the ends arranged N.-S., that in the centre, E.-W. There are a few traces of the kerbs of these early cairns protruding through the body of the long mound.

3. *The Clava Cairns.* Without doubt the best-preserved and most rewarding to visit of the megalithic monuments around Inverness are the Clava cairns. Several of these sites have been taken into guardianship by the State (Balnuaran of Clava; Corrimony) and may comfortably be inspected. Visually they are superb, yet their dating, their origin and their function are all in dispute, despite several recent excavations[12]. The group contains passage-graves and ring-cairns sharing many architectural features. The passage-graves have straight passages leading through a round cairn to a circular and exactly central chamber, with a basal wall of orthostats surmounted by corbelling. The roofs have collapsed. The ring-cairns consist of pennanular stony banks, edged with kerbstones and enclosing a central space. These sites have no entrance.

Altogether in the county, there are twenty-nine sites which may be confidently attributed to this group, with fifteen more that may have belonged. Of the twenty-nine, nine are certainly passage-graves, and twelve are ring-cairns. They tend to concentrate in three areas, all low-lying: at the head of the Great Glen; on the Aird, to the south of the Beauly Firth; and in the southern part of the Spey Valley. It is noticeable that most passage-graves are in the first area. The majority of the cairns were put up in rather inconspicuous positions. In general, the passage-graves are smaller than the ring-cairns, perhaps because of the technical problems of corbelling broad chambers. These chambers never exceed 16 foot (4.83 m.) across, whereas the central space of a ring-cairn can be as wide as 35 foot (10.7 m.). Despite these discrepancies, both types of cairn share unique architectural traits among the megalithic monuments of the British Isles.

Whereas the majority of chambered tombs have their entrances between N.E. and S.E., the entrances and tallest stones in the Clava cairns were erected towards the S.-S.W., the ring-cairn lines in particular clustering around the S.S.W.[14] Such orientations may indicate an interest in the midwinter sunset, but the alignments seem very imprecise, and it may be that, if they were astronomically determined, it was towards several celestial targets.

Both passage-graves and ring-cairns have stones graded in height, rising towards the S.S.W. They are also surrounded by stone circles. There is no other group of chambered tombs in the British Isles around which stone circles were set. There is an occasional site in Ireland, but only the Clava cairns were almost invariably encircled. Of the passage-graves, only the isolated Avielochan (INV 5) does not have a stone circle. Of the ring-cairns, only West Town (INV 50), in a remote position on the uplands near Loch Ashie, lacks such a setting of stones. The Clava stone circles, like the cairn-kerbs, are graded in height.

Several of the cairns have cupmarks on their stones, basin-shaped depressions perhaps 3 inches (76 mm.) across, made by grinding the surface with a small stone. In passage-graves these are to be found mainly in the passage and chamber, and only rarely on kerbs or circle-stones, whereas in ring-cairns the distribution is much more widespread, though well over half the markings are in the southern hemisphere of the monument. Several natural rocks in the neighbourhood of Inverness are cupmarked[15] and their proximity to the Clava cairns makes it likely that the same people were responsible for both[16]. Although there is no definitive interpretation of these markings, their frequent association with prehistoric burials, and their presence on stones supposedly aligned on the sun, suggests that they were symbols of life and fertility.

Because of the use and re-use of megalithic tombs over the centuries, the material in them today is often merely rejected detritus, fragments of the original deposits, and possibly misleading in its implications. Within the Clava cairns, there are signs of varied practices: scatters of white quartz pebbles (INV 17; 30); cremated bones (INV 9; 10; 21; 37); cists with skulls (INV 28); but no objects that can be used for dating.

Before looking into the purpose of these great megalithic monuments, it is worth asking how many people were involved in their construction. Demographic studies are notorious archaeological quicksands, but in matters concerned with the manipulating of heavy weights, it is possible to estimate a minimum number of workers needed to drag or erect a stone. At most Clava cairns the stones are of no considerable weight and are plentiful locally. The heaviest kerb at Gask (INV 32), the largest ring-cairn, is no more than about half a ton (508 kg.) and most stones are little heavier, except for those in the circle. The west stone at Balnuaran of Clava N.E. (INV 9), a sandstone block, measures about 11 x 2 x 5 feet (3.4 x 0.6 x 1.5 m.) and weighs about seven tons (7 tonnes). Perhaps fifteen persons would have been required to move it, implying a minimum community, including the young, aged and infirm, of some thirty people. If one guesses at an original total of about fifty

Clava cairns in Inverness-shire, with an average building-rate of one per generation over five centuries, as the culture slowly spread into the outlying districts, this would point to no more than two or three tombs belonging to the early phases, and a population of less than one hundred people in the county.

One of the most controversial problems of the Clava cairns has been their origins[17]. Although it is possible to detect a source for the passage-graves in the chambered-tomb tradition, the ring-cairns have no simple explanation. A recent excavation at Raigmore (INV 47) offers hints. The site was a kerbed enclosure with a low central mound, the kerbstones graded towards the S.W., surrounding pits, some of which contained charcoal from which came two C-14 determinations of 2782 ± 90 B.C. and 3033 ± 130 B.C. Similar enclosures are known from Ireland, and the first Clava monuments may have been simple circular stone settings, within which ceremonies of propitiation and supplications for fertility were conducted at specific times of the year. Some Irish sites were later covered by chambered tombs, and one may speculate that in the country immediately around Inverness people from the S.W. constructed similar encircled low mounds for their rituals, mounds which, at a later time, had passage-graves built on them. The ring-cairns which, without Clava features, are widely distributed in northern Britain, may be an indigenous development by natives influenced by the architecture and ritual of the passage-grave builders. In that sense they are derived from the chambered tombs, despite their native ancestry.

What is interesting, is the isolationism of the Clava builders. They appear confined to the Inverness area, except for the outlying group in the Spey valley. They are not to be found along the fertile coastlands of the Moray Firth, perhaps because this was already occupied by makers of beaker pottery[18]. If so, then any attempted Clava penetration into the area must have been late, for the land around Nairn was not settled in any numbers by beaker users until as late as the 16th century B.C.[19] This must be left as a problem for the future.

Two Clava sites can easily be visited. The first is at Corrimony (INV 17) in Glen Urquhart, a passage-grave excavated in 1952. A stone circle 77 feet (23.5 m.) in diameter surrounds a 50 foot (15.2 m.) cairn constructed on an artificial mound of small stones. Many broken quartz fragments had been deliberately scattered around the kerbstones during the building of the cairn. There is a gap in the stone circle at the E.N.E., where archaeologists found, not a stonehole, but a cobbled area which indicated that the gap was intentional.

The entrance to the passage is at the S.W. and leads to a central corbelled chamber, now roofless, 13 foot (3.96 m.) across. Within this was a small, slabbed area placed on sand, in which the excavators detected the stain of a crouched burial. A large stone, now lying on top of the cairn, is thought to have been the chamber's capstone. It is heavily cup-marked.

The second site is that of the great Balnuaran of Clava cemetery itself. Here there are two passage-graves and an intermediate ring-cairn on a bent N.E.-S.W. line about 400 foot (122 m.) long.

Balnuaran of Clava S.W. (INV 10) is a passage-grave surrounded by a graded stone circle, in which there is no N.E. stone, reminiscent of the cobbled gap at Corrimony. Like that site, the cairn is built on a conspicuous mound. The entrance, between two large kerbstones, is at the S.W. There are cupmarks on a stone on the east side of the passage, and on the first stone on the west in the chamber. The site was excavated as long ago as 1828, when two probable flat-rimmed pots were discovered one containing cremated bone.

The central site (INV 8) is a ring-cairn. Its kerbs and stone circle are graded in height towards the S.W. Radiating out to three circle-stones are three enigmatic cobbled settings without good parallel elsewhere. There are cupmarks on two eastern kerbstones. When excavated in 1953, the central area was found to be blackened by charcoal, amongst which was a thin spread of cremated bone.

The N.E. site (INV 9) is another passage-grave, with a 54 foot (16.5) m.) cairn, also on a wide platform. Around this, at ground level, is a fine stone circle 104 foot (31.7 m.) across. There is a splendidly cupmarked kerbstone behind the cairn at the N.N.W. In the passage, aligned S.W. is another cupmarked stone. A "few bones" were found in the chamber about 1854.

Professor Alexander Thom has suggested that observers once squatted in the chambers of these cairns to observe the midwinter setting sun[20]. A similar phenomenon has been noted, this time for midwinter sunrise, at the famous Irish Boyne passage-grave of New Grange, Co. Meath, where the sun also shines down the pasage into the chamber at its solstice. But as comparable alignments do not exist at most of the other Clava passage-graves, it is not possible to extrapolate astronomical inferences from them. One can only record at the Balnuaran necropolis evidence of the same rites that have been seen elsewhere: cupmarked stones, cremated human bones, stone circles enclosing areas for ritual, and assume that here also were sites magically used by the earliest settlers for supernatural protection against the terrors and misfortunes of their lives.

4. *Other Sites.* It is remarkable that, once the megalithic tombs have been examined, Inverness-shire has few other notable prehistoric sites of the Neolithic and earlier Bronze Ages. With the exception of one small kerb-cairn, one stone circle and a few closed round cairns, there is little else recorded, although further field-studies may reveal more cairnfields in Upper Strathnairn[21]. Such paucity is made the more strange by the presence of henges, both in the Black Isle to the north, and in Aberdeenshire to the east[22], monuments of circular earthen banks used all over the British Isles as meeting-places. Such a lacuna in Inverness may once more attest to the resistance to innovation by the native population.

What other monuments there are, are directly connected to the Clava tradition. Only a few yards north of Balnuaran of Clava S.W. is a small kerb-cairn, 13 foot (3.96 m.) across, of low contiguous stones, graded to S. - S.W., one of the E.S.E. having cupmarks and a cup-and-ring mark on its upper surface. The site was probably a shallow grave. Over its filling at the west were some quartz pebbles. It is very like other kerb-cairns in Argyll, such as Achacha and Strontoiller[23] and at Monzie, Perthshire[24], and this points to continuing contacts along the Great Glen during the 2nd millenium B.C.

Just south of Inverness is the only free-standing stone circle in the county at Torbreck, near Ness Castle. Although small in diameter, only 17 foot (5.2 m.) across, its nine stones are tall, graded towards the S.W., where one stands 7 foot (2.13 m.) high. Like the Clava kerb-cairn, the size of the circle is compatible with its being a later representation of the inner space of a Clava cairn where the important rites were enacted, and if it is indeed later, then it may reveal the growth of a new tradition along the Great Glen, founded on selected practices from the older and more monumental Clava sites. Such a continuity could be expected among the conservative peasant societies of prehistoric Britain.

During the Early Bronze Age, stone cists at Bught Park in Inverness itself, and at Craigscorry, were built which contained bronze daggers, probably brought to the area from the S.W. Early bronze axes, halberds and even bronze-smiths' moulds discovered in the county[25] all betoken the continuing use of the Great Glen during the 2nd millenium. The presence of bronze rings and the concentration of metalwork in the counties of Nairn, Moray and Banff, as well as the establishment of strong Beaker groups there, point to increasing activity along the shores of the Moray Firth. Little of this is reflected in the Bronze Age sites of N.E. Inverness-shire.

As well as the cairns in Upper Strathnairn, there is a Bronze Age cairnfield on Grenish Muir[26] where, on the sandy ridges near Loch na Carraigean, possible stone-lined fields and tiny, turf-covered mounds of stones may be the results of land-clearance during the later 2nd millenium. There is little else, except the round cairns. One, opened in the early 19th century, "the most conspicuous of a group of tumuli in the parish of Alvie . . . held . . . a human skeleton, with a pair of large hart's horns laid across it."

"We grow at last by custom to believe,
That really we live;
Whilst all these shadows, that for things we take,
Are but the empty dreams which in Death's sleep we make."

A. COWLEY.

REFERENCES

1. Scott, Sir L., "The Colonisation of Scotland in the Second Millenium B.C.," *Proc. Preh. Soc.* 17, 34, 1951.
2. Walker, I. C., "Easterton of Roseisle: a forgotten site in Moray," *Studies in Ancient Europe*, eds. Coles and Simpson, Leicester, 111, 1968.
3. Henshall, A. S., *The Chambered Tombs of Scotland, II*, 277, Edinburgh, 1972.
4. Scott, J. G., "The Clyde Cairns of Scotland," *Megalithic Enquiries in the West of Britain*, 206, Liverpool, 1969.
5. Henshall, *ibid.*, note 3.
6. Woodham, A. A., *Proceedings of the Society of Antiquaries of Scotland*, 90, 102, 1956-7.
7. Henshall, A. S., *The Chambered Tombs of Scotland, I*, 1963; *II*, 1972. Edinburgh University Press.
8. Wells, H. L., "The Inhumation Burials," *The West Kennet Long Barrow Excavations, 1955-6*, S. Piggottt, 81, H.M.S.O., London, 1962.
9. Henshall, *Ibid.* note 3.
10. Woodham, A. A., & M. F., *P.S.A.S.*, *97*, 35-9, 1963-4.
11. Piggot, S., The Dalladies Long Barrow, N.E. Scotland. *Antiquity 47*, 32-6, 1973.
12. Piggott, S., "Excavations in Passage-Graves and Ring-Cairns of the Clava Group," *P.S.A.S. 88*, 173-207, 1954-6.
13. Henshall, 12-39, 358-386, 1963.
14. Burl, H. A. W., "Stone Circles and Ring-Cairns," *Scot. Arch. Forum 4*, 45, 1972.
15. Jolly W., "Of Cupmarked Stones in the Neighbourhood of Inverness," *P.S.A.S. 16*, 300-401, 1881-2.
16. Simpson, D. D. A., & Thawley, J. E., "Single-Grave Art in Britain," *Scot. Arch. Forum 4*, 84, 1972.
17. Walker, I. C., "The Clava Cairns," *P.S.A.S. 96*, 87-106, 1962-3.
18. Walker, I. C., "The Counties of Nairn, Moray and Banff in the Bronze Age, Part I," *P.S.A.S. 98*, 76-125, 1964-6.
19. Clarke, D. L., *Beaker Pottery of Great Britain & Ireland, I & II*, 176-90. Cambridge, 1970.
20. Thom, A., "Megalithic Astronomy: Indications in Standing Stones," *Vistas in Astronomy 7*, 18-19, 1965.
21. Woodham, A. A., *Discovery and Excavation in Scotland*, 33-36, 1963; *ibid.*, 22, 1965.
22. Burl, H. A. W., "Henges: Internal Features and Regional Groups," *Arch. Journal 126*, 1-28, 1970.
23. Ritchie, J. N. G., "Excavation of a Cairn at Strontoiller, Lorne, Argyll," *Glasgow Arch. Journal 2*, 1-7, 1971.
24. Mitchell, M. E. C., & Young, A., "Report on Excavations at Monzie, Perthshire," *P.S.A.S. 73*, 62-71, 1939.
25. Coles, J. M., "Scottish Early Bronze Age Metalwork," *P.S.A.S. 101*, 1-110, 1968-9.
26. Graham, A., "Cairnfields in Scotland," *P.S.A.S. 90*, 7-23, 1956-7.

PREHISTORIC MONUMENTS

b. The Hill Forts of the Inverness Area

ALAN SMALL

The Inverness area is particularly well endowed with a whole variety of Iron Age monuments — forts, duns, brochs, crannogs and hut circles. The location of Inverness at the east coast end of the Great Glen at a focal point of prehistoric routeways which were frequently water-orientated, made the area not only attractive to settlers but also politically important. The small proportion of cultivable land has also saved many of the sites of prehistoric activity from the ravages of the plough.

Two major problems arise in any consideration of the hill forts of this area. First the question of definition. Where is the dividing line between duns and forts? Duns are comparatively small defensive structures with disproportionately thick dry-stone walls. They are usually, but not always, circular or sub-oval in shape and may have outer ramparts and ditches. A dun may be regarded as serving a single family unit, and consequently an internal area of approximately 450 square yards (375 sq. m.) would suffice. Structures such as *Dun More,* above Beauly; *Dun a Cliabhan; Dun More Tighnaleac* and *Craig Dhu* clearly fall into this category, while sites like *Tom-a-Chaisteal,* slightly above this areal limit at c. 525 square yards (450 sq. m.) are probably also single family units. A second distinctive group by size are the sites (Table 1) occupying an area of between 600 - 900 square yards (500 - 750 sq. m.). These are clearly above the size required for a single family unit, but far too small to be of any regional significance. They may have served a small group of families living in the area, or, alternatively, simply have been the unnecessary status manifestations of the wealth of a particular rich family. Provided that the necessary resources in materials and labour were available, the local topography of a site frequently dictates the size and shape of a defensive monument.

The structures above 1555 square yards (1300 sq. m.) in internal area, the main subjects of this paper, are true forts, clearly catering for a populated district rather than a single family, and the larger ones in that group must have a regional rather than local significance. The huge vitrified fort on the Ord of Kessock is so disproportional in size to all others in this area, that one wonders whether it is to be seen as a regional defence centre controlling a frontier along the Beauly Firth. The sizes given for the forts must be regarded as extremely approximate, as in most cases there is no reliable excavation data on which to base estimates. On some sites, later works make it impossible to offer any realistic measurements, e.g. the mediaeval castle at Urquhart. In the case of Castle Spioradain, the ramparts were used as a quarry during the construction of the Caledonian Canal, and, furthermore, the raising of the water level drowned part of the defences.

The second major problem in considering the hill forts is the lack of modern excavation. Many of them have suffered indiscriminate digging, for example, Dun Fionn was trenched by Lord Lovat in the early 19th century[1], but no reports of the excavations survive. Craig Phadrig is the only one of the true hill forts in this area which has seen modern excavation[2], and it is on the evidence from Craig Phadrig that much of the conclusions regarding the hill forts must be based.

The siting of hill forts, in common with duns, brochs and other defensive works, is invariably closely related to the local topography. The tops of hills with at least one precipitous side, small knolls and ridges rising above the surrounding plain, coastal promontories with narrow necks linking them to the mainland, and small islands of hard ground in marshy territory are all favourite locations. Occasionally, where the site was of unconsolidated gravels, some levelling and trimming up of slopes took place, but usually man's defences were simply additions to the natural contours of the site. The basic concept appears to have been the enclosure of the fort area by a massive rampart encircling the hill-top. Sometimes the precipitous nature of certain approaches appears to have obviated the need for a continuous rampart, but in most cases some form of man-made defensive wall was regarded as essential. At sites such as Craig Phadrig and Finavon in Angus[3], the whole area of the hill-top was not used, and the forts seem to have been constructed to meet the needs of a specific community.

The construction of the circling rampart at Craig Phadrig has been examined in detail, and the basic principles there established probably apply to all forts within the study area, including most of the duns, although the dimensions of the

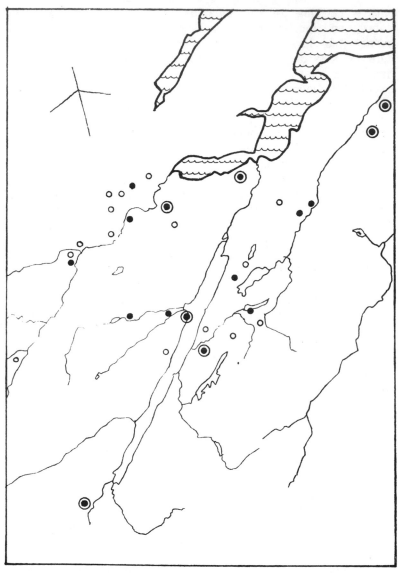

INVERNESS AND DISTRICT
DISTRIBUTION MAP 3

Timber-laced or Vitrified forts · · ◉
Stone Forts   · · ●
Duns   · · ○

SCALE ·   [scale bar: 5   0   5   10   15 KM.]
                      [5   0   5   10 MILES]

wall will vary considerably from site to site. Fig. 1 shows a sketch section of the Craig Phadrig wall. The total thickness of the wall was just under 21 feet (6 m.) and on the basis of the quantity of the collapsed debris still remaining, must have originally stood at least 26 feet (8 m.) high. The rampart consists of two revetments enclosing a rubble core. All stone was obtained locally if available, by surface collection, although for some forts quarrying must have been essential, particularly for suitable blocks for the revetment. At Burghead, the inner revetting face was built of carefully dressed sandstone slabs.

The rampart was founded on the natural turf, no previous preparation having been undertaken except the marking out of the line of the wall. In some cases it is suggested that the rampart was founded on a raft of logs, but no examples of this type appear in this area. The revetting walls were carefully constructed, each occupying about one-third of the total width of the wall at the base, and gradually thinning as the structure reached its full height. The lowest yard (m.) is invariably constructed of very large blocks to provide an adequate foundation, while above this smaller blocks were used, and frequently timber lacing was introduced into the design. Clear evidence of horizontal timber beams running from the inner revetment into the core was found at Craig Phadrig, and circumstantial

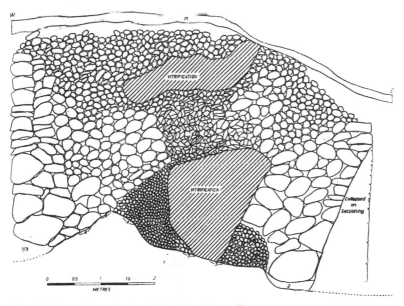

Fig. 1. A section of the Craig Phadrig wall.

G

evidence supports a network of horizontal, transverse and vertical timbers tying the inner revetment thoroughly to the core. Although timber beams appear in the outer face of some continental forts[4], they never did so at either Craig Phadrig or Burghead. Besides its value in tying revetment to core, timber lacing has the advantage of preventing a large section of the core "running" should the outer revetment be breached by attackers. If that happened, a natural causeway would be provided for the invaders. Furthermore, timber lacing has the property of spreading the weight-load in a massive structure. Brochs built entirely of dry stone, without any timber lacing, frequently show intensive shattering and cracking of stones in the lower courses due to the pressure from above. In fact, this structural weakness may be the reason why brochs appear to have been used for a very short period of time about the 1st century A.D., and many brochs were deliberately reduced in height soon after their construction.

Without excavation, it is impossible to say exactly how many of the forts under consideration were timber laced. All structures which exhibit vitrification are, however, certain to have been timber-laced. Vitrification occurs when rocks reach a fluid state and solidify into a glass-like structure. Because the forts in the Inverness area are built of a mixture of different rocks collected locally from the glacial drift, it follows that, at a given temperature, some rocks will have attained their melting point, while others remain in a solid state. Those which melt, notably those containing a large proportion of mica, will flow round the others and, as they cool, will cement the whole structure into a solid block. Examination of samples of vitrification shows that a temperature of about 5360° F. (1200° C.) has been required to produce the vitrification in most Scottish vitrified forts.

Discussion as to how this temperature was achieved in a dry-stone structure, has raged over the past two centuries. Williams in 1777, on the basis of his excavation at Knockfarrel[5], was the first to argue strongly that vitrified forts were man-made fortresses rather than volcanoes. A long period of in-decision followed with scholars arguing as to whether it was a technique of construction, deliberately done by builders in an attempt to cement a dry-stone structure into a solid wall, or whether it was the accidental result of a timber-laced rampart having caught fire[6, 7, 8]. On the evidence of a number of excavations, there is no doubt that the latter is the case, and it is worthwhile considering the sequence of events which occurred after fire started in a timber-laced fort.

Usually excavation gives no clue as to how the fire actually started. It may have been done deliberately, by attackers firing buildings inside the fort, by accidental conflagration initiated by the occupiers, natural events such as forest or grassland fires, or even lightning strikes. Indeed, the cause may have been different at each fort. Childe[3] suggested a range of wooden buildings along the interior wall of the fort at Finavon in Angus, and similar buildings may have existed in other forts. Fire in these would soon spread into the timber lacing of the rampart and, as the beams burned inwards, an intensified draught would be funnelled through the dry-stone wall. This would operate on the same principle as the flues of a blast furnace. As the temperature builds up towards the incandescence point of the boulders in the core, the intense heat will cause many of the rocks to shatter into fragments and, where the revetments are thinnest near the top of the wall, they will give way and collapse, forming a heap of heat-shattered rubble. Occasional pieces of vitrification are sometimes found in this rubble, but the main masses of vitrification usually appear in the lower part of the wall itself. The fall of the hot rubble will form an enormous heat blanket round the lower part of the walls and effectively increase the thickness of the wall by several yards (m.), giving an increased suction draught of air already partially warmed. This heat-blanket theory is well supported by the evidence from the experiments of Childe and Thorneycroft at Plean Colliery in Stirlingshire[9], where temperatures seem to have continued to increase after the initial collapse of the wall. It must be stressed that vitrification only occurs at those points where the melting point temperature of some of the variety of rocks in the core was attained. No fort is known where the rampart is continuously vitrified throughout its entire length.

Clearly, therefore, the evidence of excavation points to the end product of such a conflagration being a rampart, only about half its original height, buried in an enormous mass of rubble sloping down at an angle on either side. This is a much less substantial defence than the original structure with its towering vertical walls. It follows that vitrification destroyed the original fort, and could not have been a design feature of the builders. It is equally clear that vitrification is due to the accidental circumstances of low-melting point rocks lying in a part of the wall which attained a sufficiently high temperature for them to reach a fluid state. Many forts which show no signs of vitrification may have been built by exactly the same techniques and may also have suffered burning, but a sufficiently high temperature was never attained to melt part of the core. Thus vitrification can be regarded neither as a diagnostic feature of a particular class of fort, nor as a feature of the cultural assemblage of a particular group of people. Vitrified material can, in fact, be found in a variety of structures[10, 11]. Indeed, a farmer in Kirkhill parish reported vitrification during agricultural improvements in the 19th century. During land reclamation the peat was scraped off the surface, piled into heaps and ignited. Numerous fragments of vitrification were noted underneath these fires[12]. One wonders whether the peculiar piece of vitrification at Moniack, which does not appear to be related to any structure, is simply the product of some unrecorded experiment by a landowner. Only further excavation of non-vitrified structures can therefore prove whether they were timber-laced.

Small finds and continental parallels were the original dating criteria for fixing these forts firmly within the Celtic Iron Age, and the use of radio-carbon dates on the Scottish forts in the last decade has confirmed this pattern, viz. Finavon, 665 B.C.[13]; Dun Lagaidh, 565 B.C.[14, 15]; Craig Phadrig, 350 B.C.[2]; Craig-marloch Wood, 93 A.D.[16]; Cullykhan, 1st or 2nd century A.D.[17]; Burghead, 350 A.D.[18]. Clearly the forts were being constructed over a period of at least a thousand years, and a distribution map is of no value to obtain a picture of settlement at any given time — many of the early forts probably having been destroyed before the later ones were constructed. Indeed, the evidence from several sites, including Craig Phadrig, suggests that the primary fort survived for a relatively short time, and was refurbished later.

Although neither small finds, nor radio-carbon dates are reported for any of the small forts or duns in the Inverness area, it is likely on comparative evidence from elsewhere, that they also fit into a period covered by a similar range of dates.

All the large forts in the Inverness area have outer ramparts, in addition to the main structures. Almost invariably these appear to be of a very different character from the innermost rampart, which usually appears to have been the most substantial. This feature is common to many hill forts in Scotland[19]. At Craig Phadrig the outer rampart has been shown to be an entirely secondary feature, constructed after the initial fort was destroyed. A ruinous network at the south-western end was extended by an embankment of earth, turf and detritus from the inner rampart, enclosed by rough revetments. This encloses the east and north sides of the fort, while on the north-west the defence was completed by simply trimming back the fall of the original rampart and building a retaining wall. On this evidence, it is suggested that all the large forts may have enjoyed re-use. This is particularly true at sites such as Dun More (Cabrich), where the outworks are particularly extensive. In these cases, one can argue that the distribution of forts represents a closer approximation to the distribution of territories.

In Southern Pictland, it has been shown that there is a distinct relationship between forts and the earliest, Class I, Pictish symbol stones[20]. It is interesting to note that in the Inverness area no Class I Pictish symbol stone so far discovered is more than 3.5 miles (6 km.) from the nearest large fort. Relief is much more a limiting factor to settlement in the Inverness area than in Angus, and in the area under consideration, the relationship need no more than indicate that the environment has forced people to use the same areas throughout long periods of time. Conclusive evidence, however, of re-use of a fort in the Pictish period was obtained at Craig Phadrig, where pottery of the "E"-ware type, a clay mould used in the manufacture of an escutcheon plate for a hanging bowl, and radio-carbon dates provide a satisfactory Pictish corpus. Proof of the building of forts during the Pictish period comes from Burghead[18], and Cullykhan[17].

A study of hill forts shows that no satisfactory defence is achieved until the inner rampart has been finished. Consequently it can be argued that construction of the primary defence would be completed as quickly as possible. As a very rough approximation, each cubic yard (m.) of timber-laced wall represents ten man hours of work in the surface collection of stone, cutting of timber and construction of wall. On this basis, it is suggested that a fort such as Craig Phadrig could have been built by a team of 100 men in three months. Thus, allowing for women and children and those incapacitated, a community of between 300 and 400 people would be involved. This would represent a highly organised society under powerful leaders.

The settlement model suggested for such a society is summarised in Fig. 2. Craig Phadrig showed no sign of domestic occupation between its construction and vitrificaton, indicating that it had served purely as a defensive retreat in times of danger. Many Scottish forts are at altitudes too high for permanent settlements, and the relative paucity of domestic finds from fort excavations supports the view that many of the forts never saw permanent occupation. The typical homestead of that period appears to have been the hut circle, usually sited on slightly sloping ground, to give a dry foundation, and also where there was a depth of soil to permit some grain growing. Hut circles sometimes appear singly, or in groups, and the Inverness area is particularly rich in this type of structure. As a house type, the hut circle is well known from the Bronze Age, and may well have continued right through into the Pictish period, and in consequence specific dates cannot be assigned, without excavation. On surface indications, however, those on Ashie Moor apper to be clearly related to Dun Riach. Homesteads also occur in the coastal lowlands, particularly where deposits of glacial sands and gravels provide dry sites. In general terms, such sites were frequently selected for more substantial dwellings, such as duns, as they offered a considerable degree of natural defence, which could be easily supplemented.

In economic terms, the ideal site for settlement lay at the break of the slope, either between hill and coastal lowland, or between valley side and valley floor. This allowed the maximisation of the resources from different environments. Unfortunately, these same sites have attracted settlement through the ages right up to the present day in the Scottish Highlands, and much of the evidence has disappeared under the plough. Small patches around the hut circles would have been cultivated for grain, but this would have played a relatively minor part in the economy, as is suggested by the relative lack of finds of agricultural implements. A sickle of uncertain date was found at Dores and another, along with an iron axe, is reported from the peat moss west of Loch nam Bonnach. This is less than

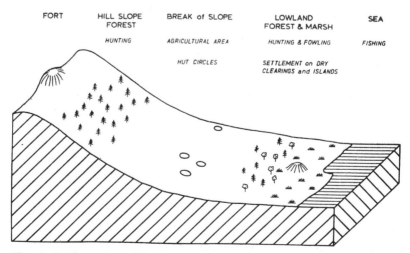

Fig. 2. Settlement model of Craig Phadrig.

a mile (2 km.) from Dun Fhambair and may be associated with it[21]. Querns occur extensively throughout the area, but the rotary type continued in use until mediaeval times, and cannot be dated out of context. Whereas Southern England became a great grain growing area during the Iron Age, Scotland, probably due to the more rigorous environment, retained the more traditional pastoral economy. Hunting was still an essential part of the economy, as is proved by the large quantities of bones recorded from the hill forts. A preliminary examination of the bones from Craig Phadrig shows a high proportion of red deer, and also possibly reindeer. The European wild boar is also recorded. Of the pastoral animals, cattle were by far the most important.

Within these communities most of the group needs could be obtained from the local environment — fuel from the much more extensive peat bogs than exist today, food from the fields, the forests, the lakes and sea, iron from bog ores, and huts, duns and brochs all built of local raw materials. Trade need only have entered into their society in a minor way. Precious metals, bronze, salt and luxury goods would have been exchanged for local surplus of things such as skins, leather goods, of which there may have been an ample supply in a region which counted its wealth in cattle. While some families may have had fortified houses within the community (possibly represented by some of the duns), the central defensive nucleus of the group was its hill fort — the last defensive stronghold against neighbouring groups keen to expand their territories.

Although a reasonable model can be created to summarise settlement patterns in the Iron Age in the Inverness area, it is impossible to assign specific territories to individual forts and society groupings until accurate datings are established for the construction and periods of re-use of each fort. At the present time, Craig Phadrig is the only fort in the region which has been shown to be in use at specific periods. Clearly it is the focus of a group making use of the rich environment of the Ness lowlands. The smaller defended homesteads to the west, at Kirkton of Kirkhill and Tom-a'-Chaisteal, if contemporaneous, may possibly be those of important people within the group. The Ord of Kessock, on the opposite shore of the Beauly Firth, would serve the south-western part of the Black Isle. Its size may reflect the large population potential of this area. Other forts which appear to serve a distinct region are, Dun Evan in Nairnside, Dun Riach, focussing on the undulating Devonian area to the north of Loch Duntelchaig, and Castle Urquhart, which clearly guards the Great Glen routeway as well as serving the mouth of Glen Urquhart. This area, where the Old Red Sandstone yielded better soils, would be naturally attractive. Indeed, almost every one of the forts and duns in this area is located on or in close proximity to Middle Old Red Sandstone areas. The forts at Dun More (Cabrich) and Lovat Bridge also fit well into a regional network, the latter emphasising the importance of riverine routes. The pattern becomes more difficult to interpret to the west of Beauly. A line of small structures control each sector of the river valley. With the exception of Dun Fionn, which is a small fort, the others are no more than defended homesteads — probably the residence of the local chieftain — the nearest equivalent probably being the late mediaeval tower-house. In this group is included the duns at Craigdhu, Erchless; the Tor, Little Struy; and the broch just to the north. It cannot be stressed too strongly that all these monuments are not necessarily contemporaneous. Indeed, there may have been only a single one in use at any given time. Only modern excavation can solve that problem.

The group of five duns to the west of Beauly are difficult to explain. While being located on good defensive sites, their geographical relations to the countryside are improbable. First, they are located surprisingly far inland, and both Dun Garblaich and the small fort, Dun Fhambair, are at relatively high altitudes of over 1000 feet (310 m.); an apparently unnecessary height, both for Iron Age conditions and probable population density at this time. Several extremely speculative solutions could be postulated, but are hardly worthy of consideration with our present lack of knowledge.

In conclusion, it is clear that only a broad hypothesis can be postulated concerning hill forts and related monuments in this area, due to lack of excavated sites. One final point, however, is acceptable — namely that some types of fort were being constructed and the same way of life pursued both in the early centuries B.C. and during the Pictish period. In fact, the division into a Pre-Roman Iron Age and a Pictish period seems to be more a semantic division in years, than a separation of two different cultural phases.

REFERENCES

1. Wallace, T. D., "Archaelogical Notes," *Trans. Inverness Sc. Soc. & Field Club,* vol 8, 87-156. 1921.
2. Small, A., & Cottam, M. B., "Craig Phadrig. Interim Report on 1971 Excavation," *University of Dundee Occasional Paper,* No. 1, 1972.
3. Childe, V. G., "Excavations of the vitrfiied fort of Finavon," *Proc. Soc. Ant. Scot.* vol 69, 49-80, 1935.
4. Dehn, W., "Die latenezeitbike Ringmaur von Preist," *Germania* vol 23, 23-6, 1939.
5. Williams, J., *An Account of Some Remarkable Ruins,* Edinburgh, 1777.
6. Woodhouselee, Lord, "An Account of some Extraordinary Structures on the Tops of Hills in the Highlands," *Trans. Roy. Soc. Edinburgh,* 1790.
7. Hibbert, S., "Collections relative to Vitrified Sites," *Arch. Scot.* vol 4, 181-201, 1857.
8. Christison, D., *Early Fortifications in Scotland,* Edinburgh, 1898.
9. Childe, V. G., & Thorneycroft, W., "The experimental production of the phenomena distinctive of vitrified forts," *Proc. Soc. Ant. Scot.* vol 72, 44-55, 1938.
10. Mackie, E. W., *The Excavation of Two Galleried Duns on Skye in 1964 and 1965: Interim Report,* University of Glasgow, 1965.
11. Mackie, E. W., "Timber-laced forts and causes of vitrification," *Glasgow Archaeol. Journal,* vol 1, 69-71, 1969.
12. Anon., "Meeting of Scientific Societies at Inverness, 30th July, 1886." *Trans. Inv. Sc. Soc., & Field Club* vol 3, 193, 1893.
13. Mackie, E. W., "Radio-Carbon Dates and the Scottish Iron Age," *Antiquity* vol 43, 15-26, 1969.
14. Mackie, E. W., *Interim Report on Excavation at Dun Lagaidh,* Univ. of Glasgow, 1967.
15. Mackie, E. W., *Excavations on Loch Broom, Ross and Cromarty: second interim report,* University of Glasgow, 1968.
16. Nisbet, H. C., "Renfrewshire — Craigmarloch Fort, Kilmacolm," *Discovery and Excavation,* 1966.
17. Greig, J. C., "Cullykhan," *Current Archaeology* No. 32, 227-231, May, 1972.
18. Small, A., "Burghead," *Scott. Archaeol. Forum* vol 1, 61-68, 1969.
19. Feacham, R. W., "The Hill-Forts of Northern Britain," *The Iron Age in North Britain,* by A. L. F. Rivet, Edinburgh, 1966.
20. Cottam, M. B., & Small, A., "The Distribution of Settlement in Southern Pictland," *Med. Arch.,* 1974.
21. Wallace, T. D., "Ancient Remains in the Beauly Valley," *Trans. Inverness Sc. Soc. and Field Club* vol 3, 134-147, 1893.

TABLE I

National Grid Reference	Name	Approx. Area in sq. yds. & sq. m.		Vitrification	Outer Defence Works
NH 466 466	Dun Garblaich	720 y.	600 m.	—	Yes
NH 473 429	Dun Fionn	720 y.	600 m.	Yes	—
NH 485 471	Dun Fhambair (Dun A Vir)	1555 y.	1300 m.	—	—
NH 513 449	Lovat Bridge	4785 y.	4000 m.	—	Yes
NH 427 239	Dun Dearduil	900 y.	750 m.	Yes	Yes
NH 531 286	Urquhart Castle	—	—	Yes	—
NH 535 429	Dun More (Cabrich)	2040 y.	1700 m.	Yes	Yes
NH 596 455	Kirkton of Kirkhill	650 y.	550 m.	—	—
NH 602 316	Dun Riach	1800 y.	1500 m.	—	Yes
NH 601 379	Caisteal Spioradain	—	—	—	Yes
NH 640 453	Craig Phadrig	3000 y.	2500 m.	Yes	Yes
NH 665 492	Ord of Kessock	13755 y.	11500 m.	Yes	Yes
NH 725 395	Doune Hill, Daviot	777 y.	650 m.	—	—
NH 828 477	Dun Evan	2630 y.	2200 m.	?	Yes

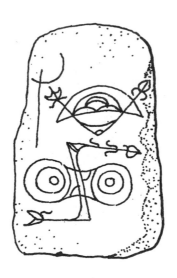

Pictish Class I
Symbol Stone.
Invereen. Tomatin.

INVERNESS, A PICTISH CAPITAL

ISABEL HENDERSON

Most people are aware that there are very few written records for the Pictish period of Scottish history. This period runs from around 300 A.D., when the Picts are first mentioned in late Classical sources, to the middle of the 9th century when, under Viking pressure, Kenneth MacAlpin led the Scots from Argyll into the eastern Pictish districts of Scotland and set up the Scottish administrative centre there.

The earliest written source that has survived for this period is a *Life of Saint Columba* written by Adomnan, the ninth abbot of Iona. The *Life* was composed towards the end of the 7th century, about one hundred years after the death of Columba. Adomnan, therefore, cannot have had any personal knowledge of the life-time of the Saint, but could have spoken to those who had personal memories of him. Adomnan himself says of his sources:

"I shall relate what has come to my knowledge through the tradition passed on by our predecessors, and by trustworthy men who knew the facts; and . . . I shall set it down unequivocally, and either from among those things that we have been able to find put into writing before our time, or else from among those that we have learned, after diligent enquiry, by hearing them from the lips of certain informed and trustworthy aged men who related them without any hesitation."

We know something of the character of Adomnan from Bede, who met him during a visit to Northumbria. Bede found that his words and behaviour showed him to be wise, modest and devout. He was a scholar and an administrator, and also a public man who, among other things, put through an important law to protect women and children. There is no doubt that Adomnan must have known a great deal at first hand about the Picts. He would certainly have known, for example, the meaning of the Pictish symbols. At this time Iona was still head of the Pictish church and contacts with the Picts must of necessity have been frequent. In a late *Life of Adomnan,* some verses are ascribed to him that refer to the death of Brude, son of Bile, a famous Pictish king who died in 693, eleven years before Adomnan's own death. The verses which could be by Adomnan, are certainly earlier than the *Life,* which tells further how Brude was brought to Iona for burial, and that Adomnan, who loved him, with great difficulty resisted the temptation to raise him from the dead. If the *Life* preserves an authentic tradition, then Adomnan was intimately connected with the royal family of the Picts and sympathetically disposed towards them[1].

Adomnan's *Life of Columba* is therefore to be thought of as in general reliable, particularly, of course, for events and circumstances contemporary with himself which he mentions in passing. However, although it is called a *Life,* Adomnan's aim was not to write a biography of St. Columba in the modern sense, but rather to reveal to the Christian world his indisputable sanctity. This means that the emphasis is not on the facts of the life and abbacy of Columba, but on his supernatural powers —his prophecies, his miracles and his visions. In spite of this pre-occupation, the *Life* remains very readable, providing a vivid picture of the life of the monastic community on Iona in its hey-day[2].

For Scottish history, Columba's importance lies in his successful mission to the Picts, which brought Christianity for the first time to the north of Scotland. Adomnan's *Life* contains the earliest account that we have of this important turning point, and is the only one that enters into any detail. Again, however, we must not expect to find a factual history of the mission. We are told nothing of Columba's motives or sense of vocation in this matter, or how he set about organising the church in the land of the Picts. We are not even told where flourishing Christian centres were established. He only mentions in passing that Columban monasteries are found within the territories of the Picts and Scots, "and have been regarded by both with the greatest respect up to the present time." The origins of these Pictish foundations, some of which must have belonged to the time of Columba, are never referred to in the *Life.*

For his purposes Adomnan is interested in the Pictish mission, not as evidence for Columba's missionary zeal, but as a means of providing a set of circumstances in which the Saint was called upon to exert particularly potent supernatural powers, comparable to the situation St Patrick was confronted with on his arrival at Tara. Most of the Pictish material in the *Life* consists of incidents taking place in or around the "fortress" and "royal house" of the Pictish king who is called Brude. A brief summary of the content of this Pictish material is the

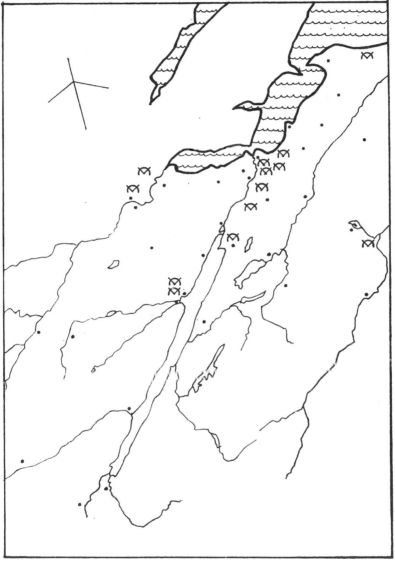

INVERNESS AND DISTRICT
DISTRIBUTION MAP 4
Early Christian Churches and Chapels   •
Pictish Symbol Stones and Crosses

SCALE.

best way to convey the nature of Adomnan's account and the difficulties one encounters when trying to use it as historical evidence.

Book I, chapter 37. Columba and a few of the brethren are singing Vespers outside the fortress of the Pictish king who is called Brude. The native priesthood, called "magicians," try to prevent their continuing. Columba reacts by singing the forty-fourth (now the forty-fifth) psalm in a voice of unnatural loudness. King Brude and his people are very frightened.

Book II, chapter 11. Columba hears of a spring that harms those who drink its water or bathe in it, and which, as a consequence, is worshipped by the Picts as a god. Columba visits it, to the delight of the magicians, who hope he will be harmed by it. Columba, however, blesses the spring and its water becomes curative.

Book II, chapter 27. At the end of chapter 25, Adomnan writes, "Now we shall tell some few things about animals." There follows in Chapter 26 an account of the Saint's encounter with a wild boar on Skye. In chapter 27, there is a long chapter on Columba's repulse of a water monster that inhabits the River Ness. Columba sees a victim of the monster being buried on the banks of the river. In defiance of the monster, he orders one of his disciples to swim across the river to fetch a boat from the other bank. The monster makes for the swimmer with open jaws. Columba makes the sign of the cross and commands it to withdraw. The monster flees, and both the brethren and the "barbarous heathens" are impressed by the greatness of the miracle.

Book II, chapter 32. The son of a convert falls ill and dies. The magicians attribute the illness to the feeble powers of the God of the Christians. Columba hears of this and raises the boy from the dead.

Book II, chapter 33. In the presence of the king, Columba asks Broichan, the chief magician, to set free an Irish girl, whom he keeps as a slave. Broichan refuses and Columba declares that if he does not give her up, then he will die. Columba leaves the king's house and goes to the River Ness where he takes from it a white pebble that he says will effect cures among the heathen people. He then predicts that an angel will come and strike Broichan, shattering the glass from which he drinks, and leaving him close to death. Two horsemen arrive from the king and ask Columba to come at once to assist Broichan, who is the foster-father of the king, and who has suddenly become ill. The girl is set free and the pebble cures Broichan. The stone can float on top of the water "like an apple or a nut." It is put among the king's treasures and cures many people. It cannot be found, however, on the day of the death of King Brude.

Book II, chapter 34. Columba wishes to leave the province of the Picts. Broichan raises mist and a contrary wind. Columba ignores this, and, calling upon Christ, hoists the sails. The boat is borne along "the long lake of the River Ness" against the contrary wind, and presently it becomes favourable.

Book II, chapter 35. Columba arrives at the fortress of Brude. He is refused entry. The Saint makes the sign of the cross and the gates open of their own accord, the bolts being forcibly drawn back. The king, "with his council," rushes out of the "domus" which stands within the walls of the fort, and meets Columba with reverence. "And from that day onwards, throughout the rest of his life, that ruler greatly honoured the holy and venerable man."

Book II, chapter 42. Cormac is looking for an island in the sea. Columba, who is staying with Brude at the time, tells him of Cormac's voyage in the presence of an under-king, who is at Brude's court. Columba asks Brude to instruct the under-king, whose hostages Brude holds, not to let any harm come to Cormac and his company should they chance to land on the Orkneys.

What use can be made of all this material? First, there can be no doubt that Adomnan had access to an authentic source, whether written or oral, which named Brude as the Pictish king visited by Columba. To suggest that Adomnan simply took the appropriate king's name from a chronological list of Pictish kings, would be unduly sceptical. There seems no reason to doubt that Brude lived near the River Ness. For Adomnan's purposes, there was no real need to say where the royal residence was at all, and he is unlikely to have taken the trouble to invent a location.

We know a little about Brude from other sources, where he appears as Brude, son of Maelchon. Bede calls him "king of the Picts," and a "most powerful king." He also appears in the Irish Annals. In 558, a few years before Columba's visit, he defeated and killed Gabran, the king of the Scots. In 584 he died fighting in the Battle of Asreth in the Pictish district of Circinn, generally thought to be Angus. This battle was fought "among the Picts themselves," and it might be deduced from this that Brude was not king of the Picts in the south. It is just as possible, however, that Brude died countering a revolt, and there is in fact no evidence of there having been any other Pictish king of significance throughout his reign of nearly thirty years. The incident in Adomnan concerning the under-king of the Orkneys is of relevance in this connection. It has a more circumstantial tone than the other incidents and certainly suggests either, that the Orkneys were included in Brude's kingdom, or, that in Adomnan's day they were part of the Pictish kingdom. It may be of significance here that, according to the Irish Annals, Brude, son of Bile, Adomnan's contemporary and friend, "destroyed" the Orkneys in 682.

According to Adomnan, Brude held the under-king's hostages. The holding of hostages as a sign of authority was an Irish practice, and Adomnan may simply have transferred the Irish custom to the Pictish court. It is possible that the Picts had a similar arrangement and that the Battle of Asreth was the result of some breakdown in the system whereby king and under-king kept faith with one another. In the Irish Annals, an expedition to the Orkneys by Aedan son of Gabran, king of the Scots, is recorded as having taken place around 580. Adomnan tells us that Columba, the head of the Scottish church, and Brude remained on good terms until the end of Brude's life, and so it has been suggested that in putting down the Orkneys, Aedan could have been acting on behalf of Brude[4]. Towards the end of his life, therefore, Brude may have been having difficulty in controlling the more distant regions of his kingdom in both the north and south. This lack of authority in the erstwhile "rex potentissimus" may simply have been due to the fact that Brude was getting old.

We do not know if Brude's permanent residence was in the north, but there is no hint in Adamnan's account that it was not. Incidents occur *while* Columba is in the province of the Picts but not *while* Brude was staying in the fortress near the River Ness. Columba, presumably, would have gone to the Pictish king where he expected to find him — at his permanent base. It is perfectly reasonable that the Pictish administrative centre should have been at Inverness around 550 A.D. The expansion of the English in the south, which later made a southern capital inevitable, was not yet under way. If Brude's kingdom did include the Orkneys and Angus, then the Moray Firth area seems an obvious centre from which to administer the kingdom — especially for a sea-faring people.

Elsewhere in the *Life*, with reference to the Scots, Adomnan mentions a *caput regionis* — the "chief place of the district." The latest editors suggest that this perhaps refers to Dun Add, the royal residence and stronghold of the Scots. The River

Add flows below the hill-fort and runs into Loch Crinan, which would have been the ship-harbour for Dun Add. Dumbarton, the British royal stronghold, is similarly sited at the mouth of the River Clyde which runs into the Firth. A Pictish royal *"caput regionis"* near the River Ness, with access to the Beauly and Moray Firths is therefore entirely in keeping with other Dark Age capital sites. The importance of the Moray Firth area is most clearly testified to by the presence of the great fort at Burghead which its excavator, Alan Small, has shown to have been in existence in Brude's time and to have been kept in good repair throughout the Pictish period.

Bishop Reeves, the first editor of Adomnan's *Life,* felt certain that the fort on the top of Craig Phadrig, 1½ miles (2.5 km) west of Inverness, was Brude's fort. The latest editors are only prepared to go as far as to say that Adomnan thought it was Craig Phadrig, and do not offer an opinion as to whether they think he was right in his speculation. The fort controls the entrance to the Beauly Firth and fits Adomnan's admittedly not very precise indications well enough, but the recent excavations conducted by Mr Alan Small have shown that at the time of Brude there was only domestic occupation and that the fort would have had none of the stronghold characteristics indicated by Adomnan or, what is more to the point, necessary for a Dark Age capital.

What of the rest of Adomnan's evidence? Did the Picts have a pagan priesthood who were the intimates of the king and one of whom was the foster-father of the king? The contest of the missionary Saint with the pagan king's *magi* or druids is a standard set piece of hagiographical writing. The classic Irish instance is the contest between St. Patrick and the druids of King Loegaire at Tara. It has frequently been pointed out that this motif is itself modelled on the contest of Moses with the sorcerers and magicians of Pharaoh and also owes something to the conflicts between St. Peter and Simon Magus in the apocryphal New Testament. The notion, however, of the Saint as, in Charles Plummer's words, "a more powerful druid," seems to have appealed particularly to Irish hagiographers and the use of these scriptural parallels could well have been prompted by the fact that they expressed aptly an actual rivalry between the church on one hand and an elite versed in non-Christian lore of various types on the other. What is certain is that the presence of magi in the province of the Picts, which is indicated in the *Life,* cannot be accepted as evidence for the existence of Druidism among the Picts, or even for the existence of Druids of the learned-sorcerer type that appear in Irish literature. There is nothing about the behaviour of the Pictish magicians in Adomnan to suggest that they are anything but stock hagiographical opponents of the Saint. This is true even of the named magician, Broichan. *Magi* or Druids were typically very influential at court, and even the fact that Broichan is said to be Brude's foster-father does not take us beyond the conventional role assigned to Druids in Irish literature.

The details of the incidents themselves are similarly conventional. The singing of hymns and psalms to ward off the animosity of the heathen is a stock motif, as is the miracle of the harmful spring changed to a curative one. It is true that there is evidence that early Celtic peoples venerated springs and wells and that on this basis we might suppose that the Picts, who were partly Celtic, might have done so also. The spring in Adomnan's narrative, however, is almost certainly literary and not based on any actual knowledge of Pictish paganism. Similarly incidents involving a contest between the hero and a water-monster are found frequently in Celtic hagiographical and secular tales. Adomnan's story could be the source of the belief in the Loch Ness monster but, alas, it does nothing to confirm the existence of the monster.

Raising from the dead was, of course, an important miracle for a saint to achieve. Adomnan calls it "a major miracle." The chapter in which Columba restores the dead Pictish boy is written with care, having literary echoes in it of passages from Gregory's *Dialogues,* Juvencus and Constantius's *Life of Germanus.* It is also given a formal ending: "cum Christo qui regnat cum patre in unitate spiritus sancti per omnia saecula saeculorum." This is the only instance of Columba restoring the dead recorded by Adomnan and it is interesting that Adomnan made it take place among the Picts. It suggests that Adomnan felt that Columba had been at the height of his powers when he was among the Picts and that the mission was successful as the result of the exertion of extreme spiritual force by Columba. Although Adomnan does not say so in so many words, the Pictish conversion was one of the major achievements of Columba's life; from this miracle we can perhaps infer that he considered it to be so.

The story of Broichan's Irish slave girl is probably entirely fiction. If we were to take it at its face value, then we could quote it as evidence for the presence of Irish slaves among the Picts, the use of horses for riding, the use of glass vessels for drinking, and, most interesting of all, the existence of a Royal Treasury. At most, however, we can only say that

Adomnan thought these concepts not inappropriate to conditions among the Picts in the sixth century. This is almost the most we can say about such interesting details as the double bolted gates of Brude's fortress, the *domus* within it, and the existence of a Pictish "council."

It has often been noted that the incident of the opening of the doors of Brude's fortress is told somewhat differently in the *Life of Comgall*. Here Comgall and Cainnech accompany Columba. Comgall makes the sign of the cross and opens the gates of the "castrum." Columba then, by the same means, opens the doors of the "domus regalis," "the royal dwelling." In the *Life of St Cainnech*, Cainnech is on Iona and accidentally strikes his head on the corner of the altar. The wound bleeds and a drop of the blood is given to the daughter of Brude, who is blind, deaf and dumb. The blood cures all her disabilities. In one of the versions of the Irish *Life of Columba*, the doors of Brude's fortress are opened by Columba and the king's son, Maelchu, together with a druid, contests with him. Through Columba's words they die. Although these Saints' Lives are all of less authority than Adomnan's *Life of Columba*, they demonstrate the freedom with which such stories were altered and added to. It is probable that the later stories are mere elaborations of Adomnan's account and that they do not provide us with any other information about Brude or his family.

There are two other incidents in Adomnan's *Life* which deserve consideration, although neither concern Brude. In Book III, chapter 14, Columba is "beside the lake of the River Ness" when he suddenly announces that he must go quickly to baptise a virtuous pagan. He arrives at Airchartdan (Urquhart) and baptises the man, his son and the household. Airchartdan is a complete transmutation of a British name into Irish and, on this basis, it has been suggested that there was a Columban monastery at Urquhart in Adomnan's time[5]. Whatever the likelihood of this, the story can be taken as showing the Columba mission in action.

There is a similar incident on Skye in Book I, chapter 33. Here the convert is also a virtuous pagan. He is described as "the captain of the cohort of Geon." No editor has been able to make anything of this except to suggest that the title seems to imply the existence of some kind of Pictish tribal military unit or band. Columba speaks to the Captain "through an interpreter" — interesting confirmation that the Picts spoke a distinct language or languages from the Irish. The Pictish leader, who is old and feeble, dies as soon as he is baptised.

His companions bury him, raising a cairn of stones over him. Is this a glimpse of Pictish burial customs, or just background writing by Adomnan? Adomnan says that the cairn can still be seen and that the stream in which the baptism took place is still called after the Captain. In the face of these assertions, perhaps we can accept the details as authentic.

From the discussions above, it can be seen that, but for Adomnan's evidence, we should not have known that Inverness had ever been a Pictish capital, and for this unique information we must be grateful. With a few exceptions, however, the background details of Pictish society which he describes are in all probability fictitious and provide us merely with an insight into what a late seventh-century writer thought it could have been like. "Merely" is, of course, the wrong word. For events which took place fourteen hundred years ago, we cannot afford to neglect an account written only one hundred years after them, and Adomnan's general assumptions, if not his specific details, must be taken seriously.

We could speculate as to what life was like in and around Brude's fortress on analogy with what we know about other Dark Ages capitals. Where the Picts are concerned, however, analogy can be seriously misleading, for we know that in some fundamental respects, for example in its system of inheritance, Pictish society was entirely different from that of its neighbours, whether Celtic or Germanic.

In the sixth century, we might suppose that the Picts were still enjoying what is known as an Heroic Age — a time when society is dominated by a military aristocracy whose chief interests are hunting and warfare. The dominant personal virtues are boldness in war and total loyalty to one's lord. In such an age, artistry found its chief outlet in the embellishment of the accoutrements of war, although dress and ornament were at all times showy. The existence of an Heroic Age in the north is demonstrated clearly by the Caledonian metalwork of the second century A.D. The massive bronze armlets, mirrors and horse-trappings, decorated with reliefs, spiral, and trumpet patterns, and set with blue glass and chequered enamel of red and yellow embody the spirit of a society at this stage. There seems some probability that the sixth-century court life surrounding Brude, the "rex potentissimus," was of this type. If this were so, then perhaps the sort of society described in the sixth-century British poem, the *Gododdin*, can be transferred to further north.

The cycle of poems known as the *Gododdin* was put together around 600 A.D. It is about a military expedition led by a British leader against the English, which sets out from his fortress-capital, Din Eidyn (Edinburgh). Like Adomnan's *Life,* the *Gododdin* is not a straight piece of historical chronicling. It is an historical epic, and no doubt rhetorical forms and emotional heightening mean that on occasions the poet departs from actuality. There can be no doubt, however, that it can tell us something of the way of life of the period. Poetry of this type was not mere entertainment, but was the recognised method of making a permanent record of the deeds of heroes. The royal fortress of Din Eidyn had a great hall, which was warmed by pine log fires and lit with tapers. Here the warriors feasted and slept, and here the lord showed his hospitality and liberality. There is minstrelsy, and mead drinking out of horn and glass vessels. The clothes of the warriors were of fine materials and brightly coloured. They wear torques and brooches. The fortress acts as the point of assembly and it takes a year for the force to be gathered together and loyalties cemented. The army consisted of cavalry and infantry. The warriors wear mail and are armed with spears, swords, knives and shields. We know that there were some Picts there. One of them may have been the father of three sons, all of whom became kings of the Picts in the mid-seventh century. This man would have been a younger contemporary of Brude.

Above all other functions, a royal fortress would be a place of assembly. As we have seen, a number of Dark Age capitals in the north are sited near firths so that a fleet could assemble at the capital as well as an army. The capital's role as a trading centre would also require access for shipping.

At the capital also, regional officers would report and receive instructions. As a result of his study of the Gaelic notes in the Book of Deer, Professor Jackson has shown that two officials which appear in later Scottish contexts in fact belong to the old Pictish system of administration[7]. The mormaer, "great official," was the highest rank of royal officer in Pictish society, who acted as the king's deputy in his district. A mormaer was a territorial magnate who held his position by hereditary right, and whose duties included collecting royal revenue. In this connection, one is reminded of the "exact-atores" who were killed along with their Pictish king in a battle in 729. Another Pictish royal officer was the toiseach, who, in a Pictish context, Professor Jackson sees as the general of the tribal army in the field. We do not know how developed Pictish social organisation was in the sixth century, but we have seen that Brude appears to have had control of the entire Pictish kingdom, and some kind of system of regional officers answerable to him would be essential. The "regulus" from the Orkneys at Brude's court could perhaps be thought of as the Mormaer of the Orkneys, who would naturally from time to time be at the capital.

A capital would inevitably be an artistic centre, royal patronage ensuring that the most skilful and innovative craftsmen were on hand. Smiths would be necessary for utilitarian needs — for weapons, tools, horse gear and domestic equipment. Fine metalworkers, however, jewellers and enamellers, would be at least as important to the Picts who no doubt shared the contemporary love of personal adornment. Objects such as brooches, torques and buckles functioned primarily as an outward show of personal wealth and prestige, but in a society without coinage they could also take on the nature of money. Professor Wilson, discussing the nature of the St. Ninian's Isle hoard, quotes Dr Kathleen Hughes's view that "in a society without a monetary economy, where exchange of precious objects would form a means of trade, there would seem no reason why churches should not keep a hoard of precious objects for economic purposes, and brooches would certainly be included in such a hoard"[8].

The interesting hoard of silver objects found at Croy may be a collection of this type, for it contains a bronze balance beam suitable for the weighing of precious metals. Alternatively, it has been suggested that it could be the stock-in trade of a jeweller[9]. Certainly it is unlikely to be the contents of a personal jewel-box. The hoard consists of three, possibly four, brooches, a fragment of a chain of finely knitted silver wire, beads of glass and amber, two silver English coins, and the balance beam notched at the top for a sliding weight[10]. The date of the coins show that the hoard must have been buried about the mid-ninth century, but the brooches could have been made considerably earlier. They are penannular, similar in design to the St. Ninian's Isle brooches and to other brooches found in the Pictish area. Professor Wilson has made a close study of these brooches, and concludes that they are of a distinctively Pictish manufacture. This type of brooch, for which a date towards the end of the eighth century is proposed, is basically characterised by being truly penannular (there is a gap in the ring), by having a curved ended plate on the hoop, and by having either lobed or a square plate terminals. The discovery of a series of moulds for brooches of this type at the Broch of Birsay in Orkney strongly supports the view that they are essentially Pictish. A small fragment of a brooch of this kind found at Urquhart Castle is now in the Inverness Museum.

The mould found during the Craig Phadrig excavations is another valuable piece of evidence of Pictish manufacture of ornamental metalwork[11]. It is one half of a two-piece clay mould used to cast an escutcheon for attaching a suspension ring to the side of a bowl. The mould produces an escutcheon with an openwork pattern composed of two opposed pelta shapes. The chronology of hanging-bowl escutcheons is by no means clear, but plain openwork patterns have frequently been assigned to early in the series which is thought to start in the fifth century. Similar enamelled designs, on the other hand, have often been dated as late as the seventh century. Mr Stevenson sees no reason to separate in time the plain and the enamelled two pelta escutcheons and prefers a date around 600 A.D. for the Craig Phadrig mould. A very similar escutcheon is found on a fragmentary bowl from Castle Tioram in Moidart[12], an area which would have been Pictish throughout the period of the hanging-bowls. The particular interest of the Craig Phadrig find is, that it provides the first piece of evidence that hanging-bowls were actually made, in contrast to being acquired by trade, in Scotland. In his preliminary note on the mould, Mr Stevenson writes that "it suggests a workshop comparable to those in the strongholds of Dunadd, Argyll, and, slightly later, at Mote of Mark, Kirkcudbright-shire."

One of the unique series of massive Pictish silver chains comes from the Inverness district. It was found in 1809, when the Caledonian Canal was being made[13]. It is the largest and the heaviest of the ten surviving chains, being 18 ins (46 cm) long and 92 oz in weight. It is made of sixteen pairs of rings and a single ring, each 2 ins (5.6 cm) in diameter. A large grooved terminal ring was with the chain when it was found, but was mislaid almost immediately. In two instances where the chains are complete, the large grooved terminal rings, which act as fasteners, are engraved with Pictish symbols. This provides interesting evidence that symbols had relevance in contexts other than the free-standing stone monuments on which they most commonly occur. The symbols are engraved with great skill and delicacy, and are said to have shown traces of red enamel inlay. The chains are clearly ceremonial pieces —presumably neck-ornaments which were part of the insignia of an important Pictish official. The nature of the symbol design suggests a date early in the seventh century for the series.

It is frequently observed that the various Pictish symbol designs are evenly represented throughout the Pictish area. No particular region seems to favour any particular symbol. Stylistically, the symbols are very alike, so much so that it is as though they had been designed or re-designed at one point in time. Whatever the origins of the designs of the symbols, this universal application and uniformity of style suggests that one powerful leader, who controlled all the Picts, was responsible for the promulgation of the symbolism — at least as it is known from the stone monuments. For other reasons, a northern origin centre for the symbolism has the support of a number of writers, with a case being made by at least two for the Moray Firth area[14]. With these considerations in mind, it is obvious that Brude, son of Maelchon, became a candidate for the role of promulgator, although some writers would consider the second half of the sixth century too early for at least some of the symbols. A date as early as this for the first of the symbol stones would, however, be acceptable to the present writer.

The symbol stones in the Moray Firth area are particularly noteworthy for the high quality of the animal symbols. There are, of course, the famous Burghead Bulls, but equally masterly are the wolf and the deer's head from Ardross (now in the Inverness Museum) and the stag from Grantown. The more immediate Inverness district has the splendid boars of Knocknagael and Dores. All these animal symbols have as an essential part of their design the use of scrolls as a means of emphasising the muscles of the animal. This is a device used in the depiction of the Evangelist animal symbols of some roughly contemporary Northumbrian Gospel Books — notably the Echternach Gospels[15]. All writers are agreed that the manuscript designs and the symbol designs stand in direct relationship to each other, although the way which the influence ran is a matter of opinion. It should be noted, however, that if the Pictish animal designs come after the manuscripts, then the whole corpus of Pictish art becomes very awkwardly compressed[16]. Unless we are to assume that the scroll design was conveyed more or less accidentally on some portable object, the contact between Northumbrian and Pictish artist must have been made in the ecclesiastical context. It is perhaps significant that these scroll-bearing animal symbols related to Evangelist Symbols, should predominate in the area where Columba brought Christianity to the Picts and where Columban foundations must have existed from the earliest period. Did a Northumbrian visitor bring with him a Gospel book in which an Evangelist animal symbol was seen by local secular sculptors? Or was a visiting Northumbrian cleric so struck by the effectiveness of the native animal designs that he took the idea of the muscle-defining scroll back to his scriptorium? Perhaps the most reasonable assumption would be that a Pictish Columban foundation in the north used one of their own native designs for an animal Evangelist Symbol in their own Gospel Book, and that a Northumbrian cleric saw the book, and copied the design. The existence of such a Columban Pictish Gospel Book, pre-dating the *Book of Durrow* — the earliest of the Gospels with this device — is, of course, an unsupported guess, but such a book would provide the neatest way of getting the designs on the Pictish stones into the mileu of manuscript illumination.

This brings us to the whole question of the development of Christianity in the area, after the Columban mission. In pagan times the capital, as a place of assembly, would undoubtedly have been a place of ritual assembly. While it is true to say that Adomnan's account of the activities of the Pictish *magi* is stereotyped, there is every likelihood that a learned priesthood of this type did exist in Pictish society, and that its cult centre was near the capital. Professor Jackson has speculated that, since the incoming Celts gave up something as fundamental as their own system of inheritance, they might very well have also given up their pagan religion and adopted that of the aboriginal population. Such a speculation, he feels, might account for the use of the archaic Non-Indo-European language in the Pictish ogam inscriptions. The old language could have been used for certain ritual purposes, and then maintained as the language of learning and ultimately of epigraphy[17]. If Pictish pagan religion belonged to the older population, then there is obviously no point in looking to Celtic sources for analogies. That there would, however, have been a system of pagan beliefs is certain, and the inevitable result of Columba's mission would have been the suppression of the priesthood who controlled them.

Although Adomnan tells us that Brude remained on friendly terms with Columba all his life, he does not actually say that Brude was baptised, or that he granted land to Columba on which to build a monastery. This is surprising, because even the stereotype story of the Saint and the Pagan King contains these incidents. Bede, on the other hand, from quite independent sources, says unequivocally that Brude was baptized and implies that he granted Iona to Columba. Irish sources say that Columba was given Iona by Conall, son of Comgall, the temporary Scottish king. It is usually supposed that both kings were consulted, thus ensuring Iona's diplomatic immunity as head of the Pictish and Scottish churches. Adomnan may have positively suppressed the Pictish rights in the matter. By the time he was writing, the boundary between the Picts and Scots had shifted, and Iona was firmly within Scottish territory. It is conceivable, also, that Adomnan foresaw that the time would come when the Picts would throw off the Irish Iona connection —an event which took place only a few years after his death. In these circumstances, the Pictish connection would be best forgotten.

If Brude did become a Christian, and it seems unlikely that he should not have done so, then he would have required at least a personal chapel, and in all probability there would have been a monastic foundation in the vicinity of Inverness. Initially this would have to be manned from Iona, but the establishment of monastic schools and the training of native clergy would be the next step. Evidence for Pictish Columban foundations anywhere in the kingdom is very sparse indeed, although we know from Adomnan that they did exist in his time. In the north, the traditions surrounding the monastery at Deer may be authentic, but apart from Deer, we are thrown back on the evidence of the sculptured stones. The collected stones, which includes a fragment of a shrine, from Kinnedar (now in the Elgin Museum) implies that there was a monastic foundation there in Early Christian times. Another fragment of a shrine at Burghead indicates, what we should suppose, that there was a monastery in close proximity to the fort. The late traditions which surround Rosemarkie, which refer to the post-Columban period, get their strongest support from the handsome cross-slab in the churchyard there. Other cross-slabs in the vicinity are at Brodie, Glenferness, Elgin and Wester Delnies[18]. These cross-slabs are symbol-bearing and they were erected, not only to the Glory of God, but to perform some function served by the symbols. The more elaborate cross-slabs would seem, however, to belong most naturally to an ecclesiastical context, whether they are memorial crosses to abbots or bishops, or whether they tell us something about the status of the foundation itself. The slabs in Easter Ross certainly suggest that this district supported at least one important ecclesiastical foundation — perhaps at Tarbat, where there are fragments of a number of particularly fine cross-slabs. Certainly the monuments at Nigg, Shandwick, Hilton of Cadboll and Tarbat require the presence of powerful and artistically ambitious patrons, whether ecclesiastical or secular, around 800 A.D.

The political history of the northern half of Pictland is virtually unknown[19]. We can suppose that during the Northumbrian occupation of the south, the north had a temporary revival as the administrative centre. After Adomnan's friend, Brude, son of Bile, liberated the south in 685, it is probable that the capital moved south again. During the eighth century, which embraces the long reign of the powerful Oengus, son of Fergus, it is likely to have remained there. The continued occupancy and maintenance of the fort at Burghead and the Easter Ross school of sculpture testifies, however, to the importance of the northern area at this time. The migration of the Scots from the west to the east in the mid-ninth century will have driven some at least of the displaced Pictish officials to the north. It is interesting to notice that place-names bearing the Pictish element *pit-* are not found in any concentration in the Moray Firth area. Dr Nicolaisen has shown that these *pit-* names are hybrids — the Pictish *pit-* being followed by an Irish second element[20]. This suggests that the names represent Irish settlement, the Pictish term *pit* meaning a piece or parcel of land having been retained by the incomers. Such an explanation makes sense of the *pit-* place name map[21]. The bulk of these names are in Angus, where Scottish settlement is likely to have been heaviest, whereas in the north they thin out, until they disappear altogether after Easter Ross. As we have seen, Professor Jackson has shown that a number of features of Pictish social organisation were retained by the Scots after their arrival in the east. This would have been true in the north as in the south, but as the *pit-* names show, it is probable that there was not a great deal of Scottish settlement in this area and that the population lost its Pictish character very slowly. Much later, a very powerful family held the old Pictish title of Mormaer of Moray, and in the eleventh century, they had almost the status of kings — carrying on in their way the tradition established by Brude, the "rex potentissimus" of Inverness.

NOTES

1. Anderson, A. O., *Early Sources of Scottish History,* I 200, n. 5, Edinburgh, 1922.
2. Anderson, A. O., and M. O., *Adomnan's Life of Columba,* Edinburgh, 1961. This is the most recent edition. It contains a translation and a long introduction. All quotations are taken from this edition.
3. *Brude* is the Gaelic form of Pictish *Bredei* or *Bridei.* See Kenneth Jackson's "The Pictish Language," *The Problem of the Picts,* F. T. Waingright (ed.), 161, Edinburgh, 1955.
4. Anderson, *Life of Columba,* 44-45.
5. Anderson, *Life of Columba,* 106.
6. See the latest edition, Kenneth Jackson, *The Gododdin,* Edinburgh, 1969.
7. Jackson, Kenneth, *The Gaelic Notes in the Book of Deer,* 102 ff. Cambridge, 1972.
8. Wilson, David M., "The Brooches," *St Ninian's Isle and its Treasure,* 104, Oxford, 1973.
9. Wilson, loc. cit., 100.
10. For a description of the hoard, see A. Ross, *Proc. Soc. Ant. Scot.* XX, 91 ff (1885-86).
11. See R. B. K. Stevenson, "Note on mould from Craig Phadrig," *Craig Phadrig* (Interim report on the 1971 excavation), Alan Small and M. Barry Cottam, Dundee, 1972.
12. *Proc. Soc. Ant. Scot.* LXXI (1936-37), Fig. 1.
13. Smith, J. A., "Silver Chains of Double Rings found in Scotland," *Proc. Soc. Ant. Scot.* XV (1880-81). 64.
14. Henderson, Isabel, "The Origin Centre of the Pictish Symbol Stones," *Proc. Soc. Ant. Scot.* XCI (1957-58), 44-60.
15. Henderson, Isabel, *The Picts,* PII. 32, 33, 34, 36, London, 1967.
16. The St. Luke symbol in the *Echternach Gospels* could have been the source of the Pictish designs, but the Lion of the *Book of Durrow* could not. See Henderson, *The Picts,* fig 24.
17. Jackson, Kenneth, "The Pictish Language," *The Problem of the Picts,* 154.
18. The monumental Wester Delnies stone was one of the elaborately sculptured class comparable to the cross-slabs of Easter Ross. The sculpture is now entirely obliterated. J. Romilly Allen and J. Anderson, *The Early Christian Monuments of Scotland,* II, 117, Edinburgh, 1903.
19. Henderson, Isabel, "North Pictland," *The Dark Ages in the Highlands,* (Inverness Field Club), 37 ff, Inverness, 1971.
20. Nicolaisen, W. F. H., "Place-names of the Dundee Region," *Dundee and District,* 146 ff., Dundee, 1968.
21. See *The Problem of the Picts,* 147.

MACBETH AND OTHER MORMAERS
OF MORAY

GEOFFREY STEUART BARROW

Moray, historically speaking, was one of the major provinces of the old Pictish kingdom and its successor, the kingdom of the Scots. The name means literally "sea settlement." Its first element *mor* is the form used in compounds of the word *mori* (Old Celtic), *muir* (Gaelic), "sea." The second element—reduced in our modern name to a single short vowel—is old Celtic *trebo* (Gaelic, *treabh*), "settlement," which may be seen in such names as the A*treb*ates, now represented by Arras, Ro*trefe,* "fort settlement," now Rattray, or Ughel*tre,* "high settlement," now Ochiltree, not to mention the scores and hundreds of southern Scottish, Welsh, Cornish and Breton names in Tref, trever and tre. Moray might have been pre-eminently the sea settlement because originally it stretched from the Sea of the Hebrides to the Moray Firth, or perhaps it got its name because it was essentially the settlement bordering the relatively calm and sheltered Moray Firth, whose harvest of fish conferred an unusually good living on the early Celtic-speaking inhabitants. The Picts were assuredly not a nation of mere landlubbers: 150 of their ships were lost in 729, perhaps wrecked on More Head or Troup Head ("Ros Cuissine"). It is possible that another ancient name for Moray was Fidach, the "Wooded Country." If this name had ever really been in use, it must have become obsolete at an early period. Logie, beside the River Findhorn, now in Edinkillie parish, was known as Logynfythenach in the 13th century, but it does not seem likely that the second part of this name represents a survival of Fidach. However far-flung the boundaries of Moray may have been at its greatest extent, its historic centre seems always to have been at, or in the neighbourhood of, Inverness, with important secondary focal points at Elgin, Forres and Auldearn-Nairn.

As one of Scotland's dozen or so major provinces, Moray would have had something of the quality of a kingdom or sub-kingdom, but also something of the quality of an ad-

ministrative district subordinated to the royal government of
the kingdom as a whole. It is an unsolved problem whether
the ancient provinces of Scotland began as relatively independent
kingdoms, which gradually coalesced, or were forcibly united,
to form a larger kingdom, or whether they arose from a
deliberate division of their territory by strong kings anxious
to secure more efficient collection of taxes or performance of
military service. On either view, Moray's importance from an
early date seems to emerge clearly enough. The king of the
Picts at the time Saint Columba (Columcille) came to Iona
(563) was Bruide son of Meilochon (Mailgwn?), whom Bede
calls "a very powerful king." Bruide seems to have ruled over
at least the Picts living north of the Mounth (i.e. Grampians),
if not over the entire Pictish nation, and it is generally agreed
that one of his chief seats — perhaps the most important —
was close to Inverness. Even if his kingdom were no wider
than the area from Shetland down to the mountains of Perthshire and northern Argyll, Bruide could not have ruled all
this territory without the help of underkings or provincial
governors. Perhaps he had both. The author of the semi-
legendary (or wholly legendary?) account of the founding of
the Aberdeenshire monastery at Old Deer certainly believed
that Buchan was already under the control of a mormaer in
Columba's time.

The strongest evidence in favour of the view that Scotland's
various major provinces were placed under officials or governors,
rather than treated as sub-kingdoms (whether or not they had
ever been such) is the fact that both native and Irish sources
call provincial rulers in Scotland *mormaers*. This is all the more
striking in the case of the Irish sources, since this term was
scarcely ever used in Ireland, and it would have been only too
easy for Irish writers to "hibernicize" Scottish potentates by
styling them kings — as, indeed, on occasion they do. Mormaer
may fairly be regarded as a Pictish term springing from the
situation peculiar to the Pictish kingdom. It means "high
steward," "great officer" or some such, and its use distinguished
the highest form of royal minister from the lesser "maers,"
some of whom may have undergone renaming in later centuries
as the "thanes" who were hereditary tenants and, at the same
time, administrators of portions of the royal demesne. Moreover, the Scandinavian sources normally refer to the chief
men of Scottish provinces by the title of "earl", and this also
suggests that underkings, if they really existed at all in late
Dark Age Scotland, were the exception rather than the rule.

In any case, it is long after King Bruide's time before

we have explicit mention of Moray in historical sources. Some of our earliest references are in the Norse sagas, which tell of the Scandinavians who have settled in Shetland, Orkney and Caithness, for whom Moray was simply another Scottish province which they might hope eventually to conquer and inhabit. One of the most prominent of these Norse settlers was an earl named Sigurd son of Eystein, who, towards the close of the 9th century, allied himself with Thorstein the Red, son of Olaf the first Norse king of Dublin and his wife Aud the Wise, a devout Christian. Thorstein had made himself ruler over a great tract of northern Scotland including Moray and called himself "king." When he was killed by the Scots, his mother Aud sailed away to Orkney and the Faeroes, and eventually to Iceland, where she and her men, many of them Irish or Hebridean, settled in the far north-west, at the head of Hvammsfjord. There Aud died and, unwilling to be buried in unconsecrated ground, was laid to rest at high-water mark. Meanwhile, her son's ally, Earl Sigurd, consolidated his hold on part of northern Scotland and is said to have built a fortress in Moray. Sigurd's story is told in the Orkneymen's Saga and his Moray fortress is of interest because in the saga it is connected with a battle between Sigurd and a Scottish "earl" called Maelbrigte. This man may well have been provincial governor of Moray, for, as we shall see, the personal name Maelbrigte occurs among the mormaers of Moray in the 11th century. Maelbrigte (died c. 892) may be placed on the same footing as his contemporary, Maelduin, "earl" of Argyll, whose captured and enslaved son, Erp, emancipated in Iceland by the Christian Queen Aud, founded an Icelandic family known as the Erplings.

Some sixty years after Maelbrigte's death, we have a report in the native "Chronicle of the Kings of Scotland," that King Malcolm I "went into Moray with his army and slew Cellach," the implication being that Cellach was the chief man of that province. Now, it is a remarkable fact, that several of the early Irish chronicles, notably the Annals of Ulster and the annals written by Tigernach of Clonmacnoise (d. 1088), take a keen interest in the leading family of Moray, whose descent is traced by Irish genealogists from Loarn, brother of Fergus of Dalriada, whom all accepted as founder of the royal dynasty of Scotland. Under the year 976, Tigernach notes (for no obvious reason) the existence of three Scots mormaers, two of whom were called Cellach — one, or perhaps both, may have been related to their namesake killed in Moray c. 940-50. If we could accept not only the basic validity of the old Irish genealogies of the 11th century mormaers of Moray, but also the probability that at least their nearer ancestors were also mormaers of Moray, we should have to find room in the 10th century for Donald son of Cathmail, his son Morgan and Morgan's son Ruadri (Rory), who was Macbeth's grandfather. The personal name Morgan (Morgrund or Morgund) has been preserved near Elgin in the name Longmorn, from Laundemorgan, literally "Morgan's clearing," but probably going back to an original *lan* (= *llan*) *Morgund*, "Morgan's enclosure." We should almost certainly be wrong to imagine that individual mormaers held office for many years at a time when kings could scarcely achieve reign-lengths of more than eight to twelve years. In the grim kind of game which mormaers played, wickets fell rapidly and a long innings was a rarity. It is likely that brothers and cousins succeeded one another rapidly until one particular generation's stock of adult males had been fully deployed, before their offspring of the next generation were ready to take power. It is also likely that in one family the same range of personal names was in use over a long period. If Cellach were one such name, another may have been Maelsnechtai ("devotee of the snow"). The sagas tell of an "Earl Melsnati" killed in northern Scotland *c.* 990, and in the late 11th century, the son of Macbeth's stepson was called Maelsnechtai. Yet another name may have been Macbeth itself, for an "Earl Macbeth" is reported to have been killed in northern Scotland *c.* 977.

We should surely deceive ourselves if we were to conjure up a romantic picture of Moray life in the days of the Pictish and Scoto-Pictish kings. No doubt the mainly Celtic, partly Scandinavian aristocracy were patrons of poets and harpers, no doubt they had a love of fine dress, golden ornaments and rich jewellery. We know that they were served over many generations by highly original sculptors who had the artistry and skill to devise and fashion stone monuments in honour of their lords and ladies which can still excite our admiration today. Although we are sadly ignorant about the kinds of house or fortress they dwelt in, we have no reason to guess that their homes were markedly meaner or less substantial than those of their immediate mediaeval successors. More excavations are needed of the kind so fruitfully conducted by Mr Euan MacKie at Dun Lagaidh, beside Loch Broom, or by Mr Iain Crawford at Sollas in North Uist, and these will surely clarify what is still an obscure picture. Nevertheless, we can hardly deny that down to the middle of the 12th century, and in some respects until the 13th, a harsh, brutally violent Iron Age

1. A burial cairn at Garbeg, Drumnadrochit, excavated in 1974. Probably Iron Age

2. Beaker and skull from a Bronze Age short cist burial at Lochend

3. Raigmore Stone Circle, central cobbled area, c. 3000 B.C. covering earlier hut sites

4. Raigmore Stone Circle during excavation, 1973

5. Craig Phadrig, inner revetment during excavation, 1971

6. Druid temple, possibly a ring cairn of the Clava type

7. Ardross Wolf Stone

8. Scots Pines, survivors of the old Caledonian Forest

9. Major James Fraser of Castle Leather

10.　James Graham, 1st Marquis of Montrose (1612-1650)

11. Castle Stewart

12. Drochaid Balbh Bhordain

13. Wade Road at Tomatin

quality characterized the struggles of these warlike mormaers and the peoples subject to them.

Before 1100, the same could be said of the kings also. A single kingship for the Scoto-Pictish nation was indeed a remarkable achievement, but it was far from meaning that the royal dynasty was peaceable and secure, or could impose a permanent "king's peace" across the land. The blunt truth is that each new king came to power, and was expected to come to power, by rebelling against his predecessor and either killing him or having him put to death. Confining ourselves solely to the 11th century, we see that King Malcolm II (Malcolm MacKenneth), an exceptionally powerful king who slew his rebels before they could slay him, actually died peacefully at Glamis after a reign of thirty years which, however, had begun with the killing of his predecessors, Kenneth and Giric. His grandson, King Duncan, was killed at Pitgaveny near Elgin (in or after battle) by Macbeth who, after his defeat at Dunsinnan Hill, was himself killed at Lumphanan by Duncan's son, Malcolm, who then proceeded to kill Macbeth's stepson and immediate successor, Lulach "the Simple." Malcolm III proved to be as tough an exponent of the difficult art of survival as his great grandfather, but even he, after ruling for thirty-five years, met a violent end during a raid on Northumberland. His brother Donald was blinded and died from his mutilation, while Malcolm's first-born son, Duncan II, was slain treacherously after barely a year on the throne.

An entirely new era was ushered in with the reign of Duncan's eldest surviving half-brother Edgar, and for over three hundred years no sovereign of Scotland died by an act of human violence. It would be difficult to exaggerate the sense of liberation and relief engendered among the people of Moray after the 12th century kings had imposed a genuine peace within the province. Our oldest surviving body of written record dealing with Moray is the group of 13th and 14th century manuscript cartularies compiled for the bishops of Moray, and for the deans and chapter of their new cathedral church at Elgin, published by the Bannatyne Club in 1837 under the composite title of *Registrum Episcopatus Moraviensis* ("Register of the bishopric of Moray"). The earliest documents copied into this invaluable collection belong to the 1170s. The most striking single fact about these manuscripts is their extraordinary silence with regard to the period before *c.* 1150. The men whose task it was to compose the legal records and preserve the most important and ancient title-deeds for the chief church of the province did not find it necessary to mention the name or the office of a single mormaer in the long line which ended with the defeat and death of Angus, Lulach's grandson, in 1130. No grant of land or act of piety by any of the old native nobility of Moray is recorded. The only human beings of the former social order referred to (and the references are all too few) are the king's thanes, the lords' *nativi,* neyfs, peasant tenants tied to the estates of their birth, and a handful of hermits, mostly in the valley of the Findhorn. The learned, educated men of Moray in the days of William the Lion and the two Alexanders (1165-1286) were not anxious, it seems, to recall the glories, if glories they were, of Macbeth MacFinlay and his ancestors. The only ingredient of the old order which anyone wished to preserve, was the cult of a few Pictish and Scottish saints revered in Moray for many centuries — Drostan (Aberlour and Alvie), Columcille (Petty), Adamnan (Insh), Cummein (Abertarff and Dulsie Bridge[1]), Fergus (Dalarossie), Talorgan (Kiltarlity), Comgan (Turriff, Kincardine on Spey, Loch Alsh) and a handful of others — and even this survival was increasingly confined to the peasantry and the clergy of the poor and remote rural churches.

It is with this background in mind that we may now turn to look at the mormaers of Moray in the 11th and 12th centuries, and at Macbeth in particular. Macbeth's reign can be understood only in the context of a long-drawn-out feud between his own ruling family of Moray on the one hand and, on the other, the royal dynasty of Scotland, and especially that branch of it which was led from 1005 to 1034 by Malcolm II, who, in order to reach the throne, had slain King Kenneth MacDub (Macduff) and his son King Giric. Another of Kenneth Macduff's sons was, it seems, Boite or Bodhe, who evidently allied himself to the men of Moray. His daughter (by a Moravian wife?) was Gruoch, a lady of strong personality (at least Shakespeare is close to history on that point!). She married as her first husband, Gillecomgain (pronounced Gilchoan and meaning "Saint Comgan's servant"), who was mormaer of Moray in succession to his brother Malcolm, killed in 1029. These brothers were sons of Maelbrigte, brother of Macbeth's father, Findlaech (Finlay). In an internecine quarrel which emphasizes their barbaric quality, they had killed their uncle in 1020. Malcolm son of Maelbrigte is apparently referred to in the Gaelic notes written into the gospel book kept at the monastery of Deer in the 12th century, where he is said to have given the monks the lands of Elrick at the south end of Old Deer parish. Tigernach's *Annals* call him *ri Alban,* "king of Scotland." This probably means simply that Tigernach regarded him as *a* king — in the usual Irish sense — in Scotland. (In the same way, another Irish chronicle tells us that Donald MacEmin, *mormaer Alban* — *"a* mormaer of Scotland," not *"the* mormaer" — fought at the famous battle of Clontarf in 1014, while Donald, son of King Malcolm III, is styled a "king of Scotland" in 1085). After Gillecomgain had been killed — burned with fifty of his "fighting tail" in 1032— leaving a son named Lulach, Gruoch married her late husband's first cousin Macbeth, despite the heritage of vengeance which the murder of Macbeth's father might be expected to bequeath. At this date, Macbeth had probably succeeded as mormaer of Moray, "thane of Moray," as the 15th century historian, Andrew Wyntoun, confusingly calls him.

Even if Macbeth had not been prompted to do so himself, he would have been expected by his wife and her kindred to pursue the greater vendetta against the house of Malcolm Mac-Kenneth. The new mormaer of Moray was a doughty warrior. The story in later writers, that he fought campaigns against the Norseman can scarcely be dismissed as fiction. Macbeth's contemporary in the north was Thorfinn Sigurdsson, "the Mighty," earl of the Orkneymen for sixty years, outliving Macbeth himself by eight. Earl Thorfinn was an ally of Macbeth's chief enemies, Malcolm MacKenneth and Malcolm III. His widow Ingibjorg, daughter of Finn Arnisson (a great friend of King Harald Hardrada, whose ill-fated invasion of England in 1066 was carried out with Malcolm III's help), subsequently married King Malcolm. Their son, Duncan II, king of Scots for a few months, was killed in 1094, perhaps by the Moraymen. It is therefore highly probable that, before and after Macbeth seized the throne, he had to do battle with Thorfinn and the men of Orkney and Caithness.

Malcolm II's successor was his grandson Duncan, son of his daughter Bethoc and Crinan, secularized abbot of Dunkeld. The fact that Malcolm II was strong enough, not only to rule for thirty years and die in his bed, but also to ensure the succession of his grandson, marks the beginning of a constitutional revolution of tremendous importance. The Scots had grasped the value of straightforward hereditary succession for the creation of a dynasty and the consolidation of royal power in the face of internal and external enemies. The historian, John of Fordoun, writing about 1380, attributed this revolution to King Malcolm's father, Kenneth II (died 995), but as a matter of historical fact, the change seems to have been welcomed and worked for by the three strong kings of the 11th century, Malcolm II, Macbeth and Malcolm III. This is

not to say that Macbeth was content to see his enemies con-
solidate their own hated dynasty. The new system meant that
rivals would be left out in the cold for good, whereas the older,
more barbaric system at least gave each party the chance to
shine every few years. Consequently, Macbeth's rebellion against
King Duncan in 1040 may well have been motivated not only
by the old blood-feud, but also by fear that a "MacKenneth
dynasty" had come to stay. Moreover, Duncan — though not
a strong king personally — had wider territories under his
rule than any predecessor, for to Scotia and Lothian he had
added Cumbria (from the Clyde to Westmorland), of which
he had been lord under his grandfather. The stakes, therefore,
were large: a bigger Scottish kingdom, and the opportunity
to found a permanent dynasty.

It was clearly as mormaer of Moray that Macbeth revolted
against King Duncan. The place of Duncan's death, given as
"Bothngouane" in the Chronicle of the Kings of Scotland, was
evidently Pitgaveny[2], three miles north-east of Elgin, in the
heart of Moray. In 1235, King Alexander II, great-great-great-
grandson of King Duncan, endowed a chaplaincy in the cathedral
church of Moray at Elgin out of the royal rents of the burgh
of Elgin, so that a chaplain could celebrate masses perpetually
for the soul of Macbeth's victim. Once he had made himself
king, however, it is by no means clear that Macbeth tried
to shift the political centre of gravity to the north. It is more
likely that he found the magnetism of the rich royal demesnes
of Angus, Gowrie, Fife and Lothian irresistible, and that, had
he been able to found a dynasty, it would soon have come to
look very like the southern-based dynasty which he tried to
overthrow. The only surviving written evidence of Macbeth's
activity as king in Scotland is a notice of two grants made
to the *célidé* — culdees — of St. Serf's Isle in Loch Leven.
By the first, "Machbet son of Finlach and his wife Gruoch
daughter of Bodhe" granted the lands of Kirkness and the
village of Portmoak. By the second, King "Makbeth", with
deepest reverence and devotion, granted to God and Saint Serf
"Mactorfin's Bogie" — Bogie near Kirkcaldy. These Fife
estates were surely not the patrimony of a mormaer of Moray,
any more than St. Serf's church was an object of Moray
veneration.

As far as the meagre evidence goes, it seems that Macbeth
ruled vigorously and not in any old-fashioned isolation. Like
King Cnut of Denmark and England a couple of decades earlier
(or King Dungal of Cumbria in the 10th century), Macbeth
travelled as a pilgrim to Rome in 1050. That he was thus

able to leave his kingdom for an arduous journey of many months and much peril proves in striking fashion the strength of Macbeth's kingship. Two years later, his reputation stood so high that a band of knightly Norman adventurers, ejected from the marches of Wales, got a safe-conduct to ride to Macbeth's court and take service with him. This is the first occasion on which Normans are known to have been in Scotland. The experiment of employing Norman "mercenaries" was not only not a success, but may actually have proved Macbeth's undoing. The arrival of these confident southerners may have aroused the jealous hostility of the native nobles, thus giving to King Duncan's sons, Malcolm and Donald, the opportunity they sought. Malcolm had taken refuge at the half-English, half-Norman court of Edward the Confessor during the reign of Macbeth, and had made an alliance with the redoubtable Siward, a Scandinavian warrior who held the earldom of Northumberland. In 1054, Siward and Malcolm took an army into Scotland and encountered Macbeth at Dunsinnan Hill, on the northern edge of Gowrie — further proof, if it were needed, that Macbeth had been ruling from the ancient and accustomed power-base of the Scoto-Pictish kings. Despite the presence of his Normans, who were killed to a man, Macbeth was decisively defeated. He survived for only three more years before being killed at Lumphanan in Mar. It may have been in thanksgiving for his defeat of Macbeth that Malcolm III —once he had despatched Lulach the Simple at Essie in Rhynie parish (1058) — made a grant of the lands of Keig and Monymusk to a community of célidé settled at the latter place and afterwards subordinated to the bishops of St. Andrews.

As events were to prove, the overthrow of Macbeth and his stepsons marked the end of the "house of Moray" as a participator, even on an alternating basis, in the royal government of Scotland. But, for the next century and a half, the rebellions and risings of the men of Moray posed a threat to the stability of the crown which every king in turn was forced to meet and overcome. Scotched again and again, the descendants of the ancient mormaers were defeated only when the last of their stock was exterminated. It would be quite unrealistic to expect that the house of Moray would accept the judgement of 1057-8 as final. The unfortunate King Lulach had left a son, Maelsnechtai, as well as a widow and a daughter whose names are unknown. The widow was captured by King Malcolm in 1078, after a campaign in which Maelsnechtai barely escaped. But since he is reported in the Annals of Ulster to have "died happily" in 1085 and had previously made a grant of land (an unlocated Pett Maldub, "Maeldubh's farm") to the monks of Deer, it looks as though Maelsnechtai had managed to make his peace with Malcolm III. The Ulster annalist calls Maelsnechtai "king of Moray," no doubt using "king" in the Irish sense; otherwise we should have to suppose that the triumphant and ruthless King Malcolm III had been forced to tolerate an under-king in his most troublesome province during the decade when he was at the height of his power.

The identity of the husband of King Lulach's daughter is not known. Possibly he belonged to the Moravian nobility, possibly he was mormaer of some neighbouring province, such as Ross or Buchan. What is clear is that the son of this marriage, Angus, was brought up to be mormaer of Moray and regard himself as pretender to the Scottish throne. It is likely that the men of Moray backed Donald Bàn, Malcolm III's brother, in his unsuccessful four-year struggle to wrest the throne from his normanising nephews. Nevertheless, the ruling family of Moray was evidently in eclipse at the turn of the century, presumably during Angus's minority, and it is not until the middle of Alexander I's reign (1107-24) that we hear of a royal expedition against rebels in the north. In 1116 the men of Moray slew Lodmund, son of Donald, said to be a grandson of Malcolm III. Wyntoun tells how King Alexander "the Fierce" led a new-fangled cavalry force north of the Mounth and across the "stock ford" into Ross — i.e., across the Beauly River near its mouth — eventually catching up with his foes and putting most of them to the sword. It may well be that this tale has a sound historical basis, and that Alexander I was punishing the Moray men for their crime of which his own nephew was the victim.

"Fewe he lefft," says Wyntoun, "to tak on hand swylk purpose efft." But the few must have included Angus, Lulach's grandson, who seems either before King Alexander's death, or at least from David's accession, to have been recognised as mormaer — perhaps by this date we ought rather to say "earl" — of Moray. Angus allied himself with Malcolm MacHeth, probably disinherited Earl of Ross, and prepared to throw off the fealty which he had evidently sworn to King David. Seizing their opportunity in the summer of 1130, when the king was in the south of England, the two northern malcontents raised a great host and marched south to win back the kingdom for the slighted house of Moray. They were met at Stracathro, after they had crossed the North Esk, by a royal army led by Edward the Constable. At its hands they suffered a total defeat. Angus was killed, and the king's troops were able to take full control of the whole province of Moray on behalf of their absent master.

It was probably at this point that David I granted the earldom of Moray to his nephew William, son of King Duncan I. William cannot have been born later than 1094 (i.e. posthumously), for his father's only charter belongs to that year and speaks of his "infants." William was twice married and it is therefore reasonable to assume that his first marriage had already taken place before 1130. The identity of his first wife is unknown, but subsequent events make it likely that she was either a daughter of Maelsnechtai, or a sister of Earl Angus. If so, William would have been earl of Moray as much in right of his wife as by formal royal grant. Indeed, it is doubtful if William remained earl after his first wife's death, for he does not seem to have been styled earl while he was lord of Craven and Coupland in right of his second wife, Alice de Rumilli (c. 1140-51?). By his first wife, William had a son named Donald, invariably named MacWilliam. This form of patronymic testifies to his upbringing in a Gaelic-speaking milieu. Donald may well have believed that when he came of age, he would succeed to the earldom of Moray, but, if so, he was to be disappointed. Well before King David's death in 1153, Moray was beginning to be settled by knights and barons brought in by the crown. We cannot doubt that some of the lands given to these new-comers had been demesne land of the old mormaers.

In 1163, native inhabitants of Moray (Murevienses) were "transferred" by King Malcolm IV. There is no clue to the precise meaning of this cryptic report in the Holyrood chronicle, but it may refer to an eviction of freeholders to make way for feudal tenants. The feudalisation of Moray was neither rapid nor all-pervasive, but it was by no means half-hearted. It involved the erection of three or four royal castles, the planning and building of new burghs, and the establishment (obviously under difficulties and making little headway until the 1180s) of a properly organized and endowed diocese and episcopal see. In the course of this development, a completely new dynasty of local nobility was brought into existence, significantly using the surname "de Moravia," "of Moray" (Murray), and a new system of sheriffs was introduced which put local government on the same footing as the south and centre of Scotland. These gradual but far-reaching changes meant the extinction of the old mormaerdom and almost all that it stood for. This fact alone would have given an air of desperation to the revolts led by Donald MacWilliam for a good many years down to 1187, by his son Guthred (1211-12), by Guthred's younger brother, Donald Bàn (1215) and, finally and most desperately, by Guthred's or Donald's son, Gilleasbuig (1228-30).

Donald MacWilliam was perhaps born in the third decade of the 12th century; if so, he would have come of age towards the end of David I's reign, and would have already been chafing during the reign of Malcolm the Maiden at the crown's refusal to grant him his inheritance. When we first hear of him, in 1179, he had long been in revolt against King William. He aimed, it was said, to take the kingdom itself and had the support of certain of the nobles of Scotland (unfortunately Roger Howden, the well-informed Northumbrian chronicler who tells us this, was too discreet to say who these nobles were). Donald himself, however, was no doubt an outlaw and had been forced to make a home for himself in the western isles or possibly even in Ireland. In 1179, King William took an army to Inverness and built two new castles, at Dunskeath on the north shore of the entrance to the Cromarty Firth and at "Etherdouer," i.e. Redcastle in the south of the Black Isle. The siting of these castles was clearly designed to protect Moray from the north-west. Donald withdrew, only to return with greater force in 1187. Again the king led a northern expedition, basing himself upon Inverness. One of his own servants, Gillecolm the marischal, from Perthshire, betrayed Auldearn castle to the rebels. Even some of the earls in the royal army were said to be disaffected. Food was running short and the king's men split up into foraging parties. Roland *alias* Lachlan, of Galloway, long practised in the guerilla warfare of the Galloway hills, led a large band of eager young warriors. They discovered MacWilliam on a moor called Mam Garvia, a name which seems to represent Gaelic *màm gairbhe,* "rounded hill of the rough place," or even "rounded hill of Garve." The spot has never been located satisfactorily, but was evidently in Ross and not far from Moray. In a fierce fight, Roland's men got the better of their foes and Donald himself was slain. At this distance of time, it would be easy to portray him as a romantic hero, nobly but desperately pitting his strength against feudal tyranny masquerading as the forces of law and order. Contemporaries who actually suffered from Donald's depredations had no romantic illusions. "By the mercy of God, peace, long disturbed, was restored to king and kingdom," wrote the anonymous monk of Coupar Angus.

Twenty-five years were to pass before a MacWilliam again

disturbed the king's peace. As before, the storm-centre was in Ross, where the nobles—presumably the old native aristocracy —stirred up Donald's son Guthred to revolt. The rebels must have been numerous and menacing and succeeded in taking the king's officers by surprise. Fighting went on, albeit sporadically, from 1211 to 1212. Brabantine mercenaries, obtained from King John of England, had to be brought in to stiffen the royalist army, whose leaders were Thomas, earl of Atholl (son of Roland of Galloway), Thomas the Durward, William Comyn, soon to be earl of Buchan, and Malcolm, son of Earl Morgan of Mar. At last, in the summer of 1212, with King William's newly-knighted heir Alexander taking part in the campaign, Guthred and his followers were defeated. The captured Guthred was led before the king at Kincardine Castle in the Mearns, and was then beheaded and hanged upside down. In the same year, Derry in northern Ireland and the whole region between Lough Swilly and Lough Foyle were laid waste by the earl of Atholl, son of the victor of Mam Garvia, perhaps by way of punishment for providing a base and support for the MacWilliams. It seems incredible that any more members of the family would now risk their lives in revolts foredoomed to failure.

But in 1215, taking advantage of the conflict with King John in which Alexander, now king of Scots, was fully engaged, Guthred's brother, Donald Bàn, along with allies who included an Irish king's son and Kenneth Mac Aht (i.e. MacHeth), descended upon Moray with fire and sword in the bad old-fashioned way. They were resisted, and what seems specially significant about this resistance is that it came from the native aristocracy of Ross. "Machentagar," reports the Melrose Chronicle, "powerfully overthrew the king's enemies, and cutting off their heads brought them to the king on 15 June (the day Magna Carta was first sealed by King John at Runnymede in England)." "Machentager," who was promptly knighted by Alexander II, was Fearchair mac an t'sagairt, Farquhar Priest's son. Before 1235, he had been made earl of Ross. Whether Farquhar was descended from the lay abbots of Applecross or, as has seemed to some more likely, belonged to a line of hereditary priests of St Duthac at Tain, there seems no doubt that he was a leader of the old native aristocracy. If such men would no longer support the MacWilliams, their cause was clearly lost.

Yet even as late as 1228-1230, one Gilascoph (Gilleasbuig) "of the race of MacWilliam," together with an unidentified Ruaraidh or Rory, rose in revolt and (among other things) stormed the earth and timber mote-castle built at Abertarff near Fort Augustus by Thomas of Thirlestane, a royal tenant, slaying Thomas himself inside it. The revolt was put down by Earl William of Buchan, whose kinsman Walter Comyn a little later got the lordship of Badenoch, perhaps as a consequence. In 1230, the infant daughter of Gilascoph MacWilliam, the last survivor of her race, was battered to death at the market cross of Forfar after a proclamation by the common crier: "a somewhat too cruel vengeance," as the anonymous chronicler of Lanercost wrote. But this savage extermination is a testimony to the fear and hatred which the ancient dynasty of Moray could still arouse among their kinsmen, descended from Malcolm MacKenneth, and among those who were devoted to consolidating and preserving a new kind of Scottish kingdom.

NOTES

1. Timothy Pont's manuscript "Mapp of Murray" (c. 1600) in the National Library of Scotland (Pont Maps No. 8) shews "Suy Chummenn" (i.e. Suidhe Chuimein, "Saint Cummein's Seat") as the name of the striking hill marked on the O.S. 6″ Map of 1871 (Nairnshire, Sheet XI) as The Doune, half a mile south of Dulsie Bridge. At the east end of this hill, a natural shelf or platform of land contains the remains of some early stone structure. The O.S. 6″ Map marks the place as "Chapel Field" and (in Gothic letters), "site of Chapel." The name Suidhe Chuimein is otherwise known at Abertarff (Fort Augustus). Saint Cummein was abbot of Iona and died in 669.
2. "The smiths' farm." Compare the 13th century "Gaelicized" form Badfothel for the Aberdeenshire place-name Pitfoddels *(Reg. Episcopatus Aberdonensis,* i, 6). The form of this name in use today represents the older "Pictish" form.

River scene of Inverness.

LIFE IN EARLY INVERNESS

D. J. MACDONALD

The title of this chapter, prescribed by the Editorial Committee, is so wide that it could mean almost anything. If, as is likely, it is meant to cover from the earliest known settlements up till, let us say, 1914, the date which really saw the end of an era, then treatment must be sketchy in the extreme. Inasmuch, however, as in all ages there were common elements of living throughout the British Isles, I will mention only such aspects as seem to derive their quality from their belonging to Inverness and its immediate background.

Geographical factors made Inverness the kind of place where even primitive peoples might be expected to live. Even in the absence of roads, it was a nodal point because valleys debouched on to the estuary of its river, and its position at sea level gave it protection from extremes of climate and weather.

By the 6th century it was already recognised as of significance, for it was here that the ruler of Pictland lived. Brude Mac Maelchon seems to have exercised at least some degree of authority as far as the Orkneys. St. Columba, who was statesman as well as ecclesiastic, came here when he wished peace between his own Goidelic Scots in Dalriada, and their Brythronic cousins to the east of Drumalban.

Therefore it would be true to say that from the earliest times Inverness was in some sense a capital, and that knowledge, however rudimentary, must have had some effect on its citizens. They may even have exhibited some kind of 6th century uppishness.

They would be aware of trade: of the felling of trees for boat-building, trees from the depths of the old Caledonian forest that clothed hill and valley, save where outcrops of rock and the frequently recurring bogs and morasses made large growth impossible.

Their movements would have been fairly limited, and such people as came to them arrived by sea or along the naturally provided avenues of travel. Most of the visitors would come from east of Drumalban and north of the Mounth. The exceptions would be traders, early missionaries following in the wake of the legions, and the first probings of the Scottish Crown.

Additional to those more or less legitimate travellers would be warring factions or plundering raiders. These last would tend to go for herds of stock, for the town of Inverness, if such it could then be called, would have had very little to offer.

The River Ness and its estuary determined the town's lay-out from the very beginning. The river being, by repute, the second fastest in Britain, would cause such dwellings as there were to be well back up the slopes on the east bank, which would appear to have been inhabited earlier than the flat lands on the west bank. Thus, what we know as Church Street and Castle Street were the oldest roads in the town. Bridge Street and Fraser Street are the descendants of the paths taken by the women with their washing tubs. No doubt there were several large stones like *Clach na Cudainn* (the Stone of the Tub) at the Town Hall, on which they placed their tubs or, indeed, used as beating stands for their washing.

High Street and Eastgate would follow as the natural way of entry from east of the town (or village).

Houses would tend to cluster round four other centres. One was the estuary, where ships would bring catches of fish, or merchandise from the Low Countries, and carry away hides and timber. Another would be the Dominican Friary, in what is still the Friars' Street area. Above all, they would shelter under the lee of the two Castles.

It is impossible to say now which was the older site. Macbeth's Castle, to which Shakespeare refers, rose above the bluff which runs along the south side of what is now Millburn. It would in some measure command the sea approaches and the road from the east. The other site, the one on which Inverness Castle now stands, would be the watch-tower for movement from the Great Glen to the South-west and from the North. The vitrified fort on Craig Phadrig represents an earlier time, belonging as it does to the era of all such hill-forts in the north of Scotland, as distinct from that of the broch dwellers.

For the "man in the street," life must have been intolerably limited by our standards, although he probably did not feel it so, and he had his occasional diversions.

In the 6th century, he may have heard St. Columba and St Moluag preach on the knoll where the Old High Church now stands. He may even have witnessed the confrontation between St Columba and Broichan, the Arch-Druid. Centuries later he may have watched the comings and goings about the Priory when two of its monks went with a Scottish mission to Bergen to help frame the Treaty with Norway that followed the Battle of Largs in 1263. He may have fished with the monks of a Thursday evening from Friars' Shotts, the spit of sand on the west bank of the river on Huntly Street.

No doubt there would be recurrent fears and uncertainty about incursions from the wilder mountainous lands to the west and south-west of the town. One occasion for resentment must have fallen in 1411, when Donald of the Isles, camped near Muir-of-Ord on his way to the Battle of Harlaw, sacked the town in revenge for their poor reception of him. Forty years ago, Inverness crowds watched from Huntly Street as the Theatre Royal and St. Columba Church went up in flames. Five hundred years before that, their ancestors gazed at their bridge being burnt down by the Lord of the Isles, "the famousest and finest of Oak in Britain," according to the Wardlaw MS. The women would not have gone that day to put their tubs on *Clach na Cudainn*.

The comings and goings of the great ones would be a matter of fair frequency in Old Inverness. When Mary, Queen of Scots, resided very temporarily at the foot of what we now call Bridge Street, being denied access to her own castle by the representative of the Earl of Huntly, she would have found herself surrounded by poor houses. Here and there stood the residences of the merchants, which were usually above their shops.

Chairs for ordinary household use were unknown at that time. People had no forks; food was picked by hand from a common dish. Hats were worn at meals. Very few people washed their faces every day. Whether the aristocrats who descended upon the town followed Cardinal Wolsey's practice of carrying an orange in front of him as he walked among the populace in order to counteract the unpleasant odours, I cannot say. He was probably in advance of his time. "Gardyloo" would be the cry of Inverness housewives, as of any contemporary town where houses were two storeyed. Milton talks of the London of his day as a city where open sewers annoyed the air. Inverness in the 16th century was not big enough for sewers — and the river was near.

The citizens had their diversions, not the least frequent of which was public execution. An old name for Castle Street was Doom Street, because along it the condemned climbed to have their final view of the world from somewhere about Ardkeen Tower.

If anyone felt like viewing the street without himself being seen, he had a peephole in his shuttered windows, which he could open or close by sliding a panel. If he were a burgher making some money by sea-trade or cattle, he probably had a "stand of harness," as he would have called his suit of armour, in a corner of his living-room. Should he feel inclined for sleep after the day's events, he would have lain down on a canopied bed, for he reckoned he had fresh air a-plenty in the course of the day.

Dr Evan Barron, in a paper read to the Field Club in 1907, paints a vivid picture of the activities which the mediaeval Invernessians would see as they watched the world go by. He says: "Wool, pelts and hides were its [i.e. Inverness'] principal exports, and it also did a large trade in timber, herring and salmon . . . In some years as many as 4000 hides, besides pelts, were exported. There must therefore have been a very considerable tanning industry in the burgh. Where there was a trade in timber, ship-building also flourished, and the fact that burgesses of the town themselves owned ships, and that 200 cows could be sent to Leith by sea goes to prove that 'the noble ship' built in 1249 for the Count of St Pol was no mere chance episode in the history of the town."

The older ones among us, brought up in Victorian ways, are apt to think this a careless age. Our Town Council, for example, found it necessary not long ago to keep one of the gates into Tomnahurich Cemetery closed to prevent through traffic from using the road. But in Queen Mary's time, the churchyard which still surrounds the Old High Church was enclosed by a broken dyke, through which horses and cows strayed to feed on the grass which grew on the graves; and no one seemed to care. On the 18th of March, 1564, however, an order from the Town Council and the magistrates required that "the kirkyard be biggit and dykit with stones for stopping of horses and bestial."

On the riverside below the parish church stood the then crumbling Friary, surrounded by six rich fields which after the Reformation became the glebe of the parish minister. Hence our Glebe Street. Across the river from the Priory rose the Chapel of the Green. In 1563 one Andrew Sutherland was tried before the magistrates for carrying away its bell. At the same court, James Kelly was charged with stealing twenty stones out of the Friary. His defence was that he was employed by a Hamburg man to carry them to his ship.

The records of the Burgh Court at that time make strange reading today. A man sues his neighbour for a boll of meal, for a barrel of salmon, for a dozen hides. Some of the punishments seem equally strange. Banishment, for example, was one of the sentences for persistent disturbers of the peace, slanderers and other undesirable persons. Some of them, however, were not always strictly enforced. In January, 1562, Elspet Barnet was found guilty of saying to Thomas Waus, a burgess, that he would hang himself as his friends did, and drown himself as his sister did, and that she would burn all his "corns." She would also burn John Ross's "corns," although "herself would be burnt for it." If she were found in the town thereafter, she was to be burnt on the cheek. Three months later, she was back. Again the same decree was issued. Two years afterwards, she was back again.

One curious entry in the Town Records for 24 March, 1736, may suffice to convey the "atmosphere" of the law in those days. It reads:

"By 4 fathoms rope to hang Peter Corbet: six shillings;
"To the officers to drink after the execution: 32 shillings.
"Paid the Town's Officers for watching Peter Corbet for 46
    nights at twelve shillings per night, £27 12/-;
"Candles furnished the officers then: £6 18/-.
"The Dempster for hanging Corbet: 13/4."

One of the citizens' recurrent fears was epidemic disease. Cholera struck terror. The last such disaster in Inverness took place not so very long before the founding of the Field Club. As one walks along the paths in the Chapelyard cemetery, one walks over the graves of the victims.

Punctuated by long periods of what to us today, our time pressurised by technology and its tabloid presentation by much of the media, would seems aeons of boredom, the early citizens of Inverness saw the wash of history move beneath its serene skies. The 17th century was the first to pile the Ossa of religious feud on the Pelion of secular strife. He would see the Mackintoshes march to the Stone of Watching to beat off the Mackenzies from over the ferry. He gaped at Montrose drinking his fleeting cup of water at the Priseag Well and then halting awhile, bound on his horse, on the old Exchange. How unlike his victorious sweep through the town from Auldearn to Inverlochy! He watched the Cromwellian ships bear stones from the Fortrose Cathedral to raise the Commonwealth's citadel beside the river mount, and heard the English speech that legend says conditioned his own mode of communication.

"The town was then, and had long been, mainly Anglo-Saxon, an English-speaking colony in the midst of Celtic and Gaelic-speaking clans," said Kenneth Macdonald, Town Clerk of Inverness, to the Field Club in March, 1895. "Its population was probably not less than 2000 and not more than 3000.

Small as it was, it possessed extensive trading privileges and as a military post it was keenly contested for . . . At the Chapelyard were the butts where the citzens congregated with their arms in times of danger for inspection and exercise.

"At the top of Bridge Street and Kirk Street, where the Steeple now rears its head, was the Tolbooth, comprising the courthouse and gaol, a poor building and probably an old one. On the ground level, under the Tolbooth stair, were two shops, one belonging to Robertson of Inshes, and the other to John Cuthbert, Elder. The Tolbooth had a steeple, with bells and a clock. The steeple was taken down and rebuilt in 1691, part at least of the cost being met out of money collected from the inhabitants to buy off Coll Macdonald of Keppoch (Town Council Minutes of 9 March, 1691). The kind of building the Tolbooth was, may be gathered from the fact that it had no chimney until the steeple was re-built."

The 18th century provided the citizens with alarms and excursions in plenty, with the comings and goings of the three Jacobite campaigns. By our time-scale, however, these were separated by long years when nothing seemed to happen. In the '15, Mackintosh of Borlum would have made a busy to-ing and fro-ing as he mustered Frasers and Chisholms to go north to meet the Earl of Sutherland's army at Alness. He may sometimes have seen a handsome young fellow come over the ferry from Killearnan, but he could not have known — and would not have cared, anyway — that Aenas Sage would one day join that Earl's army, and in 1726 become the first Presbyterian minister of Lochcarron.

Invernessian had four years to wait before he watched the army march out from the Castle and go down the lochside to meet the Rebels of the '19 and their Spanish allies in Glenshiel. But that was miles away among the barbarous, foreign-tongued brigands of the West.

That minor excitement over, twenty-six years had to elapse before the '45 gave Invernessians their first taste for centuries of a major battle on their doorstep, and the experience of living in an occupied town. Several of them went one cold, wintry day in April along the road that now takes them to a match in the Thistle Park. They went further that day, to see the last act played out in the tragedy of the Stuarts and, alas, of many Highland men, on Drumossie Moor.

When some days later, Invernessian washed down his salt fish with home-brewed ale, did he and his wife talk with bated breath of how Cumberland kicked the Provost down the stairs and on to Church Street? Then, when he heard a rumour,

K

did he rush down what is now Huntly Street to see Jacobite prisoners led out from the High Church to be shot among the stones of the graveyard.

Sir John Pringle, Physician-General to the Duke of Cumberland, quoted by Dr Whittet in his "Medical Resources of the Forty-five," wrote: "After Culloden we advanced to Inverness and encamped on the south side of the town. After our arrival the inflammatory diseases still increased and were the more severe as the climate was so cold and the camp exposed in an open country to piercing winds . . . At Inverness two malt barns received the (Hanoverian) wounded, in all 270 . . . Besides these two barns, two well-aired houses were prepared for the sick." Pringle drew attention to the smallness of the town, to the gaol filled with many wounded prisoners and to "the morbid state of the air from the measles and small-pox which had prevailed in the town before the arrival of the army."

I wonder if a "Good Morning" passed between Invernessian and the smart young officer on his way to a mathematics class in the Grammar School which we now know as the Dunbar Rest Centre. Provost Dunbar, nearly a hundred years before, had built it as a hospital. It was many things in its day, and in 1746 it was a school. Borlum had been there, and perhaps another young man whose name was to be a matter of controversy in the literary circles of Edinburgh and London, James Macpherson, the author of "Ossian." The young student of Mathematics was aide-de-camp to the Duke of Cumberland, and was one day to be General Wolfe, the victor of Quebec.

One Saturday evening in September, 1773, he saw, if he were anywhere near what we call Bridge Street, a post-chaise with a gross, heavy-jowled man and a younger companion stop at Mackenzie's Inn at the Horns, where Lipton's supermarket now stands. Had he been told that they were Dr Johnson and James Boswell in course of their Highland tour, the information was probably convey little to him.

While still wondering about the pair on Sunday morning as he went to his own kirk, he would see the big man "larding the lean earth as he moved along" to the Chapel in the Black Vennel, now Baron Taylor Street. He little knew that 200 years on, he could buy in that Chapel House the most sophisticated cameras and recording machines, such as might have made things a lot easier for his biographers. If, after church, he went for a walk by the harbour to "see the strange shipping there," he would see the same unequal couple go into the house of Collector Keith of the Customs, and no doubt told his wife that it was as odd a viewing as he had seen since Cumberland's troops had left the town nearly twenty years before.

Eighteen years after that, masons were putting up a building on New Street, a fine square, solid edifice. Maybe the masons, carefully dressing the stones, wondered why it should be called an Academy. Ah, no doubt some grand name, for did the money not come from Lovats and Mackintoshes and from some of those younger scions of the Chiefs who found the sugar-plantations of the West Indies more rewarding than the impoverished glens? Our mason would not have read Plato's "Republic," nor guessed that in the name were high hopes for this "seminary for young Highland gentlemen," as its first prospectus proudly called it.

Sometimes he saw MacDonell of Glengarry, that queer throw-back to the kind of Chiefs his grandfather knew, come "soondin' through the toon" with his anachronistic tail. No doubt the streets buzzed with echoes of the row between the said Glengarry and the Directors of the Academy over the appointment of a classics master, and the rejection of the better candidate, just because he was the Chief's nominee. *"Plus ca change, c'est plus la meme chose."* In the 15th century, it was pillage from the west that irked the citizens. In the 18th, it was the troubles the western clans brought on the town in 1715, 1719, and 1746. In the 19th, it was the town's rejection of a chief's patronage. In the 20th, it is the town's objections to County Council requisitions. Regional government will no doubt shift the focus, but not the fact of protest. Anyway, the new building would soon give its name to New Street, parvenu beside Church Street and the High.

When he grew to an old man, Invernessian and his cronies would get some fun from wandering down Academy Street on Market Days. He would see the women bending over the stalls at the side of the street, oblivious of the Academy boys pinning together the crinolines of a couple of them, then running across the cobbles to watch the fun as the two galleons in full sail tried to disengage from each other. He would also see a new phenomenon on Sunday morning: the Academy boys, led by the Rector and the Masters, all in top hats and frock coats, marching to service in the Old High.

He might not know, however, that one Rector was given money by the Directors to go by sea to London to buy scientific equipment, and did not return till he had spent all the money, and not on what he had been sent to buy. One of the Mackintoshes of Raigmore knew, and wrote up that and other scandals in a book whose circulation was limited, and whose author styled himself "Invernessicus." Invernessicus was also distressed by another affair. The Chairman of Directors of the Academy was the Provost of the Town. He was accused of causing one of the classical masters to reside for a term in Aberdeen to help his (the Provost's) son with his studies at King's College, while still drawing his salary as a teacher in the Academy.

The Academy was not the only school in Inverness in those days. Here, for example, is what Mr Hugh Barron has written in a paper in "Scottish Gaelic Studies": "Charles Fraser Mackintosh, M.P., who was born in 1828 — and built what is now Lochardil Hotel for his residence — attended the school at Dochgarroch from about 1836 until 1840, during the time that Mr Forbes was master. He seems to have made good progress under this competent teacher and won prizes for Latin and Greek in 1839. His time at Dochgarroch was followed by about a year at a small boarding school which was carried on at Torbreck, near Inverness, by two brothers, John and Walter Gair. They were assisted for some time in this work by their brother Alexander, who had at one time been minister at Glenmoriston."

Among the books used by Charles Fraser Mackintosh at school were

"Davidson and Scott's Arithmetic," modernised (Edinburgh, 1835),

"Analecta Graeca Minora," (Greek Grammar), and

"Elements of General History," by Tyler (London, 1841).

These all came from the library of his father, who was a tacksman at Dochgarroch. One wonders how the teaching in Dochgarroch School was affected by the construction of the Caledonian Canal, so admirably written up by Mr A. D. Cameron of the Academy.

These events all took place before the Disruption of 1843 hit the town. Fifty years after that event, Invernessians would see the Academy pupils, girls now as well as boys, marching to the then new Academy on the Crown lands. It was built in the old Abertarff wood, built, too, round the ghost who rattles the doors and sighs along the empty corridors o' nights.

It was a busy time for Inverness, that turn of the 18th century into the 19th. Not only did a fine new school go up, but the Northern Infirmary was begun. It was built by private donations and public subscriptions. The private donors were in the main those who had built the Academy thirty years earlier. It was a great achievement, and comes fairly early in the list of Scotland's hospitals. Its opening in 1804 was celebrated with much local pomp and circumstance, and with a marvellous *"fiesta"* in the evening. No doubt many of the citizens watched from the outside, as their descendants were in the second half of the century to watch the nobility arrive for the Northern Meeting Balls on Church Street. Such are time's revolutions, that where once only blood that was bluer than blue could enter the portals, social security benefits are now paid out to the *"hoi polloi"*. Two wars, with the consequent invasion of the sanctum, first by the American YMCA, and then, in the second conflagration, by a variety of service activities, prepared the way for the change.

Built into the Infirmary were two basement rooms to house "lunaticks" (sic). No longer would the citizens on a Sunday afternoon find relief from tedium by standing on the old stone bridge, which was washed away in 1849, to dangle juicy morsels in front of the grating through which peered unfortunates housed beneath it. It was their only contact with the world outside.

In 1864 came another forward stride in the building of the Inverness District Asylum, now Craig Dunain Hospital, marking the first serious attempt to treat the insane.

Then came the railway. There were jobs for Inverness men and women to keep the new Iron Horse going on its way. Unlike some other concerns, the Highland Railway was promoted by public-spirited men for the benefit of the community, and not for big commercial interests in the South.

Once a year, on the 12th of August, and the days preceding it, the station would buzz with life, for the "gentry" came North then for the Shooting Season. The town merchants would cultivate them for the large orders that came in from the lodges, and the Stationmaster would put on his top hat and dance attendance on "the quality."

The railway network spread. Trains now came in from Kyle and Wick. Excursions ran to the former to join a steamer sailing up Loch Duich. The engine sported a bunch of heather in front of its funnel, and message boys called their wares along the platform. Inverness Rock was *"de rigeur";* but the toilets on the train were few and far between, for there were no corridor coaches in those days. The fare was not much more than five shillings.

Newspapers were now printed in town. "The Inverness Courier" was authoritative for the local scene and was staunchly "for the town." Other papers came and went. There was, for example, "The Highlander," which produced cheerful commentary in the year of the foundation of the Field Club. The

Gaelic Society was afoot. The Rose Street Foundry, now A.I. Welders, was in being.

Dr Martin Whittet, in his history of Craig Dunain Hospital, quotes from the "Courier" of 1864, the year of the hospital's foundation, some items that bring back the life of the mid-19th century in our town — e.g. Shinty: "It is high time that the Authorities put an end to the practice of Shinty playing in the public streets of Inverness." Englishtown Asylum: "Since the opening of the District Asylum near Inverness, most of the pauper patients of Dr Hyslop, proprietor of Englishtown Asylum, have been removed as it was for their special accommodation that the D.A. was erected."

Soup Kitchen: "East End of Wells Street, Inverness. 850 Rations of bread and soup have been issued every alternate day. Tickets may be had on application to Mr Macpherson, High Street. Donations and contributions to Commercial Bank." Inverness District Asylum: "Among the visitors to the Asylum grounds, we regret to hear that on several Sundays and holidays of late, a number of unmannerly and idle persons of both sexes from Inverness have annoyed patients by going close to the windows and staring in at them. On the last Sacrament Fast, several such persons refused to go away and some patients, in consequence, became so excited that they could not be allowed out on their ordinary exercise on that day."

Four years before the Field Club was founded, the Gaelic Society of Inverness came into being. So you have in the town of that day a parallel growth of culture and industry.

Then, as now, the citizens were aware of the changing face of the town, with the disappearance of ancient landmarks. Here, for example, is what Mr Fraser Mackintosh, referred to above, said in a paper he delivered to the Field Club in February, 1893. "The great flow of prosperity which has affected the town of Inverness during the last thirty years, and which happily shows no sign of abatement, has at the same time the effect of removing many landmarks dear to the hearts of the sons of Clachnacuddin, and has given the town even in its centre an appearance (to use a description lately applied to Dundee) 'modern in style and utilitarian in aspect'." There is nothing new under the sun.

It is clear from reading a book like Miss Anderson's "Inverness Before Railways," written in 1885, that social life in Inverness in the early and mid-19th century was lived on two levels. "Since the opening of the Inverness and Nairn Railway in 1855," she says, "not only have a number of strangers come to reside in the Highland Capital, causing a spirit of competition to arise . . . and a gradual but complete revolution in the ways of what had for many years been a quiet, exclusive little town . . . Thirty-five years ago there were only a few classes in Inverness, and these were clearly defined, but this did not prevent each class from taking a kindly interest in the others."

Yet one is aware of the attitude of patronage (kindly, but none the less patronising) towards "the lower orders." When one thinks of our contemporary bank managers, harassed by various pressures, offering a wide variety of extraneous services to a demanding public, one cannot but be mildly amused by this passage from Miss Anderson's book: "In those days, when everyone was more or less hospitable, and the set of fine-looking courtly bankers, for whom Inverness was at that time noted, vied with each other in keeping open house, there was no one who dispensed hospitality with a more lavish hand, no one who was more generous to all who needed help, than Mr Mackenzie, Ness House, agent for the Bank of Scotland. Not only did his birth and connections, his singularly aristocratic appearance and exquisite courtesy secure for him the undisputed precedence, but he was about the last to maintain in Inverness the manners and customs of a former generation, and was even in those days considered the *"beau ideal"* of a Highland gentleman of the olden time."

At the other end of the scale, again from Miss Anderson: "The country girls did not then ape the fashions of their superiors in rank . . . It was a pretty sight to see them flocking into Inverness on a Martinmas Market Day, each with a bright tartan shawl, fastened by a large silver brooch, while their faces beamed with the expectation of "fairing" from their favourite "lad" . . . It was a picturesque sight also to see the "wives" in mutches . . . standing beside their carts, which extended from one end of Academy Street to the other. Ladies of the best position did not think it beneath their dignity to go in and out among the carts, examining the butter and cheese, while their children, under a servant's eye, delighted in wandering among the little stalls." Shades of the supermarket and the comprehensives!

On the other hand, we of the noisy Inverness of the 1970s, with almost daily reports of vandalism, may feel that history repeats itself, albeit with variations, when we read this; "In one respect Inverness has altered for the better" (i.e. the Inverness of 1885). "It was at one time (not a very old date) the custom for several idle young men of the upper classes to accost with impertinence and follow about the streets or roads, young girls of whatever rank in society — gentlewomen or maid-servants — they might be, and lay wagers beforehand as to the amount of annoyance to which they could subject them. There was also a regiment at Fort George about forty years ago, of which several of the officers were notorious for their impertinence to ladies. They used to sit on the parapet of the old stone bridge, making remarks on everyone who passed, and sometimes following pretty girls to the doors of their own homes. Even less than thirty years ago, there were wild young militia officers and others who used to go about at night taking the knockers off doors, hurling coaches into the river, and disturbing the slumbers of the inhabitants generally. Such customs as these have long since happily died out."

In Vol. VIII of the Transactions of the Field Club, we read: "At a largely attended meeting of the Club (on 14th December, 1915), held in the Waverley Hotel, the agenda included a paper by Mr James Barron (of the 'Inverness Courier') on 'The Making of the Field Club.' A letter was read from Mr E. M. Barron intimating that news had been received of the death of Major James Barron (in action in France) and that his father was unable to be present. The paper, which was of exceptional interest, was read by Mr William Simpson."

At the end of the paper we read: "In the same issue of the 'Courier' in which the above account appeared, there was a letter from the late Dr Aitken [the Physician Superintendent of what is now Craig Dunain Hospital], suggesting the formation of a Scientific Society and Field Club, and a meeting was called by circular, signed by Dr Aitken and the late Mr Walter Carruthers. The meeting was held on 10th November, 1875, and a resolution forming the Society was adopted."[a]

A short-lived contemporary of the "Courier" was "The Highlander," referred to above. It printed a considerable amount of Gaelic prose and verse, and gave fair coverage of Scottish news. The issue of 13 November, 1875, does not mention the inaugural meeting of the Field Club.[b] It may, however, be at least amusing to draw towards the end of this rather arbitrary romp through the ages with some equally random excerpts from that number, for they give some impressions of life in Inverness in the Foundation Year of our Society.

On the closely printed front page is a "Trade Directory and Shopping Guide" for people living outside the town. Most of the names have disappeared into history. One is P. G. Wilson, the Great Jewellery Establishment, 44 High Street. Another is the Maybole (not Maypole) Boot and Shoe Shop,

London House, High Street. At 76, Castle Street, was J. Mac-
Neill, Umbrella Maker and Repairer. A watch and clock maker
at 21, Castle Street rejoiced in the name of P. Minck.

Loch Fyne herring were on sale at J. P. Brodie's on
Castle Street in Half Firkins, Firkins and Quarter Barrels, while
"Lochourn herring" were available in Half and Whole Barrels.
C & J Macdonald, at 14 Castle Street, were fleshers.

One Glasgow firm said "Teas and Sugars are now so extraordinary [sic] cheap that every household should use them
more freely —

"Sugar (Brown — Dark) — 2d per pound.
  "   (Yellow — Bright) — 2½d per pound
  "   (White — crushed) — 3d per pound
  "   (Crystals — sparkling) — 3½p per pound."

David Hutcheson & Co., Glasgow, tell us that their steamers,
"Staffa," "Cygnet" and "Plover" will sail from Inverness to
Glasgow on Mondays and Thursdays at 6 a.m. "Steam com-
munication" could be had between Inverness and Liverpool
via the Caledonian Canal by the new Screw Steamer, "Princess
Beatrice," 448 Tons Register.

To a correspondent, D. C., Rosneath, the Editor says—
"Pray, exercise your usual patience. Other matters press at
present." The leader column begins: "We have repeatedly
directed attention to the question of food and the preparation
of it. Whether the movement will proceed wisely or not, the
teaching of cookery has begun in Edinburgh."

News items: "Mr Charles Innes has assumed as partner
Mr Wm. Mackay, solicitor, and the large business of the
establishments will be carried on under the firm of Messrs Innes
and Mackay. It is hardly necessary to introduce Mr Mackay,
who is already well known, as the first Secretary of the Gaelic
Society of Inverness, an intelligent and patriotic Highlander,
and a young man of character and marked ability."

"The Haugh Bridge Committee met on Wednesday, when
the Treasurer, Mr Black, Banker, announced that £160 had
been lodged in the bank, and that subscriptions to the amount
of £400 were outstanding. The Primus intimated a further
subscription of £20."

"On Saturday between 70 and 80 pupil teachers were
examined in Farraline Park Institution, the inspectors present
being Messrs Jolly and Sime." Mr Jolly was first President of
the Field Club, and on the 11th of January, 1876, he delivered
his inaugural address on the Scientific Materials round Inverness, and the Scientific work open to the Club.

Perhaps it would not be unfitting if I ended this chapter

with a word about the Field Club's contemporary, the Gaelic Society of Inverness, founded in 1871, one year before the Education Act of 1872. The almost simultaneous birth of the two societies is a pretty fair indication of the cultural climate at that time. Incidentally, the Gaelic Society is not to be confused with An Comunn Gaidhealach, which has similar aims but a very different approach to their realisation. The latter is a younger organisation, its birth falling in the last decade of the 19th century.

Inverness has never been a "Gaelic" town in the sense, in which, for example, Oban is, and to some extent, Glasgow. Inverness was the outpost of government for the Scottish Crown. It also lay, as it still does, on the indeterminate yet distinctive border between the East of Scotland and the West, almost a Harlaw between the Isles and Mar. Indeed, it has today a far larger element of "Gaelic" people than at any period in its history.

Owing to a range of pressures, Gaelic-speaking people had last century an inferiority complex about their native tongue. The pacification after Culloden, the well-meant but ill-conceived "civilising" efforts of bodies like the S.P.C.K. and, in some instances, of the national church, set the pace of declension. It was accelerated by the Clearances, with Border farmers and shepherds coming into the emptying glens; the succeeding advent of shooting tenants and their usually English staff; and by the coming of the railway.

The first awakening was academic rather than popular. Perhaps not un-naturally, it began with Highland exiles. "Distance makes the heart grow fonder" has its ethnic significance as well as its personal truth. The first gleam came in 1777 with the founding of the Gaelic Society of London, which is still active. There followed others in Glasgow, Perth and Edinburgh. The Inverness Society was comparatively late in arriving. There may have been an advantage in this, in that its formation was not the result of romantic nostalgia, but of an awareness that a heritage was disappearing, and that not much time was left in which to halt the process.

Its founders were Inverness citizens. Among them was Dr William Mackay, referred to above. Another was Alexander MacBain, headmaster of Raining's School, and editor of "An Etymological Dictionary of the Gaelic Language." Yet another was Mr James Barron of the "Inverness Courier," father of the late Dr Evan Barron and grandfather of Miss Eveline Barron, the present proprietor and editor.

One of the aims of the Society was "the establishing in

Inverness of a library to consist of books and MSS., in whatever language, bearing upon the genius, the literature, the history, the antiquities and the material interests of the Highlands and the Highland people." If the dream was never realised in all its grandeur, it was at least indicative of the quality of scholarship and of thought in old Inverness. The phrase "in whatever language," is itself as clear an indication as one could wish that worthwhile life in Inverness did not begin in 1970.

Was it one of Thomas Telford's assistants who once said of the citizens of Inverness that, "with the possible exception of the Provost, there is none that wouldn't be better hung." The readers of this *pot-pourri* of vignettes may feel that if he meant "hanged," he was probably right. One would like to think, however, that at least some aspects of Life in Old Inverness are worthy of being hung as pictures of living interest even today.

(a) and (b) — The *Transactions* are in error, for the inaugural meeting of the Club took place on 19 November, 1875, and so could not have been recorded in *The Highlander* on the 13th. — Ed.

FOR FURTHER READING

1. Anderson, P. J., *A Concise Bibliography of the Printed and MS. Material on the History, Topography and Institutions of the Burgh, Parish and Shire of Inverness*, 1917.
2. The Transactions of the Inverness Scientific Society and Field Club.
3. The Transactions of the Gaelic Society of Inverness.
4. Anderson, Isabel H., *Inverness before the Railways*, 1885.
5. Carruthers, Robert & Sons, *Old Inverness*, 1967.
6. Watson, W. J., *Prints of the Past around Inverness*, 1925.
7. Johnson, Samuel, *A Journey to the Western Islands of Scotland*, 1775.
8. Boswell, James, *The Journal of a Tour to the Hebrides*, 1785.
9. Fraser, John, *Reminiscences of Inverness: its People and Places*, 1905.
10. *Reminiscences of a Clachnacuddin Nonagenarian*, John Maclean, ed. by Charles Bond, editor of the "Inverness Herald," 1842.

MEDIAEVAL CASTLES AND TOWERHOUSES

EDWARD MELDRUM

"The castle is a fundamental piece of architecture"; those are the words of an eminent Scottish architect of the present day. Even now, in this technological age of progress, the mediaeval castle, whether splendidly entire or impressive in ruin, can yet exercise intense interest and fascination to all but a minority.

It is necessary to clarify the definition of a castle. A pre-historic "broch" or "dun" cannot be referred to as a castle, which is wholly a product of the Middle Ages, that period of history which, in Northern Scotland, lasted from the 12th t᷎ the 18th century. Castles were constructed from the designs and plans of mediaeval military engineers and architect/master masons: they were the fortified residences of the ruling classes, thus becoming the symbols of secular power in the days of the Feudal System, when Scotland and other West European countries were governed by that early form of military govern-ment.

Throughout the Inverness and Aird district there are many castles. Some are ruinous, some restored, some still occupied, some demolished and built over, while of others only the site remains: but all are of interest to those who care about our country and its past.

From early mediaeval times the district was divided into parishes, each of which generally coincided approximately with the estate of a feudal lord or knight. The parish nucleus con-sisted of the Castle and the Church, the latter the symbol of spiritual power; nearby was the lord's farm — The Mains (from the Norman-French "Demesne"); the Mill; sometimes the justice mound (or Court Hill), and gallows hill, for some lords had judiciary powers of "pit and gallows" over their tenants, both freeman and serf. These powers survived until after the 1745/6 Rising.

The first castles in the Inverness district date from after 1135, when David I brought a well-equipped army of Anglo-Norman, Breton and Flemish knights into Moray, which then stretched from the Spey to Strathglass and beyond, and from the Firth to Loch Oich in the Great Glen. This invasion suc-

ceeded in defeating the Gaelic-speaking forces of Angus, Earl
of Moray and his brother Malcolm, whose family, under the
Celtic laws of royal succession, claimed the Scottish throne
as descendants of the dynasty of Moray. After the subjugation
of the fertile south side of the Moray Firth, the King divided
the area among the knight adventurers of his army, and thereafter the first castles were built. But these strongholds were
not stone and lime castles, like some of the Norman keeps of
England. In the Highlands of the 12th century, castles were
timbered earthworks, known as motehills, of which there are
three main types.

1. The simple "motte" or high round or oval topped
mound, with wooden tower encircled by a timber palisading,
often surrounded by a dry "fosse", or ditch.

2. The "motte and bailey" type, where there was added
to the "motte" a lower mound with ancillary buildings, all within
a palisade, and surrounded by ditches.

3. The third type was less of a defensive castle, being a
low square or oval mound with the usual ditch. This type of
earthwork was known as a "moatstead" or "moated homestead," like that at Castle Leather (now Heather), east of Inverness. All these timbered earthwork castles no longer, of course,
have the timber palisading, tower and lesser buildings; in fact,
all that can be seen today are the earthwork mounds and
ditches.

Motehill castles were set up on natural or part-artificial
mounds in positions of strategic importance — at river crossings
and ferries, or commanding a hill pass. It has to be remembered
that, in the early Middle Ages, most high ground was forest,
most low ground was bogland; trackways were few and
dangerous, so it was quicker and safer by water. Most "mottes"
occupy what were strategic situations, and some were attacked
and dismantled in the risings of the Moraymen between 1180
and 1230. The sites of these 12th century earthwork fortalices
are found distributed throughout the northern part of the
district, along the coastal lands of the Moray Firths and in
the valleys of the Nairn, Ness and Beauly rivers.

Cantray Doune is a 35 ft (10.5 m.) high motte with a
circular summit 60 ft (18 m.) in diameter. This prominent
earthwork dates from the 12th century, when the lands of
Cantray were held by the De Moravia family, descended from
Freskyn, the greatest Scoto-Norman baron in Moray. It was
defended on the north-east by a rocky burn, beyond which
Cantraydoune farm occupies the site of The Mains (or
"demesne").

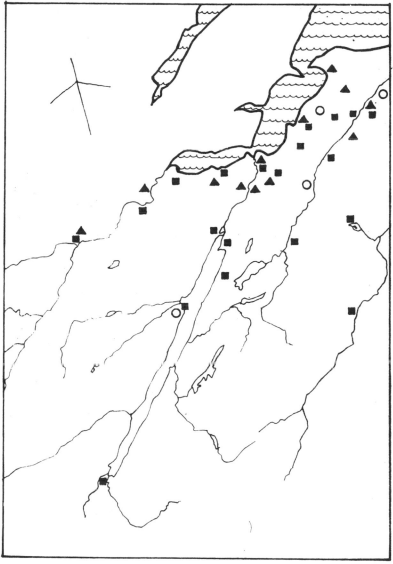

INVERNESS AND DISTRICT
DISTRIBUTION MAP 5
Motehill Earthworks   · ▲
Stone Enclosure Castles · O
Towerhouses   · ■

SCALE.

Petty Castlehill contained in the mid-12th century the timber castle of Freskyn de Moravia and of his descendant, Andrew of Moray, Lord of Petty, leader of the Northern Scots, who allied with William Wallace to defeat the English at Stirling Bridge in 1296. The "motte" of Petty stands on the 60 ft (18 m.) high raised marine terrace overlooking Petty Bay; the circular summit is 40 ft (12 m.) in diameter, and the landward defences consist of a semi-circular ditch 20-30 ft (6-9 m.) wide, at 30 ft (9 m.) below the top. Nearby is the now disused Parish Church, an ancient site.

Loch Flemington contains an island (possibly artificial), known as Castle Island, linked to the shore by a causeway, sometimes covered by water. Although there are no remains, this was the site of another timber stronghold of, as the name of the loch recalls, Freskyn the Fleming, Lord of Braichlaich— an early mediaeval parish, known also as Bracholy now included in Petty.

Cromal Mount, on the highest point of the 100 ft (30 m.) high raised beach overlooking Ardersier village, is one of the largest motehill earthworks in the district: the inner circular enclosure, 60 ft (18 m.) in diameter, is within the oval summit 140 by 100 ft (42 by 30 m.), with a huge 50 ft (15 m.) wide fosse or ditch in the landward side. The timber fortress here was probably a Royal Castle, dominating the east side of the ancient ferry-crossing over the Firth to the Chanonry of Ross. South-east lies the Mains — originally the home farm of the Castle.

Torvean Motehill — now difficult to identify because of tree-planting by the Dochfour estate — has an oval top about 100 by 50 ft (30 by 15 m.) standing about 60 ft (18 m.) above the road level. This motte commanded an old ford over the Ness, of which Holm Motehill was the eastern guardpoint. There is a main ditch 5 ft (1.5 m.) wide, with an outerscarp 3 ft (900 mm.) high at 40 ft (12 m.) below the top; and on the north-west side only is an intermediate ditch, with a width of 3 ft (900 mm.) not now easily traced.

Holm Motehill is a very good example of an early mediaeval timber castle earthwork, recently cleared of undergrowth by the landowner. It is sited between a minor road and the 50 ft (15 m.) deep den of the Holm burn. The motte summit is 30 ft (9 m.) in diameter and stands 25 ft (7.5 m.) above a steep-sided ditch on the east, the west part of which has disappeared.

Castle Leather — now corrupted into "Castle Heather" —

is a rectangular shaped low earthwork of the "moated timber homestead" type; the enclosure is about 140 by 120 ft (42 by 36 m.), with a wide ditch on three sides, possibly fed by water from the burn on the fourth side. Later this became the site of a stone castle, owned by a branch of the Frasers.

Castlehill of Lovat, at Wester Lovat, was an early earthwork, the site of the castle of the 13th century Bissets of Lovat. Although now largely built over by farm buildings, recent agricultural operations have uncovered the foundations of walls of the later stone castle of the Frasers of Lovat.

Lovat Bridge Motehill stands 25 ft (7.5 m.) above the level haugh fields of the Beauly River. A 12th century timber castle stood on the 240 by 190 ft (72 by 57 m.) summit dominating the river-crossing known as the Stockford of Ross, now replaced by Lovat Bridge.

Erchless Motehill or *Tom a' Mhoid* is a densely-planted mound used as the burial place of the Chiefs of Clan Chisholm in the 19th century. But its characteristic shape and defences make it the probable motehill earthwork of the De Aird, or Del Ard, family, whose heiress Margaret of the Aird (c. 1368) married Alexander Chisholm, son of Sir Robert Chisholm, Constable of Castle Urquhart, and ancestor of the Chisholms. The motte has a circular top 75 ft (22.5 m.) in diameter, with very steep slopes to the rocky Erchless Burn 40 ft (12 m.) below on the west side. The ditch on the other sides, 15 ft (4.5 m.) below the top, is 6 ft (1.8 m.) wide with an outer rampart.

Inverness Castle Hill, now occupied by the 19th century castellated court-house and police headquarters, consisted originally of a motte-and-bailey fortress dating from the foundation of the Royal Burgh of Inverness in the mid-12th century. The large oval-topped "motte" (300 by 150 ft or 90 by 45 m. approximately) stands about 8 ft (2.4 m.) above the triangular-shaped bailey sloping 250 ft (75 m.) to the south. The whole earthwork, probably formed out of the old raised beach, and thus partly natural, dominated both the burgh and the ford, later replaced by a bridge over the River Ness about 80 ft (24 m.) below. The timber castle was a key point in the Wars of Scottish Independence in the late-13th and early-14th centuries, being recaptured for Bruce in 1307. No stone fortifications, however, appear to ante-date 1412, when Alexander Stewart, Earl of Mar, became Governor. In 1508, the Earl of Huntly became the hereditary Sheriff of Inverness, and he constructed a great stone Towerhouse. This was besieged and captured by Mary, Queen of Scots, and her

L

army in 1562, when the Constable, Alistair Gordon, was hanged for treason. After being captured and recaptured during the Civil War, the Wars of the Covenant and the Jacobite Rising of 1715, the mediaeval castle was repaired, and a new barracks and outer wall built by General Wade, to become the first Fort George. This was destroyed by Prince Charles' Jacobite army in 1746.

Timber castles on motehills had several disadvantages — their wooden buildings were small, cramped and inconvenient, easily set on fire and very vulnerable to siege artillery. It can be assumed that many motehills, particularly the smaller examples, did not outlast the 13th century. Some were little more than strongpoints, perhaps only occupied in times of danger, while others survived as timber fortresses in continual use until as late as the 15th century.

By the middle of the 13th century, the new style of stone "enclosure" castles, also known as "curtain-wall," "courtyard," or "enceinte" castles, originating from Northern France, had reached Scotland. In its simplest form, this type of military fortress consisted of a square or rectangular (rarely circular, or oval or triangular) courtyard enclosed within high battlemented walls. Its later evolution brought the addition of square or round towers at one or more, or at all four corners. Very good examples of these "courtyard" or "enclosure" castles are at Lochindorb in Moray, Castle Roy in Badenoch and Inverlochy in Lochaber. All these were built by the powerful Scoto-Norman family of Comyn, Earls of Buchan, Lords of Badenoch and Lochaber. It was William Comyn, Earl of Buchan, who in 1228-29 quelled the last rising of the Moraymen. There is the possibility that at Rait, near Nairn, the early Comyn enclosure castle, of which only overgrown foundations remain adjacent to the early 14th century castellated manor-hall of the De Raits, was his work. The "manor" of Rait is first recorded in a list of estates in 1238.

Castle Urquhart is the largest mediaeval stone castle in the Inverness district, and one of the largest in Scotland. It occupies a formidable defensive position on a rocky headland thrusting into Loch Ness, south of Drumnadrochit. Urquhart displays the complete evolution of the Scottish castle, from prehistoric fort to late mediaeval towerhouse, but the main structure is a massive enclosure castle, irregular in plan to conform to the natural rock formation of the loch-side situation. The earliest fortress here was "Caisteal na Sroin — "Fort of the Promontory," a dun with timber-laced walls, where vitrified stonework was discovered during the castle excavations between

1912-22. The dun is now occupied by a shell-keep on the motte-like mound, and in the 13th century the double bailey was added within the stone-built enclosure walls including the donjon tower; the deep ditch, probably part of the prehistoric defences, on the landward side, was then enlarged. In the reigns of the Alexanders, Urquhart was of strategic importance in controlling the natural lines of communications along the Great Glen, together with Inverness at the northern end and Inverlochy at the southern. This great stronghold saw much action during the wars of Wallace and Bruce. Though occupied by the English in 1296 and 1303, it was finally recaptured by the Scots in 1308. Notable Constables included Sir Robert Lauder and Sir Robert Chisholm in the 14th century, and later the office was held by the ancestors of the Macleans of Dochgarroch. To the earlier buildings within the curtain walls — gatehouse, hall, great chamber, kitchen and chapel — there was added the rebuilding of the upper part of the donjon by the Grants of Grant, who in 1509 became the lairds of Glenurquhart. This high tower exhibits features of later mediaeval towerhouse architecture, particularly the wall-head arrangements, probably constructed by the master-mason, James Moray in 1627. The castle has been ruinous since it was blown up after the 1689 Jacobite Rising. Now an Ancient Monument, it attracts hosts of visitors every summer.

During the early 14th century wars against the English invaders, most Scottish enclosure castles became ruinous by intention, for it was Robert I's policy to burn the timbered towers on the motehills, and to reduce and demolish the great stone castles to prevent their occupation and fortification by enemy forces. This was a continuation of the largely successful "scorched-earth" tactics of the typically Scottish guerilla warfare initiated by Wallace. And so, even after the victory of Bannockburn, no more large castles of the "courtyard" type came to be built.

Instead, a new type of castle was evolved during the Wars of Independence. This was the Towerhouse. The earliest examples were simple towers, square or rectangular in plan, their small scale and verticality contrasting with the horizontality of the large scale 13th century fortresses. The Towerhouse is unique to Scotland, owing little or nothing to the influence of the Norman keep in England. Scottish towers often have stone vaulted interiors, cellars and storage at ground level, hall and kitchen at first floor, with entrance door at this level reached by timber or stone forestairs. Above were sleeping quarters and garrets in the roof, surrounded by a battlemented parapet with corner turrets for look-out and active defence against attackers. At first the simple towerhouse had no projecting portions, but later, and especially in the 16th and 17th centuries, with the need for enlarged and more private accommodation, L-plan towers with one wing, and Z- and E-plan towers with two wings were built. Most towerhouses had a small outer court, called a barmkin, which might have corner towers and a gatehouse.

Towerhouses were more numerous throughout the land than the stone enclosure castles because of the break-up of the estates of many noble families who, as English adherents, forfeited their lands after 1314. The once powerful Comyns lost their vast territories in the East and Central Highlands. The old earldoms and baronies were divided among lesser lairds who built, often under royal licence, defensive fortalices which, significantly in the turbulent Highlands of the later Middle Ages, when no man could trust his neighbour to keep the peace, had to be towers of strength.

Throughout the Inverness area such castellated houses, whether occupied or ruined, form historic, picturesque monuments in our straths and glens. The typical towerhouses, such as Erchless, Cawdor or Stewart, are strikingly impressive vertical towers with walls of ashlar or harled masonry, steep-pitched slate roofs, small-paned windows, corbie-stepped gables and a plethora of round and square turrets at the eaves, corbelled out at the corners and capped by graceful and conical roofs. The exuberance of the design and the elaboration of decorative features — gargoyles, dormer pediments, armorial panels, ornate sculptures — add to the undoubted attractive aspect of these old buildings set against the background of the Highland scene. The sturdy yet flamboyant towerhouses are typically Scottish in character and inspiration, and must be preserved as glorious survivals of our country's architectural heritage.

Cawdor Castle, just outside the district, is one of the finest rectangular towerhouses, built in 1454 under royal licence by William Calder of Calder (or Cawdor). Muriel, the heiress of Cawdor, by forced marriage in 1510 to Sir John Campbell, brought the castle and lands to that clan. The tower is now the nucleus of a complex of later buildings added in 1660 and later. Cawdor, which has unsubstantiated legendary links with Shakespeare's "Macbeth" (but see *Old Calder* p. 150), is still the residence of the Campbell Earls of Cawdor.

Kilravock Castle, on the high west bank of the Nairn,

up-river from Cawdor, is a very fine towerhouse, rectangular in plan, built, also under royal licence, by Huchone de Rose about the year 1460. The five-storey domestic south wing was added in the 17th century. Mary, Queen of Scots, visited the castle in 1562, and Prince Charles was entertained here two days before Culloden; Cumberland, the day after. Burns was a visitor in 1787. Still owned by the Rose family, the castle is now a Christian Guest House.

Dalcross Castle is an L-plan tower of warm red sandstone rubble masonry, built in 1621 by Simon Fraser, 8th Lord Lovat. A north wing was added in the early 18th century by Mackintosh of Mackintosh, who had by then acquired the lands. Although deserted and ruinous during the 19th century, the whole castle was handsomely restored about 1900, when the attractive arched outer gateway was built.

Castle Stewart is an impressive E-plan towerhouse dating from 1623-5, the builder being James Stewart, 3rd Earl of Moray (son of the "Bonnie Earl of Moray" of the old ballad). It is the third castle at Petty, the first being the motte and the second, now vanished, at Hallhill. The plan is unusual, the main block having lofty square towers at the south-east and south-west corners, and there are splayed angle turrets corbelled out at the north-east and the north-west corners. The castle is still in the possession of the Earl of Moray.

Inshes House is a rather plain mansionhouse dating from 1767 and later. It occupies the site of a mediaeval towerhouse built by the Robertsons of Inshes, a northern branch of Clan Donnachaidh. Of this earlier fortalice, one interesting square barmkin tower remains, with musket- and pistol-holes, and characteristic corbie-stepped slated roof, its style indicating that the castle had probably been of late 16th century date.

Bunchrew Castle was originally built by Simon Fraser, 8th Lord Lovat. His initials and those of his wife I.S. (Jean Stewart) are on a "marriage" fireplace lintel, dated 1621. There are considerable additions, dating from between 1843 and 1897.

Moniack Castle is an L-plan tower with entrance door in the re-entrant angle, at the base of a round stair tower corbelled out at eaves level to form a square cap-house and parapets. It was built in the early 17th century by the Frasers of Lovat; alterations to the roofs and the north frontage were carried out about 1830.

Erchless Castle is a lofty L-plan towerhouse, believed to have been built between 1594 and 1610, and to have been completed by John Chisholm (d. 1623), who was a Commissioner of Peace for Inverness-shire and thus responsible for the lawful behaviour of his clan. The tower, which so strongly resembles the Mackenzie towerhouse of Fairburn in Ross that the same master-mason was no doubt employed on both, was altered and added to in 1887. The last chief of the male line of Chisholm, who was invariably addressed as The Chisholm, was Duncan, who died in 1858. Erchless is still occupied and handsomely maintained.

By the end of the 17th century, and certainly after the failure of the Jacobite Risings, the need for the lairds and clan chiefs to hold and defend their strong towerhouses had lessened. The era of the arrogant lords, with their feudal powers and their flamboyant castellated towers had passed: nevertheless, the tradition of castle-building never quite died out, and the external ostentatious trappings and the decorative features of the old 'Scottish baronial" architecture continued to appear in mansions, shooting lodges and other buildings throughout the district into Victorian and Edwardian times.

Finally, some brief mention must be made of the sites of former castles, where only fragmentary or minimal remains are still visible.

At *Old Calder* was the site of an early earthwork castle, probably of the "moated homestead" type; the predecessor of Cawdor Castle ½ mile (800 m.) to the south.

Hallhill of Petty is today only a low mound, once surrounded by now-drained bogland, and known as "The Island" in the 18th and 19th centuries. The stone castle here, probably of 15th century date, succeeded the Motehill of Petty and was much involved in the feuding between the Huntly Gordons and Clan Chattan, led by Mackintosh. In 1513, it was sacked by Dougal Mor Mackintosh after its refortification by the Ogilvies.

Culloden House, a palatial Classical mansion of 1783 in the Adam style, occupies the site of an early 17th century castle of the Mackintoshes, of which the basement cellars yet remain. This castle belonged, before 1745, and after, to Duncan Forbes of Culloden, President of the Court of Session. Prince Charles spent three nights here before the battle. Some time after 1746, the castle was destroyed by fire.

Castle Mattoch, at Castletown, Nairnside, is now only a large mound, partially removed when the railway was constructed in the 1890s. The stone tower has disappeared, and the one remaining feature of this castle, the history of which is uncertain, is the moat, still waterlogged in places.

Daviot Castle was once a large and formidable stone castle, built by David, Earl of Crawford about the year 1380, and destroyed by Hector Mackintosh in 1534. One small round courtyard tower survives, overhanging the steep bank of the Nairn, to the north of Daviot House, built on the site about 1825.

Tordarroch House, recently restored as a castellated tower-house, has been since the 15th century the ancestral home of the Shaws of Tordarroch, chiefs of Clan Ay. It was a three-storeyed tower in 1746, and the Episcopalian Bishop Forbes (of "The Lyon in Mourning") stayed here in 1770.

Moy Hall, home of the Laird of Mackintosh, succeeded earlier mansions on the same site, while the ruins of the earliest stone "ha'-hoose" of the Chiefs, built by Lachlan Mackintosh in 1665, are yet traceable on the tree-clad island on Loch Moy.

Garbole Castle is said to have stood on high ground south of the graceful single-arched Garbole Bridge, where the Kyllachy burn joins the Findhorn, but nothing remains of the building, nor is its history known.

Erchite Castle stood at or near Wester Erchite farm house, into which some of the castle's stones appear to have been built. Apparently a towerhouse of the Frasers of Erchite, it commanded a magnificent view over Loch Ness before its dismantling by the Hanoverians after 1746.

Aldourie Castle is a Baronial-style mansion of the late 19th century, incorporating an earlier tower of 16th or 17th century date. This, and the next-mentioned castle, controlled at the east and west end respectively the passage across the ancient ford of Bona, which was passable until the Caledonian Canal construction raised the level of the River Ness where it leaves the loch.

Lochaleg Castle, or *Bona Castle,* or *Caisteal Spioradain,* consists of the very fragmentary ruins of a towerhouse, belonging in the 15th and 16th centuries to the ancestors of the Macleans of Dochgarroch. Some masonry walling, an inner ditch, outer ward and ditch, are the only remnants of this once strong castle on its promontory, defended by the River Ness on one side and by the Abban water on the other. The castle was dismantled and the site was much disturbed during the formation of the Canal.

Abertarff Motehill was a timber castle built by Thomas of Thirlestane, who, c. 1210, was Lord of Abertarff until his death at the hands of Gillascop. Shown clearly on a military map of 1719 are the ruins of the mediaeval Castle of Kilchumein which evidently stood on Thirlestane's earthwork, which appears to have been about 120 by 90 ft (37 by 27 m.) across, with a 30 ft (9 m.) wide fosse on the south, west and north sides, the mouth of the River Tarff defending the eastern approach.

The site of this early motehill and later castle is now occupied by the church of the Benedictine Abbey of Fort Augustus.

Fernua Castle, or *Tom a' Chaisteil,* was a minor tower-house with barmkin wall and causeway approach, all now crumbling and overgrown. The site is a strong defensive one, south of Kirkton of Fernua (or Fernaway) churchyard, on a tree-clad mound, its embankments sloping to steep-sided burns converging from east and west. The south (entrance) side is protected by a part-natural, part-artificial wet fosse.

Dounie Castle was originally a motehill castle, of which some earthworks and ditches remain. It belonged to the Bissets until 1268, after which it became, through marriage, the castle of the De Fentons, who were designated "of Beaufort." The Frasers of Lovat gained Beaufort in 1511, and the stone tower-house of Dounie was probably built in the 16th century, and thereafter occupied by the Lords of Lovat until destroyed by the Hanoverians after 1746. Still the home of Lord Lovat, the present Beaufort Castle, built on a grand scale in the Victorian Baronial style, is a gloriously ostentatious example of the architectural survival of the mediaeval castellated tradition in the North of Scotland.

LATER HISTORY

THE CHRISTIAN CHURCH

JOHN MacINNES

There is a church in Glen Urquhart named after St. Ninian, the disciple of St. Martin of Tours, who erected his white-washed stone church, commonly called "Candida Casa," at Whithorn on the Solway about the year 400 A.D.[1] It would be tempting to think that St. Ninian or his disciples had evangelised the Inverness countryside, but, despite the valiant efforts of Dr Black Scott and Dr W. D. Simpson, the majority of sober historians of today have pronounced against them. Their vote goes in favour of St. Columba[2]. That princely soldier of Christ landed in Iona in 563 A.D., had his famous interview with Brude, the pagan king of the Picts a year or two later, won a notable victory over the chief druid, the king's spiritual adviser, and baptized, either on that occasion or on a later visit, an aged Pict called Emchattus and his son Virolecus. This baptism was administered at Airchartdan (now Urquhart)[3]. Columba, taking advantage of the favourable political climate, paid a number of visits to King Brude's territory and established monastic and evangelising centres as far east as Aberdeen-shire.

The Columban Church, child of Irish Christianity, has been one of the glories of Western European religion. Its passionate enthusiasm, its genius for evangelism, its self-denying austerity, its devotion to sacred learnings, its unquestioning belief in the power of prayer, its gentleness in dealing with the raw and intractable elements of paganism, were notable elements in its spiritual knight-errantry. On the other hand, its tribalism, its tendency to keep the leadership within the founder's family, and its failure to envisage a national church, doomed it to eventual decay[4].

By 800 A.D., the Vikings had begun their savage raids on the North and West of Scotland[5]. Iona lost its pre-eminence and Dunkeld, for a time, became the mother church of the united kingdom of Picts and Scots, until St. Andrews took its place. Margaret, queen and saint, the wife of Malcolm Ceann Mor, is thought by some to have had a notable influence on the church life of her husband's kingdom. The church of the "Cele De," with its fossilised relics of Columban practice, was decadent. She aided in the process of transition to the system of the universal church. "We are unworthy to partake," replied the Cele De, when reproached for their neglect of the sacrament. She found it necessary to reprove them for their total disregard of the Lord's Day, and has thus been praised or blamed for being the true author of Scottish Sabbatarianism. She disliked their "barbarous rites" in the conduct of public worship, and encouraged "the beauty of holiness"[6].

Margaret's son, David I, that "sair sanct for the crown," was tireless in realising his mother's aims. He completed the ecclesiastical map by defining the parochial system and re-establishing the Bishops' dioceses and, as the rhyming chronicler said,

> "He illumyned all his dayis,
> His landys with kyrkys and abbays"[7].

In Moray and Ross the royal policy of quelling the Celtic unrest, and the eventual forfeiture of the ruling dynasty, gave the Scottish Monarchy a golden opportunity for putting their Norman administrative ideals into practice. Ecclesiastical jurisdiction was very much a part of this policy, and the Register of Moray, a collection of the Bishops' Charters, is exceptionally good evidence of how the mediaeval church was rearranged and set up. The Bishop of Moray moved his Cathedral from Birnie. to Elgin, and in 1224 the new building was dedicated to the Holy Trinity. It was looked upon as the Light of the North and the ornament of Scotland, with a chapter of Canons and a Constitution based on that of Lincoln. It is suggested that it was at this time that the Pontifical recently found at Brodie Castle, and thought to be the most important historical discovery of the century, came to Moray.

The new tenants-in-chief, as well as the old, rebuilt churches and started new parishes. Endowing them with one-tenth of the produce of soil, sea and river, the tiends thus gifted still remain. King William made over a "toft" of land in Inverness for the endowment of the Church there. The religious orders, pioneers of Christian civilisation, were introduced. The Benedictines came to Inverness, the Valliscaulians to Beauly[8]. In the 13th century, the Friars, Dominican and Franciscan, came to Inverness and, not being enclosed communities, they played the role of a mediaeval Salvation Army. Hospitals (*Scottice* spittal) were erected at different points, one at Elgin, another in Killearnan in the Black Isle. "Sangschules" were set up at the religious houses. Great men endowed chaplainries in the parish churches to pray for the welfare of the donor's family, dead and living, the funds of which were used in later days for the provision of school and college bursaries[9]. The church was very much alive, and the spiritual flame was not quenched during the troubled years of the Wars of Independence.

The decline of the church's vigour in the later Middle Ages coincided with an advance in the arts of civilised living. Why, then, the decay of the church? Of course, the church, through the ages, has had experience of a certain rhythm of decay and resurgence and it would take a very wise or bold man to ascribe a reason for either. In the case of mediaeval Scotland, however, there were two causes which plainly worked to the hurt of the church. The first was the appropriation of parish benefices by the cathedrals and religious houses. A miserably paid and usually almost illiterate curate was appointed to carry on the parochial duties, while the great corporations received the tiends. The second was the system known as "in commendam," whereby the king, with the pope's often reluctant consent, was able to appoint a layman, or even a child, to the headship of a rich abbey. The bulk of the revenue then went to the commendator, often a senior officer of state, or a royal bastard, while an ordained deputy discharged the duties[10]. Most of the parishes in the Inverness neighbourhood in the late mediaeval period were "appropriated" and served by deputies called Vicars.

We need not doubt the Trinitarian orthodoxy of the people's religious belief, but they inherited and did not question the large element of superstition which had come to them from pre-Christian faith and practice. Although the cult of the saints, St Bride, St Columba, St Maelrubha and St Dubhthach (Duthus) was prevalent, bulls were sacrificed to Mourie (Maelrubha) as late as the 17th century. The healing power of holy wells; the belief in magic stones and in the physical potency of cursing and blessing; the presence in lake and river of water bulls and water horses, and in hillocks of those uncanny beings, the fairies (sithichean), were all part of the spiritual atmosphere in which they lived. One gets the impression that, while belief in witchcraft was not doubted, the penalties for its practice were not so ruthless as in better educated regions[11].

In 1560, the Scottish Parliament declared for a reformation of the national church after the Genevan model. The Catholic clergy, if they were not prepared to become Ministers in the Reformed Church, were deprived of their spiritual function, though they retained two-thirds of their emoluments. The other third was allotted to the Crown and the servants of the Reformed Church. Qualified ministers were in scant supply, but readers and exhorters, often converted priests, monks and friars, were placed in the parishes to conduct services and exercise pastoral care. There appears to have been little opposition around Inverness. The Bishop did not change his allegiance, but as he was patently a man of immoral character, his decision did not carry weight[12]. Some Lairds remained champions of the Catholic cause. It followed that the clans who had been long restive under their shadow inclined to favour the Reformed side.

The Burgh became aggressively Protestant. In 1559, neatly anticipating the national policy, the magistrates ordered the religious houses to deliver their silver vessels and priestly vestments into their keeping. Their landed estates were seized and eventually became Lovat's property. In 1561, the Burgh Court arranged for the annual election of elders and deacons. Immoral persons were to be named in church in time of worship. Unmarried co-habiters were ordered to marry. The disobedient were to be banished. The burgh folk were commanded to attend church regularly. A moral re-armament campaign was under way[13].

The non-urban countryside did not follow the example of the Town Council. Indeed, the forty years after the Reformation of 1560 witnessed a considerable decay of public morality[14].

At its foundation, the Reformed Church possessed three basic documents. There was the Scots Confession, accepted by the Estates as a definition of its faith, and it was in general agreement with the theology of Geneva, Hugenot France, the Netherlands and the Rhine. If anything, it was more severely scriptural. There was the Book of Common Order, the authorised guide to the conduct of public worship. A Gaelic version was published in 1567[15]. This manual was certainly used in Argyll. The evidence is not conclusive as to its use in the Inverness countryside. Then there was the First Book of Discipline, which laid down governing principles of the church's life. It authorised the creation of kirk sessions in all parishes, the appointment of superintendents to oversee provincial districts, which normally coincided with the ancient dioceses. It was the second Book of Discipline, of 1578, which under the influence of Andrew Melville propounded the Presbyterian system of Church Government. In theory, there was to be one order of ministers and the Church with its courts was to be independent of any secular influence. Presbyteries and Synods with an independent General Assembly was the ideal, but in practice there was much equivocation and the "exercise," a council of neighbouring ministers and elders, grew into the court known as the Presbytery.

The staffing of the parishes with suitable pastors was a trying problem. The General Assembly appointed superintendents and commissioners to oversee the "planting of kirks." In Inverness, the earliest commissioner was Robert Pont, brother of Timothy Pont, the cartographer. He was not noticeably successful. In 1574, Alexander Howieson, minister at Inverness, was appointed to the like office[16]. By 1600, almost all parishes had ordained ministers.

The pattern of congregational life remained remarkably consistent until the beginning of the 19th century. Kirk sessions and presbyteries, with or without Bishops, exercised a careful control over the faith and morals of the people. Superstition and idolatry incurred ecclesiastical wrath. The image of St Finane, reverenced in Dunlichity, was burned at the market place of Inverness in 1643[17]. The "Coan," described as the idol of the Glengarry Macdonalds, was judicially condemned. In 1678, the Synod of Moray ordered the Presbytery of Inverness to condemn the pouring of libations of milk on fairy knowes, the kindling of midsummer fires, and to preach powerfully against witchcraft. In neighbouring Ross-shire, a bull was sacrificed to "Mourie" as late as 1678. Kirk sessions had to deal with cases of sexual irregularity, quarrels of spouses, breach of promise, slander, drunkenness, and breaches of the Sabbath code. They had also to look to the care of the poor, the vagrant, the physically infirm. Presbyteries organised collections for the support of poor scholars, and were able on occasions to set up parish schools. Dingwall, Kirkhill, Kiltarlity and Petty enjoyed this privilege, while Inverness had its grammar school[18].

The alternation of Presbyterial and Episcopal rule during the 17th century made little or no difference to the worship of the people in church. The people gathered to hear the Bible read by the reader or catechist for an hour before the minister's service. As there was no Gaelic Bible until 1767, the reader in the Gaelic parishes translated "currently" from the English as he stood before the people. In an English service, as in the burgh, the people sang the metrical psalms. There were no Gaelic metrical psalms until 1650, and then only the "Caogad," the first fifty psalms[19]. For a hundred years after the Reformation, the voice of Gaelic church praise was silent. The sermon was long and severely doctrinal. In times of political distress, however, there was much "preaching to the times."

A chief method of imparting theological instruction was the annual catechising. Up to 1650, John Craig's admirably pithy catechism, the noble Heidelberg Catechism of the Palatinate Church, the massive catechism bearing the great name of John

Calvin, published in Gaelic dress in 1633, were all used[20]. The Shorter Catechism of 1647 superseded all these. All persons of "examinable age," that is, of seven years and upwards, were expected to undergo the ordeal. Baptism was generally regarded in the Highlands as essential to salvation, and desperate measures were sometimes used to compel ministers to baptize children whose parents were under church discipline. The frequent neglect of the celebration of the Lord's Supper is therefore astonishing[22]. For example, it was reported that there had been no celebration in Glen Urquhart between 1647 and 1671. Fast Days and Thanksgiving Days, ordered either by church or by civil authority were frequent. Ministers had not their sorrows to seek. Rural ministers in Celtic fashion were habited in kilt and plaid and wore their hair long. This custom was condemned by the church authorities. A minister who, for right or wrong reason, disagreed with the great men of his parish, could be starved out, the heritors withholding his stipend, and lesser folk making free with his cattle and his sheep[23].

If James Fraser, admitted to Kirkhill in 1661, be taken as representative of the rural clergy, they must be regarded as men of culture. The "Wardlaw MS" is adequate proof[24]. Thomas Hog (Kiltearn) was a learned theologian, and a famed director of souls. James Fraser of Breay (Black Isle), deeply spiritual and a natural rebel, was a thinker of some originality. Bishop Murdo Mackenzie of Moray influenced liturgical practice. Large scale revivalism, of the type associated with the name of John Balfour of Nigg in the fourth and fifth decades of the 18th century, and of John Macdonald of Ferintosh in the mid-19th century, was in evidence in Inverness during the latter years of the reign of James VI. Robert Bruce of Kinnaird was an exile in Inverness from 1605 to 1613, and again from 1622 to 1625. His massive theological thinking and his deep spirituality have been an influence in Scottish Presbyterianism to our day. Although an exile by royal decree, he continued to preach in the burgh and in rural parts. People travelled from Ross and Sutherland to listen to his message[25]. A Jesuit father, reporting to Propaganda, said that the people along Loch Ness side were ardent Calvinists, having become absolutely imbued with these sentiments by a preacher sent there by James VI for banishment[26]. Bruce's imprint can be seen in the religious life of Easter Ross, the Black Isle and Moray as well.

The presence of Father MacBreck on Loch Ness side in 1648 reminds us that the Roman Catholic Church was by no means dead in Scotland. In the early years of the 17th century, the Roman Catholic Archbishop of Armagh, alive to the racial kinship of his people and the Highlanders of Scotland, and acting on the forward policy of the Counter Reformation, sent missionaries to the Hebrides, and a little later the Roman Catholic Archbishop of Dublin sent several Franciscan Friars to the Islands and to the West Highland mainland. Even later, St Vincent de Paul sent a number of priests into the Highland field. Considerable, though exaggerated, success attended their labours. In 1681, the Roman Propaganda office sent Alexander Leslie to report on the religious situation. He informed his superiors that there were 14,000 Roman Catholics in Scotland, 12,000 of them in the Highlands and Islands. Examining this figure in the light of a religious census carried out between 1701 and 1705, Professor D. Maclean concluded that a more realistic estimate would be about 5,500, but admits that a significant advance in the Roman Catholic population took place after 1712. The regions where the advance was made were the Great Glen, Lochaber, Badenoch, Strathglass and round about Boleskine and Abertarff. Kilmorack and Glenmoriston also shared in this growth, but in Inverness and six miles round it, there was only 36 Roman Catholics in 1698, and no appreciable change thereafter.

To revert to the main stream of national church affairs. There is little doubt that the National Covenant of 1638 had overwhelming popular support. It was signed by many Northern potentates. Bishop Guthrie of Moray and Bishop Maxwell of Ross were deposed by the 1638 General Assembly, the latter being also excommunicated[27]. If one may gauge popular feeling by the action of the young folk, the spectacular burning of copies of the offensive revised Prayer Book, commonly known as "Laud's Liturgy," by the boys of Fortrose Grammar School in 1638 is worth notice[28]. The Solemn League and Covenant was a disruptive factor in the national unity but, by and large, the "barons and freeholders of Moray stood firmly for the Covenant." James Fraser of the Wardlaw MS., though his heart was with the King's cause, sadly describes the wholesale devastation wrought by Montrose's men round Inverness and in the Aird.

The deposition of the "malignant" ministers of Dingwall, Contin, Urray and Fodderty during the church war between Resolutioners and Protesters was followed after the Restoration of 1660 by the deposition and severe persecution of Thomas Hog and John Mackillican, the two chief leaders of the Protester party. On the whole, the Inverness district accepted the change from Presbyterian back to Episcopal rule submissively. A

M

number of ministers refused to conform and were relieved of their cure, and later, the minister of the First Charge in Inverness and the pastor of Dores were "outed" for refusing to take the oath required by the Test Act. A feature which dimmed the post-Reformation euphoria was the large number of exceptions made to the Act of Amnesty for acts done during the inter-regnum, but the congregational life of the church settled down to its usual course.

There was little or no difference between the Episcopal and Presbyterian order of worship. The Episcopalian clergy insisted on the saying of the Lord's Prayer and the singing of a doxology at the end of a psalm, both good Reformation practices which had been discontinued by Presbyterians under English sectarian influence. The kirk sessions oversaw the moral life of the parish as before, and also cared for the poor and infirm. Some sessions managed to establish schools. Inverness had its ancient Grammar School, and Kiltarlity in 1671 and Kirkhill in 1682 had each a parish school. The Petty School was also flourishing then and continued its usefulness into the 18th century[29]. Other parish schools there appear to have been none, but men of substance were accustomed then and during the next century to hire a teacher for their own families. The session was the courst of first instance in cases of petty crime. Applicants for divorce or for declaration of nullity of marriage were referred to by the presbytery, who passed the task to the bishop. The official referred to as "the Commissar" appears to have had the final say. Church collections were made for specific objects, as for the building of a bridge at Inverness, the repair of a street in Dingwall, the ransom of seamen or merchants captured by Barbary pirates. The collection for the "Gaelic bursary," that is, the student attending college in preparation for the ministry, was an annual event. The custom of making sinners mount the stool of penance during church worship or of fixing their necks in the "jougs" attached to the outer wall of the building while the service was going on, was maintained.

The "Field Presbytery" of Moray and the considerable body of unyielding Presbyterians in Easter Ross and the Black Isle were a source of annoyance to the episcopal authorities. In 1672, the Moray covenanters ordained James Fraser of Breay to the ministry, and he became a frequent preacher at conventicles. There was scarcely any offence more heinous in the eyes of rulers of the Church, whether Episcopal or Presbyterian, than the performance of sacramental acts by members of an outlawed religious sect. Hence the fury aroused by the celebration of the Lord's Supper at Obsdale, Rosskeen, in September 1675. John Mackillican, late of Fodderty, and Mr Anderson of Cromarty were the offending ministers. Troops arrived with orders to disperse the conventicle and arrest the ministers. The people had dispersed before their arrival and Mackilligan hid under the ample riding cloak of the corpulent Sir Robert Munro of Foulis and so escaped arrest[30]. He, however, as well as Thomas Hog of Kiltearn and James Fraser of Breay, suffered imprisonment later on in Blackness Castle and on the Bass Rock[31].

The defection of Angus Macbean, of the First Charge of Inverness to Presbyterian nonconformity and his subsequent deposition in February, 1688, might by some have been regarded as foreshadowing the coming revolution in church and state, but neither in the burgh nor in the surrounding countryside were there any overt desires for change. By and large, the people had accepted Episcopacy and, as Presbyterian difficulties in re-shaping the church after the Revolution Settlement showed clearly, the Episcopal ministers had won the trust of the people. On proper occasion, they might deny him his stipend, lift his cattle, threaten him for reproof administered from the pulpit, but they would not consent that a Whig minister should displace him.

Neither the non-committal reply of Bishop Rose in 1689 to William of Orange's demand that the Church of Scotland should support his assumption of the throne, nor the Jacobitism of many of the Episcopal clergy, led to the re-establishment of Presbyterianism; it was rather the political move in Parliament of withholding finance from the Crown. The Estates resolved to establish Presbyterian rule in the church and committed the labour of reconstruction to the "antediluvians." the survivors of the clergy ejected at the Restoration. A Northern Commission was created to supervise this work. John Forbes of Culloden, Grant of Grant, Brodie of Brodie and Sir John Munro were members. The Episcopal clergy were classified as 1., Non-jurors who refused to take the oath of allegiance and whose benefices were declared vacant; 2., Men who took the oath, but would not conform, and were protected in their benefices; and 3., Men who conformed.

There were no converts among the Inverness clergy, and the resistance to the Presbyterian "take-over" was strong. In the burgh, the minister of the Second Charge died in 1691. The attempt to declare the church vacant so as to instal a Presbyterian was frustrated by mob violence, and the church remained vacant for eleven years[32]. Hector Mackenzie of the

First Charge was in a strong enough position to compel his Presbyterian colleague to an equal division of all services, English and Gaelic. James Fraser of Kirkhill was too highly respected to be disturbed. Robert Cumming of Glen Urquhart remained unmolested in his parish until his death in 1730. The minister of Moy kept his parish until 1705, and his successor, Alexander Leslie, had an arduous but ultimately successful task in making Presbytery popular. Daviot refused to receive back its surviving antediluvian minister; Michael Fraser retained his benefice. Dingwall in 1704 and Beauly in 1720 were the scenes of sectarian riots. In each case, the local activists were aided by roving bands of Macraes from Kintail, who had assumed the role of strong-arm champions of prelacy[33].

The future of the Episcopal remnant, as a church separate from the establishment, lay with the non-jurors. They effected a much needed change in public worship. Drawing on the theological thinking of the "Aberdeen Doctors" and the great 17th century English divines, they established the rule of Bishops on a sounder foundation than on the fiat of an earthly king. Their profound belief in the Divine Right of Kings and their involvement in the affairs of '15 and '45 entailed much suffering and persecution. Yet in 1770, when Bishop Robert Forbes, Bishop of Ross and Caithness, (of The Lyon in Mourning) visited Daviot, Moy and Inverness, large crowds of the faithful turned out to listen to his message of encouragement. In 1803, there were still 300 Episcopalians in Killearnan, reported the parish minister, but in 1841, only a few remained[34].

The Presbyterians faced the task of rebuilding with courage and intelligence. Once they took over a parish, almost the first task was to create a reliable kirk session, composed of men able to command both physical and spiritual respect. Tradition has preserved the names of some elders who by their zeal and piety won fame and influence. They were leaders in praying societies and fellowship meetings and were regarded as trusted directors in the religious life[35]. The church was fortunate in the help rendered by the Royal Bounty Committee of the General Assembly and by the Society for the Propagation of Christian Knowledge. The former employed missionaries, who were fully trained ministers, to assist the parish clergy in ministering to a remote district in the parish. These men, usually houseless and churchless, endured hardship, but received a useful apprenticeship for their calling, and some, like John Robertson of Kingussie, and John Macdonald of Ferintosh, became distinguished preachers. The S.P.C.K., which owed its Scottish inception to James Kirkwood, an Anglican clergyman, was from

1709 engaged in promoting schools in the Highlands to supplement the parish schools, but their teachers had the additional task of acting as catechist, taking services and visiting the people[36]. Several of these teacher-catechists were Gaelic poets (of a sort), such as Maclachlan of Abriachan and Peter Stewart of Moy[37].

The provision of religious literature was undertaken by the General Assembly and the S.P.C.K. The Gaelic metrical psalms were published in Kirke's rendering in 1684, and in the Synod of Argyll's version in 1694. The Gaelic Shorter Catechism and Confession of Faith were issued in 1725, and the Scottish Gaelic New Testament in 1767[38]. Apart from the Shorter Catechism, taught to every child of "examinable age," the chief means of instruction was the sermon. In an evangelical parish, the sermon was severely doctrinal, and pointedly directed towards the conversion of sinners. The moderate preachers, who began to appear in many parishes before 1750, were prone to discourse on the sublimity of the virtues, especially benevolence. The goodly custom of family worship was successfully inculcated. There was a sustained attack on certain social customs, such as riotous behaviour at "Lykewakes" and "penny bridals," and also on lingering superstitions.

Towards the end of the 18th century, the evangelical party, historically opposed to the law of patronage, was in the ascendant. This party could count some famous names in the Inverness district, like John Graham of Ardlach; Dr Fraser of Kirkhill; Hector Macphail, Resolis; James Calder of Croy and his son Charles[39]. Then there came the brothers, Robert and James Haldane, and the agents of the Society for the Propagation of the Gospel at home. They touched most parts of the Highlands, preaching, distributing tracts and setting up Sunday Schools. In Inverness and district, they attracted multitudes and established praying groups. In Gospel-hardened Dingwall, they found "great stupidity as to the Gospel." Their Gaelic minstrel was Peter Grant of Strathspey. With the rising tide of evangelicalism, there developed an interest in Foreign Missions, though we can recall that, as early as 1735, the S.P.C.K. sent Neil Macleod, a Skyeman, to minister to men from the braes of Inverness and to their Red Indian neighbours in Georgia.[40]

The great church event of the mid-19th century was the Disruption of 1843. There had been little Presbyterian dissent in the Northern Highlands. Secession churches in Nigg, Wick and Thurso, were the memorials of long past dissensions. The whole of the Highlands was, however, affected by the rising tide of the new evangelical fervour. The Independent and Baptist deviations of the Haldane brothers and their followers had the result of confining the new enthusiasm within the confines of the church. The feeling of political helplessness in face of the "improving" policy of the landlords, resulting in the eviction of multitudes of crofters and small tenants in the four northern counties, produced bitterness and hostility. They protested in the one way open to them. The cry against the intrusion of ministers presented by the landlord patrons (though the Crown was really the largest owner of patron rights in the Highlands) became universal. The result was that in 1843 the Free Church could claim the allegiance of the vast bulk of the people north of Inverness. It is interesting to examine the book called "Disruption Worthies of the Highlands"[41]. There we have honourable mention of John Macdonald, Ferintosh, "The Apostle of the North"; Donald Sage of Resolis; Alexander Stewart of Dingwall, a disciple of the famed Charles Simeon of Cambridge; and Archibald Cook of Daviot. There are none from the burgh. Is this a case of the sweet reasonableness of the Inverness folk?

There was a growing concern during the first half of the century about the spiritual and educational needs of the Highlands. This is reflected in the setting up in 1811 and 1812 of the Edinburgh and Glasgow Gaelic Schools, whose object was to teach people to read the Gaelic Bible. They were widely supported and very successful. They were followed by the Inverness School Society, which began in 1818. Their valuable "Moral Statistics" reveal that there were, in the province of Moray, over 9000 people unable to read. In six years they had 65 schools and over 3000 pupils.

Outside the Presbyterian fold, the Episcopal Church gave up its non-juring testimony on the death in 1788 of Prince Charles. Its people were heartened in 1784 by the action of the American Church, whose first Bishop, Samuel Seabury, rejected by the Church of England, sought and received consecration, and thereby the Apostolic Succession, from the Scottish Bishops, including Arthur Petrie, Bishop of Moray and Ross. In this action, the world-wide Anglican Communion can be said to have its origin. Encouraged by the growing interest in the Middle Ages, fostered by the writings of Sir Walter Scott, himself an Episcopalian, the Episcopal Church enjoyed a steady revival in the 19th century. In place of the ruined cathedrals of Elgin and Fortrose, Robert Eden, Bishop of Moray and Ross from 1851 to 1886, built a new Cathedral in Inverness, the first new cathedral to be completed in Britain since before the Reformation. Bishop Maclean (1904-43) was a liturgical and Aramaic scholar of international repute.

The Roman Catholics, too, won their legal freedom at the end of the 18th century. Under the auspicious eye of the Fraser family, many Frasers and Chisholms had been able to continue their worship in Strath Glass and Beauly unmolested. The controversy between Scottish and Irish Roman Catholics in the South of Scotland did not influence the North. After many years under a Northern Vicar Apostolic, the Inverness district was placed under the Bishop of Aberdeen when dioceses were established in 1878. That same year also saw the foundation of St. Benedict's Abbey at Fort Augustus, on the site of the Hanoverian Fort, as a school and religious centre for the Highlands.

The Established Church enjoyed a slow but steady convalescence after the shock of 1843. In the burgh, Alexander Clark, of the First Charge wrote many books. He was responsible for the erection of the West Church. He was succeeded by Donald Macleod, who had the name of being a brilliant pulpit orator. In 1853, Alexander Macgregor was admitted to the Second Charge. He was a Gaelic poet, a good Highland historian and a winning preacher. The East Church, formerly a chapel of ease, became the property of the Free Church. The Patronage Act of 1712 was repealed in 1874.

A movement for the improvement of the conduct of public worship originated in the Established Church even before the Disruption. John Wesley, on his visit to Inverness in 1767, criticised the unattractive church services. In 1812, Dr Harry Roberts of Kiltearn published his "Scotch Minister's Assistant." It was the first essay at a Book of Common Order since the Directory of 1647, and the sensible rules of the Directory had long been either forgotten or disregarded. Scripture lessons began again to be read in church as part of the worship, instead of being made the occasion of a verse by verse lecture. Prayers began to be shorter. Tentatively in the South, even more cautiously in the North, hymns were introduced, and an occasional organ was placed in a church. The custom of sitting during the singing was slowly replaced by standing. The old custom still remains in the present Free Church. Every innovation caused some heart-burning. In the end, innovations were accepted in both the Established and Free Churches.

In the Free Church, and also to a lesser extent in the parish churches, the great sacramental assemblies, which began to be popular in Easter Ross in the early 18th century, and in which the "Men," the lay religious leaders, found their chance of fame and influence on the Question Day, were social as well as spiritual occasions[42]. Folk of different parishes met and cultivated friendships. In the 1860s, a movement for the union of the Free Church and the United Presbyterian Church began in the Lowlands. It was looked on with profound suspicion in the North. Dr Kennedy of Dingwall became the eloquent champion of anti-unionism. The U.P.s were voluntaries. They were opposed to state aid to the church, and were fiercely accused of planning to overthrow the lordship of Christ over the nation. Dr Kennedy won. The union proposals were dropped. But soon another occasion of offence arose. Professor Robertson of the Free Church College, Aberdeen, had written articles for the Encyclopaedia Brittannica in which he expressed radical views on the historicity of Deuteronomy and some other Old Testament books. He was suspended from his teaching office. But the higher criticism of the Bible became a stock theme of denunciation on the part of the more conservative of the Highland ministers[43].

This feeling was strengthened by the Lowland pressure for the relaxation of certain clauses in the Confession of Faith. In 1893, the Free Church Assembly passed a Declaratory Act which allowed that men holding office in the church were not required to believe the more repellent inferences drawn from the Doctrine of Predestination. The challenge was accepted by two ministers of the Free Church. They left to form the Free Presbyterian Church, which is still a force in the North and is vigorously represented in Inverness today.

The long delayed union of the Free Church, led by Principal Rainy, and the United Presbyterian Church took place in 1900. The United Free Church was born. The union was followed by the secession of a minority, principally Highland ministers and elders. They repealed the Declaratory Act and won their claim before the House of Lords that they were the owners of all the property of the great Free Church. Parliament had to intervene to make a realistic division of the spoils. The Free Church today are the successors of the rebels of 1900. They play a valuable part in the spiritual life of our Highlands today, and serve to remind us all of the good old days.

The first World War interrupted the negotiations for the incorporating union of the Established Church and the United Free Church. These were resumed after the war, and resulted in the historic Act of 1929. The united Church was declared to be free from secular control of its creed and discipline. The difficult task of the union of Parish and U.F. congregations, and the equally laborious work of church extension in the new housing areas had been commendably accomplished. Inverness has added several new congregations to its already impressive list. There are, of course, spots on our love-feasts. Non-church-going has increased. The evening service has become a shadow. There has been a steady erosion of Sunday discipline. Interest in the Foreign Mission enterprise has diminished since the mission churches have become autonomous.

The ecumenical movement has, however, resulted in happier relations between the separated churches. The increasing social work of the churches, impressive in its scale, has become largely undenominational. The support given to Christian Aid and similar organisations is not exclusive to any particular denomination. There will be difficult days ahead, but it is the immoveable conviction of the Church that the Christian cause will not perish, and that the gates of hell will not prevail against it.

REFERENCES

1. Scott, A. B., *Pictish Nation and Church.*
2. Duke, J., *Columban Church.* Simpson, W. D., *Historical St Columba.* Simpson, W. D., *Celtic Church in Scotland.*
3. Reeves, W. (ed.), *Life of St Columba — by St Adomnan,* p. 203.
4. Duke, J., *Columban Church.*
5. Mackenzie, W. C., *History of Hebrides and Highlands and Islands of Scotland.* Sawyer, P. H., *Age of Vikings* (2nd. Ed.). Jones, Gwyn, *The Vikings,* p. 90.
6. Burleigh, J., *Church History of Scotland,* p. 18.
7. *Wynton,* vol II, pp 181, 183 (Hist. of Scotland Series).
8. Batten, E. C., *Priory of Beauly.*
9. Duke, J., *Church of Scotland to 1560,* ch. IV and p. 101.
10. *Church History of Scotland,* pp 90 ff.
11. Mackay, W. (ed.), "Records of Presbytery of Inverness and Dingwall," *Scottish History Society;* Mackay, W., *Urquhart and Glenmoriston,* passim.
12. Mackay, J., "Church in the Highlands," *Chalmer's Lectures.*
13. Mackay, W., *Inverness in the Middle Ages.*
14. Mackenzie, W. C., *Highlands and Islands.*
15. Maclachlan, T., *Foirm na n-Urrnuidheadh,* 1873. 3rd ed., 1972 by R. L. Thomson.
16. Lees, J. C., *County of Inverness,* p. 50. *Fasti Ecclesiae Scotticae* (Synod of Moray). Craven, J. B., *Diocese of Moray.*
17. Mackay, W., *Records of Presbytery of Inverness and Dingwall,* Introduction.
18. Barron, E. M., *Scottish War of Independence,* introduction, p. xlvi.
19. Mackinnon, D., *Gaelic Bible and Psalter.*
20. Thomson, R. L., *Adtimchiol an Chreidimh* (new edition), Scottish Gaelic Text Society, 1962.

21. MacInnes, J., "Baptism in the Highlands," *Records of Scottish Church History Society*, p. 14. 1957.
22. Burnett, G. B., *Holy Communion in Reformed Church of Scotland*, passim.
23. Mackay, W., *Records of Presbytery of Inverness and Dingwall*.
24. Mackay, W. (ed.), *Wardlaw MS*.
25. Barron, E. M., *Scottish War of Independence*, introduction, p lxii, etc.
26. Maclean, D., *Counter Reformation in Scotland*, p. 155.
27. Burleigh, J., *Church History of Scotland*, ch. IV, and pp. 220 ff.
28. Barron, E. M., *Scottish War of Independence*, introduction, p. xli.
29. Mackay, W., *Records of Presbytery of Inverness and Dingwall*.
30. Noble, J., *Religious Life in Ross*, p. 75.
31. MacCrie, T., and others, *The Bass Rock*.
32. MacInnes, J., *Evangelical Movement in the Highlands*, p. 23.
33. Ibid., pp. 24, 31.
34. Noble, J., *Religious Life in Ross*, p. 266.
35. Kennedy, J., *Days of the Fathers*. MacInnes, J., *Origin and Early Development of "The Men." Records of Scottish Church History Society*, 1942.
36. Annual Reports of S.P.C.K. Royal Bounty MS. Minutes.
37. See Rose's *Metrical Reliques*. Laoidhean Spioradail le Ughdaren Eugsamhail.
38. Mackinnon D., *Gaelic Bible and Psalter*.
39. MacInnes, J., *Evengelical Movement in the Highlands*, ch. IV.
40. *Account of the S.P.C.K.*, 1774.
41. *Disruption Worthies*, Edinburgh, 1877.
42. MacInnes, J., *Origin and Early Development of "The Men,"* p. 54.
43. Macdonald, K., *Social and Religious Life in the Highlands*.

St. Stephen's
Inverness.

OLD HOUSES AND CHURCHES

WILLIAM GLASHAN

During the period 1950-70, an unusual number of the older buildings at Inverness were demolished, but changes had always been taking place, as can be appreciated from the study of old surveys and the drawings of Delavault and Slezer. There were thatched houses on the site of the Crown Church after the Crown School had been built and most of the houses in the Burgh had been thatched in earlier times. Fires and neglect led to continuous rebuilding.

The Burgh developed on the East Bank of the Ness around Castle Street, Bridge Street, High Street and Church Street. The gardens behind the houses were gradually built over, there being narrow closes leading to the buildings behind. It was not until the 19th century that the Burgh expanded up to the Hill district. There had been houses along the West bank of the Ness from early times, connected by a bridge to the East bank.

CHURCHES IN INVERNESS

The Old High Church[1] was the Parish Church of Inverness. Of the mediaeval building, only the tower remains, with an 18th century parapet and spire. After being in ruins for a period, the church was rebuilt in 1770, and known as The English Church, because no Gaelic was used in the services. It is a plain rectangular building with galleries round three sides and an apse on the South side. Set in the Churchyard facing the river, it has a pleasant simplicity, the tower being very effective.

At the East end of the Old High Church and fronting to Church Street is the Gaelic Church[1]. Rebuilt in 1792, it was the "third charge" of the Old High. It is a severely plain building with arched windows and is now a Free Church. This church had a remarkable pulpit, "The Black Pulpit," which was very ornate and probably very old. It was removed to a warehouse after the Free Church came, but vandals broke in and smashed the pulpit to pieces.

Behind the Gaelic Church, in the Churchyard and close by the gateway from Church Street, is the Robertson of Inshes'

Mausoleum (1660), an elaborate and imaginative work of its time.

The West Church in Huntly Street was the "second charge" of the Old High. Facing the river, it is a plain classical building with columns and pediment. The low tower has a dome on top; its placing at the rear looks curious now, but originally it faced on to a bowling green[2]. It was built in 1834 and opened in 1840[1].

In Church Street, opposite the Gaelic Church[3], was an Episcopal Church[4] built about 1800 with a cupola, and demolished between 1821 and the middle of the century. This was not, however, the place where Dr Johnson and James Boswell worshipped in 1773[5].

The East Church was built in 1798[1] and the North Church (in North Church Place, alias Chapel Street) in 1837. These were Chapels of Ease for the Old High and in 1843 both became Free Churches. The East Church was considerably extended; the additions included the staircase and tower, with an enlarged gallery; Dr Ross was the architect. Immediately behind the East Church, where the Hall now is, was a Roman Catholic church, later demolished[6, 3].

St. Mary's Roman Catholic Church in Huntly Street was built in 1837 and is good Gothic Revival by Robertson of Elgin, architect, who also designed St. John's Episcopal Church in Church Street. Some of the details of both churches were almost identical. St. John's had a fan-vaulted roof and an uncompleted tower. After being used as a garage for some time, with most of the front still intact, it was demolished and replaced by an office block.

St. Andrew's Cathedral was dedicated in 1869 and consecrated in 1874. Previous Bishops of Moray had had their seat at Elgin, but Bishop Robert Eden (1851-86) considered that Inverness was the best centre for the Diocese and set about the great enterprise of building the Cathedral. The Inverness congregation that then met in a small church in Bank Street, latterly the Y.M.C.A. (recently rebuilt), formed the nucleus of the first congregation. The architect was Dr Alexander Ross. The Cathedral is cruciform and Gothic Revival in style, with an arcaded nave, transepts, chancel and two western towers, 100 feet (30 m.) high. There was a cast-iron fleche at the crossing, but it was removed in 1961 because of structural defects and replaced by a copper cross. The original drawings show the towers finished with spires 200 feet (60 m.) from the ground; the chancel was to have been much longer, with a semi-circular apse and an ambulatory with flying buttresses; there was also to have been a Cloister.

Queen Street Church, Huntly Street, was built about 1895, the architect being Pond Macdonald. There is a tower with an ogee-conical spire. The front is Italian Baroque and there is a great flight of steps. The side elevation, like that of the West Church, is very plain. The interior is quite good and the pulpit excellent. The tower and the main roof were strengthened in the 1960s. This was the third of the Queen Street churches. The first was in Queen Street and was a plain barn, probably used as a school after being abandoned as a church; later it was converted to houses and finally demolished in the 1960s. The second church was in King Street, and was Norman Revival. It became, in turn, a skating rink and a warehouse.

The original North Free Church, mentioned above, was replaced by the present church in Bank Street next to the Old High. It was built in Gothic Revival style, Dr Ross being the architect. The tall spire has its sides and buttresses quite vertical, which contrasts unfavourably with the fine tapering lines of the Old High. There is a splayed base to the front of the tower, but it has been cut vertical on the Church Lane side, and this looks awkward.

St Columba High Church in Bank Street (originally the English Free Church, built 1843) is also Gothic Revival, with a good spire, now marred by the removal of the elegant flying buttresses which marked the transition from square to octagon. The church was badly damaged by fire during the 1939 War and was restored (Leslie Grahame Macdougall, architect), which gave a different character to the interior.

St Stephen's Church in Southside Road was "disjointed" from the Old High, and built about 1900[1], Robert Carruthers being the architect. It is Gothic and has a small needle spire. For sheer quality of design, I think it is the best of the Inverness Churches.

The Crown Church, beside the Academy, was built about the same time as St Stephen's, the architect being one of the Rhind family, several of whom were architects. It is also a good Gothic church. It is unfortunate that the tower was never completed, as it was well placed to have been seen down several streets and from several parts of the town.

SECULAR BUILDINGS IN INVERNESS

The oldest surviving house is Abertarff House in Church Street, an excellent example of Scots Domestic. Dating from 1593, it was occupied by the Frasers of Lovat, among others. For years it was hidden by houses in front of it, and became ruinous. It was restored by the National Trust for Scotland and is now occupied by An Comunn Gaidhealach.

Dunbar's Hospital, in Church Street, opposite the Old High, was built in 1668, and was given to the Burgh by Provost Alexander Dunbar. It was first used as a Hospital, then as a School (called the Old Academy[6]; or the Old Latin School[3]). At various times it housed a Library, and the Fire-engines; and the Female School and the Female Work Society were here before they moved to Ardkeen Tower in 1836[6]. During the cholera epidemic in 1849, it was again used as a hospital. The building has very good decorative dormer heads and crow-stepped gables. Slezer's Prospect shows a turret on the roof, and Captain Wimberley[8] mentions a turret, but Delavault does not show it — nor even the middle chimney stack which now exists.

Bow Court adjoins Dunbar's Hospital. It was probably built just before 1729, replacing a building demolished in 1722[9]. It belonged to Lady Drummuir, who owned a number of properties[11] in Inverness, having inherited them from her husband, Alexander Duff, who had been Provost and M.P. A tablet on the School Lane side has the arms of the Duffs of Drummuir and an inscription, "Katherine Duff, Lady Drummuire, gifted the six Incorp. Trades and Masons of Inverness the ground on which this building stands. 1729." The inscription had been puttied up and painted over except for the date, and was discovered when the stone was being cleaned. The building shown on Wood's Plan[3] as Trades Property, is the one adjacent to the N.E. wing of Bow Court. I infer that the panel had been built into the earlier Trades Building and had been removed to the wall of Bow Court and the inscription obliterated when the Trades Building was rebuilt in 1830.

Bow Court is a U-shaped plan, and consisted of two separate houses, entered through a pend. Four of the rooms were panelled. When the harling was removed in 1971, it was seen that there had been doors from Church Street into the two kitchens. The profile of the original Trades Building against Bow Court was found, and there was evidence of a building adjacent to the S.E. wing, the fire-places and flues being incorporated with the S.E. gable of Bow Court. At one period, one of the houses was occupied by the Rector of the Academy and the other as a hostel for boys. In 1972, the building was reconstructed as shops and flats, with arched arcades on the Church Street front: architect, William Glashan.

Lady Drummuir's house, where she was hostess to Prince Charles and later to the Duke of Cumberland, was on the site of No. 43, Church Street, and was demolished in 1843. Lady Drummuir was 77 in 1746[9], and it was her daughter, Lady Mackintosh, who bore the burden of the visits, and it was she who said, "I have had two Kings' bairns living with me in my time, and I wish I may never have another[10]."

Some of the old houses opposite Lady Drummuir's had fine dormer heads and these are preserved in the Clydesdale Bank; see also one of Delavault's drawings[11].

The Burgh Steeple, at the corner of Church Street and High Street, was built in 1791, William Sibbald being the architect; he also designed the spires of St. Andrew's Church in Edinburgh and of Inveresk Church. The Steeple was built by public subscription under Provost Inglis. The upper part of the spire was badly bent in an earth tremor in 1816[6] and had to be rebuilt. In the larger of the two balls below the weathercock is said to be a bottle of whisky from the Millburn Distillery[9]. The Court House, now the Prudential office, adjoins the Steeple and was built just after it and in the same classical style. The balustrading along the top has unfortunately been replaced by solid masonry.

The Northern Meeting Rooms in Church Street were built in 1790[12] and demolished about 1960 to make room for the Social Security building. This was a very severe classical building with good interiors, and was used for great social occasions. There was, earlier, a drapery store on the ground floor. The building was badly damaged by fire in 1805, following an explosion in Baron Taylor's Street. In rebuilding, an attic storey was omitted.

No 23, Church Street was a dignified classical building; used latterly as a solicitor's office, it was originally a town house of the Frasers, and for some time, a bank. It was demolished to make way for the recent Bank Street - Bridge Street re-development scheme.

Other town houses of county families were[9] those of the Mackintoshes of Aberarder, now Martin's shop, in Academy Street, and of the Mackintoshes of Raigmore in Church Street, recently demolished.

At the bottom of the North side of Bridge Street was the building known as Queen Mary's House, which was demolished in 1968. The only mediaeval parts were the vaulted cellars, a small section of which is rebuilt in the entrance of the Highland and Islands Development Board building on Bank Street. The house was said to have been the residence of Queen Mary in 1562[9]. It became ruinous and was rebuilt and altered several times from the 18th century onwards. It was a plain building, but the Burgh lost in character when it was replaced.

Between Queen Mary's House and the Court House in Bridge Street were two 18th century buildings with cornices and balustrades. On the Bank Street side of Queen Mary's House were two pleasant houses in pink stone walling, with little gardens and climbing plants, and next to them, the Parish Council building and the Courier's office. The last named is the only survivor of this group.

The Suspension Bridge, now demolished, was built between 1852 and 1855[9]. It grouped well with the Castle and was asymmetrical, the higher pylon being at the East end with a big arch in the centre for traffic and two smaller arches for pedestrians. The previous bridge was of stone, and had seven arches[11]. Turner and Delavault did drawings of it. Built in 1685, there was a cell below the roadway on one side of the centre arch, which was used as a prison; this bridge fell during the flood in 1849. When the Suspension Bridge was being demolished, the abutment of the West arch of the old bridge was uncovered and could be seen for a time before being surrounded by concrete.

Close to the N.E. end of the old stone bridge stood Castle Tolmie, which was demolished after 1849. It had good dormer heads which were re-used in an extension to Redcastle[9]. A later building called Castle Tolmie was built at the S.E. end of the Suspension Bridge, Robert Carruthers being the architect; it comprised three houses of an interesting design, grouping well with the Castle and the Bridge. Although in good condition, it was demolished to make way for the "contemporary" block of shops and offices. Before the second Castle Tolmie was built, the site had a pleasant row of small houses called Gordon Place, which is shown in one of Delavault's drawings[11].

The South side of Bridge Street was demolished about 1962 for street widening. The buildings varied from late 18th to late 19th century. The best of them was the Workmen's Club, a Neo-classical building with columns and arches, the architect being John Rhind, a former Provost of the Burgh.

On the West side of the river is Balnain House, an early or mid-18th century mansion. It is a well-proportioned plain classical building with walls battered and entasised, and with dressed angle quoins. There was once a portico at the front door with wooden columns painted to resemble marble[9]. It had a large garden stretching back to King Street and including one side of Greig Street. It was called Fairfield House in 1821[3], and was owned by C. Munro. Later, the owner was Captain

Fraser of Balnain[9]. The building was also known as the Blue House, because one owner had been a planter of indigo. Restoration is now intended.

The Royal Northern Infirmary was begun in 1803[6] and was extended from time to time. Most of the wards were built in the 1920s, the architect being Sir John Burnet. The Chapel was designed by Dr Ross's firm; the nave is for Presbyterian worship and the transepts for Episcopalian and Roman Catholic services respectively.

Macbeth's Castle is said to have been on the Crown. The Castle in its present position has been destroyed, rebuilt and altered many times. Its appearance in 1746 can be seen in Sandby's drawing[11]; it showed a mixture of styles; it had been repaired in 1718[9, 6], and extended by a barrack wing on the North. At that period it was called Fort George (not to be confused with the later Fort George at Ardersier). Prince Charles took the Castle in 1745 and had it blown up to prevent its falling into the hands of the Hanoverians. The French serjeant who lighted the fuse was killed, but his dog was blown over the river and escaped with the loss of its tail[12]. The Castle lay in ruins until 1835, though a small part was used by the Weavers. It became a quarry for builders; one ornamental stone with the date 1620, built into the front wall of a house in Culduthel Road is said to have come from the Castle.

The first part to be rebuilt was the Courts, at the South end. The architect was William Burn, of Edinburgh. The foundation stone was laid in 1834 at the same time as that of the Observatory building (Ardkeen Tower[13]), there having been a procession of the Magistrates, Masonic Lodges and children of the Infant and Female Schools for both ceremonies. The Courts are built in a pink stone and in a castellated, vaguely Tudor style.

The second part to be rebuilt[9, 12], was the Prison, which was converted for use as County Council offices when Porterfield Prison was built. This part of the Castle was built in 1846, by an unknown architect but the building resembles the Calton Jail in Edinburgh, which was designed by Archibald Elliot. This is perhaps the better part of the Castle; it is quite picturesque, but though the Castle is popular with visitors, its merit lies mainly in its siting.

Ardkeen Tower[13] at the corner of Culduthel Road and the Old Edinburgh Road, was known as the Observatory Building, or as the United Charities Building. It was originally occupied by the Infants School, the Female Work Society and the Juvenile Female School, united as "The United Charities,"

The dome was used as an Observatory by a separate body. The building was enlarged in the late 19th century, a second storey having been added on the Old Edinburgh Road front and the rear angle filled in with several rooms. The second storey unfortunately conflicts with the dome, but was made to convert the building to a private house.

Ardkeen Tower was formerly approached by a monumental flight of steps at the corner of the streets, and the entrance hall was under the dome. The former hall is now the drawing room; it is elliptical and has a fine view from the windows. The dome has lost its weather-vane. A tablet in the pediment has the words "United Charities 1830" painted on top of the half-obliterated words "Observatory Buildings." The building was stated to be "Mr Wilderspin's plan," but this may refer to the method of conducting the school. The original scheme was apparently of a more ornate design, but, as carried out, it is a good classical building.

Behind Ardkeen Tower, on the site of the first houses in Old Edinburgh Road, was the Burgh Reservoir[2] which was still in existence in 1868. The water was pumped up from the river by a pump powered by a water-wheel at the Islands; the wheel was adjustable to the level of water in the river[9, 14].

Raining's School, at the top of Raining's Stairs, was built in 1757[9] and named after Dr Raining, a Norwich merchant and philanthropist. It is a solid, stolid building, very plain and with little pretensions to good design, but it could be made quite pleasing with a careful restoration.

Dr Bell's Institution[9] in Farraline Park was built in 1841[6] and is externally one of the best buildings in Inverness. Built in Greek Revival style it has a Doric portico and pediment, with wreaths in place of the orthodox tryglyphs. The windows have their jambs tapering as in the doorway of the Erectheum. The architect was probably Archibald Simpson of Aberdeen.

Dr Bell was a Prebendary of Westminster[9] and the Bell's Institution was built from funds from his Trust. From the same source was built the first Central School. The Ordnance Sheet of 1864[2] shows a pleasant lay-out of grounds where now are the Bus Station and Car Park, with two Gate Lodges, one of which is now a cafe and the other a chiropodist's surgery. On either side of the grounds were play-sheds, with curved fronts. Behind the Institution was a reformatory.

The old Royal Academy was in Academy Street[6, 12] and was built in 1792. The building has now a bank and a supermarket on the ground floor and a dentist's surgery and offices above. A wing of class-rooms extended behind, with two playgrounds and the Rector's house occupying the area now Messrs Macrae & Dick's garage[2]. The upper floor is almost as it was originally, but the portion at the corner of Strothers Lane is an addition. The Old Academy was a plain building of no great merit.

Opposite the Old Academy is the entrance to the Markets, an excellent and lively classical composition with three arches and sculptured sheep and cattle. The Markets, rather tawdry now, are interesting and have good roofs, especially the large centre one. They form a good covered shopping centre and are worth a re-decoration.

The Customs House in High Street (formerly the Post Office) was probably designed by Archibald Simpson of Aberdeen. It is good early 19th century classical, the details being Greek. The ground floor is now ruined by insensitive shop fronts. The map of 1868[2] shows shops at street level; the upper floors had rooms for music and dancing[6].

The Bank of Scotland in High Street was built in 1848, Thomas Mackenzie of Elgin, being the architect, for the Caledonian Bank. It is a dignified and imposing building with Roman Corinthian columns, a sculptured pediment and a rusticated base. It is well sited cn the axis of Castle Street.

The Town House, opposite, is a late 19th century building in a Gothic style. It once had a big turret in the centre, but this was removed some time ago. There is a dignified entrance and staircase, a large Hall and a Council Chamber (in which the Cabinet met on 7 September, 1921, under David Lloyd George, to discuss the Irish Question, the only time the Cabinet has met outside London[11]). The crystal candelabra in the staircase and the Council Chamber came from the Northern Meeting Rooms. The Burgh Arms on the West gable came from the old stone bridge. The old Town House, on the same site, was built in 1708[6] as the town residence of Lord Lovat, but became the Burgh Town House in 1716[9]. It had an arcade of seven arches at street level and was otherwise a plain classical building. It was not as wide as the present building and there was The Commercial Hotel (formerly The Horns) on the West of it[11]. The old Market Cross and the Clach-na-Cudainn stand against the Town House as they did against the earlier building.

Looking eastwards along the High Street, one can see high up on the Crown, a Regency building, now comprising three houses, known as Crown House, or Abertarff House (not to be confused with Abertarff House in Church Street). It was the town house of a branch of the Frasers. Near it is the present Royal Academy, the oldest part being "collegiate" in style.

No 14, Culduthel Road, and Aultnaskiach House (near Culduthel Road) are early 19th century houses which were very like each other. The former is as originally built, with a semi-basement, but at Aultnaskiach House the ground floor has been lowered for a large area in front, and the basement floor modified to become the ground floor. The land being on a slope, the rear remains as it was originally.

Drakies House, on the Perth Road, opposite Raigmore Hospital, is dated 1820 and is a two-storey Renaissance House.

GROUPS OF BUILDINGS

Union Street and Queensgate were built in the second half of the 19th century and formed harmonious groups of Victorian classic shops, of offices and hotels. In the middle of the North side of Union Street was the Methodist Church, formerly the Music Hall. Unfortunately it was burned down and leaves a sad gap. In the middle of the North side of Queensgate was the Post Office, built in 1888; it had an Italianate elevation with columns, arches, balustrades and urns, and the buildings on either side were in sympathy. When the Post Office was reconstructed in the 1960s, the front was demolished and replaced by a "contemporary" one, with the same number of windows and doors and of the same height, but with concrete facings, paying no heed whatever to the rest of the street.

Portland Place, beside the Harbour, is a pleasing Regency group. Built in 1828[9] the houses have classical porticoes approached by steps.

Douglas Row, on the East bank of the river, is a line of plain little houses, sufficiently varied to escape monotony, with a quiet, old-fashioned air. On the West side of the river, there are houses of similar character, mostly higher; they have been reduced in number since the 1950s. Nearer the Ness Bridge, some of the houses have gables facing the river, crow-stepped; they are overshadowed by a dominating cinema, now used as a bingo hall.

Ardross Street and Ardross Terrace are good groups of Victorian houses, probably by Dr Ross. They have mostly been converted to offices or hotels without much external change, except for one insurance office opposite the Cathedral, which is a perfect example of bad manners. The Palace Hotel and the Columba Hotel were also probably by Dr Ross. The Columba was extended in 1937 by a Newcastle firm of architects. On the site of these hotels was Ness House[2], which was demolished about 1870. The house itself was near the corner of Young Street, and the garden covered the whole area of Ardross

Terrace up to the Cathedral, it had trees, bushes and winding paths.

Church Street, High Street and Castle Street had numerous closes or pends running off them. All the Bridge Street closes were demolished in the 1950s and 60s. The earlier houses had gardens behind them, and these were gradually filled in with back wings to the houses. Some of the remaining closes are picturesque, and those between the High Street and Baron Taylor's Street could be developed as pedestrian shopping precincts. There is a pleasant little close off Church Street to the North of Dunbar's Hospital, with little whitewashed cottages.

In Telford Street, there is a row of houses[15] built for the Canal contractors to live in. They are built of Redcastle stone, and of a good plain classical style. John Mitchell, Telford's Superintendent of Roads, lived in one of them. Mitchell's son, Joseph, who succeeded him, built and lived in Viewhill, now a Youth Hostel opposite Ardkeen Tower; he is famous as well for his roads and churches as for his part in the development of the Railways.

Cromwell's Citadel was built in 1652[12] and the next few years. Stones for its building were taken from Beauly Priory, Fortrose Cathedral, Greyfriars Church and Kinloss Abbey. It was an irregular pentagon with bastions at the angles, and was to hold 2000 men; it had a harbour[3]. Only the Clock-tower remains, surrounded by oil tanks. The Citadel was abandoned only five years after its completion, and was demolished, the stones being re-used for the second time for, among other purposes, the stone bridge (1685)[12] and Dunbar's Hospital (1668).

BUILDINGS OUTWITH INVERNESS

At Kirkhill (Wardlaw)[7] there is a ruined church. A Mausoleum has been added with an interesting Belfry. It has a conical top, surrounded by four lesser cones. The builder is stated to be William Ross. It closely resembles the Tolbooth at Tain.

Fort Augustus was built by Wade in 1729 on a plan not unlike that used later at Fort George at Ardersier. During the '45 it was held at different times by both sides. Damaged, and eventually dismantled in part, it was given to the Benedictines, and the Abbey and School were built, and these have been extended and developed since, but parts of Wade's building can still be seen. The architects for the earlier work on the Abbey and School were Joseph Hansom (who invented the Hansom cab) and Peter Paul Pugin, whose father, A. W. N.

Pugin, collaborated in the design of the Houses of Parliament in London.

Fort George at Ardersier was started in 1747[6], the work lasting some twenty years, and remains almost as built. It has a beautiful geometric plan, best appreciated from the air, and is considered to be the finest 18th century fort in Europe. The Chapel is a plain, solid dignified building, with a combination of military and ecclesiastical character.

Culloden House, in addition to its involvement with the Jacobite Risings in its earlier state, is perhaps the largest Renaissance mansion in the district. It may have been designed by William Adam, who designed Duff House, Banff, and who was the father of Robert and James Adam. The Dovecote is a very good one; although now in bad repair, it is hoped that it will be restored.

Culcabock House was certainly built before 1746, because a few of the Jacobite soldiers were slain in the kitchen by Hanoverian troops. This is a pleasing small mansion; the two largest rooms have segmental ends, and the one on the first floor has a camped ceiling and is very well proportioned. There is said to have been an earlier house on the site.

Dr Alexander Ross designed so many Episcopal Churches in towns and districts around Inverness, including St. Paul's, Strathnairn, Dingwall and Dornoch, that it was sometimes said jokingly that it was no wonder that it was called the diocese of Moray and Ross.

Of all the architects mentioned above, Dr Ross must be regarded as outstanding. He was the Sir Christopher Wren of the North and, with Mr Macbeth and other partners, he did great work throughout the Highlands. Dr Ross's father, also an Alexander Ross, came to Inverness as an assistant to Archibald Simpson while Raigmore House (now demolished, except for certain fragments) was being built[16].

From the earliest huts by the river to 1600, and from then to today, the buildings of Inverness have been built, demolished and replaced. Each style has had its admirers and its detractors. We do not know what was said by either side when, in 1848, the Caledonian Bank unveiled its new facade in the High Street, breaking the seemly 18th century street scene. We do know what was said in the 1960s about the Bridge Street development. We look today at Inverness, at our few 18th century buildings and recall the Age of Reason, and the unrest of that century. We see the self-assurance of the 19th century in Union Street, some of its flamboyance in the High Street and at the Castle;

there was nothing modest there. What our successors, reading this in the future and looking at their Inverness, will say of the buildings of the 20th century, we cannot tell.

REFERENCES

1. *Fasti Ecclesiae Scotticanae*, 1915.
2. Ordnance Survey, c. 1868. (Property of the Inverness Field Club).
3. *Wood's Plan of Inverness*, 1821.
4. *Statistical Account of Scotland*, 1793.
5. Boswell, James, *Journal of a Tour to the Highlands*, 1785.
6. Douglas, Smith and Fraser, *A History and Description of Inverness*.
7. Hay, George, *The Architecture of Scottish Post-Reformation Churches*.
8. Wimberley, Captain, *The Hospital of Inverness*, 1893.
9. Fraser, John, *Reminiscences of Inverness*, 1905.
10. Taylor, Alister & Henrietta, *The Book of the Duffs*, 1914.
11. Delavault, and others, *Old Inverness*. R. Carruthers & Sons, 1967.
12. Mackintosh, Murdoch, *A History of Inverness*, 1939.
13. *United Charities School*. Drawing and description in Inverness Burgh Library, post-1830.
14. Barron, James, *The Northern Highlands in the 19th Century*, 1903.
15. Cameron, A. D., *The Caledonian Canal*, 1972.
16. Verbally from Mr Alistair Ross, the son of, and successor to, Dr Alexander Ross.

With the exception of No. 2. the above works may be consulted in the Inverness Public Library.

The Steeple
Inverness

THE LOCAL CLANS AND JACOBITISM

JEAN MUNRO

There can be no doubt that the townsfolk of Inverness considered themselves menaced by the wild Highland clansmen who lived on their doorstep. By the mid-16th century, the burgh laws laid down that only those owning lands within the bounds might enjoy its freedom and benefits. For example, in 1556 the Town Council stated that "for diuerse and sindrie guid causis . . . the intakyn of clannit men and strangeris nocht beand merchandis nor making thair dale [daily] habitation within our bruch nor haweing of fre land in the same is express incontrar our borrow lawis[1]."

Some years before this, there had been reference in a statute confirmed by the Earl of Arran in the name of the infant Mary, Queen of Scots, to "the gret hurt and scaith quhilk hes bene this lang tyme bigane usit throw indrawing of owtlandis men of grete clannis nocht habill nor qualifyit to use marchanice nor mak daylie residence . . . within the said burgh." Apparently these men had "be divers and sindry sinester weyis purchast their fredomes throw solistatioun and laubouris of grete clannit men and utheris adjacent to the said burgh[2]." One of the sinister ways was to bring pressure to bear on the widows of burgesses to make over their property within the burgh, instead of allowing it to pass to the husband's nearest suitably qualified male kinsman.

These two documents are interesting, not only in stressing the "hurt and scaith" aspect of the problem, but also in showing that "clannit men" had any wish to become involved in the affairs of the burgh.

A little more than a century later, in 1671, the Council, seeing that "this Burghe lyand in the mouth of the hylands quhair thair ar many disaffected personis subject to povertie and givin to thift and roberrie . . . think it expedient and verie necessar that everie inhabitant of this Burgh be sufficientlie furnished with waponis for thair own defence and defending His Majesties interest sua far as in thame lyes . . . [3]."

A royal burgh like Inverness, which had probably received its first charter from King David I before 1153[4], was based on the trading privileges and monopolies which it enjoyed. The early inhabitants formed a colony round the royal castle and river mouth, and some of them were indeed "strangeris" in their surroundings, having come from the south or east, or even across the seas to follow their trade. As late as 1500, the majority of traders seem to have had names markedly different from the Gaelic ones that surrounded them. It was a lowland place, in that people living there and on the Black Isle, even as late as the 18th century, would speak of going "into the Highlands" when referring to the hinterland of Inverness-shire and Ross. But it is easy to over-emphasise the gulf that lay between the burgh and its neighbours, and there was early interchange between the two — for example, a relative of the Robertsons of Struan came north to Inverness some time before 1488, and settled there as a trader[5]. But the burgesses and humbler inhabitants of Inverness certainly favoured peace and economic stability of a kind which did not accord with the way of life of their Highland neighbours.

Who were these "clannit men" who pressed so closely about the burgh? Although modern clan maps, with their brightly coloured sections, suggest neat divisions on the ground, which were certainly not to be found in the 16th, or any other century, the clans did have fairly definite spheres of influence, and those nearest Inverness were the Frasers, the Chisholms and the Clan Chattan.

By 1545 these clans were well established. The Frasers had come from the south of Scotland when King Robert Bruce drove out the Comyns in the early 14th century, and by 1367 Hugh Fraser had gained possession of Lovat through marriage with an heiress[6]. Two years later, Robert Chisholm followed his father-in-law, Sir Robert Lauder, in the office of Constable of Castle Urquhart and, again through marriage with an heiress, moved part of his family from their lands near the English border to take up residence in Strathglass[7]. Representatives of all the leading clans or tribes which formed the confederacy of Clan Chattan, Mackintosh, Macpherson, Shaw, MacGillivray, MacBain and MacQueen, signed a band in 1543, by which time they were already settled in Strathnairn, Strathdearn and Badenoch[8].

By tracing the development of these clans, and looking at some special incidents, we can learn something of the relations between the burgh and the clans. Although the Clan Chattan was in some ways the most important of the burgh's neighbours, the Frasers and Chisholms provide good examples of a more normal clan. As we have seen, the chiefs of both these clans were incomers, and must have taken over many natives when they acquired their lands. Within a hundred years or so, each had created a clan round him.

The Gaelic word *Clann* means children, and the central theme of a clan is kinship. Younger sons were granted parts of their father's land, where they founded cadet families, which provided the officers in war, and leaders in peace. For example, by 1544 the Frasers had established five such cadet branches, a total which increased to twenty-six by 1650[9]. The Chisholms, with a much smaller clan country, never reached this total, but had several similar cadet houses. But, while all those living within Fraser or Chisholm lands regarded their chief as the father of the clan, they were by no means all descendants of the founder. Many of them certainly came to share his blood through marriage, and, after a century or two, it would often be hard to determine the exact degree of kinship.

Some came into the clan because, as tenants, they chose to follow Fraser of Lovat or The Chisholm in peace and war. In return for the personal loyalty of his clansmen, and their most welcome addition of strength and manpower, the chief gave them his protection which, by the mid-16th century, involved making himself responsible to the King for their good behaviour. In 1430 and 1538, Lovat and Chisholm had received charters from the King, giving them the right to hold law courts within their own lands, and they were expected (not always with justification) to keep order there. Where a case involved men of different clans, then the Sheriff of Inverness would try the case, and each chief would be required to bring his offending followers to court, or pay a fine on their behalf.

Today clansmen are generally recognised by their surnames, and it is not easy to appreciate that in the 16th century Highland life, surnames were only regularly used by the chiefs and cadets. Everyone else used a patronymic — such as Alasdair macDonald vic Iain (Alasdair, son of Donald, son of Iain), whose son would be Roderick macAlasdair vicConnel. This indicates no clan membership and leads to much confusion for later genealogists covering the period during which surnames became fashionable for all. When a surname was taken, it could have been that of the local clan to which Alasdair and Donald belonged by blood, or it might have been the patronymic "frozen" in one generation. Again, by-names were used in small communities — Reid (red), or Beg (small), either of which could become a surname within any clan. Occupational names, too, are frequent, and nearly every clan would have had its Smiths and Wrights. Another variation which occurs and produces modern "septs" is that in which the name of the chief is adapted. Among Fraser surnames are many in which Simon, a favourite among the chiefs, appears, such as Simson, Syme, MacSimon and even MacKim. Also members of the Fraser clan were MacGruers and MacTavishes who lived around Abertarff and Stratherrick and followed Lovat, although those of these names living in other parts of Scotland belonged to other clans.

Apart from the Frasers and Chisholms, almost all the wild Highlanders surrounding Inverness belonged to the Clan Chattan, a unique confederation which grew up around Mackintosh. There were two categories of members, although, once joined, their status did not differ. The first were those "of the blood" of the old Clan Chattan, whose heiress Eva, Mackintosh married and brought from Lochaber in the early 14th century. The first Shaw and Farquharson were traditionally Mackintosh descendants, while the Macphersons, Cattanachs, Macphails and Macbeans are all said to have been related to Eva. The second category of members of Clan Chattan neither shared, nor claimed to share, any common blood. They were independent small clans, whose chiefs voluntarily placed themselves within the confederation, most probably for protection. The Macgillivrays, Davidsons and Dallases are among those who bound themselves to follow Mackintosh in his capacity of Captain of Clan Chattan. The Macleans of Dochgarroch felt themselves too far removed from their chief in Mull, and chose to ally themselves to the confederation, while the MacQueens are said to have descended from a Macdonald who came from Moidart in the service of the bride of one of the Mackintosh chiefs, settled in Strathdearn, and enrolled his family under the banner of Clan Chattan[10].

The confederation was a loose link between these various elements, based on protection, and no formal constitution survives or was probably ever thought of, but a series of bonds or bands were entered into by most, or all, of the members, pledging mutual support on specific occasions, the earliest of which was signed at Inverness in 1543. The most important in the series was that signed at Termit near Petty on 4 April, 1609. The special circumstances which gave rise to this band was the minority of the chief, and an attempt by Huntly to drive a wedge into the confederation by setting the Macphersons against the Mackintoshes. At Termit, three leading Macphersons joined with representatives of the six other clans of "the haill kin of Clan Chattan" to bind themselves in general support of the Captain and Chief and "to concur, assist, maintain, and defend each others . . . in all actions of arms, deeds, and occasions whatsoever." The document was witnessed by the Provost and common clerk of Inverness and by one of the burgesses[11].

A clan, then, was based on an enlarged family unit, dependent on the chief, and it would seem at first sight that the townsfolk of Inverness would not be unduly concerned with the life of "clannit men." Those younger sons of chiefs and cadets who chose to leave their clan country and come to live in the burgh were quite clearly made to adopt new loyalties. In 1580, two burgesses were found who lived at some distance from the burgh bounds, and they were given the choice of moving their households, or losing their status. John Vass agreed to leave his family home at Lochslin in Easter Ross, but Robert Dunbar of Durris said that he could not come and make his residence in Inverness, for the great hazard of his life, because a deadly feud standing as yet unreconciled between him and some of the clans to the west of the burgh[12]. Eight years earlier, John Munro of Urquhart had similarly pledged inability to claim property in the town, because a feud between the Mackenzies, Clan Chattan and the Munros "within the space of tuay yeiris unrecunsalit" made it unsafe for him to dwell there[13].

Clan feuds are notorious, and arose partly from man's natural instinct to defend his territory, set against the pressure of space on the richer land. But there was another factor which led to constant friction. By the mid-16th century, there was a major problem which challenged the so-called "clan system." Lovat and Chisholm both held crown charters for their lands and therefore acted in the dual capacity of clan chief and feudal landlord. But certain chiefs, for one reason or another, were not so fortunate, and they and their clansmen suffered considerably in consequence. Mackintosh did not have a royal charter for his clan lands around Moy or in Badenoch, although he did have one for Lochaber lands full of Camerons and Macdonalds. His clan lands were held, after 1544, from the Earls of Huntly, whom circumstances cast in the role of an enemy. In this situation, feudal theory demanded that Mackintosh clansmen follow their landlord, Huntly, but kinship remained the stronger element. James VI recognised this fact when, in 1587, an Act of Parliament was passed allowing certain specified clans who were dependent upon chiefs or captains "be pretense of blude or place of their duelling," to follow those chiefs, "althocht agains the will ofttymes of the lord of the grund[14]."

This Act certainly helped matters to some extent, but it provided no solution where feuds had already grown up, as that between the Camerons and the Mackintoshes had done. Much blood was shed over the years in this feud, which was not resolved until the 1660s when, at one stage of the negotiations, the citizens of Inverness found themselves spectators at what might have turned into a major battle. In 1664, Mackintosh tried to raise an army to start another round in the struggle, but found that, for one reason or another, many of his friends were unwilling to turn out on his behalf. The Earl of Moray managed to arrange that the two sides, under Mackintosh and Lochiel, should come to Inverness to negotiate. The stage was set. On 15 June, Mackintosh with 500 men took up position on the haugh to the east of the River Ness, while Lochiel with 300 followers set up camp below Tomnahurich on the west bank. Neither side moved, but the Bishop of Moray and Robert Cumming of Altyre, acting as mediators, were rowed backwards and forwards across the river with proposals and counter-proposals. Eventually agreement was reached, by which Lochiel was to buy the rights over his lands from Mackintosh for £40,000[15]. The clans left their places in good order, but unfortunately they had hardly reached home when it became obvious that Lochiel could not possibly find so large a sum of money. Once more the men were gathered — this time in Lochaber — but, before battle, another arrangement was made by which Lochiel borrowed the money to pay Mackintosh. The sequel was not a happy one, but it lies beyond the scope of this study.

During the 16th century, the Crown tried to extend the rule of law deeper into the Highland region, and the problem of the enforcement of that law became a very real one. The King of Scots at this time had neither a private army, nor a police force, and had to rely on a "loyal" clan (that is, one on whose support he could then count) to discipline an unruly neighbour. Letters of Fire and Sword — a commission to search for, and apprehend, any number of named criminals, "if need be, with fire and sword" — were issued for this purpose to whatever chief had the power to carry them out. This was practical, but it was not easy for the criminal clansmen to appreciate on which occasions an attack was caused by personal greed or spite, and on which by royal warrant. The consequence was, that all too often such action proved to be, not a salutary lesson, but the prelude to a series of reprisals, which in turn called for more discipline.

This chain reaction can be found constantly on the larger

scale of Highland history, but it can also be seen to affect individuals such as Robert Dunbar of Durris and John Munro of Urquhart. As late as 1671, the Town Council expressed concern at the danger of reprisals at the hands of escaped prisoners and their friends. They claim that "they find that the caice and condition of the Magistrats of this burghe is farr different from the caice and conditione of the Magistrats within any other burghe within the kingdom," and request that the whole council and inhabitants will stand by them to keep them "hairmless and skaithless in ther persones, goods and geir[16]." The case that was concerning them at the time, was the escape of Alexander Chisholm of Comer from the tolbooth in October, 1668, and the magistrates were apparently still fearful of the "danger that may aryse throw his escape."

It was not only the magistrates who feared the wrath of the Highlanders. Mr Thomas Huistone, minister of Boleskine, complained to the Presbytery of Inverness of "his house being laitly seized upon by Lochabber Robbers, himselfe threatened with naked swords and drawn dirks at his brest, his money and household stuff plundered, and seeing that one of their numbered suffered death laitly therefor at Inverness, the rest of them were lieing in waite for his life and threatening his ruine and damage, so that in the evening he is affrayed to be burnt to ashes or morning[17]."

Small personal feuds were so far accepted as to be written into legal documents. A bond drawn up in Inverness in 1605, shows The Chisholm lending his half-brother 1,000 merks on condition that he will take his part in all "causes, querrellis, contraversies, deidlie feuds or actiones quhatsumever." If support were not forthcoming, the borrower had to repay the sum "within xv dayis nixt efter my fault." Lovat and Mackenzie were appointed judges between the parties in case of disagreement[18].

The magistrates' plea in 1671, that their burgh was in a different case from any other, may have been founded on the fact that Inverness was the seat, not only of the burgh court, but also of the sheriff court which covered nearly all the Highland area, including the modern counties of Ross, Sutherland and Caithness, as well as Inverness. An Order of 1688 states, that if MacDonald of Morar and MacDonald of Castletoun refuse to pay their arrears of taxes, despite quarterings of soldiers on them, they are to be arrested and imprisoned in the tolbooth of Inverness[19]. In view of their fear of reprisals, it is not surprising to find that the magistrates were generally quick to grant bail to such powerfully connected prisoners.

The strength of clan feeling is illustrated by a case which came to the Privy Council in Edinburgh in 1662. A number of Macleans were living in Strathglass as kindly tenants — occupying land in the Chisholm country for no rent, and on a vague, but strongly felt, right — when a charge of witchcraft was brought against them. This was a charge which was always difficult to refute, and the 14 women and one man must have given up hope when they were thrown into prison and The Chisholm applied to the Privy Council for a Commission to proceed against them. But help reached them from a very distant source after the husband of one of the women turned to their chief, Sir Allan Maclean of Duart, far away on the island of Mull. He at once petitioned the Privy Council on behalf of "his kinsfolk and friends," and accused The Chisholm of having "most cruelly and barbarously tortured the women." One of the bailies of Inverness was appointed to examine them, "at the door of the prison vault," and, luckily for The Chisholm, found no mark of torture on them. The end of the story is not known, but it seems clear that the Macleans owed their escape from death to their chief, in spite of the fact that their ancestors had left Mull some three hundred years before. A Highland historian (Dr William Mackay) remarked that he knew of no incident that more vividly reflects the best features of the old clan system[20].

One of the most frequent sources of contact between the burgh of Inverness and the "clannit men" was, some may be surprised to learn, through trade. Inverness was an early point of export and the items most in demand were salmon, skins, hides, timber, and linen and woollen cloth. By charter, the burgesses had the monopoly of trade, but al¹ these products had to be supplied by the neighbouring Highlanders. The chiefs and cadets were by no means too busy to exploit the rather limited resources of their homelands. In 1558, the Records of Inverness show that Clanranald had come into Inverness with "merchandace" for John Nilson — an apparently peaceful action which led to trouble when another burgess, Nicoll Kar, tried to recover a debt that Clanranald owed to him. In the ensuing brawl, "Johne set on the sayd Necoll to the intent to haf slane hyme," and involved two of Clanranald's men in the attack. The burgh court found in favour of John[21]. Three years later, it was Glengarry who was in the burgh selling "ane red kow" to Mathew Paterson[22].

The more distant chiefs of the west coast found themselves at odds with all the royal burghs, including Inverness, when they began to charge herring-fishers anchor dues and rents for huts, as well as payment for seaweed used to cover the fish, and a percentage rate on fish caught near their shores. In 1586, the Privy Council heard one of several long complaints from the burghs on the subject, and regulations were laid down to limit the rate charged. But the clansmen were in business.

Attempts were made by Lovat to exact a toll on the use of the passage of Loch Ness. Fraser of Struy tried to sue a burgess in the burgh court in 1564, for the price of a licence for one year[24]. Eleven years later, Glengarry successfully complained to the Privy Council that Lovat had tried to prevent him and his clansmen from carrying wood in boats to Inverness[25]. The right of burgesses and other inhabitants of the burgh to use the loch for trade was confirmed in James VI's charter to Inverness — the Golden Charter — granted in 1591 and, incidentally, some of the Highlanders also felt the benefit[26].

Glengarry was not the only chief to sell timber. Alexander Chisholm of Comer brought an action in the burgh court in 1565 against John Robertson, burgess, for non-payment for 46 dozen oak boards — a case which Chisholm won, after the sheriff had called witnesses from beyond the jurisdiction of the burgh[27].

Not only did the burgh buy from the clansmen, but there was a return trade, by which manufactured or imported items found their way into Highland homes. Mackintosh of Cullernie, or rather his wife, was owing £5 to the local agent of a Hamburg merchant for a puncheon of wine in 1557[28]. A keg of wine from the cellar of Alexander Cuthbert reached a customer in Glenelg in 1585[29]; and six years earlier, Moir Nykloidd in Lochaber was reported as owing 22 merks for "ane fyne quheit pled wyth the pertinentis eftir hir discretioun[30]."

As these few random examples show, payment was only too often the problem, as ready cash was scarce to the point of non-existence in many parts of the country at this and even later times. For example, Hector Maclean in Dochnacraig admits in 1687 that he cannot pay cash to John Dunbar, merchant in Inverness, but makes instead a disposition in his favour of certain oxen and a 20 gallon copper kettle[31].

A slightly different solution had been found in 1603 by Lachlan Mackintosh of Dunachton for paying his son's Edinburgh school fees. There exists a receipt by Mr Robert Stevin, one of the teachers of the High School, for fifty-two buttons and a knap of gold, weighing six ounces and a half, which are to be re-delivered on payment of 300 merks at Martinmas next[32].

Martinmas not only saw the end of the harvest and some payment of rent, but also, and most important of all in the Highland calendar, it was the time of the great cattle trysts. Even in the 18th century, Highland bills were, in the words of Bailie John Steuart of Inverness, "payable at Creef," where the greatest of the markets was held. In 1734 the Bailie sent at least three letters — to MacDonald of Scotus, MacLeod of Ebost and Alexander MacGillivray from Petty — by bearer direct to Crieff[33]. In the following year, he told Coll Macdonald of Barrisdale that the bill for 60 bolls of oatmeal "must be payed precisely by 15 of July nixt at our Market and at Crief market be equall halves[34]."

The chief's responsibility for the behaviour of their clansmen sometimes extended as far as private small debt. Donald MacDonald of Glengarry allowed himself to "becum actit in the burrow buikis of his awin fee motywe will" as surety for Ewin McAne VcConquhie in Killenan, who owed money to a burgess. Glengarry not only undertook to bring Ewin to court but, if he failed to do that, he agreed to allow the burgess "to poind and distreinye quhatsumevir gudis or feir pertenyng onye of his cuntre folkis dwelling within his boundis and cuntreis[35]."

Now and again, in spite of their wish for independence, the citizens of Inverness had to rely on their neighbours for help. But it was an accepted crime against the liberty of the burgesses if a citizen tried to "purchase lordship" — in other words, to seek or accept help in a dispute from people of influence outside the burgh[36]. This meant that if a clansman chose to become a merchant or small tradesman in the burgh, he should no longer count on the support of his chief. This was not always so well known and understood outside the burgh as it was inside it, and there were a few occasions when the council had to recruit "pretty able men brought from the country" to re-inforce the town guard[37].

One of these occasions was in 1665, following an incident, described elsewhere in this volume, at the fair called "Cabog Day." The death of two visiting Glengarry Macdonalds was the excuse for their chief, recently raised to the peerage as Lord MacDonnell and Aros, to demand satisfaction. He was then living just outside the burgh bounds at Drakies, and one of his contemporaries wrote: "Some do construe that Glengarry stays there for to give the greater latitude to his rude clan

O

to sally, sorn upon, and pillage their neighbours." The town council, "finding that there are great threats and boasting made for invading them . . . find it expedient therefore to write to certain particular gentlemen and noblemen (especially the Earl of Moray) desiring their presence here with such as they will be pleased to bring along with them." It was probably the heartening presence of these "strangers" that enabled the council to refuse Glengarry's demands for reparation, and a special offensive and defensive alliance under which "wheresoever the people of Inverness or any person of them sees my Lord MacDonnel, his friends, followers or any of them, that then and immediately they should lay down their arms on the ground in token of obedience and submission." The Privy Council, when applied to, merely fined the town £4,800 Scots[38].

Another Macdonald, Coll of Keppoch, threatened the town in 1689 when, with 900 men, he arrived to keep a rendezvous with Claverhouse at the start of the Killiecrankie campaign. He was the first on the scene, and found the situation full of possibilities. He had just been defeated, in Lochaber, by the Mackintoshes and their allies in what was, in fact, the last clan battle in Scotland, and he was anxious to assert himself in revenge. So, alone near Inverness, he threatened the town with destruction. Lord Macaulay describes the scene: "The danger was extreme. The houses were surrounded only by a wall which time and weather had so loosened that it shook in every storm. Yet the inhabitants showed a bold front; their courage was stimulated by their preachers. Sunday the 28th of April was a day of alarm and confusion. The savages went round and round the small colony of Saxons like a troop of famished wolves round a sheepfold. Keppoch threatened and blustered. He would come in with all his men. He would sack the place. The burghers meanwhile mustered in arms round the market cross to listen to the oratory of their ministers. The day closed without an assault; the Monday and Tuesday passed away in intense anxiety; and then an unexpected mediator made his appearance." This was Claverhouse, who on the morning of 1 May rode up with a small body of horsemen and quickly undertook to settle the dispute. Keppoch claimed that he was only asking for what was lawfully his, as Inverness owed him large sums of money. Eventually the town agreed to pay £2,700 Scots, which the citizens tried in vain to recover from the Privy Council, but it was probably a small price to pay for the removal of the clans from their gates[39].

This incident must have been specially disappointing for the burgh, because the council had just achieved a piece of very practical co-operation with some of the clan chiefs. The river-crossings at Inverness had always been important, and from time to time local chiefs had contributed timber for keeping up the bridges. In 1654, The Chisholm, Fraser of Struy and Grant of Glenmoriston supplied joists after an old bridge had fallen "by the inadvertancy of a carpenter" in an accident which involved about 200 people and, though "4 of the townes men broke leggs and thighs," and 16 suffered bruises, "by Providence not one perished[40]." Fifteen years later, it was decided to replace the wooden bridge with a stone one. The magistrates appealed for £3,000 and, among those who contributed, in cash and not stone, were Mackintosh, MacLeod of MacLeod, MacDonald of Sleat, Lovat, the lairds of Cawdor, and Grant, and the Earl of Huntly. MacLeod gave £1200 on condition that his coat of arms was carved on the bridge[41].

The building of the bridge introduces a peaceful note into this account of the relations between Inverness and the clans. This note, though apt to be transitory, had not been entirely absent during the previous century. The clans were not always at feud with one another. The minister of Wardlaw tells how, after Lovat was appointed Governor of Inverness Castle in 1574, he used to train his young kinsmen and clan with drill and all manner of games — "They used swimming, arching, football, throwing the barr, fencing, dancing, wrestling and such manly sprightly exercises and recreations." Apparently Lovat "caused the countrymen to come into Inverness *per vices* 50 or 60 at a time, and were dayly exercised upon the levell of the Castlehill or down in the Links, by one Lieutenant Thomas Carr, a townsman and my Lordships own domestick servant . . . So that not onely the young men of the name of Fraser got good occasion of disciplin and education by this meanes, but many mo(re) of the adjacent clans out of emulation flokt in, the Munroes, the Rosses, Mackenzies, M'kintoshes . . [42]."

Horse-racing was popular on the haughs beside the river, and the same minister of Wardlaw describes how, in May 1662, "the concourse of people flokt . . . to behold the course." Many of the chiefs were present, including the lairds of Grant, Mackintosh, Foulis, Ballnagown, the Lord Macdonell, Lovat and Kilravock. "The Provost and Magistrates of Inverness with the citizens, came in procession over the bridge to their bounded march and, with the usual ceremony, hung the silver cup with blew ribbons uppon the hookes off the painted port, the Sadle and the Suord set uppon the top of it." The races lasted two days and, on the first evening, "the magistrates gave the nobles a sumptious treat[43]."

Lovat himself and his bride had been "most sumptuously treated at Inverness by the magistrates" the previous year as they passed through on their wedding journey[44], while the bridegroom's parents had also been well entertained on a similar occasion in 1642, with "wines at the Cross and tables covered," after the magistrates had "mustered the train bands of the town to keep off the rable[45]."

There is no doubt that the clans suffered — the clansmen as well as the chiefs — through their entry into national politics in the mid-17th century, when Montrose called them out to support the Stuarts. Some change was inevitable as society developed. James VI and I, backed by his English resources, tried unsuccessfully to tame the chiefs, and his successors would have had to carry on the process, if they had not needed military support for themselves. Economic and social change was also reaching the clans and altering the relationship between the chief and the clan — the keystone of the old clanship.

The adherence or opposition to Jacobitism on the part of each clan is by no means the simple matter it is sometimes assumed to be. This is not the occasion to analyse individual motives, but personal relationships played a part, as well as the more obvious religious and political loyalties. Some clans played a consistent role — probably few equalled Alexander Robertson of Struan's feat in being 'out" in 1689, 1715 and 1745 — but it is misleading to generalise. There were Campbells who fought with the Jacobites in 1745 from individual conviction, though most of the clan was strongly Hanoverian. Circumstances were also important as, for example, among the Macleans whose chief was a prisoner — almost a hostage — throughout the '45. The record of the local clans can best be read in their own more detailed histories, but the story of the Frasers, Chisholms and the Clan Chattan illustrates the diversity of attitude within each clan and between different Risings. The leaders of the three clans were inconsistent in their adherence, and none was able to lead a united clan in the '45.

In covering a very wide field, enough has been said to show the essential elements of the clan "system," and some of the causes of friction between the burgh and the clans, as well as their more peaceful relations. The next contribution will demonstrate that the clans' warlike reputation was not entirely undeserved.

REFERENCES

1. Mackay, William, & Boyd, Herbert Cameron (Eds.), *Records of Inverness,* vol I, p. 3, New Spalding Club, 1911.
2. *Register of the Great Seal,* vol iii, No. 3233.
3. *Records of Inverness,* II, 211.
4. Pryde, G. S., *The Burghs of Scotland,* p. 11, 1965.
5. Mackintosh, C. Fraser, *Antiquarian Notes,* p. 373, 1865.
6. Fraser of Reelig, C. I., *The Clan Fraser of Lovat,* p. 8, 1952.
7. Dunlop, Jean, *The Clan Chisholm,* p. 7, 1953.
8. Mackintosh, A. M., *The Mackintoshes and Clan Chattan,* pp. 124/5, 1903.
9. *The Clan Fraser of Lovat,* p. 20.
10. Dunlop, Jean, *The Clan Mackintosh,* p. 16, 1960.
11. *The Mackintoshes and Clan Chattan,* pp. 196-9.
12. *Records of Inverness* I, p. 286-7.
13. *Records of Inverness* I, p. 216-7.
14. *Acts of the Parliaments of Scotland,* iii, p. 218-9.
15. *The Mackintoshes and Clan Chattan,* p. 250.
16. *Records of Inverness* II, p. 249.
17. Mackay, William (Ed.), *Inverness and Dingwall Presbytery Records,* Scottish History Society, p. 5, 1896.
18. Chisholm Writs in private hands, 6th February, 1605.
19. Paton, Henry (Ed.), *The Mackintosh Muniments,* No. 626. 1903.
20. Mackay, William, *Sidelines on Highland History,* pp. 75-86, 1925.
21. *Records of Inverness* I, p. 21.
22. *Records of Inverness* I, p. 58.
23. *Register of the Privy Council* IV, p. 122.
24. *Records of Inverness* I, p. 115.
25. *Collectanea de Rebus Albanicis,* p. 34, Iona Club, 1847.
26. Mackintosh, C. Fraser, *Invernessiana,* p. 255 et seq. 1875.
27. *Records of Inverness* I, p. 123.
28. *Records of Inverness* I, p. 10.
29. *Records of Inverness* I, p. 304.
30. *Records of Inverness* I, p. 266.
31. *Mackintosh Muniments,* No. 619.
32. *Mackintosh Muniments,* No. 205.
33. Mackay, William (Ed.), *The Letter-book of Bailie John Steuart of Inverness,* pp. 385-6, Scottish History Society, 1915.
34. *Letter-book,* pp. 388-9.
35. *Records of Inverness* I, p. 283.
36. *Records of Inverness* I, p. 32.
37. *Records of Inverness* II, p. 223.
38. Barron, E. M., *Inverness and the Macdonalds,* pp. 70 et seq., 1930.
39. Macaulay, Lord, *History of England* (Everyman edition), II, p. 462.
40. *Records of Inverness* II, p. 210.
41. *Records of Inverness* II, p. 285 et seq.
42. Mackay, William (Ed.), *Chronicles of the Frasers, The Wardlaw Manuscript,* p. 171, 1905.
43. *Wardlaw MS.,* pp. 447-8.
44. *Wardlaw MS.,* p. 439.
45. *Wardlaw MS.,* p. 277.

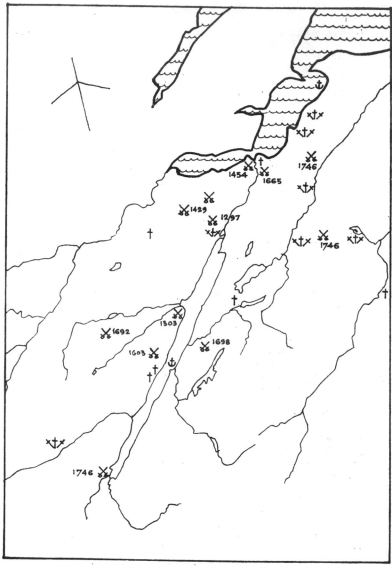

INVERNESS AND DISTRICT

DISTRIBUTION MAP 6

Murders · †   Battlefields · ⚔   Massacres · ×†×

SCALE ·   5 KM.   0   5   10   15 KM.

5   0   5   10 MILES

BATTLE, MURDER AND SUDDEN DEATH

ALLAN MACLEAN

Inverness is one of the strongest sites in Scotland. It is difficult for an army to be transported by sea, and therefore, in military terms, the strategy of a campaign is dependent on the lie of the land. Mountains and rivers form boundaries, and therefore need to be guarded. The lowest river crossings were vital strategic points, and frequently battles were fought near them; for example, the many battles and skirmishes in the Stirling area, including Bannockburn, were to gain possession of the first crossing of the Forth. Looking at the map, it is clear that the region round Beauly was one of importance.

The map, however, shows Inverness, to have been a far stronger position than Beauly. On the east, the sea and mountains channel all reasonable movement towards it. The River Ness is strategically as important as the Beauly. One only needs to stand at the Castle at Inverness today to see, looking over the Cathedral, that the river is very short, and any crossing of it from the South has to be within six miles of the castle. Furthermore, if the Firth is to be crossed by boat, the Kessock Ferry is a far safer crossing than Ardersier-Fortrose, and even that crossing is within twelve miles of Inverness.

It would not, therefore, be surprising to learn of many battles fought in the neighbourhood, but, in fact, records have scant accounts of any major encounter. This does not mean that the importance of Inverness has necessarily been exaggerated. Inverness was really only important in National Wars. The battles for Inverness were fought at a distance, at Auldearn (East of Nairn), at Harlaw (in Aberdeenshire), or Inverlochy (near Fort William). The barrier of hills across Strathmore and Strathearn and in Aberdeenshire were a back-cloth for frequent forays into the Lowlands. Control of the Highlands was dependent, in the long run, on controlling all the Highlands simultaneously. Cromwell and the Hanoverians, the two forces who succeeded in this, planted citadels and forts to maintain their grip.

When, however, the last fight for the control of Inverness

took place, it was very close to the town indeed, within four miles, on the top of Drumossie Moor.

Records of the 12th and 13th centuries which survive show that Inverness was used as a base for attacks into the hills. At the time of the English invasions, King Edward I of England came north to Moray on two occasions. He reached Elgin in 1296 and from there he managed to gain control of the chief strongholds. Castle Urquhart was placed under a new Constable, Sir William Fitzwarine, with a strong garrison. Edward's hopes that he had subdued Scotland were shattered by the rise of William Wallace and, in the North, of Andrew de Moray, a great feudal baron. Moray, with Alexander Pilches, a burgess of Inverness, his Lieutenant, led a force which in one summer liberated the North and, joining forces with Wallace, won the victory at Stirling Bridge in September, 1297. At the start, they concentrated on Inverness and Urquhart.

The Constable of Inverness, Sir Reginald Le Chen, was worried by this and called Fitzwarine from Urquhart for a conference on the Sunday before Ascension Day, 1297. On his way back, Fitzwarine was attacked by Moray and Pilches. Although the place is not known for certain, it seems likely that it was at *Battlefield*[1], near Dochgarroch. This was the view held by Dr William Mackay, the eminent local historian. A waterfall there is called Eas a' Chath (Cascade of the Battle), and it is on the old route from Inverness to Urquhart, which climbed the hill behind Dochgarroch. If this is the place, Moray probably lay in the woods above the road and sprang on to Fitzwarine passing below. Two of Fitzwarine's principal followers fell into Moray's hands as wounded prisoners, along with eighteen of his best horses. Fitzwarine was lucky to escape and to reach Urquhart.

King Edward heard of this and ordered some of his forces at Aberdeen to relieve Urquhart, stating: We learn that certain malefactors and disturbers of the peace, roaming about, have killed some of our servants, and imprisoned others . . . and are maliciously laying ambushes for our beloved and faithful William Fitzwarine.

Eventually Urquhart, like Inverness, fell to the Scots, and Edward, on his return to Scotland in 1303, had to attempt to recapture them. Inverness opened its gates without resistance, but *Urquhart*[2] prepared for a siege. Edward's forces determined to starve the garrison at Urquhart into surrender. Eventually, in the winter, when the stores ran out, it was clear that the garrison had to escape. The drawbridge was lowered and a poor expectant mother came out. She told the English that she had been caught in the castle at the beginning of the siege and wished to have her child in better circumstances. The English let her through and, as they did so, the garrison rushed out, hoping to surprise the besiegers, but in the ensuing struggle they were killed to a man, including Sir Alexander Forbes, the Governor. The only person to escape was the expectant mother, who was, in fact, the Governor's wife.

The 15th century is largely a history of Macdonald incursions into the North, and although Urquhart and Inverness were captured and recaptured, frequently there was no fighting; sometimes the doors were ready opened.

National History again touches Inverness in the Civil Wars of Charles I when the Royalists were under the command of Montrose. They were mostly a Highland force, fighting the Covenanters. For the account of Montrose's relationship with the city of Inverness, one can largely rely on the Wardlaw Manuscript, the work of James Fraser of Phopachy, later Episcopalian minister of Wardlaw (Kirkhill) after the Restoration, but in this matter, as a Fraser, he was generally in sympathy with the Covenanters.

Montrose decided to blockade one side of the town and garrison, and Huntly was to blockade the other. The garrison in the Castle was strong and, two years before, the Covenanters had encircled the town with an earthen wall, a deep trench, ramparts and palisades. Every parish in the district had been ordered to help build the fortifications, which included four strong gates. Huntly, however, though glad to see Montrose leaving Castle Gordon, had no intention of joining forces with him. Montrose, despite this, closed in the *Siege of Inverness* on 29 April, 1646[3]. According to the Wardlaw MS., he "fixt his gunns upon the top of the old castlehill, called Castrum Vetus, under a hawthorn tree due east, and batters hot." This old Castle Hill is part of Inverness now known as the Crown, and it therefore appears that Montrose's guns were in the vicinity of the Crown Church of Scotland. They clearly held a good position, but the siege, despite reinforcements of Mackenzies and Macdonalds, without the help of Huntly would have taken a long time.

The Frasers had been noticeable for their adherence to the Covenant and it may have been for this reason that Montrose allowed his troops to pillage in the Aird. Report has it that there was not a beast untaken nor a house undisturbed in the 26 miles between Inverness and the head of Strathglass, and the people were only safe in the "sconces" which had been built at Kirkhill (in the Fort Field on the home farm at Kingillie), by Fraser of Culboky, at Lovat Castle, the Fort of Beauly, Eilean Aigas, or the Doune at Struy.

The accounts of Montrose's siege of Inverness are not very helpful, but it appears that the Covenanters secured their position and pulled down some stone houses and kilns "near the bridge-end, south-west," to prevent shelter for an attack by Montrose. One cannot be sure on which side of the river this means, but they were probably on the site of the Columba Hotel, and certainly when Montrose was captured and brought through Inverness in 1650, an old woman at the West end of the Bridge is reported to have said, "Montrose, look above, view these ruinous houses which you occasioned to be burned down when you besieged Inverness[4]."

Montrose stationed three troops of horse, which he could ill spare, at the Fords of Spey to report any movement of the enemy. Accounts again differ as to the reason, but Lord Lewis Gordon, Huntly's son, detained these troops at Rothes, while Middleton, with the Covenanting army of 600 horse and 800 foot, crossed the Spey and marched through Moray. If Montrose had been surprised by this army, he would likely have suffered a worse defeat than any he had had so far. Luckily for him, Middleton's trumpets sounded somewhere about Stratton or Culloden, and Montrose's camp was alerted.

Montrose had nothing with which to withstand so strong a cavalry force, so, after only a week, he was forced to raise the siege. In his escape, he had to leave his camp to Middleton, together with all the provisions and ammunition. What particularly riled Montrose was the loss of his two brass ordnance cannon, with which he had been attacking the Castle. The river was very shallow and, quoting the Wardlaw MS., he "managed his retreat so well, that with little losse, he came to the Capplach and so marched with his few forces over the Stock foord of Rosse, and leagured two miles above Beuly in the Wood of Farly." The Stock Ford was the old ford across the Beauly river.

One would suppose that if Montrose had been west of Inverness and making direct for Beauly, he would have gone by the flat land and quick going of the Aird, as Middleton did in pursuit. Maybe Montrose wished to avoid the sconces at Kirkhill and Lovat, but he probably crossed the Ness at a well-known ford above the Islands and, to avoid Inverness altogether, he went into the hills above Dunain and Doch-garroch. He may have first thought that he would marshal his troops in the hills, but then, realising that he had enough time and was travelling light, without much baggage or ammunition, he aimed for a strong position across the Stock Ford. I agree with Dr I. F. Grant, that probably they went straight over the hills to Belladrum. She places Montrose's camp as "somewhere to the west of the present Beauly war memorial[5]," and I am content to leave it in Fraser's words of "2 miles above Beuly in the Wood of Farly." In the next paragraph, Fraser terms it "Strachines wood in Fairlie," and I take this to be above Ruisaurie.

Middleton, according to Fraser, was well content to let Montrose slip through his fingers, and on arriving at Inverness was welcomed and able to refresh his troops. He did not stop, but, taking the direct route through Kirkhill parish, "he leagured that night in the Moore of Blair ni Cuinligh, a little above the Stockford of Ross." Montrose was in sight opposite him and Blair ni Cuinligh is a wood near Lovat.

The following two days, the two commanders corresponded with each other by messengers and trumpets, and it is said that Middleton was as afraid of Montrose as Montrose was of him. Although Montrose probably held the stronger position, he was almost without ammunition and not so strong in men, and he needed to reserve them for more fighting. Under cover of a great smoke from firing his camp, he escaped, and Middleton went to Lovat and then crossed over by Beauly Ferry to Ross.

Dr Grant has drawn up a hypothetical route now taken by Montrose. She says: "He probably made his way over the hills so as to cross the Ness at a ford just below the Loch and so made his way across Strath Errick and Strath Dearn. There were numbers of hill tracks by which he could have marched, for the old Highlanders passed constantly from one Strath to another."

Montrose, finally giving up hope of securing Huntly's support, and while raising other help from Royalist clans, received a letter from the King telling him of his fatal surrender to the Scots Covenanting Army, and ordering Montrose to disband his army. The siege of Inverness had been a fiasco, and Montrose, in August 1646, sailed into four years of exile, only to return in 1650, to be captured and to end a tale of glorious failure.

Meanwhile, although the Royalist commander had disbanded his army, the Royalist clans were still carrying on some form of guerilla warfare. Early in 1649, maybe as a result of hearing of the King's execution, the Mackenzies surprised the garrison which Fraser of Breay had left in the Bishop's Castle at Fortrose. Next, on 22 February, 1649, the Royalist forces, mostly Mackenzies and Mackays, crossing the Kessock Ferry, assembled at Merkinch (then a flat island) at 9 in the morning in full view of the Castle. Marching up the west bank of the river, they crossed the Ness, then flowing shallow, and drew up their battalion above the township of Allt-na-skiach, which in present day terms means that they halted about Heatherley Crescent and Sunnybank Road. Immediately a trumpeter and two single horsemen went to the Castle and demanded its surrender[6].

There was confusion in the town. The Governor, Sir James Fraser of Breay, was in the South and the Castle was under the command of a Major Murray. He at once set about fortifying the Castle Street gate, the one nearest the besiegers. While he was organising this work, a beam of wood fell on his head, which apparently "raised his passion and rankled him." As he returned down Castle Street, he found that his soldiers were mutinying. Immediately drawing his pistol, he shot at a man with a drawn sword, Serjeant John Mackenzie, and as he killed him, he shouted, "Take that for heading a mutiny!" As he came to the bottom of the street, he was told that the Magistrates could not be trusted. The garrison was depleted because lieutenants had taken troops out of the town for various reasons, and Captain Cranstoun had drawn up the remaining troops in the High Street. He called out, "Major Murray, Instantly horse and be gone, else you are betrayed," and immediately they rushed out of the town along the Eastgate and Millburn roads.

The Royalist forces were able to seize the town and take over the Castle that same day, without any fighting. It was a contrast to Montrose's siege. At once the ramparts of Inverness were demolished and levelled to the ground.

The town remained in Royalist hands until May. Hearing that Middleton was again in the North, the Royalist clans, Mackays and Mackenzies, raised 1500 men. They met on Sunday, 3 May, at Inverness. With ample supplies, munitions and arms, they set off for Moray the next day. Camping at Balveny Castle, they were surprised by a small force of Covenanters, 400 being killed and 1000 made captive. These captives were led back to Inverness and "thence conducted over the bridge of Ness, and dismissed every man armless and harmless." This is in striking contrast to the treatment which the victor of Culloden, less than a hundred years later, meted out to the unfortunate inhabitants of Inverness, and indeed of most of the area round.

Under the Protectorate, the Citadel was built at Inverness,

but this was almost totally demolished at the Restoration, only the small tower surviving to this day. It never saw any military action, and Inverness itself, though a central point for military operations, and thus frequently filled with soldiers, was rarely itself the scene of fighting.

Dundee came on his recruiting expedition of 1689. He arrived on 1 May, and by the 8th had left for fear of a battle with General Mackay, who was then at Elgin. Dundee needed to raise more troops, and when Mackay arrived, the town was open for him.

In 1715, the Castle was taken by the Mackintoshes on 13 September. They then attacked Culloden House, hoping for arms and ammunition, but, like the Mackenzies a month later, they were unsuccessful. Inverness was recaptured for the Hanoverians on 13 November by Rose of Kilravock, after only two months in Jacobite hands.

Prince Charles arrived at *Moy Hall* on Sunday, 16 February, 1746, with an advance guard of about 500 Camerons. A small guard of about 30 men were around the house that night, and news that the Prince was there, even of the size of his guard, reached the Hanoverians in Inverness. A plan was made that about 1500 men under Lord Loudon should march out of town and surprise and capture the Prince. But a boy (maybe sent by the Laird of Mackintosh, who was under Loudon's command) managed to escape with the news and to reach Moy by a different route, probably by Daviot. In the meantime, Lady Mackintosh, the famous "Colonel Anne," had posted Donald Fraser, the Smith of Moy, and four men with loaded muskets beyond the Prince's guard, as an advanced guard on the (old) military road to Inverness. They walked up and down in the terrible storm of that night on the moor, about two miles distant from Moy. At last they saw against the skyline a large body of men marching towards them at no great distance. With great presence of mind, Fraser posted his four men at strategic points and, as Loudon's men approached, they fired their muskets. As the account says: Upon this the blacksmith huzzaed and cried aloud "Advance, Advance, my lads. Advance (naming some particular regiments), I think we have the dogs now!"

Loudon's men, by the flashes of lightning, saw the peat stacks and thought that they were men, and the whole situation made them think that they were being attacked by the entire Jacobite army. They were panic-stricken, and all 1500 fled to Inverness. Loudon's account says that he got half way undiscovered and a detachment which he had sent to prevent intelligence, "going a nearer road contrary to orders, fired at four men, which alarmed the rest." It is said that one, if not the only person killed, was Donald Ban Maccrimmon, Macleod's piper, among the Hanoverian men. It is also said that he had a premonition of his fate and composed the famous *"Cumha Mhic-criomain,"* or Maccrimmon's Lament, before he left Skye. Loudon's troops were mostly made up of men from local Whig clans, and when the Jacobites arrived at Inverness the next day, the Hanoverians had abandoned the town. This affair is known as *The Rout of Moy*[7].

The role of Inverness in the campaigns that led up to Culloden is too well known for consideration here. It is, however, remarkable for how much of the so-called "Jacobite Year," 1745-6, the town and castle of Inverness were in Hanoverian hands. It goes a long way to illustrate an oft-forgotten fact, that the Highlands were not Jacobite to a man. Only a few of the clans were Jacobite; many were neutral, or pro-Whig Hanoverians. It was partly this loyalty of many of the people in and around Inverness to the Hanoverians which makes the aftermath of the Battle of Culloden so disgraceful— and unforgiveable. Most of the citizens had not taken any part in the battle and, while the burning of the Episcopal Chapel may be understandable in the light of their open Jacobitism, the wholesale destruction of much of the town and the harrying of the glens is in marked contrast to the aftermath of the Battle of Balveny.

While the Inverness area may not have seen much fighting on the national scale, it certainly witnessed some terrible conflicts between local families and clans. The battle-site nearest to Inverness is at *Clachnaharry.*

Although there is a monument on the site, there is still some doubt as to the date and the dispute which led to it. The most likely date is 1454. The Munros had been in the South and were returning with their *spreidh* (booty). It was customary for the owner of the lands through which such a troop went to receive a *stoig-chrich* (cut of the takings). Some dispute broke out at Moy between the Mackintoshes and the Munros. Feeling was such that the Mackintoshes pursued the Munros, catching up with them at the ford above the Islands at Inverness. The Munros had time to send the booty over the hill beyond Kinmylies, and then, according to one account, waited for battle on the flat ground by Clachnaharry. The details are not certain, but all descriptions depict it as a particularly bloody conflict, in which both sides suffered great losses, but which the Munros won[8].

The Mackintoshes and other Clan Chattan clans were, not surprisingly, involved in many of the other battles recorded in the district. Many fights were brought about by wrongful occupation of lands. The feud with the Comyns may well have been of this type. One traditional account is worth recording.

The Comyns, having driven the Mackintoshes for refuge on to the *Island in Loch Moy*[9], proceeded to dam the loch in order to cover the island and drown the occupants. When things were getting desperate for the Mackintoshes, one of their numbers, in the dead of night, swam out to the dam. He bored many holes in the wooden planks which made up the barrier, and plugged them with stoppers. By a skilful use of ropes, he pulled all the plugs out at once, and the rush of water broke the supporting turf bank. The Comyns were encamped below the dam and were overwhelmed. This must have happened about 1440, for in 1442 the Comyn lands of Meikle Geddes and Rait were transferred to the Mackintoshes.

At the beginning of the next century, the Mackintoshes were in dispute with the Ogilvies and the Earl of Moray. Petty had been granted to the Ogilvies, with the knowledge of Moray, who also had rights there. The Mackintoshes claimed that it was their property, and in 1513 Dougal Mor Mackintosh, a cousin of the Chief and a great local malcontent and warrior, attacked the newly-built *Hall Hill,* or castle of the Ogilvies at Petty[10]. The Mackintoshes slew a son of Ogilvie and killed the 18 men composing the garrison. Hall Hill is in a field near Wester Dalziel. Twenty years later, the Mackintoshes were still in conflict with the Earl of Moray and the Ogilvies. In 1531, Hector Mackintosh, the acting Chief, invaded Moray's country, plundering Dyke, laying siege to Darnaway Castle and, on the way back, attacking Hall Hill and putting 24 Ogilvies to the sword.

There are various tales of retaliation for these raids, and one in particular is of note. The Earl of Moray held a Court at *Tordarroch* on behalf of his young nephew, the Chief of Mackintosh[11]. His real reason was to find a clue as to the whereabouts of Hector. Eighteen men who had taken part in the plunder of Dyke refused to divulge their leader's hiding place, and were hanged "over the balks of the house where the court was holden." Matters do not seem to have stopped there, and in 1534 the Mackintoshes laid siege to *Daviot Castle* and burned the houses there, including "the slaughter of women, men and children to the number of twenty persons[12]."

What position the people of *Petty* took in these controversies is not clear, but in 1593 they suffered badly for their support of the Mackintoshes[13]. The Earl of Huntly, in order to take his revenge on the Mackintoshes, entered Petty with a large force and killed about 200 of the inhabitants, as well as gaining much booty.

Only a few years before, in 1574, the Mackintoshes had had their eyes on the old church lands at Ardersier[14]. The Campbells of Cawdor were also interested, and in the resulting fight, the Mackintoshes and "utheris of the Clanquhattan" did much damage to the village, "depaupering of the tenantis and occupearis thereof and debarring of the saidis personis . . . fra any manner of fisching in that pairt callit the stell of the ness of Arthurscheir be braking of ther coubilis (boats) and cutting of ther nettis."

Ardersier was not the only place which kept boats. Cromwell had a "stately frigate" as a patrol on Loch Ness; partly built, it was driven on rollers to Lochend, where it was completed[15]. And tradition tells of a battle on Loch Ness in the early 15th century. The young bride of Gruer Mor from Portclair was on her round receiving wedding presents from her friends. When she reached Foyers, she was grossly insulted by Laurence Grant. In revenge, Gruer sailed from Portclair with galleys full of fighting men. Grant, with his men, rowed out to meet them, and in a desperate fight on Loch Ness in a bay to the west of Foyers, now called *Camus Mharbh Dhaoine* (Bay of the Dead Men), he was defeated[16]. Nevertheless, he was able to reach the Western shore, but in the woods above Ruiskich, at a place called *Ruigh Laurais* (Laurence's slope), he was overtaken and killed. Gruer then seized Foyers.

The same woods above Ruiskich were the scene of a battle nearly 200 years later, in September, 1603. With the rise of the Mackenzies, the Macdonalds were jealous and, probably as a result of the loss of Strome Castle, Allan Dubh, the son and heir of Ranald Macdonald of Lundie in Glengarry, led a raid against the Mackenzies in Redcastle. This included the burning of the Church at Kilchrist (Gilchrist near Muir of Ord), some say with many Mackenzies inside. On their way home, laden with booty, the Macdonalds camped on a level moss at the foot of Mealfourvonie. Unknown to them, the Mackenzies, eager for revenge, were not far behind. Rounding the South-eastern corner of the hill, they saw the Macdonalds on the plain below, ever since known as *Lon-na-fala* (Meadow of Blood), and swept down on them[17]. The fight was fierce, but the Macdonalds were tired, so that the Mackenzies eventually got the upper hand.

One account goes on: There was never one left alive of

14. Wade Road between Raigbeg and Slochd

15. Ford on Wade Road, between Sluggan Bridge and Lethedryveole

16. Achcullin, Abriachan, showing the canopied chimney scarcement ("hanging lum"), small press and turf walling above

17. Old reaper at work

18. Whisky still. The man in the centre lived to a ripe old age, dying as a result of falling down a flight of church steps.

19. The boys of Abriachan School, c. 1910

20. Winter storage, Beechwood Farm, Inverness

21. *Gondolier* at Fort Augustus

22. Round House, Inverness Station, demolished 1963

23. Inverness Market, 1886, before the fire

24. Inverness Castle and Suspension Bridge, late 19th century

5. Bank Street, with St. Columba High, Inverness, late 19th century

26. The old Town House, Inverness, demolished 1878

27. Inverness Harbour, early 20th century

28. Horse and cart crossing Kessock Ferry, early 20th century

29. and 30. The Rose Street Foundry, Inverness, then and now

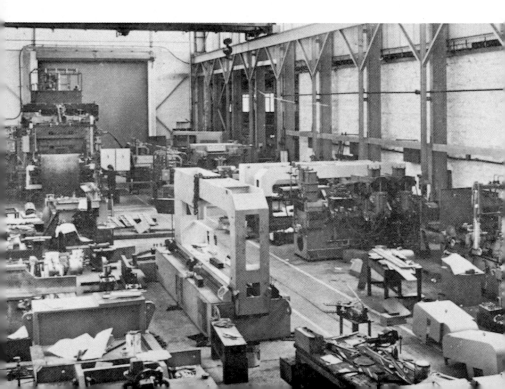

them but Allan himself who escaped naked, without cloathes or arms by a leap that he gave desperately over a most ill-favoured lynn (pool), which he nor any other man did never before nor afterwards. Allan being asked thereafter how he got such a leap done, answered that providence had brought him through, and he would choose rather to die than try it again, though he were put to such necessity. Others add to the story, that a Mackenzie chased him across, but had to cling to a tree, which Macdonald cut with his dirk, shouting as Mackenzie fell to his death, "I have left much with your race today, let me leave them that also." Allan plunged down the slopes of Ruiskich and, diving into the water, was picked up by a Fraser from Foyers, who had seen his escape from the other side.

The account given above, a Mackenzie document, and all the romantic guides, place the jump at *Allt Sigh,* but Dr William Mackay, basing his account on local tradition, places it at the less well-known tributary, *Allt Ghuis*[18].

Another fight happened in the same hills, later in the century, 1691 or 1692. Some years before, a vagrant woman from Lochaber had given birth to a child in Glen Urquhart. He was looked after by the people of Shewglie and called *Gille Dubh nam Mart* (Black Lad of the Cows). Local people did not forget his origin, and they taunted him about it, so that eventually he left and went to Lochaber. Using his knowledge of Glen Urquhart, he led a band to raid Inchbrine, while the locals were at the peat moss. Returning soon after, the Glen Urquhart men followed the raiders, who had taken the old path over Coire Buidhe and Glen Coilty. They caught up with them on a small rocky plateau on the south side of the burn which flows through Coire Buidhe, since called *Carn Mharbh Dhaoine* (Rock of the Dead Men[19]). By arbitration, the raiders agreed to give up their loot, and the Glen Urquhart men began to carry it away. As they did so, a hare, later thought to have been a witch, ran between the parties, and a Glen Urquhart man shot at it. The Lochaber men thought that the shot was intended for them, and so a fight ensued. It was a sharp struggle and eventually the Glen Urquhart men, much depleted, were forced to retire. The raiders were free to take their booty, and one account says that they went back for more, first.

Many battle sites involving local clans are outside the Inverness area, such as the famous battle of *Blar-na-leine* (Field of the Shirts) between the Frasers and Clanranald of Moidart, which was fought at Kinlochlochy in 1544. Of such skirmishes, accounts survive of manoeuvres without exact locations. One such is the most interesting conflict between Simon, Lord Lovat, and some men of Atholl in the hills above Inverfarigaig in 1698, which was termed the *Day of Alltnagoire*[20].

The north end of Loch Ness was the scene of one encounter, traditionally more brutal than most. The antecedents are not clear, but about 1450 a conflict arose between Cameron of Lochiel and Hector Buie Maclean, Seneschal of Urquhart Castle. According to the Camerons, Hector was a "robber baron from the North" who had been attempting to occupy Lochaber. The Macleans claim it to have been a raid of revenge against Cameron atrocities, but Hector Maclean certainly had important prisoners in Bona Castle at Lochend, including Cameron of Glen Nevis. It is not certain who killed whom first, but it ended with Maclean displaying the dead Camerons from the battlements, and Lochiel killing two of Maclean's sons and other of his followers in view of the Castle. Ever since, Castle Bona has been known as *Caisteal Spioradain,* because of the terrible haunting by dead Macleans and Camerons[21].

Another battle of which few details survive was *Mam a' Chath* (Moor of the Battle) on the Caiplich. All accounts place it as the site of a battle between the Frasers of Lovat and the Macdonalds. The Macdonald Lords of the Isles had been attacking Lovat and this battle put an end to their incursions. The Wardlaw MS. dates it as 1464, but it is more likely to be 1429, when the Macdonalds made a raid into the North, and Lovat was Sheriff Depute of Inverness[22].

A battle in the same range of hills is marked on some maps at *Blar-nam-Feinne* (Field of the Fingalians) and sub-titled "Site of Battle fought here between Malcolm King of Scotland and Thorfinn a Norwegian Earl." There is no clue as to which King Malcolm this was, and it is more likely to have been King Macbeth. If this battle is authentic, it would be in the 11th century[23]. There are several cairns on the site, and more about a mile away.

In more recent times, local fights could blow up over more trivial affairs than wrongful occupation of lands. The Wardlaw MS. describes a "rude ryot and slaughter at a fair in Inverness called the *Cabog Day*[24]. In 1665, a big fair was being held in Inverness at the Horse Market to the south of the Castle, at the top of Culduthel Brae. A woman was selling cheese and bread, and an Inverness man, Finlay Dubh, picked up a cheese to ask the price. On being told, he let the cheese, "whether designedly or by negligence," run down the hill into the river. The woman then asked him to pay, and in the ensuing discussion, several came to the woman's side to see justice done, and Finlay's friends came to his support. Soon a riot broke out, and the guard were called in. Even this had no result, so the Provost rang the alarm and appeared himself. The people called for justice and the guard, "being opposed and abused," let off their guns. Two of the crowd were killed, both Glengarry Macdonalds, and ten were wounded, of whom two later died. The guard was clearly to blame and the Glengarry Macdonalds threatened revenge. They sued the Town Council, and the action was taken to the Privy Council, who decided that the town should pay the Macdonalds £4800 damages and any surgeon's fees. It is not stated whether the woman was ever paid the cost of her cheese.

Only a year before, Inverness had been terrified by two fires at *Culcabock*[25]. It appears that the Robertsons of Inshes had lent money to the Grants of Glenmoriston, who then found they could not repay it and had to give the estate of Culcabock to the Robertsons in exchange. The Grants, unhappy about this, in dead of night burned two corn barns at Culcabock on 4 January, 1664, and eleven more stacks on 20 March. They later kidnapped Robertson and kept him for a time in Glenmoriston. The matter was finally settled by the Judiciary in Edinburgh. In earlier times Robertson, if he could not muster support, would have been murdered by his opponents.

William Mackintosh, the Chief of Clan Chattan, was murdered in his bed in Inverness on 22 May, 1515, by a kinsman who hoped thereby to succeed to the estate. Lachlan Beg, William's brother, who did succeed, found enemies in a nephew to whom he had been particularly kind, and in his own foster-brother. They murdered Lachlan on 25 March, 1524, while hunting at Ravoch (Raigmore) in Strath Dearn, near Tomatin. They were later captured, imprisoned for 8 years in Loch-an-Eilein, and then, being found guilty, tortured, and then one was beheaded, the other hanged[26].

A murder took place in the 17th century, when recruits were needed for the Swedish wars. Many Scots volunteered, but Lord Lovat at a Court near Beauly named several extra men for the service. One, Donald Macwilliam was unwilling to go and fled up the hills of Convinth beyond Boblainy[27]. Alexander Urquhart, Lord Lovat's chief gentleman, caught up with him and Donald asked to be left alone. Urquhart laid hold of him and Donald killed him. Many searched for Donald, but eventually he was given up by Thomas Fraser of Boblainy, a friend, who tricked him and sent his head to Lovat.

There are accounts of many other murders in the district,

but they are often concerned with personal vendettas. The largest number, however, were political and under the orders of the Duke of Cumberland in 1746. One single instance will suffice to illustrate their barbarity.

Major James Lockhart, a person who had been imprisoned by the Jacobites and had bribed a guard to set him free, was in command of a troop in Glenmoriston. Seeing three men, unconnected with the Jacobites, harrowing a field, he shot the three without a word of warning. Then he ordered Grant of Dundreggan to gather together his cattle[28]. Since it was difficult to get them all at once, Lockhart stripped Dundreggan and made him witness the three bodies being hung at the gallows. Grant's own life was only spared when it was learned that, so far from being a Jacobite, he had been helpful to the Hanoverians. His cattle were, however, removed, his house burned and his wife's rings and clothes stolen.

But one death in Glenmoriston showed such courage that it outshines any other event in the district, the death of Roderick Mackenzie[29]. Even the date of his death is not known, nor who exactly he was. He served as an officer in the Jacobite forces and probably there learned of his resemblance to Prince Charles, and tradition has it that he used this on several occasions to make the Hanoverians think that the Prince was somewhere different from where he actually was. A party of Hanoverians in Glenmoriston in July, 1746, taking him for the Prince, attempted to seize him. Mackenzie made no attempt to undeceive them, but refused to be taken alive. As they shot him, he cried out, "You have killed your Prince." The delighted troops sent his head to higher authority and the exertions of the Hanoverians were slackened for a time. Roderick Mackenzie's self-sacrifice probably saved the Prince. A cairn marks the site of his death and his grave is across the road, near the river. In 1973, the Inverness Field Club placed a carved teak cross on the grave.

"From Battle, Murder, and from Sudden Death, Good Lord deliver us."

REFERENCES

1. Mackay, William, *Urquhart and Glenmoriston,* p. 20-22, 1914.
2. *Urquhart,* p. 26-7.
3. Mackay, W. (Ed.), *Chronicles of the Frasers* (Wardlaw MS.), SHR 47, pp. 314-5, 1905.
4. *Wardlaw MS.,* p. 354.
5. Grant, I. F., *In the Tracks of Montrose,* p. 212, 1931.
6. *Wardlaw MS.,* p. 334-40.
7. Forbes, Bishop, *The Lyon in Mourning,* SHR 20, p. 149-50, 1895.
8. Mackintosh, A. M. M., *The Mackintoshes and Clan Chattan,* p. 80-1, 1903. *Wardlaw MS.,* p. 85-7.
9. *Mackintoshes,* p. 72-3.
10. Mackintosh, Charles Fraser, *Antiquarian Notes,* Second Series, p. 383, 1897.
11. *Antiquarian Notes,* ii p. 383. *Mackintoshes,* p. 120.
12. *Mackintoshes,* p. 121. Mackintosh, C. Fraser, *Invernessiana,* p. 206, 1875.
13. *Mackintoshes,* p. 171.
14. *Mackintoshes,* p. 158. Innes, Cosmo (ed.), *Thanes of Cawdor,* p. 179, 1859.
15. *Wardlaw M.S.,* p. 416.
16. *Urquhart,* p. 71-2.
17. *Highland Papers* i, SHR, p. 49, 1914.
18. *Urquhart,* p. 129-31.
19. *Urquhart,* p. 221-2.
20. *Memoirs of the Life of Simon, Lord Lovat, written by himself,* p. 78-95. A graphic account of this bloodless victory for the Frasers, which is not explicit of its exact locality.
21. *Memoirs of Lochiel,* p. 19, 1842. Maclean, Charles Maxwell, *Clan Tearlach o'buidhe,* p. 44-5, 1865.
22. Macdonald, A., *Old Lords of Lovat and Beaufort,* p. 29, 1934.
23. Various accounts of Inverness describe battles to the west of the town, mostly at the end of the 12th century against Donald Ban of the Isles. Torvean and Tomnahurich are cited, but the battles appear to be fictitious.
24. *Wardlaw MS.,* p. 479-80. Barron, E. M., *Inverness and the Macdonalds,* 68-72, 1930.
25. *Urquhart,* p. 179-87. *Wardlaw MS.,* p. 453-55.
26. *Mackintoshes,* p. 104 and 114.
27. *Wardlaw MS.,* p. 256.
28. *Urquhart,* p. 295-6. *Lyon in Mourning* iii, p. 57.
29. *Urquhart,* p. 296-7. *Scots Magazine,* article by Iain Cameron Taylor July, 1967.

COMMUNICATIONS

a. Roads

LORAINE MACLEAN

Today's traffic engineers speak of Trips, meaning journeys. A Trip is said to have three essential characteristics, an Origin, a Destination and a Purpose; it has two variable characteristics, a Mode (a method of travelling, by foot, horse, bicycle, car, lorry or bus) and a Route. From the beginning this must have been true, even if the Destination could not always be named or described, nor the Route foreseen.

When our first predecessor reached the lowest crossing of the River Ness, he found it marked by the radiating tracks of the animals that used it. From that day, the tracks have widened and lengthened, but they still bring people to that crossing, and even when the new bridge over the Kessock Narrows to the Black Isle is complete, the river must still be crossed by the traffic coming north up the A82 through the Great Glen and wishing to reach Aberdeen, or the developments in Easter Ross.

In the 13th century, our A96 was foreshadowed by the *Via Regis* (the King's Road) from Aberdeen, which divided to the east of Inverness, one branch arriving at the Castle by the Eastgate, the other crossing the narrows between Ardersier and Chanonry Point. There were tracks on either side of Loch Ness, though they did not run on the present lines; where they came down to water-level there were strongholds to control the traffic at the fords. There was no great need for an A9 from Perth to Inverness until the 18th century, and its route from Inverness to Beauly varied with the position of the Stockford of Ross, the crossing of the Beauly river which is now made at Lovat Bridge, but which seems to have changed with the movement of a firm bottom to the river.

Until the early 18th century, the roads were little better than tracks, good enough for horse, cattle and foot passengers, and there was then no other traffic overland. Heavy freight was sea-borne. The roads were, technically, un-made.

When George Wade, the Irishman who was Commander-in-Chief in Scotland from 1724 to 1739, started his main road-building operations by work between Fort Augustus and Fort William, he was improving these original routes. In twelve years he had built real roads from Inverness to Fort William via the south side of Loch Ness, and from Inverness to Dunkeld over the Drumochter Pass. These were roads made up to the standard of the time, from 12-16 feet (3.5 - 5 m.) wide, excavated down to the gravel sub-soil, the surface earth thrown up on either side, and then the surface of graduated stones laid on the gravel base. These hollow roads held the snow in winter, but winter travellers were few, and no work on the road was attempted between October and May.

"Toby" Caulfeild, another Irishman, had been Wade's principal assistant and in 1732 he became Inspector of Roads. In 1734, he settled at Cradlehall, outside Inverness, and continued his road-making from there until his death in 1767. In the years between 1740 and 1767, he built roads from Poolewe to Coupar Angus, from Fort William to Dumbarton, from Dunkeld to Stirling, beside many others, but his most lasting work is perhaps the couplet,

"If you'd seen those roads before they were made,
    You'd lift up your hands and bless General Wade."

Though Wade spoke of travelling in his coach with "great ease and pleasure" in the 1730s, Lovat, in 1740, took eleven days to go from Inverness to Edinburgh, 158 miles (255 km.). in his coach, breaking his axle three times on the way. It was easier to ride, but Lovat was an old man. In 1773, Johnson and Boswell found no road fit for wheeled vehicles north of Inverness. In 1785, the Highland roads were handed over from military to civil engineers, and in 1786 a candid assessment said that the average rate of travel was 1 m.p.h.

The day of the great Scottish road-builders had come, and Thomas Telford and Joseph Mitchell spent their lives developing road communications as well as those of water and rail. J. L. Macadam (1756-1836), Surveyor General of Roads from 1827, invented the road-surfacing method that bears his name; later the graded road-material was coated with a mixture of pitch and tar before being rolled to make a more weatherproof surface — tarmacadam, or tarmac. The gradients were improved and the roads re-aligned as was thought necessary. The green line of the old road can often be seen near the present metalled surface.

In 1809, a direct coach began to run between Inverness and Perth, gradually increasing its speed from a three-day journey for the 117 miles (188 km.) until it left Inverness at 5 a.m. and reached Perth at 9 p.m. By 1811 there was a daily coach from Aberdeen. In 1819, the Commissioners for Highland Roads reported that a coach could leave Inverness at 6 a.m. and reach Thurso by noon of the next day; and by 1828, Telford said there was now no ferry between Tain and Thurso.

In 1847, according to a "Guide to the Objects of Interest" in and around Inverness, there were three Royal Mail coaches leaving the town daily, to Perth at 1.45 a.m., arriving there at 12.30 a.m., fares to Perth, inside £2. 5s., outside £1. 12s.; to Aberdeen, via Elgin and Huntly, at 2 a.m., arriving there at 7 p.m., fares to Aberdeen, inside £2, outside £1 1s.; to Tain, via Invergordon, leaving at 1.15 a.m., arriving there at 1 a.m. "in time for the Perth and Aberdeen mails," fares to Tain, inside £1, outside 14s.

As well, the *Defiance* ran daily to Aberdeen, leaving "the Caledonian and Union Hotels," as did the mail coaches, "every lawful morning, at 6 a.m.," arriving at 6 p.m., for the same price. The *Star* went daily to Elgin, the *Duke of Wellington* to Perth in the summer and autumn, and the *Marquess of Breadalbane* to Glasgow "by Fort-Augustus, Fort-William, Glencoe, Lochlomond and Dumbarton," from the beginning of June to the end of October, leaving at 8 a.m. and arriving at 5 p.m., for £2 and £1 10s. In the summer, there was an extra coach to Nairn.

According to Mitchell, in the hey-day of coaching, when from Perth to Inverness the average speed was 10-12 m.p.h., it was done in great comfort. Lord Glenlyon and some friends started a coach between Edinburgh and Aberdeen. "Their coaches were luxurious and handsome, the horses beautifully matched and of the first character, harness in good taste and of the best quality . . . Time was kept to the minute." As a result, the *North Defiance* was started "between Inverness and Aberdeen, on the same principle, and then the mail and other coaches were obliged to follow suit and travel with equal speed and punctuality." But not all journeys were so comfortable. "On the top of or inside coaches, in gigs, in carts, on horseback, on ponies and on foot . . . by night and day, I had to make my way and many a snowstorm and bitter blast and wet jacket I had to endure . . . travelling some 7000 or 8000 miles a year for about forty-five years, I never had an accident."

When Joseph Mitchell had completed the Highland Railway (then called the Inverness and Perth Railway) over Drumochter in 1863, long-distance travel by stage coach was over, but the other roads round Inverness were as busy as ever, carrying people and goods to and from the markets and rail-head, as they still do today. A century before, in 1760, there was no chaise for hire in Inverness, "nor was the common cart used in the town till the same year, when it is said that one of these vehicles was introduced by subscription!" By 1903, however, there were plenty of cabs running from the Exchange in High Street, with advertised prices. To Culduthel Wood cost 4/-; to Lunatic Asylum, Porter's Lodge, 2/-; opposite Dochgarroch House, 4/-; to Tomnahurich gates, 1/-, but to the top, 1/6. Fares could also be arranged by distance, one mile or under, 1/-; 6d for every additional half-mile, or part thereof; or else by time, "Making Calls, Shopping, etc. — 1s for first half hour and 6d for every additional quarter," but "For an airing into the country — 3s for first hour and 2s 6d for each succeeding hour." "From midnight till 5 a.m., Double Fare. From 5 till 8 a.m., Fare and a half."

Up to the Second World War, Market Days in Inverness, as elsewhere, filled the narrow streets with herds of cattle and flocks of sheep on their way to and from the auction ring, but the days of the drove roads to the markets of the south had long passed and, with them, a way of life. These wide roads along which moved the great herds of cattle tended to avoid the towns as far as possible, but instead to go up the glens where there was water and grazings and soft going for the beasts.

Today the main roads round Inverness are largely wide enough not to need passing-places, but there are still many single-track roads up the glens, and some main roads, even of A-category, have passing-places. Not everyone that uses these, despite the notices put up to inform them, realises that the passing places are to allow vehicles to overtake as well as to meet, and this can cause much annoyance when urgent traffic, such as a doctor's car or an ambulance, is needlessly delayed.

Even now, more passenger-journeys are made and passenger-miles covered in the Highlands by bus than by any other means of public transport, and the buses also carry mail, newspapers and other necessities. The Post Office has recently started a service of carrying passengers and small freight, as well as mail, where buses do not go.

The discovery of oil in the North Sea has given a great impetus to road improvements in Inverness and the district round. New houses, such as the proposed new town of 16-20,000 people between Balloch and the present A9, will need roads. Most people can only see the heavy loads necessary for the increasing industry arriving by road, though many are now beginning to think that much could be carried by water or rail.

Speaking to the Ancient Monuments Society in 1969, Thomas Sharp, C.B.E., D. Litt., F.R.I.B.A., M.T.P.I., said, "Years ago we planners used to think in terms of planning our towns to meet the needs of traffic. Such town planning would be madness now; we must plan and control the traffic to meet the needs of the town." The people of Inverness are looking to the completion of the Kessock Bridge as a means of ensuring that the blocking of streets by over-sized lorries, trucks, caravans, cars, motor-cycles and pedestrians can become a memory. Perhaps they are setting their hopes too high. The A9 is being altered yet again, at a cost overall from Perth of £60 million, to make it safer and to line it up with the approach roads to the bridge. That the Raigmore Stone Circle, some 5000 years old and built over still more ancient hut sites, has been destroyed before a complete excavation could take place, is part of the price that seemingly must be paid.

Some of the latest thinking on the proposed new line of the A9, helped by aerial surveys and the use of computers, is turning towards the line of the old military road, surveyed on foot or on horseback by Wade; a road that was a silent witness of the Rout of Moy in 1746. Even in those days, no compensation was paid to the landowners through whose property the road was to pass, for it was considered to be an improvement. Some agreed, but some, no doubt, said as bitterly as a farmer did not so long ago of a proposed line, "Of course 'they' would not put the road *there,* it is not good farming land!" Wade and Caulfeild would be amazed if they could see the machinery that has replaced their 300-500 troops and wheelbarrows, at 6d a day extra pay for privates and 2/6 for ensigns. When the War Office stopped this allowancet for officers, much resentment was caused, as can be read in the correspondence of Major James Wolfe, the future conqueror of Quebec. The sort of road that should be built to carry today's traffic would be beyond their dreams — a dual carriage-way that would allow fast traffic to get past the slower lorries, caravans and those wishing to travel slowly to enjoy their journey and the view through their windscreens. Perhaps the traffic on their roads would be to them a nightmare.

But, writing when the top speed is limited to 50 m.p.h., when every car has been issued with a petrol-ration book, when the cost of petrol may go to £1 a gallon, it seems possible that soon the traffic will be reduced to a mere shadow of what it has been. Travellers may yet turn again to public transport and to bicycles, they may walk once more along the old green ways and drove roads that still lead into and out of the hills.

"Twa hunner an' forty year lang syne,
Cam sodgers' brig an' highway.
Noo, tarry roads dae commerce fine,
Yet I'll haud Wade's for my way.
For when we're young an' faring' furth
We'll ken the tumult cease —
Whaur deer an' whaup hae mind for us,
An' Heilan' folk aye kind for us,
Then we'll tak' heart an' find for us
Auld drovers' ways o' peace."

I.B.C.T.

BIBLIOGRAPHY

Johnson, Samuel, *A Journey to the Western Islands of Scotland*, 1775.
Mogg, Edward (Ed.), *Paterson's Roads*, in which no road is given north of Edinburgh.
Douglas, Smith and Fraser, *History of Inverness, and Guide to the Objects of Interest in its Neighbourhood*, Inverness, 1847.
Mitchell, Joseph, *Reminiscences of my Life in the Highlands*, London, 1884. Republished by David and Charles, 1970 and 1971.
Mackenzie, Alexander, *Guide to Inverness, Nairn and the Highlands*, Melven Bros., Inverness, 1903.
Salmond, J. B., *Wade in Scotland*, Edinburgh, 1938.
Haldane, A. R. B., *The Drove Roads of Scotland*, Nelson, 1952.
Haldane, A. R. B., *New Ways through the Glens*, Nelson, 1962.
Taylor, Iain Cameron, *Highland Communications*, An Comunn Gaidhealach, 1969.
Transport. Occasional Bulletin No. 4. Highlands and Islands Development Board Publication, 1973.

COMMUNICATIONS

b. Bridges

Dr JAMES BRUCE

When General Wade began the construction of his military roads in Scotland in the first half of the 18th century, stone bridges in the Highlands were few, and the traveller whose progress was barred by a river of any size had to make a detour to a convenient ford. Wade was responsible for the building of some 40 bridges, and his successors added appreciably to this number. Later, in the 19th century, Thomas Telford built scores, of which a large proportion survive to carry traffic of a nature never foreseen by their designer. Many of these old bridges, situated in places of great natural beauty, have a grace and simplicity which are a source of pleasure to the traveller, but the ravages of time, neglect and modern vandalism have resulted in once soundly-constructed works becoming ruinous and decayed. Some have already vanished without trace. These notes have been written in the hope that, by directing attention to those which still remain, interest will be aroused, and that the public will make its voice heard when inevitable modern developments threaten their preservation and survival.

The list which follows does not pretend to name all the old military and Parliamentary bridges in the Inverness and Great Glen area, but it is an attempt to indicate some which may appeal to those who find satisfaction in the contemplation of the stone arch over a stream. They are listed roughly in the order in which the traveller would meet them in the course of journeys along the old military or later Parliamentary roads. Neither age nor builder plays any part in the arrangement. Occasional diversions from the main route will be necessary to visit an example off the beaten track. The area is roughly that of the Inverness District covered by this book, but some excursions into neighbouring counties will be made.

Faillie Bridge (712380), a well-preserved single-arched specimen, crosses the River Nairn near the site of a vanished Wade bridge. Half a mile (804 m.) south, at *Scatraig* (712373), a simple Wade bridge, now very far gone, carried the military road to Moy over the Mid-Lairgs burn. The same stream is crossed by another Wade bridge of a similar pattern a mile (1609 m.) upstream (715361). Afforestation now surrounds it and will soon hide it completely. There is no parapet and the deck has been cemented.

At the ruins of *Ortunan* (843238), there is a little-known crumbling bridge, almost certainly by Wade. *Insharn* (843223) has a single-arched specimen in fair condition. Nearby, where the grass-covered track of Mitchell's 19th century road runs down from the bridge over the railway at Slochd Cottages to meet the burn, are the mouldering remains of an old stone bridge (843242), whose existence is largely unknown despite its proximity to the A9 trunk road. The arch has partially collapsed and those parts which still stand are dangerously unstable. On the other side the track climbs to meet Wade's road, crossing on the way a small tributary by a simple arch similar to those of Wade design (842243).

Sluggan Bridge (870220) is a handsome arch on the line of Wade's road, replacing the original Wade bridge, long since swept away. It is now much decayed, and there is little prospect of restoration work being undertaken, despite its classification as an Ancient Monument. The pack-horse bridge at *Carrbridge* (906229) is a well-known tourist landmark.

A small stream, un-named on the 1" O.S. map, flows eastwards near Avielochan dairy, three miles north of Aviemore. At this point the military road lies east of the present A9, immediately behind the farm buildings. By following the track southwards through a birchwood, the stream is reached where it is crossed by a small Wade bridge, becoming ruinous, but with the arch still intact (903164).

Feshie Bridge (852044), near Kincraig, carries the B970 over the River Feshie at a popular picnic site. About six miles (9.5 km.) south-west, *Tromie Bridge* (789996) competes with it both in the beauty of its situation and the appeal of its architecture.

Drochaid Balbh Bhordain (722959) is a Wade bridge known only to those who explore the secret places, on the line of the military road between Kingussie and Etteridge. It is a simple one-arched example. Dr D. J. Macdonald's translation of its name is "The Bridge of the Silent Flood Gate." This bridge is not shown on the 1" O.S. map.

Close to the *Falls of Truim*, in picturesque surroundings, the river is crossed by a stone bridge (680924) which is a well-preserved specimen of Wade's. It is best seen when the surrounding trees are in their autumn colours. A bare mile (1.5 km.) south are the remains of *Crubenmore Bridge* (677913).

This is now dangerous, part of one arch having collapsed.

Dalwhinnie has a fine example at *Wade Bridge* (639828), two miles south of the railway station. This grass-covered two-arched bridge has no parapet. Weather and time have combined to loosen some of the stonework. Lying, as it does, close to the present A9, where road alterations are taking place, this Ancient Monument is worthy of preservation.

On the military road from Dalwhinnie to Fort Augustus, over the Corrieyairack Pass, a few of Wade's bridges remain, but those on the stretch from Glen Truim to Drumgask have been so restored that they should perhaps be regarded as 19th century products. Near Dalcholly House, the River Mashie is crossed by a simple bridge (600937), which has the appearance of a restored Wade specimen.

Garva Bridge (522948), also known as St George's Bridge, by which Prince Charles Edward crossed the Spey in 1745, is one of Wade's better-known works. It lies on the route used by drovers in the early 19th century. Between Garva Bridge and the summit of the pass there are several single-arched Wade bridges, all more or less decayed. That at *Melgarve,* on a loop a few yards to the north of the present track (469961), presents an attractive aspect viewed from the south, but closer inspection reveals a gaping hole in the deck and large gaps in the north parapet. It is by-passed by a recent wooden erection. The original bridge built by Wade over a tributary of the River Tarff has long been replaced by an iron one.

Between Inverness and Fort Augustus, the first Wade bridge met is that at *Inverfarigaig,* on Wade's 1732 road (B852). It lies close to the modern replacement, but is so overshadowed by it as to be almost unnoticed (523238). It can be viewed from a spot a short distance up the steep zig-zag road which rises from the loch side, or inspected from close quarters by climbing down the bank from the modern bridge.

Whitebridge (489154) has a beautiful single-arched Wade bridge, much admired by tourists, but sadly in need of repair. The best view is obtained by walking a few hundred yards upstream. This bridge was badly damaged by floods in the 19th century, but was restored to its present form.

Some three miles (4.8 km.) from Fort Augustus, there is a ruinous Wade bridge over the River Doe (406089), where the track of the old road diverges briefly from the A862.

The track of Wade's road from Fort Augustus to Fort William leaves the present highway at the north end of Loch Oich and immediately crosses the Calder Burn to run along the south-east bank of the loch. Of the original Aberchalder bridge nothing remains except the abutments, the stone arch having been replaced by a wooden erection. The modern *Bridge of Oich* (338035) is seen to the best advantage from the point where Wade's road, which runs parallel to and close to the track of the old railway, reaches the loch side. There are one or two very small bridges, little more than culverts, on the south-east side of Loch Oich, probably original Wade structures, which pass almost unnoticed.

Wade's bridge in Glen Gloy, *Nine Mile Bridge* or *Low Bridge* (224864) carries the old road over the River Gloy close to the modern highway, but lies hidden. Still in use by farm traffic, it has been repaired with more regard for utility than artistry. The name Low Bridge distinguishes it from the better-known *High Bridge* (201822) over the River Spean. Now a dangerous ruin, difficult of access, this is most conveniently viewed by following the track of Wade's road downhill from the Lochaber Historical Society's notice-board for about 200 yards (183 m.) until a gap is seen through the trees on the right. This leads to the water's edge, from whence the best view is obtained at a point where an upright rock, vertically striated, stands close to the bank. The ground drops steeply to the river and great care is required. After heavy rain, the approach should be shunned.

Turret Bridge (338918) is a simple one-arched bridge, to see which entails a journey to near the head of Glen Roy. If the bridge disappoints, the journey will not.

At Invermoriston (419167) are the crumbling remains of Telford's bridge. Further upstream, *Torgyle Bridge* (309129), built 1808-11, still carries the 20th century's traffic, but his bridge at *Ceannacroc* (227107) has been superseded by a modern one more suited to today's needs. The original one, despite the loss of coping stones, still looks sound.

On the military road, now a mere track, between Achlain in Glenmoriston and Fort Augustus, a couple of interesting single-arched old bridges survive. These, although of the post-Wade area, are similar in design to the General's. That at 349102 is at a convenient resting place from which to look across Inchnacardoch Forest to the east.

Within the area covered by this article, the post-Wade military road from Fort George to Grantown has several bridges worthy of mention. At *Clephanton* (824503) an attractive hump-backed bridge crosses the River Nairn. A simple one at *Highland Boath* (898447) is probably a 19th century restoration. *Dulsie Bridge* (932415) is a superb example in a striking setting. This bridge came through the famous Morayshire floods of the early 19th century unscathed. South-east of Dulsie Bridge, the remains of a post-Wade bridge still stand near B9007 at 944402, its former service now taken over by a modern, but unappealing, replacement.

The Nairn valley has several old bridges in addition to Whitebridge and Clephanton. *Cantray Bridge* (800480), *Holme Rose* (815488) and *Tordarroch Bridge* (675336) are all of interest, the last-named being a particularly good example of a 19th century hump-backed bridge of a type fast disappearing. Beyond the headwater of the Nairn, the B815 crosses the River Farigaig by an attractive arch at *Dunmaglass* (607245).

Lovat Bridge (516450), over the River Beauly, was built by Telford in 1811. It was severely damaged by floods some years later and was restored with alterations. It remains, however, as a noble example of the bridge-builder's art, and although it will soon become redundant, it is surely worth preserving. Its fate is at present undecided by the authorities. A fine view can be had from 100 yards (91.5 m.) upstream, on the left bank.

In the neighbouring county of Ross and Cromarty, Telford's *Contin Bridge* (455567) still carries the main road over the Blackwater. Farther north-west, at *Little Garve* (397628), still stands one of the most beautiful of the old bridges, carrying the old military road over the Blackwater. Seen from a short distance downstream, it is a subject worthy of an artist's brush. It is a sad reflection on today's sense of values that no funds are available for its preservation, and it is already showing signs of deterioration which, if not arrested soon, will inevitably result in its loss.

Is it too much to hope that in this age of materialism some means will be found of preserving for posterity such examples of beauty combined with engineering skill as still remain to us, and of which we are but the temporary trustees?

COMMUNICATIONS

c. Railways

JOHN AIRD

On the subject of railway communications in the Highlands, volumes could be written. The social and economic conditions existing here in the middle decades of last century contrived to make the story of communications, and, in particular rail communications, in the Highlands of absorbing interest. In the confines of this article, however, it is necessary to restrict our account to what happened in Inverness itself and its immediate environs.

In the decade following 1840, all the principal railway routes connecting Edinburgh and Glasgow with the South had come to be built. Further north, the railway was opened in stages from these two cities to Perth, which was reached in 1848, and to Aberdeen in 1850.

As early as 1840, considerations had been given to the idea of linking Inverness with the south by rail, but nothing happened until 1845, when the Great North of Scotland Railway, based on Aberdeen, was incorporated for the purpose of building a railway from Aberdeen to Inverness. The proposed route would serve the towns of Huntly, Keith, Elgin, Forres and Nairn, and would, of course, traverse a relatively well-populated countryside. This was a circuitous route, but it had the advantage of not having to cross any mountain barrier, with its attendant steep gradients for the ability of locomotive hauled trains to ascend steep inclines was a matter about which the railway engineers of the time had relatively little knowledge. The Great North scheme would thus have provided a through route to the south, and almost immediately a rival scheme was promoted. This was to provide a route from Aberdeen to Inverness also, but by a different route, serving Ellon, Turriff and Banff, thence along the coast to Elgin. A separate, but associated company called the Inverness and Elgin Junction was to link this route with a line to Inverness.

In Inverness itself, however, neither of these schemes was greeted with any enthusiasm, principally because of the apparently unnecessarily long detour by way of Aberdeen. There

arose a strong desire to promote a more direct route to the
south, which would have the effect of reducing the distance
to Perth by over 50 miles, and in 1845 a group of influential
persons from Inverness and District, including prominent landowners, headed by a civil engineer called Joseph Mitchell, got
together to consider what could be done to achieve their object.
Mitchell produced a scheme which was a bold one for those
early days.

His route was to leave Inverness and Elgin Junction at
Nairn, whence it would proceed southwards via Glenferness
and the valley of the River Dulnain to Carrbridge, where it
would enter Strathspey. It would then follow the valley of the
Spey to Newtonmore, climb through the pass of Druimuchdar,
and then descend by way of the valleys of the Rivers Garry
and Tay to a junction with the line between Perth and Forfar.

There were two serious drawbacks to this scheme; first
of all, there was the question of the gradients which would
be involved in taking the railway over a 1320 foot summit at
Glenferness and one of almost 1500 feet at Druimuchdar. The
second was, that the proposed route would pass through a
comparatively desolate and sparsely populated countryside, from
which the railway could expect little revenue. A Bill for the
promotion of this railway was submitted to Parliament, but
there was much opposition and it was defeated. Mitchell's bold
scheme was before its time, but he was not a man to be
despondent about such a set-back, as we shall presently see.

In the meantime, however, a modest start was being made
to railway communications in the Highlands. The Inverness
and Nairn Railway Company was incorporated under powers
obtained under an Act of 1854 to link the two towns. This
was a railway which had peculiar difficulties in construction,
because it was completely isolated from the rest of the Scottish
railway system, and all plant and equipment had to be brought
by sea, which caused certain delays. Despite this, the line was
opened with due ceremony on 5 November, 1855. No time
was lost in extending the line eastwards.

A new company called the Inverness and Aberdeen Junction
was formed, and was authorised to continue the line from Nairn
to Keith, where a junction was to be made with the Great
North of Scotland Railway. The Inverness and Aberdeen
Junction Railway took over the Inverness and Nairn Railway
in 1861 and, because of financial difficulty, the Great North
abandoned their plan for continuing their line from Keith to
Inverness — at least in the meantime.

But the demand for a shorter route from Inverness to the

south revived in the late 1850s. Railway engineering and locomotive design had advanced sufficiently in little over a decade
to make it appear much more feasible to construct a railway
through the Grampians.

A new company, with the title of the Inverness and Perth
Junction Railway was proposed. Its route was to leave the
Inverness and Aberdeen Junction Railway at Forres and proceed southwards, climbing to a summit on Dava Moor, thence
descending to Grantown and the valley of the Spey. It was
then to run through Kingussie and over Druimuchdar Pass,
very much on the same route as the line already proposed
in 1845. At Dunkeld it was to form an end-on junction with
the Perth and Dunkeld Railway, which was already in existence.

Opposition to the Bill for the new line was strenuous, but
this time it was unsuccessful, and Parliamentary consent for
the line was duly passed. Work proceeded, with Joseph Mitchell
as engineer, and the line was opened throughout from Forres
to Perth on 9 September, 1863. The advantages of the new
line were obvious — travelling times were considerably reduced,
and there was a corresponding reduction in fares. On 1
February, 1865, the Aberdeen and Inverness Junction and the
Inverness and Perth Junction Railways were amalgamated to
form the Highland Railway, with its headquarters at Inverness.

There were, however, other influential bodies, none of
them based in the Highlands, who were interested in promoting
railways to Inverness. There was evidently a belief (subsequently
found to be erroneous) that there was a lucrative business to
be shared with the Highland Railway by any other company
which succeeded in reaching the Highland Capital. We have
already mentioned the Great North, which had nevertheless
succeeded in getting no nearer to Inverness than Keith. But
this was not for the lack of trying, and until the end of the
century the Great North attempted by various means to obtain
powers to run its own trains to Inverness, either over the metals
of the Highland Railway, or by its own route. The other proposed line to Inverness came from a totally different quarter.

In 1883, a new Company, nominally independent but backed
by the North British Railway, was formed. It was called the
Glasgow and North Western Railway, and its intention was
to build a railway from Glasgow via the east side of Loch
Lomond to Crianlarich, across Rannoch Moor, through the
Pass of Glencoe and across Loch Leven and thence to Fort
William, with an extension to Inverness. The distance by this
route from Glasgow to Inverness would have been approximately 160 miles, as opposed to 207 miles by the existing route

via Perth. The Parliamentary Bill for the Glasgow and North Western line was vigorously opposed by the Highland, who justifiably saw it as a threat to its livelihood. It succeeded in convincing Parliament that there was insufficient traffic to justify more than one railway from the south to Inverness, and the Bill was rejected. No sooner had this crisis been passed, however, than the threat was renewed from a slightly different quarter.

Authority was obtained for the construction of the West Highland Railway, from Glasgow to Fort William. The route was to be similar to that of the Glasgow and North Western scheme of a few years earlier at its southern end, but at the northern extremity it was to cross Rannoch Moor in a more northerly direction and reach Fort William from the north-east, using the valley of the Spean. The Highland, seeing the possibility of a threat to it in a different form, had opposed the West Highland's Bill, but in this it was unsuccessful and the West Highland route to Fort William was opened in 1894. But at Spean Bridge, the West Highland Railway was only 55 miles from Inverness, and the Highland Railway realised that this could be a great temptation to the North British Railway, which really controlled the West Highland.

In 1895, the West Highland and North British Railways sought powers for the extension of their line from Fort William to Mallaig. This was, not unexpectedly, opposed by the Highland Railway, on the ground that it would abstract traffic from their existing terminus at Strome Ferry and ultimately their extension to Kyle of Lochalsh, work on which had already started. The Highland was, however, persuaded to withdraw its objection, and the Bill for the Mallaig extension was passed. As a consideration, the West Highland and North British companies undertook not to promote, or assist in promoting, any railways through the Great Glen for at least ten years.

A few months later, a local Company, under the name of the Invergarry and Fort Augustus Railway, was incorporated for the purpose of building a railway from Spean Bridge on the West Highland Railway to Fort Augustus. A large proportion of the capital required for this undertaking was contributed by the then Lord Burton. Despite the expected strong opposition, this Company obtained Parliamentary sanction to proceed, and its Act was passed in August, 1896. The result of all this was that the North British and West Highland companies now regarded themselves as released from their undertakings of the previous year, because in the following year,

1897, no less than three schemes were promoted for the completion of the link between Fort Augustus and Inverness.

The first was by the Invergarry Company itself, and the other two were by the North British and Highland Companies respectively. The North British scheme could be regarded as predatory, while the Highland's Bill was a blocking move designed to keep the North British out of the Great Glen. After a fierce Parliamentary contest and a lot of costly litigation, all the Bills were thrown out. And so the Invergarry and Fort Augustus Railway was left to look after itself. The line was opened in 1903, but it was soon found that the cost of heavy engineering works had exhausted its finances and there was no money left to buy locomotives or rolling stock.

First the Highland Railway was induced to work the line, but it was not a paying proposition, and that Company withdrew after a few years. The North British then took over the running of the line, but nothing prospered. In 1914, the North British purchased the Invergarry Company outright, paying less than one-tenth of its original cost, and assisted by a grant of £4,000 from Inverness County Council! So the hopes of the promoters of this little line were never realised, and what might have in other circumstances have formed part of an important through route, became no more than an uneconomic branch line.

But all these activities in the Great Glen obliged the Highland Railway to think about a more direct route between Inverness and Aviemore, especially as a further threat was developing in the east. A company called the Strathspey, Strathdon and Deeside Junction Railway proposed to built a route from Ballater to Nethybridge via Cockbridge and Tomintoul. This grandiose scheme was backed by the Great North of Scotland Company, which had itself applied for powers to extend this line to Inverness via Carrbridge. The Highland therefore decided that it must take steps to shorten its route to Inverness, so it applied for the necessary powers. These were granted in July, 1884, and the two schemes supported by the Great North were thrown out.

The Highland Railway, having obtained the powers for the new line, was not in any great hurry to use them, and construction proceeded slowly. The line was only opened to Carrbridge in July, 1892, and it was not until November, 1898 that it was completed to Inverness. The route is steeply graded, and there are a number of impressive engineering works, including the viaducts at Slochd and Tomatin, and the impressive one at Culloden over the River Nairn. The engineer was

Murdoch Paterson. After the opening of the route much of
the main line traffic was transferred to it, although through
services to the south were still maintained over the older route
via Forres and Grantown. The principal rail network from
the south was now complete, and it is to the north of Inverness
that we now turn.

At first the promoters of a railway from Inverness to
Dingwall, headed by Sir Alexander Matheson of Ardross, had
been deterred from going ahead by the existence of several
water barriers, which would entail the construction of costly
bridges. Before even leaving the Burgh of Inverness, a substantial bridge would be necessary to span the River Ness and
a swing bridge over the Caledonian Canal would be required
at Clachnaharry. Between there and Dingwall, the Rivers Beauly
and Conon had to be crossed. Nevertheless, the ceremony of
cutting the first sod of the line took place on 19 September,
1860, and the railway, known as the Inverness and Ross-shire,
opened its line to Dingwall in June, 1862.

The existing station at Inverness was extended to include
additional platforms for the Ross-shire trains. The railways to
the North and to the South diverged immediately on leaving
the station, and connecting them to form the third side of a
triangle was a line forming part of the Harbour branch, and
later known as the Rose Street curve. This lay-out has remained
basically unaltered to this day. It may be of interest to note
that, although the Dingwall railway was originally a single
line, the section between Clachnaharry and Clunes was doubled
during the years before the First World War. There was also
a station at Clachnaharry, but this was closed in 1913.

Brief reference should now be made to the branch lines
in the Inverness area. There were relatively few of these and
many years were to elapse before even the first of them was
to open. In July, 1890, powers were obtained for the construction of a branch line from Muir of Ord to Rosemarkie,
primarily to provide more rapid transit facilities for the fish
traffic from Fortrose and Avoch. The line was opened as
far as Fortrose on 1 February, 1894, but work on the extension
to Rosemarkie was never started. On the opposite side of the
firth, on the line between Inverness and Nairn, there was a
station built to serve the garrison at Fort George and was so
named, although the Fort was some 3½ miles distant. It was
considered desirable to provide the Fort with better rail communications and the necessary powers were obtained to construct a branch line to Ardersier, and when the line was opened
on 1 July, 1899, the juction station was re-named Gollanfield

and the name of Fort George was given to the terminus at Ardersier.

There were two other railway propects which never came to anything, although one of them was actually started. This latter was a scheme for a railway to connect the town of Cromarty with the Inverness to Dingwall railway at Conon. The line was authorised in 1902, and because of difficulties relating to the acquisition of land, construction started from the Cromarty end. Work proceeded very slowly, and by 1914 only six miles of track had been laid. With the outbreak of war in August of that year, all work was suspended, and some time later the track which had been laid was lifted. Work was not resumed after the war, and the project was abandoned. The other scheme, in 1897, was for a railway from Inverness to Lochend on Loch Ness, which, it was hoped, would help to improve communications between Inverness, Fort Augustus and Fort William. Unfortunately, no proper arrangements had been made with the Highland Railway for access to Inverness station, and for the working of the line by that Company, and when Parliamentary powers were sought, the Invergarry and Fort Augustus Railway objected on the grounds that if the proposed line were authorised, it would effectively block the completion of its line to Inverness! The Invergarry Company's objections were sustained and the matter proceeded no further.

Such then is a brief outline of the growth of railway communications in the Inverness district. All the principal lines remain open, save that from Forres to Aviemore via Grantown, which was closed in 1965, and, if the number of passengers carried has declined in recent years, industrial developments in the area have helped to generate new freight traffic. Unhappily, the Fort George and the Fortrose branches have suffered the fate of many branch lines, and were closed completely in 1958 and 1960 respectively, largely due to the effect of competition from the bus and private car.

BIBLIOGRAPHY

Vallance, H. A., *The Highland Railway*, David and Charles, 1963.
Nock, O. S., *The Highland Railway*, Tom Allan, 1965.
The Highland Railway Company, Stephenson Locomotive Society, 1954.
Ellis, C. Hamilton, *British Railway History*, Allen and Unwin, vol I, 1954, vol II, 1959.

COMMUNICATIONS

d. Water

A. D. CAMERON.

The mountains divide people, the seas unite them and, until the early 19th century at least, the easiest and cheapest means of communication was by sea. The most flourishing royal burghs in the Middle Ages tended to be on the coast, on the edge of the land, certainly, but also on the edge of the sea. The connection was close between ports like Leith, Aberdeen and Inverness on the western fringe of the North Sea and ports across it in Europe. In fact, a port such as Inverness had more regular contact with Danzig on the Baltic than it had, say, with Glasgow.

Writers on the creation of royal burghs rightly stress the protection afforded by their proximity to royal castles which were built to control the main lines of communication. Professor Dickinson notes in Inverness, among other burghs, "the main street running direct to the castle, that is, to the centre which the burgh first served[1]." Here in Inverness, an outpost of royal power, it was just as important to see where the main street (Church Street) was running from. It ran from the harbour, on which the town and castle depended for supplies coming in from the south by sea.

Situated about seven miles south-west of the converging arms of land at Chanonry Point and Fort George, which almost turn the Inverness Firth into an inland sea, Inverness offers safe anchorage and shelter to vessels against the worst of the weather. The port itself is never closed.

Inverness Harbour

In earlier days, ships came farther up river to the old pier (between where the Waterloo Bridge and the Railway Viaduct now stand). Said to have been built in 1675, it was probably re-built or better built then, as it is hard to imagine a port with Inverness' amount of trade with no pier facilities at all. John Slezer's *Prospect of Inverness*[2] (1693) shows three ships in the old harbour and he comments, "It hath a harbour fit for smaller vessels." Farther upstream, in his picture, several boats lie beached on the Maggot. An interesting illustration in Edmund Burt's *Letters from a Gentleman in the North of Scotland* (1754) shows women wading in the water at about this point and carrying their menfolk on their backs to their boats. In John Home's *Plan of Inverness*[3], produced in 1774, the sites are marked of this old pier and the new harbour built between 1725 and 1732, which cost £2750 and was paid for by a levy on all the ale brewed or sold in the town. This harbour, although later called the New or Citadel Quay, was at right angles to the river outside the southern defensive mound of "Cromwell's Fort." Having spent this sum on harbour works which were never completed, the Town Council decided to spend no more and the harbour

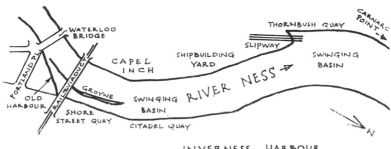

INVERNESS   HARBOUR

seems to have survived the next sixty years on an expediture on repairs of less than £100. This was a period of inflow of harbour dues to the Common Good, to be used in any way the Council saw fit, of minimal expenditure and, inevitably, of the decay of the harbour.

Surprisingly, trade did not decline. The value of harbour dues more than doubled between 1800 and 1807, almost certainly because of the dramatic build-up of materials for the construction of the Caledonian Canal which began in 1803. Stimulated by this increase in traffic, but probably far more by the fear that trading vessels would desert the harbour for new facilities being provided at Muirtown Basin on the Canal, the Town Council undertook harbour improvements, first repairing Citadel Quay and then, between 1813 and 1817, building Thornbush Quay, capable of taking vessels of 250 tons, on the west side of the river. In spite of these improvements, the Town Council's fears of Canal competition were justified and they complained to the Canal Commissioners in 1826, "In the last eight years [the shore dues of the port of Inverness] have diminished, though the trade and population of the Burgh have increased considerably."

In 1847, the year when the £150,000 reconstruction of the Caledonian Canal was completed, the Town Council again decided that competition could only be met by modernisation and considerable expenditure. Control of the harbour was transferred to Inverness Harbour Trust, consisting of seven councillors, five merchants and five ship-owners. The Trustees had the right to borrow money and all the income from harbour dues was at their disposal, to be used for harbour purposes only. Their scheme of modernisation in the 1850s, under the guidance of Joseph Mitchell as harbour engineer, gave the harbour its present shape. The river was made easier to enter by intensive dredging until a depth of 21 feet (6.5 m.) was achieved and a minimum bottom width of 120 feet (36.5 m.). The dredged sand and gravel was dumped on land to build up embankments to define the west side of the harbour and protect the low-lying Capel Inch from floods. Thornbush Quay was extended and another embankment was formed to carry a towpath out to Carnarc Point to help sailing ships into and out of the harbour. In his *Port of Inverness*[4], Joseph Cook describes this scene.

"Imagine the sun high in the heavens, a full spring tide, the sails of the old windmill on the Ferry Road are almost motionless, there is a brig just entering the river mouth . . . The crew run a rope ashore to Carnarc Point, where await three horses to take her in tow, they hitch on and begin their long pull up the river. It is a slow job, but it is the horses' daily task, and they move along with a rhythm . . . they move over Thornbush Quay, and at length reach the tow path on the Capel Inch. As the ship bends into the channel she gets further away from the tow path, and more rope is played out. Slowly but surely the horses reach the old Customs House, and the ship is almost abreast of the old quay, a shout comes across the water, 'Let go,' the tow rope is hauled in and the ship soon moored in her berth[4]."

After modernisation, the harbour became a busy place until keen competition came from the railway which first captured the passenger traffic and then the freight. Fewer steamers called at the port. Further improvements to Shore Street quay in the 1880s allowed big coal-carrying vessels to use it and, aided by lower freight charges of 3/- to 3/6 per ton, compared with 6/8 charged by the railway, the harbour became the centre of the coal trade, importing and distributing no less than 46,700 tons in 1909.

On the east side of the river, the harbour was scoured out, Citadel Quay was repaired and a groyne was constructed to form a safe sheltered harbour. The Shore Street Quay was built at the expense of the Railway Company, whose railway bridge cut off the old harbour from the Citadel Quay[5].

Ship-building

It should not be considered surprising that the Count of St Pol in Flanders, needing a ship to take him on a Crusade in 1249, should choose to have it built in Inverness. The port was easily accessible across the North Sea and well placed to become a centre for the building of ships. The burgh embraced both sides of the river and, with ample supplies of timber growing on the low land upstream, the most economical way of transporting it was to float the logs down the river. Timber-floating continued on Highland rivers into the 19th century and George Burn, the builder of Lovat Bridge, found himself at the receiving end of it before 1813. Four times he had a service bridge smashed by single logs swept against it — an interesting and frustrating example of transportation by water interfering with the construction of a new means of communication across water. As long as ship were made of wood, ship-building was an important local industry, carried on in yards on both sides of the river until the 1870s. Farthest upstream on the Merkinch side, beside the railway bridge, was Munro's ship-building yard; near the Thornbush slipway was Macgregor's, where the last schooner to be built was the *Sovereign* in 1878; on the Shore Street side, John Cook's yard occupied the site of the present sawmills and there were two substantial yards within "Cromwell's Fort." With ship-building went sail-making and rope-making. The cloth was woven in two factories, Grant's in the Fort and Anderson's Thornbush Hemp Manufactory near the Quay. Sail-makers worked in Shore Street and the old Tannery building. Rope-making took place in Rose Street and also beside the Canal. According to the *New Statistical Account,* four hundred to six hundred tons of hemp and three or four cargoes of timber and tar a year were imported to Inverness, mainly for these industries. In Merkinch and the Shore Street area lived a community connected with ships and the sea — ships' carpenters, blacksmiths, sail- and rope-makers, and sailors.

Trade

Successive charters in the Middle Ages granted or confirmed to Inverness the monopoly of trade for the whole land area to the north and west, reserving to its merchants the right to buy or sell timber, skins, hides, fish, wool or cloth. Nearly 5,000 hides are said to have exported from Inverness in 1406, as her contribution to Scotland's customary exports of hides, furs and fish. In the first half of the 18th century, Bailie John Steuart, as his *Letter-Book*[6] shows, was a prominent local merchant, with wide connections in Europe. To Danzig, Rotterdam, Le Havre, Bordeaux, Lisbon, Barcelona and Leghorn, as well as to England and the Western Highlands sailed the dozen little ships in which he had an interest. Chiefly they carried skins, salted cod and herrings to the Baltic and Holland, and salmon and herrings to France and the Mediterranean. In 1720 the barque *Marjorie* carried lamb, fox and otter skins to Danzig and returned with a variety of goods, tarred rope, flax, linen, iron, glass and soap.

With ships of such small capacity, about fifty tons, it was essential for a merchant to prevent his ships ever sailing without a cargo. Sending the *Margaret* to Gairloch for salmon in 1722, he supplied sixty salmon barrels filled with oatmeal and requested, "Let your meal be emptied out of the barrels without loss of time, that the salmon may be packed." The *Margaret* also carried salt in barrels, which were to be filled with 25,000 cod. The salmon were sold at Le Havre, the ship re-loaded with Burgundy, brandy and claret and, calling in at London on its return, collected, among other things, half a hundredweight of sugar, a tin watering can, two garden spades and a dozen prayer books. Salt, a necessity in the fish trade, was imported from Hamburg, Rotterdam and Lisbon, luxuries like spices, tea and sugar came from Holland, and raisins, lemons, coffee and olive oil from Leghorn in Italy — all by sea.

Salmon were exported to the Continent in time for Lent and, according to a letter to Rotterdam in 1725, if all were not sold, they were to be "keeped under pickle till the month of September and then, if repacked and washed clean, might sell at Bilboa or Havre as new salmon." Steuart was also involved in brandy and claret smuggling on the west coast, where among his customers was the Governor of Fort William, but the trade became dangerous because of the excisemen and uneconomic because a competitor was selling brandy at 10/- a gallon. To the garrison at Fort William also went meal and barley by sea, just one of many customers on the west coast supplied by Steuart. Meal for Fort Augustus was carried to

Lochend by packhorses, at a charge of 6d per horse, and loaded on the Government galley or other ship and transported along Loch Ness.

Through the Great Glen

Regular patrolling of Loch Ness was started by Commonwealth troops in the 1650s. Having built a forty ton ship in Inverness, they hauled it overland on log rollers for six miles to Loch Ness where, armed with four pieces of cannon, it was employed to stop Highlanders crossing the loch and to supply troops at Fort Augustus with stores and ammunition. The tradition of having a galley on the loch was continued by General Wade and in the early 19th century, when the projected canal was being surveyed, its commander, Mark Gwynn, took soundings of the loch in it for Thomas Telford.

The Caledonian Canal, started in 1803 during the Napoleonic Wars, was an attempt to open up a safe communication by water between the Atlantic and the North Sea, particularly for frigates of the Royal Navy, but it took much longer to complete than was expected and the War was over before it was opened in 1822. Four years earlier, however, ships were sailing direct from Inverness to Fort Augustus with meal, coal and building materials and as soon as the whole Canal was opened, boats from Wick were delivering large quantities of salt herrings to Ireland. At a stroke, Glasgow was put in close touch with east coast ports such as Aberdeen and Dundee, and with the Baltic, and all this trade was passing through Inverness. The difficulties of sailing ships making progress against contrary winds in the Great Glen prompted the Canal Commissioners to provide steam-tugs in the 1840s. The development of big iron-hulled ships powered by steam, however, meant that for them the Canal was now too small and the Pentland Firth held fewer perils.

Coasting vessels, fishing boats and some Baltic traders found the Canal a useful waterway and passenger traffic began to build up. The Canal put Inverness in touch with Glasgow and in 1847 four steamers were engaged in the Inverness to Glasgow run, a voyage which took two days and cost £1 10/-, cabin class, 10/-, steerage. Coaches and omnibuses turned up to collect passengers at Muirtown and carts for their baggage, to convey them all to the town's hotels. Soon there was a rival service from Liverpool. On the Canal, from the 1870s, *Gondolier* and *Glengarry* provided a daily service between Muirton and Banavie. More and more people were coming to admire Highland scenery and they came by water. Steamers and hotels turned tourism into a local industry.

Through passages by passenger ships are now no more, due to bus and rail competition, but short trips on the Canal by the *Princess Louise* in the '30s and *Scot II* today show the interest there is, not only in the "Monster," but in travel by water. Ocean-going yachts and motor cruisers in increasing numbers are taking advantage of the relative emptiness of this waterway through the Great Glen, which previously the fishing boats had to themselves. Occasionally, unusual loads which are too big for road or rail are towed through, such as the digesters for the Pulp Mill at Corpach, or the giant transformers, towed by *Scot II* to Foyers in 1973.

Passengers from the Harbour

Starting in 1804, a smack sailed once every three weeks to London; in 1815 it returned from London to Burghead in seventy hours, thirty-four hours less than the mail coach, but ten to twelve days was the normal time. When Joseph Mitchell went to London in 1823 to become a pupil to Thomas Telford, he sailed from Aberdeen, cabin class, receiving four meals a day on a voyage lasting six days for a guinea, the result of a price war between two rival companies. From Inverness in the 1840s, the steamer *Northern Star* carried passengers and cargo every second Monday on the London run, calling at Fortrose, Cromarty and Invergordon, Findhorn, Burghead, Lossiemouth, Banff and Aberdeen. *The Duke of Richmond* called at the same ports weekly on her way to Leith, while the *Maid of Morven* sailed twice weekly to Little Ferry in Sutherland[7]. At low tide, these steamers moored at Kessock Ferry pier. The ferry still functions with an atmosphere of excitement for passengers, a feeling of going abroad.

The Harbour since the War

Almost unnoticed by the people of the town, the harbour provides a service on which they rely, by handling materials for the town and the Highlands. True, the coastal trade has declined and some commodities, such as coal, cement and lime, which used to come in by sea are now carried north by rail or road. It appeared ironic to the Harbour Master that the 42,000 tons of coal which arrived in railway waggons in Inverness in 1950 should be transferred to lorries outside the window of his office on Shore Street Quay. For a time, between 1958 and '66, five or six coal boats a month were regular callers at the port, feeding the Gas Works with 25,000 tons of coal a year, until the new gas plant on the Longman came into operation.

Construction work in the Highlands brought trade to the harbour. For hydro-electric schemes in the late '40s and '50s, regular supplies of cement were imported from Belgium and Germany, and in 1972 a Dutch tug brought in a pontoon with dredging materials for the oil-rig yard at Ardersier. Before 1950, sectional wooden houses, which are now the homes of Inverness people, came in by sea from Sweden, while others, to be erected in west coast villages, continued their journey through the Caledonian Canal. Ships from the Baltic bring in timber regularly and give an international flavour to the port.

Oil for central heating and petrol for cars arrive by sea at Citadel Quay, are pumped into storage tanks on what was once "Cromwell's Fort," and are distributed all over the Highlands by road. The rise in the demand for oil is such that oil tankers now provide the greatest revenue to the Harbour Trust and more than compensate for the loss of the coal and cement trade. In the month of March, 1972, for example, twenty-four out of thirty-five ships using the port were tankers. Not only are more tankers calling, but they are bigger. In 1966, the Harbour Master reported that they were now capable of carrying 50% more fuel. Five years later, when the *Esso Penzance* delivered a cargo of 3,200 tons of oil, it established a record for the port.

Less frequent imports include salt from Germany to be used on Highland roads in winter, alumina and creolite for the aluminium industry, lime from England and basic slag from Holland. Occasionally barley has been imported for distilling from England, Denmark and even Australia and, on rare occasions, some has been exported.

On the whole, since the war Inverness has been a receiving port, one into which cargoes are imported but from which almost nothing is exported. In 1947, 44,000 tons of shipping departed without a cargo: in 1959, the figure was 60,000 tons. This may appear to be a waste of shipping space as road congestion increases, but many railway waggons and lorries also return south empty after delivering loads to the Highlands.

Exports from Inverness are minimal in quantity, but of astonishing variety. Some commodities are exported only occasionally, oats and barley to Ireland and Europe, dried milk to Holland, and timber to Shetland, as well as welding machinery built by AI Welders. In 1971, and again in 1973, the *Aberthaw Fisher*, using the "roll-on" method, took aboard welding machinery which could not have been lifted by the harbour cranes and would have been difficult to deliver from Inverness by any other way than by sea. Some cargoes are "once and for all" exports, scrap rails from the railways on the Quay to Italy, Spain and Holland, old hangars from Dalcross to Denmark and Holland, and the machinery from the aluminium works at Foyers, which went to Norway[8].

Foreign countries have been quick to appreciate the value of the catches of Kessock herring brought into Inverness, particularly since the boom season of 1965, when some 375,000 crans were landed. Cargoes were exported to Norway, Germany and even to Iceland. Since then, Norwegian refrigeration ships have stationed themselves in the harbour to deal with the fish immediately, and in 1969 a fish processing factory was established at Thornbush.

Operated by the Harbour Master, Captain Malcolm Macleod, and a small staff, providing a pilot service and with a stevedore to arrange for the handling of cargoes, the harbour is an asset to the town. It more than pays for itself, even although its charges are low, 4p per registered ton on merchant ships, 5p on pleasure boats. On the goods most commonly imported, the rates are: petroleum spirit, 23p per ton, wooden battens, 11p per 50 cu. ft., grain, 10p per ton, salt, 8p per ton, and herrings 5p per cran.

The port is outward looking, international in a way that the rest of the town is not, maintaining a link across the sea with the Baltic ports and capable of dealing with more trade with the Common Market countries. If, because of economic growth or the particular needs of the oil industry, demands on it intensify beyond a certain point, its facilities will have to be improved, e.g., Citadel Quay extended, the channel deepened, more powerful cranes installed. Alternatively, greater use could be made of Thornbush Quay, but in both cases the size of ships that can be accommodated is limited by the width of the swinging basins, where ships turn round before heading out to sea.

REFERENCES

1. Dickinson, W. C., *New History of Scotland,* vol I, p. 112 n.
2. Reproduction in *Old Inverness,* Robert Carruthers & Sons, 1967.
3. *Transactions of Inverness Field Club,* vol II.
4. Cook, Joseph, *The Port of Inverness,* 1931.
5. *Letter-book of Inverness Harbour Trust,* 1847-57.
6. Mackay, William (ed.), *Letter-book of Bailie John Steuart,* Scottish History Society, 1915.
7. Cameron, George, *History of Inverness,* 1847.
8. Harbour Master's Monthly Reports, 1945-73.

FOR FURTHER READING

Mitchell, Joseph, *Reminiscences of My Life in the Highlands,* 2 vols, 1884. Reprinted by David and Charles, 1971.

Haldane, A. R. B., *New Ways Through the Glens,* Nelson, 1962.

Cameron, A. D., *The Caledonian Canal,* Terence Dalton, 1972.

White Bridge · 1782

R

COMMUNICATIONS

e. Air

ROBERT McKEAN

Inverness is the main growth point of air services in the Highlands and Islands network. Total traffic has increased by 114% since 1966, with the major rate of growth on the Inverness-London route an an annual average of 35%, due to the introduction of direct services which are now 12 non-stop flights a week in each direction. There is also a significant annual growth rate of 25% between Inverness and Glasgow. Other sharp annual increases are between Inverness and Birmingham; Manchester and Belfast; Orkney and Shetland. The Inverness-Stornoway sector continues to register increases in traffic, but this rate of growth may slow down with the introduction of the new car ferry service between Ullapool and Stornoway.

Scheduled air services were operated before the last war to airfields in the Highlands and Islands, but the provision of good airfields has been a persistent problem. During the war, a number of airfields were set up for defence reasons and, when the war was over, these were available for use as Civil Airports.

Scottish Airways Limited was incorporated as a private company on 12 August, 1937. It was formed out of Northern and Scottish Airways Limited (formed in November, 1934), and Highland Airways Limited, to co-ordinate the internal interests of British Airways Limited with the surface travel interests of the London, Midland and Scottish Railway and those of David MacBrayne Limited. The holding company of Scottish Airways Limited was Western Isles Airways Limited.

But by then Inverness had had its own airline for some years.. In April 1933, E. E. Fresson registered Highland Airways Limited to operate air services in northern Scotland from Inverness, with a capital of £2,675. Highland Airways operated into and out of the Longman. On 29 May, 1934, Fresson inaugurated the first regular British internal air mail when he piloted a DH Dragon Moth G-ACCE to Kirkwall (Wideford) carrying

2,000 letters. This company continued to operate until merged with Scottish Airways Limited in 1937.

The introduction of air services is a natural development in a region where geography presents difficulties and no little discomfort for those using surface transport. Some surface transport will always be essential, but where mountains or water have to be negotiated, air transport offers many benefits. Air transport is naturally dependent on the provision of airfields, and that is a problem on account of the shape of our land.

When British European Airways (BEA) was set up by Act of Parliament in 1946, it was given the task of operating all United Kingdom and European services, and there followed rapid development in all areas, including the Highlands and Islands where the potential traffic was then small but the benefits to travellers were great.

In those days, aircraft were in very short supply. Those towns in Scotland which had comparatively large airfields — and these included Inverness, the Airport having moved to Dalcross — relied on domestic services being operated by Dakotas (DC3's) and services to other parts provided by De Havilland Rapides (DH89's). By December, 1963, the Dakota had generally given way to the Herald and Viscount, and the Rapide was succeeded by the De Haviland Heron. The trunk routes, Glasgow and Edinburgh to London, saw the Dakota replaced by the Vickers Viking, then by the Vanguard, Comet, Trident and BAC Super 1-11.

This is a necessarily short historical background to air transport as it affected Inverness in early days. Within Scotland itself, there were a fair number of operating companies on airline and charter flying before September 1939, and there had been a few short-lived services from speculators — the airline business could be a bit of a jungle.

During the 1960's services in Scotland were being adapted to Scottish needs. Many routes were operated as through services, some of them starting in the south of England and ending up in the Shetlands. This practice enabled higher aircraft utilisation rates to be achieved, and, of course, opened up the country to the rest of the United Kingdom and the world. Edinburgh and Glasgow were then the terminals of the BEA trunk routes from the south. Flights to Inverness could be either an extension of these services, or part of a separate Scottish pattern of services. The advent of air services connecting important areas of the Highlands and Islands undoubtedly has been a great step forward in improving internal communications throughout the regions, and the Inverness-London direct services have generated considerable traffic growth, of both passengers and freight.

BEA (now Scottish Airways Division of British Airways) has been operating since the war, and because of low traffic density and short distances, has lost money on its Highland services. It has carried these losses by cross-subsidising, despite the suggestion made some years ago by the Air Traffic Licensing Board that BEA should receive an Exchequer Subsidy for these services. It was recognised that these unprofitable services could not be discontinued without causing distress, hardship and further depopulation. Loganair has, during the last few years, been building up a complementary service.

Transport subsidies account for only part of the total social cost of maintaining the economy of the Highlands and Islands. The question raises very broad issues, but we cannot ignore a matter which is of such basic concern to the transport needs of the Highlands and in particular the Inverness area. The Highland and Island aspect of Scottish Airways Division services cannot remain as they are over the next decade. Either depopulation will have reached the point at which many communities have ceased to be viable or, as I firmly believe to be more likely, effective regeneration will be well advanced with improved communications and a more buoyant social structure.

Thanks largely to the efforts of the Highlands and Islands Development Board and others, Inverness is experiencing important industrial developments, which have improved the economic stability in the area, and, as a result of the oil exploration programme, there is promise of great prosperity. Financial aid in some form is a prerequisite of plans for development. The need to subsidise the provision of Airports and air navigational services will continue. Certainly, improvements are possible by Government supporting air services considerably more than in the past. The "spin-off" of an improved air transport system in Scotland is not, however, for British Airways' Board to judge. The cost of improvements would still be extremely small in comparison with other subsidies provided in the national interest.

Scottish Airways' plans are dependent upon the plans of Government Authorities being studied with those of the operator. Since the company is in most cases the sole operator, much depends upon the level of reliability the Government accept as appropriate to Scottish operations, where terrain and weather present fairly exceptional problems. Development of Inverness Airport should go ahead to allow it to be upgraded as quickly as possible to jet operations. It is Scottish Airways' intention to schedule the BAC Super 1-11 500 into Inverness in 1975-76 at the latest. This fast airliner will be used on the London route initially and, later, to Stornoway and possibly to Benbecula.

Broadly speaking, in Scotland affinities are up and down the East Coast and up and down the West Coast, with Inverness facing more in both directions than either Glasgow or Aberdeen. These traffic flows will be influenced considerably should there be oil exploration in the west and, given reasonable break-even load factors, tourist flows can be influenced by organisation. The aim should be to develop services as much as possible from the three bases of Glasgow, Aberdeen and Inverness, with all points served from these three bases being connected, with morning and evening services in each direction. Traffic flows will not permit total elimination of two sector routes. The aim, so far as Inverness is concerned, should be for services to be operated something as follows: —

From Inverness to: Glasgow/Prestwick; Oban; Mull; Fort William; Skye; Benbecula; Stornoway; Dornoch; Fearn; Wick; Aberdeen; Dundee; Edinburgh; Orkney; Shetland.

Schedules between all these places should be planned to make the maximum number of connections at the main points and, where traffic flows between other points merit it, services with small STOL (short take-off and landing) or VTOL (vertical take-off and landing, i.e. helicopters) aircraft would operate as required. Services from Prestwick direct to the main tourist areas will be justified as traffic grows.

Availability of airfields, even with considerable subsidy to serve the traffic densities foreseen, does not hold out any prospect of Scottish Airways being able to operate with one type of aircraft only. It is logical to minimise the number of types, which will be three in 1975 and might be reduced to two in the 1980s. In 1975, the aircraft types will be: (a) BAC 1-11 500 series; (b) Viscount 800 series; (c) Skyliners.

Scottish Airways and Loganair should aim towards having common equipment. Until such time as this can be achieved, however, Loganair's smaller equipment should continue to be used to connect those points which would otherwise involve two-sector operations from the main centres. Sectors between Benbecula-Stornoway, and Barra-Benbecula are examples.

Scottish Airways and Loganair are the only operators of scheduled services within Scotland. Scottish Airways, as part of the now huge British Airways, is involved in all types of scheduled air transport. The organisation and economics of air services in the Highlands and Islands cannot, therefore, be seen in isolation. It is necessary to consider the services of Loganair as well as those of Scottish Airways. Since traffic levels do not justify competition within Scotland, it is desirable that the two companies should work together in harmony. Joint management possibilities should be explored carefully.

Scottish Airways Division is the one airline with a very long tradition and with sufficient local expertise and experience to continue the main operation of air services in Scotland, and Inverness is a very important area, around which future developments should take place.

Communications have always shaped the well-being of countries and, today more than ever, growth of industry depends very much upon the ease and speed in which people, especially businessmen can travel. Air travel has had, and will continue to have, an immensely important place in our life and only air travel can offer the ease and speed to match the rapid growth and constant change in industry and ideas throughout the world. Provided Inverness Airport is given Government aid to improve its runway and to supply it with up-to-date navigational aids, the air communications in this area cannot fail to improve with a consequent increase in traffic.

Ard Kean Tower Inverness

THE MODERN SCENE

COMMERCIAL AND INDUSTRIAL
PROGRESS

PAT HUNTER GORDON

Introduction

The type, size and control of commerce and industry carried on in a town is a reflection of its location, the resources round it, its past, its present and, indeed, to a certain extent, its future. A town is made up of people; commerce is still carried on by people, and even when the completely computer-controlled robot factory arrives, people will still be necessary to programme the computer and maintain the robots. Individual events and the great tides of history leave their mark on commerce and industry; sometimes suddenly, as the closing of a mine has created a ghost town, sometimes more slowly, as the increasing size of ships affects shipyards on the upper reaches of a river. The Royal Burgh of Inverness is no exception to the general rule.

In 1973, the removal of the Stone Circle at Raigmore, dated by the carbon-14 method at about 3000 B.C., from the path of the new A9 road revealed underneath it a hutted settlement. One can imagine Inverness' first settlers to be nomadic fishermen, who perhaps first visited, then settled, what would have been the wooded, sheltered and fertile shores of the River Ness, and thus established a community in an important location on the crossing of the North to South and West to East communications. In a chapter describing Commerce and Industry, it is necessary to go back to origins, because whatever caused a settlement to start may have, and, in the case of Inverness, has had and will continue to have, a very important influence on its Commerce and Industry.

Early History

Its location astride the River Ness dictated that Inverness should have strategical and tactical importance, out of which emerged its castle to protect the river crossings, with houses clinging round for protection. This population needed supplies, and small businesses arose to cater their demands.

The community was for a long time largely self-supporting. It was noted for boat-building, there being at least three boat-builders, and for sailmaking. Hemp was imported from the Baltic, made into ropes and bagging and re-exported to London and to the East and West Indies. It had a large tanning and tallow industry. It was a malting centre, with four distilleries and twelve brewers of ale. The important landowners and local clan chiefs were educated in the town and mixed freely in its trade and commerce. They also travelled widely, as much to Europe as to England. This mixing of intellect and isolation created an independence of thought and action which character-ised the inhabitants of Inverness, and resulted in enlightened action being taken by the Council for the good of the town.

The first great change in this situation was probably the military road-building programme of General Wade from 1726, which partly opened up the Highlands. The building and main-taining of Fort George, Fort Augustus and Fort William, the need to supply them, the discovery and the use of the fighting qualities of the Highland soldiers, all led to an increased interest in the Highlands. It was the Napoleonic War, in which Highland troops played a prominent part, and which made many High-land farmers rich with the production of black cattle, that was instrumental in sympathetic consideration and approval being given to the building of the Caledonian Canal.

This great engineering enterprise brought to Inverness Thomas Telford, the great bridge, canal and road builder, whose genius, not only for building, but also for inspiring and teaching, produced the Mitchells — father and son — and may easily have inspired already independently-minded Invernessians to adopt new ideas and methods. Joseph Mitchell, whose portrait hangs in the Town House, Inverness, became a prominent member of the newly-formed Institute of Civil Engineers in London. These men also supervised the re-building of the great road from Perth to Inverness. The cost in 1810 was £400 per mile, it rose to £8,390 for the reconstruction during the 1920s, and the new 24-foot carriageway of the 1970s is estimated at £500,000 per mile.

Could it have been the influence of these engineers that made Inverness one of the first towns in Scotland to have its own Gas Works, opened by the Inverness Gas and Water Company in 1826, with gas street lighting? The *Inverness Courier,* the first gas customer in the town, wrote on 6 December, 1826, "We congratulate our fellow townsmen and every other person feeling an interest in the improvement of this burgh on the introduction of gas lights." In 1973 one road

(Diriebught Road) and one or two closes off the High Street are still lighted by gas. (See Note A.)

Communication to Inverness was by coach or cart, or by sailing vessel to one of the four wharves, Clachnaharry, Muirtown, Thornbush or the main Citadel Quay, round which were built storage sheds for merchants and wholesalers. At the Citadel was the Rope and Hempen-cloth Manufactory established in 1765.

The Clearances and the Highland Sporting Estates

The two next changes affecting Inverness were, first, the Clearances, which were partly caused by the second, the fashion of the Highland Sporting Estate, established by Queen Victoria at Balmoral, and made possible by the wealth created by the industrial revolution and by the merchant adventurers of Britain trading into the far corners of the earth. The clearances probably had less impact on Inverness than the creation of the Sporting Estate which, for the first time, introduced to the Highlands a division between town and country, to the social detriment of both, although its effect in Inverness itself was partly offset by the growth of a professional class. It is difficult for the present generation to visualise the organisation required to build a mansion house and stables in, say, Glen Affric, when even the move of the family meant sending ahead carts of hay to be located at strategic intervals, an advance party to open the house, light the fires, fill the lamps with paraffin, air the beds, and finally to welcome the arrival of the family and their personal staff.

During this period, Inverness's population increased at a greater rate than that of Scotland as a whole, and many commercial and trading enterprises flourished to deal with the building and supplying of the great estates. Yet Inverness still remained at the end of a slow and often hazardous coastal journey, or a stage coach or waggon trip from the existing, but distant, rail-head. Even in 1973, there are many people in Inverness who remember the stage coaches coming in and setting out with four horses on the route to Whitebridge or Beauly.

Arrival of the Railway

This is bringing us near to 1875, when the Inverness Field Club was first formed, when the formation of the Highland Railway made probably the greatest single change to Inverness until the discovery of North Sea oil in 1972. In 1844, the railway had been extended, so that a traveller could journey from London to Aberdeen, then, by a different line, to Huntly. The journey on to Inverness was done by stage coach. In 1854 the first sod marking the beginning of the Highland Railway was cut by the Countess of Seafield in a field east of the present Millburn Distillery. Local landlords and businessmen were together prominent in this promotion. Alexander Matheson of Ardross was the first Chairman of Directors, whose names can be read on a plaque in Inverness Station. In 1855, the Lochgorm Railway Workshops of the Highland Railway were opened, at first only for carrying out repairs and alterations. The Perth-Inverness line from Dunkeld to Forres via Aviemore was opened in 1863, being only two years in building. The Aviemore-Carrbridge-Daviot line was not built until 1898. The North line and the Kyle line followed, completing the importance of Inverness as a communications centre.

In 1869, steam engines were designed in Inverness, and were built, together with carriages and wagons, at the Lochgorm Works. The importance of this development in Inverness cannot be over-emphasised, because it created a demand for engineering services and produced highly qualified and skilled engineers in Inverness. This need, although it has at times grown tenuous, has remained with Inverness until now, when the need is greater than it has ever been. The famous 4-6-0 steam locomotive was designed by David Jones, Chief Mechanical Engineer of the Highland Railway, assisted by David Hendrie, the Chief Draughtsman, in an attic overlooking the Station Square. It is interesting that in 1973 the Chief Civil Engineer of British Railways, Mr A. W. McMurdo, is the son of a distinguished engineer of the Highland Railway and of an Inverness school teacher.

In 1875, Inverness was a town in which, in spite of the growing independence of the country estates, usually financed by outside capital, country and townsman carried out business enterprises together because limiting communications made such co-operation necessary; a town even then of many churches and public houses, but, above all, a town still made up of many independent businesses, because until fairly recently it had had to be largely self-sufficient.

The arrival of the railway started the move of wholesale traders from the quays to Falcon Square and Eastgate, adjacent to the station, from whence they provided wholesale supplies of dry goods, groceries and other imported stores, not only to Inverness, but also to the surrounding towns and villages. The suppliers of building and other heavy materials remained near the quays. This general pattern remained until after the 1939/45 war.

While Holm Mills, Howden Nurseries,, the *Inverness Courier,* and other well-kent names had already been established for many years, the arrival and extension of the railway, the building of the large estates and the building up of the Inverness that altered little between 1870 and 1900, created a climate in which other businesses were established.

Early in 1870, Mr McGruther and Mr Marshall joined up to act as merchants, shipping coal and lime in sailing vessels and small puffers; over a century they became shipping agents, merchants of all building materials, acting for ship owners, and are now developing into suppliers to North Sea oil firms. In 1872, a company called The Northern Agricultural Implement and Foundry Company, Ltd., was founded by local businessmen with Cluny Macpherson, Chief of Clan Macpherson, as its first chairman, to centralise the manufacture in Inverness of farm implements.

In June, 1878, Mr Roderick Macrae of Beauly assumed as partner Mr William G. Dick, of Redcastle (whence came all the Tarradale red stone of which Inverness buildings of that period were built) to operate from Edwards Court, Academy Street, Inverness, and to offer the following services: "First class open or closed carriages, Landaus, Wagonettes, Transport Carts, Phaetons, Dog Carts and Gigs." Anyone visiting this firm, which is one of the leading motor industry firms in Inverness and the North, can see the ramp up which the horses were led to their stalls.

The Town Council took over the water supply from the Inverness Gas and Water Company by an Act of Parliament in 1875 (it still owns the reservoir site) and over the years it has developed the drainage and sewage system and has established secure and plentiful water supplies for the town from Lochs Ashie and Duntelchaig.

In 1870, the Government, through the Post Office, bought the Telegraph System. Telephone companies began in 1879/80 with private companies which had to pay royalties to the Post Office, because of a legal argument which said that a telephone was a telegraph. In September, 1884, Mr Bennet, Manager of the National Telephonic Company, at a meeting in Inverness said that it would require 30 subscribers at £10 each to make a telephone exchange viable. He explained the benefits, and Provost (later Sir) Hector MacAndrew was the first subscriber. The number Inverness 1 is now equivalent to Inverness 33001 which is the number of MacAndrew and Jenkins. The first exchange was opened on 19 January, 1885, on the first floor above Coopers in Union Street. (See Note B).

In 1890, Messrs Will and John Burnett of Dundee took over a bakery called Milnes in Dempster Gardens. It had a shop in the High Street.

In 1891, Mrs Hamilton, who for 14 years after the death of her husband, had carried on the agricultural auctioneering business founded by her husband's father, Jacob Hamilton, sold out to a group of local farmers. The business, started in the 1830s by the riverside, was then on the site of the present Royal Academy. About 1890, it moved to be close to the railway yards. In 1905 the Company (Hamilton's Auction Marts Ltd.) was reorganised with Mr William McDonald as Chairman and Mr John Robertson as Manager.

In 1896 an important event took place at Foyers. Mr (later Sir) William Murray Morrison of the British Aluminium Company, advised by Lord Kelvin, built the first electric reduction plant powered by hydro-electricity to produce aluminium. It operated with its original turbine and water wheel until 1970 (in spite of having a German bomb dropped on it between 1939 and 1945), when it became too small to be any longer economic. This, the first hydro-electric scheme, is now being turned into a giant pumped-storage hydro-electric scheme. From this small beginning grew the complex hydro-electric system which was to revolutionise Inverness in the 1950s. Before moving on, it is again interesting that the eleventh hydro-scheme built in the United Kingdom was erected in 1929 by the Royal Burgh of Inverness at the Bught, where the Power-House and water lade are still visible.

In the 1890s, in his lodgings in Inverness, Mr Alexander Newlands, later Chief Civil Engineer of the Highland Railway, arranged for the Stationmasters all over the Highland Railway to keep rainfall records. With these records, and a planimeter to map out the catchment areas, he produced and read a paper to the Royal Society of Arts in 1918, which could well have formed the basis of today's hydro-electric schemes.

In 1895 the company formed by Cluny Macpherson in 1872 gathered together and reorganised a number of small foundries and ironworks into one company to be known as the Rose Street Foundry and Engineering Company Ltd. Sir Henry MacAndrew became Chairman. A farmer in Easter Ross, John Gordon, whose youngest son, Sam Hunter Gordon, had, after considerable family altercation, left farming and started as an engineer on Clydeside, became a director. The establishment and progress of the new Company would not have been possible had it not been for the prior establishment of the railway workshops and the work thereby generated.

In 1899, the Inverness Electric Lighting Order was passed by Parliament, and in 1904 the North of Scotland Electric Light and Power Company Ltd. submitted an offer for lighting Academy Street, Church Street, High Street and Inglis Street, Union Street and Queensgate, all at £16 per lamp per annum. (See Note C).

Over the years the small businesses of Inverness, which had originally been operated mainly from the owners' houses, had moved into specially built buildings, and the period between 1872 and 1914 saw a very large part of the town rebuilt and the establishment of prosperous owner-operated commercial premises. The iron-bound wheels of horse-drawn vehicles rattled over the stone-cobbled streets, so that straw was laid thickly in front of houses where there was sickness. Round Inverness there were the great estates, the railway, the Royal Navy at Invergordon, the trade in salt herrings with Russia, where the salt was as appreciated as the fish, with a hundred fishing boats operating out of Inverness, and the growing numbers of ex-officers and overseas civil servants who retired to the Highlands, all of whose needs helped to keep the shops busy. An off-shoot of a famous Piccadilly Grocery Store (Morell's in Queensgate) was established, presumably to serve the country house clientele, but it rapidly became appreciated locally and lasted until after the 1939/45 war.

The Sporting Estate created in Inverness at least five shops dealing in guns, cartridges, rods, fishing tackle and all the other necessities of the business — at least two employed taxidermists who could stuff expertly stags' heads, eagles and wild cats. All five lasted into the 1950s, and at least one taxidermist was still working in the late fifties/early sixties. Alan Macpherson, of Macpherson's Sporting Stores, remembers as a small boy taking hides from the shop to Chisholm's Tannery, which operated on the North Bank of the River Ness above the Grant Street (Waterloo) Bridge.

But before 1914, the two breweries still operating in Inverness, the Thornbush Brewery and Buchanan's Haugh Brewery, went out of business, probably because improved communications brought in beer made more economically on a larger scale in the South.

In the early 1900s and before, Inverness was an important fishing port, having the best sheltered anchorage in the Moray Firth area in Muirton Basin and in Loch Dochfour, where up to 30 trawlers and drifters would winter. In 1908, the Rose

Street Foundry built the Thornbush Slipway to construct and repair drifters and trawlers, while the triple expansion steam engines for the vessels were designed and built at Rose Street. Mr Sam Hunter Gordon, who was to pioneer engineering activity in Inverness for the next half century, was invited by the Directors, of whom his father was one, to return from Vickers' in Barrow-in-Furness to manage the new shipyard.

In 1911, Mr Gordon took out a licence for building electric submersible motors, which were fitted to pumps to replace the hand-operated pumps on British warships; these were built and tested in Rose Street before being fitted. In 1914, together with Captain Munro, C.M.G., R.N., King's Harbour Master at Invergordon, he designed anti-submarine protection which was used, not only to protect Invergordon and Scapa Flow, but also wherever fleet protection was required, as far afield as the Dardanelles. The nets of steel wire were constructed by the women of Inverness in the disused Thornbush Brewery. The Slipway was fully used to build drifters, large numbers of which were used for minesweeping. Great areas of timber all over the Highlands were cut down for use in the trenches. Inverness itself, as might be expected, was an important Headquarters and Communication Centre.

Period 1918-1939

While the end of the 1914-18 war resulted in immediate local employment in replacing the resources used up during the war, the period between the wars was, for Inverness, one of slow decline. There was a return to the country house way of life for those who still had the capital and were alive, and, even in the 1930s, the Glorious Twelfth of August was preceded by days or even weeks of preparation, ending in the *Royal Highlander's* arrival in Inverness with the tweedy but polished potential grouse killers; but it was only a shadow of the pre-1914 era.

The arrival of the motor vehicle just before that war created a number of new opportunities, but horse-drawn taxis (or cabs) were common in Inverness streets in 1939, and James Wordie & Co., who were the railway carriers, were delivering by horse and cart until 1961. In the late 1920s the side roads were still made of water-bound macadam, and the road menders with their neat piles of stones, all hand-chipped to an almost identical size, were situated at intervals along the roads. Their strong tea, brewed up in an open tin (which an Australian would call a billy), was a tremendous treat to a passing child to taste.

During this period, Hamilton's Auction Marts embarked

on a policy of expansion and in 1923 had marts in operation at Nairn, Forres, Dingwall, the Isle of Skye, Thurso and Forsinard, with Inverness as headquarters.

During this long period of decline, many individual businesses disappeared under the competition of larger enterprises serving bigger markets in the South. Chisholm's Tannery and Lauder's Tweed Mills were among those that went. In 1923, the Highland Railway was taken over by the London, Midland and Scottish Railway, and the work from the workshops was phased out to the L.M.S. workshops at Cowlairs and St Rollox in Glasgow, and at Crewe in Cheshire.

Mr Sam Hunter Gordon, having been one of the first in Britain to use arc welding, had set up the manufacture of arc welding rods in Inverness. However, as the use of arc welding spread, the manufacture of rods was made more efficient, and eventually the profit on each rod was less than the transport costs to the main markets in the Midlands of England. The directors of the Rose Street Foundry sold the arc welding business and bought a bankrupt business started by two men called Ashton and Ibbotson in Bradford, which was pioneering a machine for joining pieces of metal together rapidly and economically. The company, called "A.I." after its founders, with its technicians and three machines for welding the rims of wheels together which would not work, were moved to Inverness and the machines were made to work. The company, in its foundry, made the cast-iron chairs for fastening rails to sleepers; in 1929 this had to be closed.

With the aid of Government grants, Buckie built a sheltered harbour fifty miles nearer the fishing grounds, so that the fishing fleet operating out of Inverness slowly moved to Buckie. During the war, three drifters of steel, the first called the *Nebula,* were built at the Thornbush. After the war, the largest boat ever built at Inverness, the *Udney Castle,* a 500-ton, twin-engined coaster, was built for an Aberdeen firm, but there was no continuity of work.

The Thornbush Slipway was kept alive by the building of huge battle-practice targets with a body of solid wooden baulks and a latticework of masts, which the British Fleet shot to pieces each year, and which had to be rebuilt. The way of the pioneer is not easy, and it was not until about 1936 that the new A.I. industry became established, when an order, made necessary by Hitler, was received from Mr Herbert Austin, of motor-car fame, for 34 automatic welding machines to make engines for the Bren gun, the Brititsh Army's light automatic.

S

While there was no official regional assistance, the Admiralty, the L.M.S. and other railways, and Inverness County Council with orders for cast-iron mileposts (which still exist) helped to keep business going. Even so, with a less determined character than Sam Hunter Gordon in it, the Company would have gone under. Hamilton's Auction Marts were also going through a difficult period, and J. Logie McDonald, the son of William McDonald, who was Chairman of both companies, had a difficult financial task.

It is probably impossible for anyone who did not live in Inverness in the '20s or '30s to realise the impact on the town and countryside of the massacre in the trenches in France and Belgium. Not only the battalions of the local regiments, mainly Camerons and Seaforths, had suffered, but also the Inverness Battery and the Lovat Scouts, and thousands of men in the other armed forces and in the merchant navy had lost their lives or been wounded. Their loss was irreplaceable.

In an attempt to provide social work, Lord Roberts' Memorial Workshop (now Pickford's furniture store) was built to employ disabled ex-servicemen, The Northern Counties Institute for the Blind, founded in 1868 and supported by public subscription, is still providing certain services under the National Assistance of Act of 1948. It employs 30 people, of whom 21 are blind and disabled, producing annually £50,000 of bedding. Its Outdoor Services Department helps 521 blind persons and 145 partially sighted in their homes, and it still carries on some of its original charitable functions, now updated to radios, talking books, etc. Haven Products also helps disabled people. It is an off-shoot of a scheme set up in 1945 on the Hillington Industrial Estate in Glasgow to help severely disabled ex-servicemen. It later joined with the Scottish Red Cross, and Red Cross House was set up in Inverness in 1966. The workshop, opened there in 1968, is now on the Longman Industrial Estate, employing 25 disabled people and with room for expansion.

Commercially, a trend still being followed had set in — smaller businesses were being amalgamated into bigger businesses. Outlets of the large national chain stores had started to appear, probably the first being Boots and Woolworths. In 1927 there were 22 individually-owned drapers and clothiers in the High Street. Burnetts had grown in size to compete with bread baked in Glasgow and brought in by train. The local bakers and butchers were, however, still very important members of the community, which included shops like Victor Conn in Inglis Street, making high-class confectionery. The wholesalers are more difficult to identify individually, and a separate note on wholesalers is included in Note D.

Mr R. Donald and Mr W. Hamilton, of Macrae and Dick, were largely responsible for starting Highland Airways Ltd. In May, 1933, an air service under Captain E. E. Fresson, O.B.E., who pioneered the air routes to the Western Isles was opened between Inverness and Orkney, the double journey taking under 2½ hours. It was followed on 30th May, 1934, by Britain's first Air Mail Service, also from Inverness to Orkney.

The period between the wars was also the time for a great public controversy on the use of the water-power resources of the Highlands. The British Aluminium Company had already built, in 1909 at Kinlochleven and in 1929-34 in Lochaber, two large hydro-electric schemes to operate aluminium reduction plants. Industry wished to develop further schemes for cheap power to produce economically materials such as calcium carbide for use in the South. A body of public opinion, largely led by the *Inverness Courier,* argued that Industry would take the cream of the water-power, and the profit and the products would go south, creating very little employment in the Highlands. This body of opinion wished to see the water-power of the Highlands comprehensively developed for the benefit of the Highlands, and at least three private Bills placed before Parliament were defeated on the floor of the House of Commons.

Period 1939-1945

In the Second World War, Inverness again became an important Headquarters and Communication Centre. Invergordon was too accessible to German bombers to harbour the main Fleet, but some 35 miles of coast from Inverness to Lossiemouth virtually became one great aerodrome. Again the local regiments were early involved in the fighting, with the 51st (Highland) Division probably becoming the best-known single fighting division in the British Army. Again the timber resources of the area were used, with Canadian and Newfoundland Forestry Units being brought in for this purpose. Units of the re-formed Polish Army, many individuals of which eventually settled in the North, were stationed round Inverness. The famous Commando Training Centre was in Inverness-shire at Achnacarry, while at Aviemore the *Kompani Linge,* the Norwegian Commandos, trained for their operations in Norway. The last two are remembered by Memorials in their respective areas. A large temporary E.M.S. Hospital was built on the old Raigmore Estate, and is still being used as the main Inverness Hospital in 1973.

Industrially, Inverness was also harnessed. Holm Mills was fully used. The Rose Street Foundry took on women in place of skilled engineers and, among a number of other vital machines, made all the welding machines for Operation PLUTO, in which 70 miles of 3-ins. diameter pipe was welded together, wound round a 40-ft diameter drum, and floated across the English Channel with one end held on shore at the Isle of Wight, the other end landing at Cherbourg — pipes through which the invading Allied Armies were supplied with essential fuel for tanks, vehicles and aircraft. The Company was also the only one in the world to weld air-screw hubs from pressings, which saved the country thousands of man-hours of labour, and tons of special steel — 40 sq. inches of weld taking the 4000 Brake Horse Power developed by the Spitfire, Mosquito or relevant aircraft. After the war, the Company received a Commendation and an Award from the Royal Commission of Inventors for these two efforts.

The Naval force of Headquarter Ship, Landing Ships, Infantry with Landing Craft, Assault and Landing Ships, Tanks, which carried Britain's assaulting divisions on to the Normandy beaches on D Day in June, 1944, was based in the Moray Firth and carried out exercises on evacuated parts of Easter Ross. The Thornbush Slipway was redesigned to slip and store up to three Landing Ships, Tank, at one time, to act as a local repair and maintenance unit.

In 1941, amid the defeat, gloom and depression of the early part of the war, the Government set up the Cooper Committee, which recommended that Scotland's hydro-electric resources should be developed, and also recommended the setting up of the North of Scotland Hydro-Electric Board, whose main aim should be the economic rehabilitation of the Highlands. It would seek to attract industry by offering cheap power; to develop power resources for other needs, including those of isolated districts, and, while giving priority to local demands, it should be prepared to export surplus production. In 1943, in the middle of Britain's great struggle for survival against Nazi Germany, the Westminster Parliament passed the Bill piloted by a great Scottish Secretary of State, the Rt. Hon. Tom Johnston, who made domestic reform a condition of accepting office. He warned any Opposition in the House of Commons that he would give their addresses to the soldiers of the 51st Division when they returned home from the war.

Period 1945-1965

After the war, serious efforts were made to halt and reverse the depopulation problem of the Highlands, but the natural events on which man can have no real influence continued. Inverness continued to grow as a centre of local government and service. The population of the countryside continued to decline as farming became more mechanised. The young people and skilled people continued to look for their future elsewhere. The Twelfth of August declined in importance year by year, as landowners could no longer afford to staff the country houses and properly to maintain the sporting estates. The loss of this temporary annual increase in trade was offset, however, by the growth of the tourist industry, as the car became available to a greater number of people.

The Highland District Committee of the Scottish Board for Industry sat from 1946 to 1958 examining Highland problems and reporting to the Minister, but it had no power. The Highland Panel, presided over by Lord Cameron, a great fighter for the Highlands, was equally in an advisory capacity. The North of Scotland Hydro-Electric Board (see Note E), by creating work in the Highlands, by bringing civil and electrical consulting engineers in force to Inverness, by building roads and by connecting 98% of the possible consumers in their area, undoubtedly created the conditions in which success could be achieved. But even the Board with their great powers, and the energy, enthusiasm and dedication of their Chief Commercial Officer, Mr Jimmy Baillie, found, in this difficult period, that for every two paces forward, there was one back. They had, however, some great successes, not only in Inverness, but in their area — successes such as J. Arthur Dixon, Ltd., and Partridge Wilson and Company Ltd., established in 1963 on the Longman Industrial Estate. A Portland Cement Storage Unit, built on British Railways property in the same year, is still giving good service in 1974.

A.I. Welders Ltd., under Mr Sam Hunter Gordon, in 1951 spawned off another world-beating enterprise — Cable Belt Limited, an invention of a draughtsman, Charles Thomson, to overcome a problem that had baffled engineers for 50 years, and thus revolutionised the long-distance conveying of materials like coal, limestone, iron, copper and gold ore. It is when industry starts to breed that the battle is won, and Partridge Wilson equally spawned off Industrial Coils Ltd., but a recession between 1965 and 1969, and the distance from markets, meant the moving south of both Cable Belt and Industrial Coils, and the end of this small sign of natural regeneration.

In 1955, when road transport was de-nationalised, Highland Haulage Ltd. was formed by three young managers, and spread strongly until taken over by a large, southern-based, transport group in 1960. It still operates, although no longer independent. Inverness is also the Area Headquarters of Alginate Industries (Scotland) Ltd., which collects and processes seaweed to produce the alginate used in food products and textile printing.

Commercially, Inverness started early in the frozen food business. One or two local firms started up, either to take advantage of local raw material like "Scampi," the small Norwegian Lobster that the Moray Firth fishermen used to throw back into the sea, or to stock and distribute the frozen food packaged by the large firms in the South. The experience of the war, cheaper travel and the influx of Sassenachs into Inverness, changed the eating habits of the burgh and district.

Inverness was famed for years as a malting town. Millburn Distillery and Glen Albyn and Glen Mhor Distilleries have been producing for 100 years, making their own malt, although great problems arose when America introduced prohibition in 1923. All these distilleries are now owned by two large Scottish concerns, although the last was privately owned until recently. Millburn produces an excess of malt for other distilleries in its group. In 1968, three young men from England set up in Inverness the Moray Firth Maltings Ltd., which has re-established Inverness as an important malting centre.

Period 1965-74

On 1 November, 1965, the Highlands and Islands Development Board (H.I.D.B.) was established as a regional development authority, with the specific task of creating development in the seven crofter counties. It could be said that it also had its share of disappointment in its early days, because of the industrial climate and the need for the Board to take risks to get things started. Now established in Inverness, with a staff of about 200, it has made its presence felt in tourism, fishing and the increasing number of cattle in the Highlands. A number of industries of a mixed variety, employing both men and women, have been set up since 1965 as a result of its efforts, the change in industrial climate, the grants available from the H.I.D.B. and the fact that many people now feel the Highlands to be a better place to work in than Glasgow or Birmingham. Firms such as Precision Relays Ltd., Markon Engineering Ltd., Tarka Controls Ltd., Inverness Chemicals, Castle Stuart Foods Ltd. (helped to start by abundant milk surplus and a very active Milk Marketing Board) and Stuart of Inverness have all started in the last few years. The successful operation of these companies is sufficient to make an interested observer feel that, after many years, there is now every opportunity for industry to succeed in Inverness.

The hospital at Craig Phadrig has been built and money spent at Craig Dunain. A new Raigmore Hospital is being built, the first block being opened in 1970, which will ultimately replace the present Raigmore and the Royal Northern Infirmary. The names of those who contributed to the R.N.I. between 1799 and 1933 should be preserved in any new building as a testament to the efforts of individuals to help the common good of the district, and because of the historical connection of the names and bodies concerned.

In late 1969 and early 1970, the discovery of oil in the North Sea brought two large American platform builders — one with a British partner — to sites at Nigg Bay, Easter Ross, and at Ardersier on the boundaries of Inverness and Nairn. The importance of the H.I.D.B. in guiding this development of the Inner Moray Firth area and in spreading the benefits to other parts of the Highlands, cannot be over-emphasised.

Hamilton's Auction Marts are today the largest firm of agricultural auctioneers based in the North of Scotland, covering all areas from Caithness to Morayshire, under the chairmanship of Mr Murdo Rose. In 1959, Burnetts were taken over by Rank, Hovis and MacDougal and run their products from Inverness on a line from Fochabers to Fort William, and north to the Islands.

The garage business has grown and changed. Macrae & Dick have spread from Inverness to Nairn, Tain, Fort William, Dingwall, Wick, Thurso and Aviemore. Both James Ferries and Chapmans are still locally owned. Fraser & Eland have been taken over by southern-based groups and expanded, while many new businesses have been opened.

The slaughter-house in Inverness had operated for years at Citadel Quay; it was unkindly said by the locals to have been condemned for over 100 years when the Town Council built a new slaughter-house on the Longman Industrial Estate, and ran it for six or seven years. It is now operated by P. B. Flockhart, providing wholesale meat to local butchers and caterers. The hides are uplifted by an Aberdeen company.

On 4 December, 1967, the Inverness Courier celebrated the 150th anniversary of its first publication, management having been during this time in the hands of three families. Miss Eveline Barron, the present editor and sole proprietor, is well-known to Inverness. In a time of amalgamations, particularly in the arena of local newspapers, the Courier has not only maintained its independence of ownership, but also, to the great delight of its readers, its individual opinion.

The shops of Inverness have changed. From the 22 drapers and clothiers in the High Street and Eastgate in 1927, we now have perhaps three independent shops in that area. From six manufacturing silversmiths in 1900, we now have one. There were four clockmakers in 1900, today, none. Prime shopping sites are taken by Insurance Companies or Building Societies. Two major Supermarket chains are established. From five or six locally owned men's shops and as many, or more, individual tailors, we now have one locally owned men's shop, and three or four multiple tailors; the drapers and shoe shops are nearly all chain stores. Gone are many well-known Inverness names, Young & Chapman, Shand & Lindsay, MacDonald's Maison Victoria — the Inverness inventor of the Steam Permanent Wave — Munro the Cycle, Smith the Klondyke, the hatters, Miss Shackleton, and Munro, and many others, a process considerably hastened as the boom effects of North Sea oil development have become felt. The Fairfield Dyeworks closed down in the late 60s. It is invidious to mention too many names, but we still have Gilbert Ross, Fraser & McColl, Fred J. Kelly, Camerons in Church Street, the Highland Fish Shop, T. Mackenzie, the Chemist, and others operated under private or local capital. A number of small craft industries based mainly on individual talent have grown up to supply the tourist industry.

In the three years between 1970 and 1973, since the discovery of North Sea oil, the industrialisation of Inverness has proceeded fast, with the establishment of steel stockholders, steel fabricating firms and sheet metal companies, and with the setting up of service companies and offices to deal with a need created by the expansion which has come, and will continue to come, due to North Sea oil.

A. I. Welders Ltd., in 1973, just after a complete 100 years of local control, became associated with a Scottish-owned, London-based Company to finance its world trade in its existing business, and to take advantage of the opportunities offered by North Sea oil. To many generations of Invernessians the Foundry "hooter" sounding four times a day has been a familiar sound. We will finish this article with it sounding a very optimistic note for the future of the Commerce and Industry of Inverness.

NOTE A — INVERNESS GAS

The Inverness Gas and Water Company was granted statutory authority under an Act of Parliament in May, 1826. In the early days of the undertaking, meters were supplied only at the customer's request, charges being made on estimated usage. By 1873, things had gone so wrong that the Town Council promoted the Inverness Water and Gas Act of 1875, empowering the Commissioner of Police to buy the undertaking. This was successful, the managers between 1875 and 1943 being James Thomson and his son, Andrew. Efficient plant and organisation increased output and decreased cost until the gas works in Manse Place, between Academy Street, Rose Street and George Street, became one of the major communal services. There was a story that children with whooping cough would be helped by a visit to the gas works, and the writer duly paid such a visit to the ammonia plant in the 1920s to sniff it in. Gas was then based on coal.

Lamplighters were a familiar sight in the streets at dusk and dawn, turning on the light at night with a special long pole and snuffing it out in the morning. It was not until the late 1930s that the lamplighters were replaced by automatic clocks.

The gas industry was nationalised in May, 1949, and a study showed that a new plant at Inverness based on oil as a raw material, and linked by pipeline along the East Coast, would be a viable entity. As a result, the plant now sited on the Longman was opened on 2 December, 1965. Natural gas was discovered in the North Sea in that year, and Inverness may be converted to natural gas by 1977.

NOTE B — INVERNESS TELEPHONES

In 1870, one could telegraph in the North from Inverness to Edinburgh, Glasgow, Perth, Aberdeen and to smaller towns. It is interesting that the inventor of the telephone, Alexander Graham Bell, was music master at Elgin Academy in 1869, before emigrating to Canada and moving on to the U.S.A.

The first automatic telephone exchange in Great Britain was installed by the Rose Street Foundry & Engineering Co. Ltd. in Skibo Castle for Andrew Carnegie. While fixing the wiring in the rafters, one of the men, Mackay Gillanders, set the castle on fire. The rest of the men put the fire out quickly. Andrew Carnegie was so pleased that he paid the men a bonus. They then withdrew to decide whether Mackay Gillanders should get any share of the bonus, because he had started the fire, or whether, for the same reason, he should get a double share.

The small exchange first opened was moved from Union Street in 1922 to the Post Office building in Queensgate, with 500 to 600 subscribers. In 1961, it was moved to the new building in Friars Lane, converted to automatic equipment and ready for the introduction of S.T.D. In 1973, it had over 8000 subscribers and the new building is likely to be too small.

NOTE C — INVERNESS ELECTRICITY

Inverness Town Council were early into the business of the provision of electricity for lighting, with a Provisional Order entitled Inverness Electric Lighting Order, 1899. This had to be renewed twice before the first offer was considered by the Council on 9 January, 1904.

The first supply was 240-480 V. three wire D.C., which was later supplemented by a large A.C. steam-driven turbo-alternator at Waterloo Place, with an ancillary Refuse Destructor boiler wired in parallel with the boiler in the Generating Station. The Town Council took over the supply in 1925, and so it remained until after nationalisation in 1947, when the supply was taken over by the North of Scotland Hydro-Electric Board. The D.C. system was changed over during the early 1950s, and the supply at Waterloo Place was shut down in 1952, the last items to be shut down being the Rotary Convertors, which had to be kept going until the D.C. changeover was complete.

NOTE D — WHOLESALE BUSINESSES

In the early days of the wholesale business, wholesale traders established themselves at the point of supply of ship, coach or railway, where they warehoused bulk imported goods, broke these into the required smaller quantities, and supplied shops, traders and caterers.

Building Supply Merchants and Wood Merchants have stayed on at the Harbour, where the bulk of the heavier supplies come in, while most of the dry goods, grocer and greengrocer wholesalers established themselves close to the Railway Station in Falcon Square, and Eastgate.

A well-remembered figure of pre-war years was George Gallon, a wholesale fruiterer in Falcon Square, who always had a box of bruised fruit at the door, and a smile, a piece of fruit and a kindly word for children, or for those who could not afford to buy.

The first change in this system came with the arrival before the war of Coopers and the Co-op, both chain stores, supplying themselves. After the 1939-45 war, this trend continued, with the establishment of other multiple chain stores providing their own goods to their own shops, and later supermarkets. At the same time, larger wholesalers from the south, being able as a result of size to give more economical service over a wider range of goods, were taking over the local wholesaler.

A further development has been the wholesaler joining a national symbol group, such as Spar or Mace, to give the small firm the advantage of large-scale buying and national branded goods. "Cash and Carry" warehouses, where prices are kept low by cash-only deals and no delivery, are now established in Inverness. They are of value to small retailers. van traders and caterers.

The frozen food business has seen tremendous growth in the last 10 to 15 years. Inverness now has a frozen food "cash and carry" and the establishment of Salvesen's at Dalcross Industrial Estate, with national refrigerated transport facilities, is not only a boost to commerce, but also to the export of frozen fruit, such as raspberries, of which a large area round Inverness has been planted, and of frozen game and meat.

The wholesale business has provided Inverness with many of its well-known figures, requiring as it did, men of broad vision and knowledge, who had to take calculated risks and who have given great service to the town in their business and in public service. Two such men in this generation are Provost W. A. Smith, and Mr Jack Forbes. It is hoped that the trained managers who replace these individuals will give the same love and service to the life of Inverness as their predecessors.

NOTE E — NORTH OF SCOTLAND HYDRO-ELECTRIC BOARD

It is not possible to over-emphasise what the Board has done for Inverness and for the Highlands and Islands, both commercially and industrially.

In 1973, the Board's water-power developments in the North of Scotland produced an average of about 3,000 million units (one unit is approximately one bar of a radiant fire for one hour) from 54 main hydro-electric stations, with a capacity in excess of 1,000,000 kilowatts. The pumped-storage scheme at Cruachan, together with thermal and diesel stations, produce another 800,000 kw. The Foyers pumped-storage due to come on stream in 1974, will add another 300,000 kw. of generating capacity.

What this has meant to Inverness between 1948 and 1970 is that something like £100,000,000 has been spent in the Highlands on wages alone, in building hydro-electric works. At the peak of the construction work, nearly every consulting civil and electrical engineer of note had an office in Inverness. Stores and supplies were shipped through Inverness. To obtain access to the scheme, hundreds of miles of new roads were built or improved, roads that became part of the infrastructure for commercial use. The available power enriches the life of the rural areas, with reflecting benefit to Inverness in trade and tourism.

Barmkin Tower. Inches.

LAND USE

a. Agriculture

JOHN GRANT

In selecting a period against which to write on agriculture, the past 40 years' span is attractive, as one can cover most of it with the benefit of personal memory, and as there can never have been a similar period which saw so much change and agricultural progress.

The extent of change and development may be indicated by some examples. At the beginning of the period there was a harvest when an abnormally early snow-storm falling on uncut corn flattened all crops, so that harvesting by binder was impossible. A personal memory of that year was of eight scythe men, with a full complement of gatherers and stookers behind them, cutting in one 10-acre field — a ridiculous set-up for the modern farmer. Where could such manpower be found today, or where would be the need, when a modest-sized combine harvester could deal efficiently with such crops at over one acre per hour?

In those days, too, we had on our farms beef cattle of size and substance, and farmers sought to reduce that size to meet the butcher's demand for smaller joints for the modern families of that time. How acceptable would those larger cattle be for today's meat trade! How the pre-war farmer would have laughed to see the Continental cattle we import today. The hill farmer got very little for his lambs in the thirties, but he had, as his main additional worries, to contend with pasture wastage by rabbits and bracken, and sheep losses from tick and from blowfly parasites. He has had to wait until 1972 to see lamb prices really get ahead of costs, but, while he has now a new lists of pests and diseases, the chemist has helped him with ticks, blowfly and bracken, and nature has checked the rabbit. Without the advantage of experience and memory, one can hardly appreciate the extent of these scourges, nor could the pre-war farmer have anticipated the present fears of parasite and pest immunity, or of pollution.

Inverness District

The district is truly Highland. From a narrow strip of useful arable land fringing the Inner Moray and Beauly Firths, the land rises through an upland belt to a mass of hard heather-covered hills. It has considerable character, as the Findhorn, the Nairn, the rivers of the Great Glen, the Beauly and its tributaries produce a variety of glens. These glens, with the exceptions of the Lower Nairn and Findhorn, are narrow, with little alluvial land to give quality to the farms. On the other hand, the shelter created has a considerable effect on the climate and thus on the farming. The change in land quality from the arable land of the east coast to the hills on the south and western boundaries is described by the parish figures for "crops and grass" and "rough grazing" — (Table I) — the overall ratio of 1 : 9.2 in favour of rough grazing emphasising the predominance of hill lands.

TABLE I[1]

	Crops & Grass	Rough Grazing
Boleskine and Abertarff	1,833	78,766
Kilmorack	4.378	130,710
Kiltarlity	5,960	22,895
Kirkhill	3,646	1,817
Urquhart	3,879	72,930
Ardersier	1,586	297
Croy	2,867	589
Daviot	4,750	42,670
Dores	3,305	14,116
Inverness	8,678	9,625
Moy	1,899	77,811
Petty	6.594	318

The following rainfall figures — (Table II) — also give a useful picture of the variations in climate and farm quality.

TABLE II[2]

Annual Rainfall — Averages for 1916 - 1950

	Inches
Nairn	25
Dalcross	26
Inverness	26
Muir of Ord	30
Moy	40
Foyers	37
Invermoriston	46
Cannich	47

Although there is no sharp definition in land type or farm character, and no such thing as an average farm for any category, farming in the area might be classified under three headings, "mixed — arable," "upland," and "hill." As the purpose of this article is to present some record of local farming as well as to describe change and development, actual farms have been selected, where records for the period are available and where the farmers have been good enough to allow these to be used. This gives greater accuracy to the picture. Comments can be more easily made on a local basis and to some degree set against a national background.

MIXED ARABLE FARMING

This is essentially restricted to the narrow strip bordering the Beauly and Inner Moray Firths, land which varies from a fairly heavy loam on the Beauly side to the light sandy soils of Petty, land which is not of top arable quality and on which most farmers have chosen to have substantial stock as well as arable farming interests.

TABLE III

Excerpt from June Agricultural Returns of a typical "mixed arable" farm

	1935	1950	1972
Land:			
Total Acreage	282	282	503
Crops:			
Oats	65	54	92
Barley	15	40	204
Turnips	45	42	22
Potatoes	2	20	5
Mashlum	—	10	—
Grass:			
Hay or Silage	22	10	68
Grazing	133	106	112
Livestock:			
Horses	10	3	—
Dairy Cows	4	—	—
Beef Cows for Breeding	—	—	62
Calves	—	—	60
Fattening Bullocks	65	109	—
Breeding Ewes	73	57	90
Lambs	71	81	142
Hoggs	64	19	—
Sows	1	6	59
Other Pigs	40	20	193
Hens	130	225	—
Labour:			
Permanent — Over 21	5	5	3
Permanent — Under 21	1	1	—
Casual	2	1	—

The June agricultural returns quoted above describe a typical farm and discussion of the various items may trace changes over the years and establish the present position. The years 1935, 1950 and 1972 have been chosen — 1935 to depict pre-war farming and the depression of that period. At that tme, farming had suffered greatly and no real improvement was in sight. By 1950 the war was behind, the 1948 Agricultural Act had been passed to set a pattern for post-war farming, there had been ten years of greater prosperity and full production was the theme. 1972 is not only the last full year for which records are available, but also the last year before Britain's entry into the E.E.C. In the past 22 years, the pattern of farming has changed markedly, but although farming has changed to reflect changes in the economic climate, the general structure has remained. Our adoption of the economic and administrative structure of Europe looks like bringing much more drastic change.

Land Tenure and Ownership

Land is held by tenant and owner-occupying farmers, but, because it includes a few large estates, the pattern for the area has been set primarily by the circumstances and legislation of a landlord-tenant system. Although there have been some amendments in broad terms since 1948, the tenant farmer has enjoyed security of tenure. This has had the great advantage of giving confidence to tenant farmers, and farming has benefited. Landlords have in some cases been more reluctant to let and have taken farms into their own hands where possible.

There is considerable variation in size of farms, from really large family businesses to part-time small-holdings. Governments have seen the small farmer as a social and economic problem and out of keeping with the advance in technical knowledge. Official encouragement and, since 1967, the inducement of "golden handshake" schemes to outgoing farmers have made no great impact — farmers do not retire readily — but over the period and in fact throughout farming history, amalgamation of units and the creation of stronger farming businesses have gone steadily on, reflecting, in farmers, personal ambition and achievement and, in estate management, better land utilisation and economy in buildings. These factors have all operated and the effects are evident in the Inverness area. Increase in the farm business is shown as having taken place on our average farm and, set against the other figures, demonstrates the accompanying advancement in technical efficiency.

Crops and Crop Husbandry

Many expressed fears that intensive wartime and post-war cropping would cause a general decrease in soil fertility, but, in fact, the opposite has been true. This has mainly been due to increased use of lime and fertilisers and the extension of this lime and fertiliser usage to grass — in fact, to greater acceptance of grass as a crop, instead of something which was left to nature. In the Inverness area no real problems in soil structure have yet occurred. The tremendous range of selective weedkillers now available give good control of most annual weeds. The most troublesome weeds of arable farms now are couch grass and wild oats. The wild oat (avena fatua) in particular is proving difficult to control. Crop yields are not entirely a measure of soil fertility, but yields quoted for Scottish crops— Table IV — are reassuring.

TABLE IV[3]

SCOTLAND

Estimated yield per acre of: —

	Barley cwts/acre	Oats cwts./acre	Potatoes tons/acre
1935	19.8	16.5	6.7
1945	19.6	16.6	7.1
1955	27.4	19.3	7.1
1965	30.9	22.4	8.4
1970	32.7	25.6	11.4

The cereals grown in 1935 on our sample farm were "Yielder" and "Victory" oats and "Common" barley, all suitable for more acid soil, a lower fertility level and for binder-harvesting and stacking. Grain yields might be around 25 cwts per acre. Perhaps half of the oats would be fed on the farm. The barley might also be for feeding or, in a good season, sold for distilling. Plant breeders changed the cereal pattern with the introduction of high-yielding, short-strawed barley varieties, suitable for more intensive farming and greater use of fertilisers —first came the Danish varieties, "Kenia" and "Maja," and later the most dependable Swedish variety, "Ymer." The list of varieties and countries of origin is now long.

Developments in machinery were equally significant. The combine grain drill came into general use in the early 1950s and, with the low phosphate levels common in soils at that time, had a significant effect on crop yields. The combine harvester reduced labour problems, was better able to deal with lodged crops, and reduced grain losses in harvesting. With it and the baler, the traditional corn stack disappeared. Potential grain yields are now almost double those of pre-war days and, with the yield balance being in favour of barley, it has now replaced oats as the dominant cereal both locally and nationally. Barley is still used predominantly for feeding, but most arable farmers hope to get their best away for distilling. The farmer has the option, if he is adequately equipped, of drying or preserving and storing his barley on his farm, or of contracting to sell "off the combine" to a local merchant or maltster.

The turnip crop has generally declined in Scottish farming, the main reason being its heavy labour requirement. Few farmers could finance, nor would today's workmen readily undertake, work on the pre-war scale. Turnips would probably have disappeared were it not for the introduction of selective weed-killers, new sowing techniques, precision seeders and mechanical harvesters. If growing costs can be kept down, it should still be grown, as it is a useful break crop, well suited to local light soils and capable of giving a large bulk of fodder for feeding on the land to sheep or, in courts, to cattle.

The story of potato growing is less straightforward. Between the wars a small acreage of ware was grown for local markets, but in the late thirties some farmers were going in for seed production, taking advantage of the district's favourable climate and soil, and operating under the Department of Agriculture's Potato Certification Scheme, to sell in English and Southern Scottish markets. War-time saw greatly increased potato growing and this continued into post-war years until the English market for Scottish seed began to contract. The official certification scheme gave varietal purity and very good control of foliage diseases, but in recent years tuber diseases have become more troublesome, and the husbandry measures now necessary and the Certification Scheme operated extending to stem-cutting, virus tested seed are so exacting that seed potato growing is becoming the job of a few, but more highly specialised, potato growers. With the restricted and specialised seed market, and the varied and exacting demands of the increasing potato processing trade, this trend is likely to continue.

Higher fertiliser use and increased mechanisation have completely changed methods of grass conservation. There is now almost no hand labour in hay or silage making; both systems can be easy and speedy. The low rainfall of the Moray Firth coast makes it very suitable for hay-making and so, where hay is wanted as a cash crop, or where baled hay is attractive for winter feeding, hay-making has continued. Many farmers

T

have, however, gone over to silage. It goes better with intensive grassland management. It, too, entails complete mechanisation, the breakthrough in silage-making being the advent of the forage harvester. The most advanced system at present is probably that based on the high dry matter tower and belt feeding.

An interesting feature has been the development in recent years of soft-fruit and vegetable growing. Table V shows the extent and distribution of these crops — the main crop being raspberries. Vegetables are grown for the fresh market, but most of the soft fruit is for quick freezing. Climate and soil are such that quality crops can be grown; and facilities for freezing are available. Further development of this crop will depend on the market and the availability of labour for harvesting.

TABLE V[4]

	Vegetables	Soft Fruit
Inverness and Bona	52¼	12½
Petty	1	—
Croy and Dalcross	3	88½
Kirkhill	¼	89¾
Kiltarilty	—	1
Urquhart and Glenmoriston	—	5
Kilmorack	1½	78
TOTAL	58	274¾

Livestock

A number of very good dairy farms are situated in the coastal belt and around Beauly, Inverness and Nairn — both Ayrshires and Friesians are represented, but Friesians are particularly strong and increasing in numbers. The area is, however, essentially one for beef cattle. Traditionally a feeding area, it had also a few very good herds of pedigree beef cattle. There was, in the '50s and '60s, some reduction in cattle stocks, particularly of breeding herds. Pedigree herds tended to become the reserve of the wealthier few. The Inverness area, however, did not go out of cattle to the same extent as many other arable areas and now, with the great demand for beef, the trend is definitely to increase. The incentive of the beef cow subsidy and scarcity and cost of store cattle have also brought back some breeding herds.

The area has also a tradition for sheep-rearing and feeding —the light soils being well suited to the job. Breeding flocks were of half-breeds, or Cheviots, and most feeding lambs were based on the same breeds. Low prices cleared sheep from many low-ground farms and, although better returns have strengthened demand for feeding sheep, breeding flocks have not yet returned to their former numbers.

Pigs and poultry are now confined to a few, larger intensive specialist enterprises. Small flocks of hens and the odd lots of pigs — pin money units — have almost completely disappeared.

Machinery and Buildings

The development of farm machinery and the changes which mechanisation has brought to farming have been tremendous. When one considers the extent of this mechanical revolution, it is difficult to believe that many farmers still had horses at the end of the war. Mechanisation has changed all aspects of farming — from land reclamation and crop husbandry to crop handling and storage and stock feeding.

Improvement of farm buildings has also been extensive but, because of the capital involved, and as it had to follow and be adapted to progress in crop and livestock husbandry, it was slow to start. An early development was in grain drying and storage. Extension of steadings has, in many cases, followed and been facilitated by amalgamation of holdings and, to a large extent, new buildings are being built as adaptable large single span units. There is still much to be done in farm buildings, but, if capital is available and the demand for livestock persists, progress could be rapid.

Labour

The sample farm shows a drop in farm staff from 8 to 3, even although the farm has almost doubled in size. This is typical of the Inverness district and of all Britain. It has brought a profound change to the farming scene. There is much less hard work and less of the "social" atmosphere which went with it. The regular farm worker has always been highly skilled in a variety of crafts. This is still very true, but his skills must now increasingly embrace those of the mechanical engineer, and his knowledge of crop and stock husbandry be increasingly technical. An entry in our sample farmer's diary for 1935 shows the grieve's wages as £66 per year, with perquisites of a cottage and 3 tons of coal; and 6 pints of milk daily. Annual deduction for National Health and Unemployment Insurance amounted to £3 2s. 10d. annually. Overtime payments would be few. This would be about the end of an era and system, as the Agricultural Wages Act of 1937 set the pattern for weekly wages scales and working regulations in use today. In the first wages schedule for 1938, the minimum grieve's wage is given as 36/6d. a week. Comparison with the present day has little meaning, because of changed standards and value of money. Perquisites, apart from the provision of a cottage, have almost disappeared. The present Agricultural Wages Board Order gives the minimum wages for a grieve as £23.40 per week, and for a tractor-man as £20.85. Most farm workers are, however, paid above the minimum rate. This is as it should be, as in skill and efficiency they compare very favourably with industrial workers.

Upland Farming

The upland farm comes much closer to what most people would picture as a typical Highland farm. In farming terminology, "upland" has a stronger relationship to land quality than to elevation, and can be taken to describe farms on second quality land throughout the area, although in general occupying the intermediate position between the arable coastal fringe and the hills. There is no typical size, the range being between

TABLE VI

Excerpt from June Agricultural Returns of Typical "Upland" Farm

	1935	1950	1972
Land (Total Acreage):			
Arable	151	202	207
Rough Grazing	650	719	964
Crops:			
Oats	41	58	47
Barley	—	—	—
Turnips	19	21	19
Rape	—	7	7
Potatoes	1	2	1
Rotation Grass:			
Hay	10	14	17
Silage	—	—	—
Grazing	80	100	116
Rough Grazing:	650	719	964
Livestock:			
Horses (first tractor bought) in 1947	5	2	—
Dairy Cows	2	2	2
Beef Cows (A.A. Cross)	15	31	61
Bulls (A.A.)	1	1	2
Breeding Ewes (Blackface)	220	250	306
Rams (Leicester)	5	7	9
Pigs	2	—	—
Hens	50	160	—
Labour:	2	2	1

part-time crofts and quite large units. They are generally family farms. Arable land is of secondary quality; usually a light loam running out to peat at the hill side, and to better alluvial land when the farm is in a glen and lying down to a river. Bad drainage, frequently associated with impervious subsoil or merely with alluvial flats or unruly rivers and burns, can further reduce land quality. Arable land is usually limited, but most farms have "outruns" of rough grazings on river banks, moorland and hills. These outruns usually include some firm, dry land, with hill or woodland shelter, and provide extra grazing which, used in association with the arable land, greatly increase the farms' stock-carrying capacity.

Details of crop and stock describe such an upland farm and indicate some changes which have taken place (Table VI).

The arable land is hard and dry; the outrun has some birch woodland and extends to high heather hill. As for the arable farm, the farm boundaries have changed over the years and for typical reasons — extension of the farm business by taking over a neighbouring farm, a small area of land reclamation, loss to forestry of part of the inby hill, addition of a block of higher rough grazing lands.

Mechanisation, increased labour efficiency and improved technology have similarly greatly improved the efficiency of upland farming. Most striking has been the increased soil fertility. This came, as on lowland farms, from better technology and agricultural prosperity, but the Lime Subsidy and the Marginal Agricultural Production Schemes, introduced in 1937 and as a wartime measure, respectively, gave a stimulus and produced a uniformity of land improvement which would not otherwise have been achieved.

Traditionally, upland farms working on the 6 and 7 course rotation had at least half the arable land in grass and, being stock-rearing farms, depended greatly on it. Increased soil fertility, the increase in grass quality which it brought and recognition of grassland management as essential, have been features of post-war years. The increase in livestock numbers is a measure of this change. Most farms still hold to the general structure of the 6-course rotation, perhaps changing from oats to barley, and adjusting the acreage and position of the turnip crop, but others, usually those farming more intensively, have gone further or completely over to grass, conserving it as silage. Strip grazing and paddock grazing are in use on some farms to intensify grass utilisation.

The livestock increase is predominantly in cattle, and, alongside this increase, eradication of diseases, first tuberculosis and now brucellosis, have been tremendous items in farming progress. There are, in fact, great changes at present in beef cattle breeding. The market demands larger and leaner beef carcases and farmers, while renewing or building up herds in achieving brucellosis accreditation, are striving to establish breeding stock suited to this demand. There is as yet no uniformity. Traditional Aberdeen Angus and Shorthorn crosses dominate breeding herds of beef cows, but there is now more variety, particularly from dairy crosses, of which Friesian crosses are preferred. For crossing bulls, there is a greater range. The Aberdeen Angus still predominates, but a few farmers, looking for greater size, have introduced Herefords, Lincoln Reds, Devons, Welsh Blacks and, in a few cases, Charollais and Simmentals — for such, artificial insemination services have been useful. It may well take some time before farmers decide which cattle will best suit their farming systems and markets. The present scarcity and cost of feeding stuffs, if persisting, must inevitably affect their decisions.

On most farms, cattle numbers outstripped steading accommodation. This has been met by new building and by outwintering. Cattle outwinter well, but the system brings labour problems and difficulties in food transport and land poaching. Labour economy has dictated abandoning the traditional byre and, in new building, present interest is mostly in cow-cubicles and semi-scraped courts.

On upland farms, sheep husbandry, reflecting the intermediate place in land quality, is mainly based on the hill breeds, but with a Leicester or Down ram used for crossing. Post-war attempts to intensify by breeding sheep of greater fertility — based mainly on the Finnish Landrace — have had little success.

Upland farms and farming are at this moment in good heart. The present rise in cattle and sheep prices has lifted them out of a depression which was developing a few years ago. This depression was due to the fall in prices which reached its lowest point in 1966/67 and to the general problems of small farms. The effect of rising costs is felt first on second quality land, particularly if it is not supplemented by a good outrun.

HILL FARMING

There is a large area of hill land, but no easy way to describe a typical hill farm. Definition is difficult. As has already been stated, much hill land provides outrun for upland farms. Much of the more extreme, higher and outlying hill land is in deer forests carrying few sheep. Between these two extremes, sheep farms vary greatly in size, land quality and climate; all factors which influence the type of sheep and the stocking rate. Most hills are on "black" heather, but on the western side are a few "green" grassy hills. In general terms, the heather hills are stocked with Blackface sheep, while Cheviots may be carried on the green hills. To give an acreage stocking rate is almost impossible, but 6-7 acres per ewe is common. Land quality and climate influence, not only breed and stocking rate, but also the size and type of sheep carried. Cattle do not contribute much to real hill farms, their places being dictated by the amount of arable land and grassy hill available.

There has been great progress in hill farming. This may not be so obvious to the casual observer as the changes in other types of farming. New cottages, sheep fanks, clipping sheds, fences and such capital improvements have been effected, but, although encouraged by official subsidy schemes, and sometimes by factors outwith farming, income from sheep farming remained static for many years, capital has been scarce and development restricted accordingly. The real progress has been in sheep husbandry practices.

Traditionally, sheep farmers set hardiness and ability to survive unassisted on the natural hill grazings, as the first essential in hill sheep. They feared any practice which might interfere with the ewe's ability to "rake" the hill, or which might, by making life easier for her, reduce her hardiness. Wartime and post-war years saw this change. As a first step, pasture improvement was accepted, new techniques for re-seeding hill swards were developed and management systems involving controlled grazing in fenced pastures were introduced. Some farmers have tried inwintering sheep in adapted buildings or specially built sheep sheds. This is, of course, no new practice, but in modern sheep farming it has not developed to any extent — feed and building costs have been too high.

Research work published in the early '50s brought new knowledge on the nutrition of the pregnant ewe, and since then hand feeding of ewes has gradually been accepted — a revolution in hill sheep farming practice. Progress in control of sheep diseases and parasites has also been great. Again, this has involved changes which many sheep farmers accepted with apprehension, but which have now become part of normal sheep husbandry.

FARMING TODAY
Farming, although in good heart, is now in a period of great change and uncertainty — change from the British to the E.E.C. system of agricultural price fixing and marketing;

change in market demands and extension into the European market; change through acceptance of E.E.C. administration and husbandry regulations; uncertainty as to the political position and the strength of agriculture in our increasingly urban community. There is increasing competition for land, from forestry, recreation, urban extension and industry; land prices no longer signify the agricultural value. Land use must certainly be the most important future problem and one on which short-term expediency should give way to long-term thinking and the recognition of true values.

REFERENCES

1. Department of Agriculture and Fisheries for Scotland Returns.
2. Figures supplied by the Meteorological Office.
3. D.A.F.S. Agricultural Returns.
4. D.A.F.S. Agricultural Returns.

Wardlaw Church, Kirkhill

LAND USE

b. Woods and Forests

ROBERT INNES

The area covered in this book is important in the history of Scottish Forestry, indeed of British Forestry. Some of the early thoughts on Arboriculture were included in a book published by Brigadier Mackintosh of Borlum in 1729. The area contains some of the finest native pinewoods in the North of Scotland, in Glen Affric and Strathfarrar, and a few estates with a long history of good forest management. The first Chairman of the Forestry Commission was Lord Lovat in 1919, and there is an important forest research centre at the Lon Mor in Inchnacardoch Forest near Fort Augustus.

In 1969, Inverness was selected as the site for a Scottish Forestry Education and Training Centre based on the Inverness Technical College, with facilities for work in the nearby Culloden Forest.

The area is well covered with trees, the acreage planted by the Forestry Commission being more than double that in private ownership. The Forestry Commission forests are grouped into five administrative units. First, in alphabetical order, is Glen Affric, where there are 69740 acres (27896 ha.), 14355 acres (5742 ha.) of which are actually tree-covered. It was in the natural woodlands of Glen Affric that the television series, "The Last of the Mohicans" and "The Pathfinder," were filmed. Second is Culloden, with 18612 acres (7445 ha.), of which 13752 acres (5501 ha.) are planted. This forest contains the battlefield and some of the graves are among the trees, but it was open moorland in 1746. Third is Farigaig, the smallest and newest of the five, lying to the east of Loch Ness, not far from Foyers, where of 11345 acres (4538 ha.), nearly 7500 acres (3000 ha.) are planted. Fourth is Glen Urquhart, 26745 acres (10698 ha.), less than half of which is planted with trees, the greater part is mostly agricultural land still. Fifth and last, yet one of the earliest of the Forestry Commission's lands, is Inchnacardoch, running up the steep slopes west of Loch Ness a little north of Fort Augustus. Here there are 31555 acres (12542 ha.), of which less than half are planted.

Most of the area is mountainous, rising from sea-level to 3375 ft (1150 m.) at Sgurr na Lapaich, north of Loch Mullardoch in the west, and to 2702 feet (820 m.) at Carn Coire na Creiche in the Monadhliaths. Mountains and uplands constitute some 80% of the district.

The bedrock of the area has not been surveyed in detail, but an examination of the geological maps shows large areas of undifferentiated schists of the Moine Series on either side of the Great Glen, but predominantly so to the west of Loch Ness. The coastal area between Inverness and Nairn rests on Old Red Sandstone with some westerly extension of this rock down both sides of Loch Ness. Covering the bedrock is a mantle of glacial drift and boulder clay of varying depth.

Soils lying on or derived from the Old Red Sandstone are in the main moderately fertile and freely drained, and it is on such soils that intensive arable farming is practised. Soils elsewhere tend to be poorer, and those on the valley slopes are capable of producing good crops of coniferous timber after suitable cultivation and drainage.

Recent work on pollen analysis shows that the first trees to arrive in Scotland were the aspen and the birch, and these were followed by pine, oak, alder, ash, elm, lime, hazel, juniper, holly and bird-cherry. It is interesting to note that all these species can be seen today.

The early forests developed with little interference from man, and would have stretched unbroken, save only by mountain, swamp and water, to the margins of the sea[1]. Only when man turned from being a hunter and a fisher to the growing of crops and the domestication of animals was there a threat to the trees. The grazing of animals reduces natural regeneration in the woodlands, and might have had a greater effect on the forest than the cutting of trees.

The Bronze Age people used timber for a greater variety of purposes than their predecessors. These were the people who built forts and crannogs and used timber for lacing the stonework of the forts. It was the destruction of these by fire which resulted, where the stone was fusible, in vitrified forts, for example, those at Tor Duin in Inchnacardoch Forest and at Craig Phadrig, just outside Inverness.

In mediaeval times, timber was needed in ever-increasing quantities for building castles, churches and dwellings. The Kings granted land to many religious houses[2] for the support of the monks. These communities invariably established themselves within, or on the verge of, extensive areas of natural woodlands. The location of these houses gives some indication of those areas where primaeval deciduous forest survived on fertile land worth reclaiming for agriculture[2]. The only one in this district was the Valliscaulian Priory at Beauly.

The Highland woods were discovered in the 17th century by the lowland Scots. A report at the time states that in Glenmoriston "great long woods of firr trees doth grow," and the woods of Stratherrick and Abertarff are also mentioned[1]. In a deed of 1634, reference was made to the woods at Lochletter and Delshangie in Glen Urquhart.

But for extraction difficulties, the Highland woods might have disappeared. The natural woods in the valleys of the Farrar, Cannich, Affric and Moriston owe their existence today to their inaccessibility in the past, and it is only recently (1959) that the woods in Glen Affric have been peneterated by a road.

In 1634, there are records of iron-smelting in Glen Urquhart. The ore, being heavy and compact, was more easily transported to the woods than the timber to the ore. The smelting of iron did more than any other industry to destroy the native woodlands of Scotland. Anderson states that there were eighteen locations of iron-smelting in Inverness-shire, and of these, two were in Glen Urquhart, one at the head of Strathglass, one at Dores, and nine in Strathnairn[2]. The writer came across the site of a furnace in Glengarry in 1953, near the farm of Greenfield, where Forestry Commission ploughing operations had exposed quantities of pig-iron. The smelters preferred broad-leaved trees, such as birch and beech, which have high heat-producing qualities, but, where there was a shortage of these, they had no hesitation in using pine.

In 1643, there is a record that "one Captain George Scott cam to Inverness and there built a ship of a prodigious bignes for buck and burden, non such ever seen on our North seas." She sailed the day before the Battle of Auldearn, 9 May, 1645. Timber of both fir and oak was used in her construction, from Lord Lovat's Dalcattach Forest in Glenmoriston. The building of the citadel in Inverness by Cromwell's forces was done with oak from England and fir from the woods of Hugh Fraser at Struy.

The risings of 1715 and 1745 virtually stopped all estate improvement and forestry development, while the subsequent activities of the Board of Commissioners of the Forfeited Estates had a disturbing effect on many Highland estates. Vast quantities of trees were cut annually on the estates of Lovat, Chisholm and Struy by the Commissioners. In 1765, there was a large sawmill at Beauly, supplied by logs which were floated down the rivers.

Towards the end of the 18th century, Highland landowners changed their style of living by adopting that of their English counterparts. To achieve that needed more money, and one way to get money was for the owners to lease parts of their estates to wealthy sheep-farmers and industrialists from the South. Some went further and sold their land to the same kind of buyer.

At the beginning of the 19th century, attempts were being made to make good some of the destruction of the earlier period. The exploitation of the accessible native woods continued, however, at a steadily increasing rate. It was about this time that some woods were destroyed to improve the grazing for sheep. According to Nairne, the first sheep farm was established at Corrimony in Glen Urquhart by men from the South in 1797, and this was soon followed by one at Knockfin, not far from Tomich in Glen Affric.[3]

The most extensive forest estate at the end of the 19th century was Lord Lovat's estate of Beaufort. This estate had, over the past century, attempted to manage its forests according to the standards of the time. Although there were large areas of native woodlands in the upper reaches of the rivers lying to the north-west of Loch Ness, these were never managed— only exploited where possible.

The 19th century's enthusiasm for planting was not maintained into the 20th century. There were a number of reasons for this, not the least being the enhanced returns which landowners got from developing their land as deer forests or grouse moors, or for sheep grazing. All these brought an immediate return, while trees took a long time to grow, and timber was easily and cheaply imported. There were, however, some Highland landowners who could foresee a time when imported timber prices would rise, and when the United Kingdom might suffer a shortage. These men, notably Lord Novar and Lord Lovat, foresaw that the extension of commercial forestry was only possible if undertaken by the State.

Lord Lovat, assisted by his brother-in-law, Captain Stirling of Keir, undertook a survey of the Great Glen to demonstrate what possibilities there were for forestry in the Highlands and to give force to their strongly held views that a Forest Authority should be set up to extend, on a large scale, the forest area of the country. Their findings were published by the Royal Scottish Arboricultural Society in 1911, eight years before the Forestry Commission came into being, and the areas subsequently planted by the Forestry Commission followed very closely those assessed as plantable in that Report.

Before the outbreak of the First World War, Britain was almost wholly dependent for her timber supplies on imported wood from northern Europe, the United States and Canada. On the outbreak of war, the European supplies were cut off. Large quantities were, however, still being shipped across the Atlantic until the Germans began their policy of unrestricted submarine warfare in 1917. Many timber cargoes were subsequently sunk and, to compensate for the losses, the home sources were exploited to the full.

To replace the large acreage of timber felled for war purposes and to ensure that Britain would never again be largely dependent on foreign supplies of timber in wartime, the Government in 1919 decided to set up a State Forest Authority — the Forestry Commission — to undertake a large afforestation programme. Lord Lovat became its first Chairman. One of his first acts was to feu his sporting estate of Inchnacardoch, near Fort Augustus, to the newly created Forest Authority to form the first Forestry Commission forest in Scotland.

In the years that followed, the economic climate in the first post-war decade did not encourage even moderate investment in forestry. Many of the privately-owned felled areas were invaded by birch and other hardwood species and many were grazed by domestic animals, which checked the regeneration of trees.

As has been said, the Forestry Commission acquired by feu charter the sporting estate of Inchnacardoch, near Fort Augustus, and the adjacent sheep farm of Auchterawe in 1919. In 1920, they purchased the wooded slopes by Port Clair from the Glenmoriston Estate. In 1923, the valley slopes of the south side of Glen Urquhart were bought from the Countess of Seafield to form Glen Urquhart Forest. In 1924, the Forestry Commission acquired more land from the Glenmoriston Estate to form its Creagnaneun Forest. Ten years later, some 2300 acres of the Guisachan estate, not far from Cannich, were bought.

The Forestry Commission set about the planting of the areas acquired in the '20s with purpose and vigour. A great deal of the ground was covered with natural hardwood growth, mainly birch and oak, and, before planting could take place, much of this had to be removed or partly removed. Destruction of the existing woodland cover on an area removes a means of vertical drainage by transpiration, and the ground tends to become waterlogged where there is no slope. The early planters removed surplus water by cutting drains manually. On rich ground, the young trees were planted directly into the soil surface, and on ground not requiring drainage, the same method was used. The direct planting of peatland proved disastrous, mainly because the peat was not adequately drained. On private Highland estates the main species planted was Scots pine, with some European larch in a mixture. The Forestry Commission, on very slender evidence, opted to plant spruce, mainly Norway spruce, on a wide variety of soils, many of which were unsuited, or too poor, for that species. Many of these plantings failed completely, others developed slowly and patchily. These unsatisfactory plantations were later interplanted with pines and larches which overtook the checked spruce and eventually outstripped it. In the changed environment, the spruce started to grow. Examples of these mixtures can be seen today along the Auchterawe road in Inchnacardoch Forest.

The first Divisional Officer of the Forestry Commission to be posted to Inverness — Frank Scott — had worked for a time on a private estate in the Lothians and while there he recognised the merits of Douglas fir as a tree which will grow more quickly and produce more timber than Scots pine in the same period of time. He used this species, which was brought to this country in the mid-19th century by the well-known Scottish botanist, David Douglas, both freely and successfully on the slopes of Inchnacardoch, Port Clair, Creaganeun and Glenurquhart. Much of this Douglas fir is now 50 years old and will be felled from 1974 onwards, to supply sawlogs to the new sawmill at Corpach near Fort William.

In 1924 the Research Branch of the Forestry Commission selected an area of high-lying peatland in Inchnacardoch Forest —the Lon Mor — as an experimental area. The main object of the work there was to see how far the hitherto "unplantable" soils could be improved to produce crops of timber. By the end of the 1920s, some of the reasons for earlier failures had been discovered. Trees could be grown on peatlands, provided the planting techniques were designed to provide air to the roots by turf-planting, i.e., by planting through the upturned turf of peat and placing the roots in the sandwich layer between the turf and the surface of the peat. The results of this method of planting were indeed promising, and phosphatic fertilisers helped the young trees. The techniques for success were now clear; what was needed were suitable tractors and ploughs to produce mechanically the turfs on which the trees would be planted, and the necessary drains to ensure that the tree roots would not become waterlogged.

Many tree species were also planted to see which were

the most suitable for the peat soils. The choice became restricted to a few, of which Lodgepole pine *(Pinus contorta)* and Sitka spruce *(Pices sitchensis)* proved to be the best, although Japanese larch and hybrid larch have also done reasonably well.

The success of the experimental work, carried out between the wars at Inchnacardoch Forest, brought a range of soil types, hitherto regarded as unplantable, into the plantable category. This considerably widened the area on which commercial crops of trees could be grown. It was now possible to purchase large areas of land of rather poor quality which, after appropriate treatment, could be transformed into good forest soils, capable of producing satisfactory crops of timber. It also enabled the Forestry Commission to achieve the relatively large planting programmes set by Government for this part of the country.

When the Second World War broke out, the early plantings of the Forestry Commission had not reached the stage where they could be harvested for timber, and once again the country had to rely on the private estates for its timber needs, though some of the plantings of the Forestry Commission provided some of the pitprops the coal mines required. Large quantities of timber were felled on the Beaufort estate of Lord Lovat, but the native woods in Glen Strathfarrar and Glen Affric were saved.

After 1945, within the area being described, many landowners increased the acreage of plantations on their estates by means of the Dedication Scheme, or by one or other of the Grant Schemes. There were 42 Dedication Schemes and 5 Approved Woodland Schemes in December, 1973, totalling some 14,000 acres (5600 ha.). The comparable area in Forestry Commission ownership was 60,300 acres (24,120 ha.).

Not much land was acquired during the war by the Forestry Commission, but active steps were taken after the war to increase the reserves of plantable land. Existing forests were substantially enlarged and new forests were created. Land at Cullachy was added to Inchnacardoch Forest, and land at Dundreggan to Port Clair Forest, now part of the Administrative Unit of Inchnacardoch. Glenurquhart Forest was increased by the acquisition of land on the south side of the glen; Culloden by land at Dalcross, Dundavie and Holme Rose. New forests were created in the valleys of the Nairn and Findhorn, and to the east of Loch Ness at Farigaig. Perhaps the most important, from the conservationist point of view, were the purchases by the Forestry Commission of the contiguous estates of Fasnakyle and Loch Affric in 1951, and the later one of Cougie, high in the hills just south of Glen Affric, by which the Commission acquired large areas of native pinewoods. Lord Lovat retains the ownership of the other important remnant of the native woods, in Glen Strathfarrar.

The acquisition of the estates in Glen Affric presented the Commission with some unusual forest management problems, not the least being the need to conserve the natural amenity of the area. The purchase price of Fasnakyle included a large sum for the timber and, to recoup part of the cost, some selective fellings were carried out, and a road was built along the south side of Loch Benevean to facilitate the removal of the timber. The case for perpetuating the remnants of the Caledonian pinewoods was set out in 1959 in "The Native Pinewoods of Scotland," by Steven and Carlisle, and presented by Professor Steven to members of the Society of Foresters when they visited Glen Affric in 1959.

To implement his recommendation, some 2000 acres (405 ha.) of native pinewoods on the southern slopes of Loch Benevean were enclosed as a reserve. It was estimated then that the trees there had about another 70 yars to live, the oldest being about 250 years old. To regenerate the wood in 70 years would require some 30 acres to be planted annually, and it was planned to do this by planting in blocks of about 5 acres (2 ha.). The groups were to be sited in existing gaps where possible, but felling to enlarge gaps to the required size would also be accepted, and all planting stock was to be raised from seed collected from the native trees. It was hoped that some areas would be naturally regenerated, since sheep and red deer had been excluded by deer fencing. Natural regeneration was, however, slow to appear and even the planted trees fared badly in the early years. Capercailzie bred rapidly and the conditions which had been created ideally suited this bird — there were stout branches of the old trees on which to roost, and succulent shoots and buds of the young trees on which to feed. The red deer, too, broke into their former wintering grounds. Tree growth was slow initially, but some 15 years later, about 160 acres (72.5 ha.) have been successfully planted, and natural regeneration, not only of pine, but also of birch and rowan, is prolific.

More attention was paid to the mechanical development of ground preparation techniques than to the harvesting of timber. The decision to build a pulp mill at Fort William provided the impetus to find better and more efficient means of harvesting timber. It was quickly realised that the methods used to date would not produce the annual needs of the pulp-mill, so other methods had to be investigated. Cross-cut saws were replaced by power-driven saws, horses by Scandinavian double-drum winches and operating methods were radically changed. This led to a massive improvement in productivity in the early 1960s. The methods pioneered by the Forestry Commission were quickly adopted by the private forestry sector, so that productivity there has been increased, although it has not quite matched that of the Forestry Commission. The problem that forest industry faces in the North of Scotland in the coming years is the competition for labour from firms offering more highly paid jobs, especially those associated with North Sea oil.

Within recent years, the Forestry Commission has taken a much broader view of its role in the countryside. Formerly, the main objective was to produce crops of commercial timber almost to the exclusion of everything else. Although timber production is still its main objective in using its land, the Forestry Commission is giving more thought to the need to provide shelter and downfalls for sheep and red deer; to conserve areas which are important habitats for some of the rarer flora and fauna; and to provide for public recreation.

There is a great deal of informal discussion with the Department of Agriculture for Scotland, the Red Deer Commission, the Nature Conservancy, the Countryside Commission and the National Trust on matters of common interest. One of the Forestry Commission's objectives now is, as has been said, provision for public recreation, and much work is currently being done in this field in close association with the County Planning Officers. Provision is being made for more car parks and picnic sites in Glen Affric, and a caravan/camping site is planned at Cannich. Normal afforestation work has, in many cases, improved habitats for Highland animals and birds. There are Forest Walks at Reelig Glen, where the Douglas firs are famous, in Inchnacardoch Forest, in Farigaig Forest (the newest of the forests) and in Culloden Forest, where the ancient Clootie Well (now christened St Mary's Well, but far older than Christianity) is one of the unusual sights. These walks have proved very popular in recent years and there is an unsatisfied demand for more. There are booklets available describing what can be seen on each walk.

The early plantings at Inchnacardoch, Port Clair, Creagnaneun and Glenurquhart Forests have now reached the stage where they will be systematically felled from 1974 onwards, and the areas cleared of trees will be replanted. Most of the timber will go to the modern sawmill currently being

U

built at Corpach, the smaller parts will go to the adjoining pulp and paper mill.

In felling and replanting, and in the planting of bare land, much thought is now being given to the way the forests fit into the landscape, and the advice of the Forestry Commission's Landscape Consultant has been sought on these matters. Steps, too, are being taken to improve the amenity of the forests by the introduction of native hardwoods where they are absent, and to the conservation of those which already exist. Hard, incongruous lines between different species are giving way to a varying mixture of trees where they meet. Insofar as it is possible, the planting patterns are now being designed to simulate the natural state.

One of the farsighted men of the late 19th century, David Nairne, ended his address to the Gaelic Society of Inverness thus, "In conclusion, it need only be added that while Inverness-shire has reason for congratulation upon its arboricultural advancement, the forests, here as elsewhere, can never attain perfection until law or the State step in and insist upon continuity in tree production." The date of his address was 18 March, 1891.[3]

REFERENCES

1. Steven and Carlisle, *The Native Pinewoods of Scotland*, 1959.
2. Anderson, Mark L., *A History of Scottish Forestry*, 1967.
3. Nairne, David, "Highland Woods and Forests," *Trans. Gael. Soc. of Inverness*, vol 17, p. 220, 1891.

THE PRINTED WORD

EVELINE BARRON

There seems to be some doubt about the date when the first bookseller and the first printer were established in Inverness. George Cameron, in his "History and Description of Inverness," 1847, the first guide book to deal solely with Inverness town and county, says that the first bookseller's and stationer's shop was opened in 1775, and that before then articles in the stationery line had been sold by the postmaster alone. Yet a book appeared entitled "Meditations on Interesting Subjects," by the Rev. Hugh Rose, Nairn, bearing the imprint "Edinburgh: Printed for William Sharp, Bookseller in Inverness, 1762." In 1773, when Dr Samuel Johnson and James Boswell visited Inverness on their memorable Tour to the Hebrides, Johnson bought a book (Cocker's "Arithmetic"), which he gave as a present to the innkeeper's daughter at Anoch, Glenmoriston.

In 1774 there appeared what is understood to be the first book printed in Inverness — The Psalms of David in Gaelic. The title-page states, in Gaelic, that it was printed in that year in Inverness for sale by A. Davidson and W. Sharp, bookseller. A facsimile of that title-page is the frontispiece to P. J. Anderson's "Inverness Bibliography," published by Aberdeen University Press in 1917, when that distinguished Invernessian was Librarian to the University. So 1778, the date given in James Suter's "Memorabilia" for the first printing office, must be wrong.

For many years, books and pamphlets continued to be published by booksellers, sometimes in combination, as in Cameron's above-mentioned "History," when three, Kenneth Douglas, James Smith and Donald Fraser, are given as the publishers. Most, however, of these books were printed out of town. It was not until newspapers became established in the 19th century that books began to be printed here, generally after having first appeared serially in whatever paper later produced them in book form. For, to command a large enough sale to recompense the writer, as well as to pay for the printing costs, closeness to the market was, as it still is, essential — unless, of course, as was often the case, subscribers or prepaying purchasers, were secured, so that the printers, at any rate, could be sure of their money. It was also the custom that the list of subscribers appeared in the book.

An interesting example of this is to be found in a book of Gaelic poems, printed in Edinburgh in 1792 and written by Kenneth Mackenzie of Castle Leathers (now Heather), near Inverness, at least 420 names being listed at the end of the book. What makes this little book even more interesting, in view of the current clamour for the preservation and expansion of Gaelic, is the bard's dedication (in English!) to the Earl of Buchan. "Your well-known regard for the antiquities of your country, and the encouragement you have always shown to any attempt for reviving the ancient Gaelic language have induced me to prefix your Lordship's name to the following Gaelic songs . . ." Cannily, the bard ensures that at the foot of the title-page, otherwise all in Gaelic, the words appear firmly in English, "Price Three Shillings."

As most of the printed words produced in Inverness since early last century have been printed in newspaper offices, it is best to deal first with those papers. "The Inverness Journal" was the first newspaper to be published north of Aberdeen. It was established on 7 August, 1807, by one of the town's leading booksellers, Mr John Young, who had been the first to show enterprise in stocking a fairly full range of current literature, and had issued several works in Gaelic and English, including an edition of Macpherson's "Ossian" in 1806.

Mr Young's shop was situated on the south side of the High Street (then 22, now 45), and the printing office was on the second floor until its removal to the foot of Stephen's Brae. Ten years later, the "Inverness Courier" was first established in this same High Street office. It would appear that communications for publication in the "Journal" were numerous and varied, and the supply of advertisements was also good. Issued weekly on Fridays, it was a well-printed sheet of four pages, five columns to a page, the price being 6d. a copy, or by subscription, £1 7s. 6d. per annum. Indeed, the general presentation and content of the "Journal" were so creditable as to presage a long and prosperous career, but unfortunately Mr Young died on holiday in Lisbon in 1815, and the whole course of journalism in Inverness was changed.

The copyright and plant were acquired at the almost incredible sum for the time of £7000, which included £2400 for goodwill, by Mr Lachlan Mackintosh of Raigmore, who had some years previously returned from India, where he had established a successful mercantile house, and who had set his heart on becoming the secret owner of the "Journal." Mr Mackintosh, however, omitted to bind the disposers of the "Journal" not to start another paper in Inverness, and this they promptly proposed to do, so Raigmore gave them an extra £1000 to give up the idea and to bind themselves not to do so in the future. To begin with Raigmore did not openly identify himself with his paper, which was published "for himself and other proprietors, every Friday, by Mr James Beaton."

About the time that Raigmore became proprietor of the "Journal," there were somewhat questionable transactions going on in connection with certain lands in the neighbourhood belonging to the town, and the "Journal" launched forth in unmeasured terms as to "the wickedness of these scandalous proceedings." What was known as the alienation of town lands was in progress, and Raigmore exposed the business with a directness and scathing denunciation which made spicy reading. The magistrates and other authorities in the town found this intolerable, and in 1816 steps were taken to establish a rival paper, to be called the "Northern Star." In September of that year, however, the prospective publishers intimated that "circumstances with which they had but lately become acquainted made it absolutely necessary to delay publishing for a short time." This was a polite way of saying that no more would be heard of the "Northern Star," and Raigmore was delighted.

But another newspaper was desirable, because Raigmore would not allow his opponents to say a word in the "Journal" in their own vindication. Accordingly, in 1817, the "Inverness Courier" was launched, to the fury of Raigmore and, for years, fierce denunciatiton of each other took place, much to the entertainment of the community.

The first editor of the "Journal" was David Carey, who was a poet and novelist of considerable ability. Born in Arbroath in 1782, he first entered his father's thread manufacturing business, but his taste for literature soon led him to work in Edinburgh for Constable. In 1807 he moved to Inverness to edit the "Journal," remaining for five years. Before this he had published several collections of poems, and was also the author of other works, including satires in the Whig interest. In 1819 he published "Craig Phadrig: Visions of Sensibility, with Legendary Tales and Occasional Pieces of Historical Notes," chiefly valuable for the Notes, which contain much information about the early history of Inverness.

Carey was followed as editor by James Beaton, a capable and plodding journalist, well-known in the North for his literary and scientific attainments. He was a first-rate Celtic scholar and antiquary, but he became ill, and had to retire in 1816. James Fraser was the next editor, but he died in office and in the prime of life, in March, 1829. He was followed by David Stalker, who figured in a celebrated assault case arising out of an article which had appeared in the "Journal," reflecting upon several townspeople. Sheriff George Cameron of Dingwall, at that time a writer in Inverness, was put on trial for horse-whipping Raigmore. Henry Cockburn, afterwards Lord Cockburn, appeared for the defence, and. in his address to the jury, played on the name of the editor — Stalker — saying that "he was put forward as a stalking-horse," as the writer of the offensive article.

Raigmore died in 1845, and in July, 1846 the "Journal" was sold to Donald Macdonald, who intimated his "full determination that the paper would be conducted on the same Conservative and Independent principles as regarded the affairs of Church and State which it had maintained for nearly 40 years." The paper continued until 1849, when it was temporarily withdrawn because of the ill-health of Mr Macdonald, and this turned out to be the beginning of the end. In July, 1852, Donald Macdonald died, aged 39, and was buried in Daviot Churchyard. He had considerable literary attainments, the best detached specimen of his style being a pamphlet on the Perth and Inverness Railway, and his interest in local matters was intense.

The original Prospectus of the "Inverness Courier" is dated 31 October, 1817, and bears the imprint of W. Ettles, bookseller, an Elgin man at one time in partnership with the John Young who started the "Journal" in 1807. It is entitled "Prospectus of a newspaper to be published weekly at Inverness, and to be called "The Inverness Courier and General Advertiser for the Counties of Inverness, Ross, Moray, Nairn, Cromarty, Sutherland and Caithness." This is the full title still borne on the front page, except that the name of Cromarty is earlier in the list. At that time there was strong party feeling in the burgh, springing, not from politics, but from local questions, on which the "Journal" expatiated at great length and with much vehemence. There is no record of the names of the original promoters, except three who are mentioned as being proprietors eleven years later, James Suter, of "Memorabilia" fame, Provost Ferguson, and Roderick Reach, later the popular London correspondent of the paper. Mr Reach, a solicitor, was the chief literary asset on the committee of promoters; he probably wrote the prospectus, and may also have been the acting editor. The prospectus also stated that the promoters "stood upon open neutral, independent ground . . . resolved to speak their own minds boldly, and afford the means of doing so likewise on every subject of public interest, under no other restraint than those imposed by a regard for personal feelings and for the rules of decorum and good taste." The prospectus promised that where national policy was concerned, the new paper would "neither be fiercely intemperate nor tamely indifferent," and that a distinguishing feature would be the interest and variety of provincial news, and the promoters were solicitous to direct the interest of their countrymen to the investigation of the history and antiquities of the Northern Counties.

The first issue appeared on 4 December, 1817. In its early days the "Courier" consisted of four pages, each of five columns, and the price per copy was 7d., the same as the "Journal," which had started at 6d. But newspapers then were heavily burdened with a paper duty of 3d. per pound weight, a stamp duty of 4d. on every copy, and a tax of 3/6 on every advertisement.

The first editors of the "Courier" were Mr and Mrs John Johnstone, both so intimately identified with the work that is impossible now to distinguish between them. Mr Johnstone was nominal editor, but Mrs Johnstone was evidently the leading writer, and was generally spoken of at the time as the editor. It was on the recommendation of William Blackwood, Edinburgh — "Blackwood's Magazine" had started in the spring of the same year and advertised in the first issue of the "Courier" —that the Johnstones were appointed. Mr Johnstone "was a man of various knowledge . . . always getting others to work if he did not work himself," but it was Mrs Johnstone who gave a literary flavour to the paper, which it has never lost. She wrote much on domestic subjects, she made judicious selections from the London journals, few of which penetrated Highland glens; and, in her critical notices and abstracts of new books, she aimed at moral effect as well as refining the taste. De Quincey later called her the "Scottish Maria Edgworth." These first editors continued until the end of 1824, when the proprietors found that they could not afford the Johnstones' salary of £400 a year. They moved to Edinburgh and started "The Weekly Chronicle," and Mrs Johnstone produced, among other books, "Meg Dod's Cookery Book."

After their departure, the paper is described as having been issued by "James Mackay, editor and publisher," but his tenure was probably nominal. In the 1902 edition of John Noble's "Miscellanea Invernessiana," in the appendix contributed on Inverness newspapers by William Mackay, bookseller, it is stated that Mr James Suter, one of the promoters, took charge and wrote extensively for its columns.

In April, 1828, the new editor, Robert Carruthers, arrived. He was a native of Dumfries and in his 29th year, and had been recommended by the editor of the "Dumfries Courier," who had encouraged his literary gifts while he was an apprentice bookbinder and bookseller in that town. He had married and gone to England, where, in spite of his lack of schooling — he left at 12 — he undertook the management of the county school at Huntingdon, conducted on the Bell or Madras system (as later was Farraline Park in Inverness) and there he wrote a history of that town and a volume on "The Poetry of Milton's Prose." He became friendly with the poet Thomas Campbell, and other literary figures of the day, connections he was to keep up and increase after coming to Inverness.

He had not been long in Inverness when he received a visit from Hugh Miller, the Cromarty journeyman mason who was later to find fame as a geologist. Carruthers had rejected for publication a poem by Miller on the River Ness, but that did not prevent the two men from becoming friends, and in June 1829, the "Courier" printed and published a volume of poems for Miller. When, about July, 1829, "Letters on the Herring Fishery" began to appear from Hugh Miller, Carruthers realised that a great prose writer had arisen in the land. As well as contributing these "Letters," Miller acted as correspondent at Cromarty, mingling news notes with reflections and first revealing his rare power of satire. It was later that the observations which he had made during his work in quarries, turned him into a man of science. Even after Miller had become editor of the no-intrusion and Free Church organ, "The Witness," which held a position different from that of the "Courier," Carruthers continued to welcome Miller's geological works, giving them prominence in his columns, and he gave a long and favourable review to "My Schools and Schoolmasters." Much later, Miller described Carruthers as one of the ablest and most accomplished of Scottish editors.

In 1831, the "Courier" became the property of Carruthers, the price being £500 for the copyright, and "proper valuation" for the machinery etc. In 1836, the move took place from High Street to the building the "Courier" still occupies at the corner of Bank Lane and Bank Street, and, as the taxes on newspapers had been reduced two years before, the number of pages was increased to eight over the next decade or two. In addition, Carruthers was busy and eminent in the wider world of letters. He edited the works of Pope, and an edition of Boswell's "Tour of the Hebrides," as well as "Chamber's Cyclopaedia of English Literature." He also helped Lord Macaulay with information for his "History of England," and became friendly with Thackeray, De Quincey and Douglas Jerrold, while among the "Courier's" London correspondents, after the Reachs (father Roderick and son Angus) was Shirley Brooks, who was later to become editor of "Punch." In 1871 the honorary degree of Doctor of Laws (LL. D.) was conferred by the University of Edinburgh upon Carruthers, and in 1878 he died, having been in Inverness for 50 years.

He was succeeded as editor by his fourth son, Walter, his third son, Robert, taking over the business side. Walter Carruthers had joined his father in 1853, having been a Parliamentary reporter for the "Morning Chronicle," with verbatim shorthand. He was a Founder-member of the Field Club in 1875 and was one of its early presidents. Carruthers was prominent in seeing that the Ness Islands were improved and embellished, and was one of the first to suggest Tomnahurich as the best site for the new cemetery. He died in 1885, and James Barron, who had been co-adjutor with him, became sole editor and, on the death in 1888 of Robert Carruthers, principal proprietor.

James Barron was a Morayshire man, born in the parish of Edinkillie in 1847; he had joined the "Courier" in 1865 and after 1873 was the working editor and leader writer. Like Walter Carruthers, he was a founder-member of the Field Club. By 1910 he had become sole proprietor of the "Courier." Until his death in February, 1919, he guided its policies and fortunes with skill and wisdom, and his own articles, especially during the 1914-18 war, were inspiring, uplifting and comforting. Among other activities, he was twice President of the Field Club and editor of the "Transactions" from 1875 practically up to his death, although, after Volume VII (1906-12) had been published, he had been given an assistant — his own advertising manager, William Simpson. He produced three volumes of "The Northern Highlands in the Nineteenth Century," covering the years 1800 to 1856, all but the first seven years consisting of extracts from the "Journal" and then, after 1817, from the "Courier." His last big effort, very much a labour of love, was the centenary issue of the "Courier" on 4 December, 1917. During his editorship, the "Courier," after an unsuccessful experiment of coming out three times a week from August, 1880 until the end of 1885, became a bi-weekly on 1 January, 1886, publishing on Tuesdays and Fridays, as it still does.

James Barron was succeeded as editor by his younger son,

Evan Macleod Barron, as his elder son, James jnr., had been killed at the Battle of Loos, in 1915. Evan Barron, a solicitor by training and profession, continued the traditions of the "Courier" in every way, and was as outspoken for what he believed was the good of the community as any of his predecessors, and was the leader of many a doughty fight for the rights of the Highlands and the Highland people. He was a distinguished historian; his books included "The Scottish War of Independence," still acknowledged to be the authoritative work on that stormy 13th-14th century, "Prince Charlie's Pilot," "Inverness in the Middle Ages," "Inverness in the 15th Century," and many shorter works. Most of his writings are to be found in the "Courier" files, especially in the leading articles, for even if in his later years he did not put pen to paper himself, he either dictated or outlined nearly every one which appeared right up to his sudden death at the age of 85 in April, 1965.

One of the "Courier's" claims to fame between the wars, was the first "story," in May, 1933, of the sighting of the Loch Ness Monster, sent in by the paper's Fort Augustus correspondent, then as now, Alec Campbell, who called it either "beast" or "creature" throughout. Evan Barron declared that if it were as big as Campbell had said, it was a monster, and that was the word to use. In the mid-thirties, Aberdeen University conferred the LL.D. upon Evan Barron, who, among other distinctions, had been four times President of the Field Club, and once Chief of the Gaelic Society of Inverness.

Dr Barron was succeeded in ownership and editorship by his niece, Eveline Barron, who had been his junior partner since 1952, having been on the staff, except for war service in the W.R.N.S., since 1935. She has continued the fighting tradition and, when space permits, the literary one, but even although 10 and 12 pages are now possible and regular, advertising leaps up to keep pace. It fell to her happy lot to preside over the 150th anniversary celebrations of the "Courier" in 1967. A permanent commemoration of the occasion was the publication of "Old Inverness," a collection of coloured prints, most of them by Pierre Delavault, art master at the beginning of the century at Inverness Royal Academy, and originally published by the "Courier" in 1903. Several other plates, coloured and black-and-whites, were also included and explanatory text was kept to the shortest compatible with clarity.

A little later, in 1969, the history of the "Courier," including reports of the celebrations and a variety of illustrations and photographs, was published with the title "A Highland

Newspaper" to make it a companion, in a way, to Evan Barron's "A Highland Editor," a commemorative book about his father, James Barron. Like her grandfather, uncle and late aunt, Anne Barron, Eveline Barron is a member of the Field Club, seeing that reports of its activities appear in the paper as speedily as space permits.

In 1881, on 5 January, appeared the first issue of "The Northern Chronicle," an 8-page paper, costing one penny, printed and published by the Northern Counties Newspaper and Printing and Publishing Co., Ltd., Margaret Street. It was founded in the interests of the Conservative Party in the Northern Counties, and in its first issue stated "It will oppose dis-establishment. In its columns prominence will be given to all matters affecting the interests of farmers, the class upon whose welfare all other classes in the northern counties mainly depend." It appeared on Wednesdays and its first editor, until 1907, was Mr Duncan Campbell, whose "Reminiscences of an Octogenarian Highlander," appeared in 1910, over the "Chronicle" imprint. The first chairman of the company was Charles Innes, of Innes and Mackay, solicitors, who was succeeded by William Mackay of the same firm, founder in 1871 of the Gaelic Society of Inverness and an early member of the Field Club. Dr Mackay (he was later made LL.D.) also produced, either on his own, or in collaboration with another Inverness solicitor and Field Club President, Herbert C. Boyd, several extremely interesting and informative works, for example, for the New Spalding Club of Aberdeen, "Records of Inverness" in two volumes, drawn from the Burgh Court Books and other local records, with the introduction, "Inverness in the Sixteenth Century," reprinted as a separate book. Over the "Chronicle" imprint appeared his "Glenurquhart and Glenmoriston," in 1914.

The "Chronicle" was to publish many books on Highland and clan history, the chairman in its last independent years being Dr Mackay's son Captain "Willie" Mackay of the same legal firm, a past President, like his father, of the Field Club and still, in August, 1973, happily active in cultural research. The paper continued its Conservative and agricultural way until it was taken over in the 1950s by the "Highland News" (1883) and "Football Times" (1880), the latter having been acquired by the former around the turn of the century. In 1969, the "Chronicle," by then under the ownership of the Thomson Organisation, headed by the Canadian-born Roy Thomson, now Lord Thomson of Fleet and North Bridge, was finally merged with the "Highland News."

The "Highland News" began life in Dingwall on 8 October, 1883, as "The Organ of the Temperance League." On 30 May, 1888, it ceased to fulfil that function and began to be printed in Inverness for its new editor and proprietor, Dr Philip Macleod, who supported "Advanced Liberalism and Land Law Reform." It continued to be owned and run by well-known Liberals until well after the Second World War. The offices were in Hamilton Street, where they remained until the paper had to "flit" to Diriebught a few years ago to make way for road widening. For many years it was published on Saturday morning, and the "Football Times" in the evening of the same day. Then, not long after its acquisition by Thomson, it began to appear on Friday afternoon, and then around mid-day, but the change did it more harm than good, as there was local indignation at this impinging on a "Courier" day. It soon changed to Thursday, which is still its publication day. That aroused the ire of the tabloid-sized "Highland Herald," which had been founded in 1947 and appeared on Thursdays, leaving for many years, until the "Chronicle" was discontinued, Monday as the only day on which Inverness had no newspaper of its own.

As mentioned earlier, the "Highland Herald" was started in 1947, by Alastair Grant, an Invernessian then working on a Glasgow newspaper, who died suddenly a few years later. It was carried on by his surviving partners, Dugald Macrae and Harry McCathie, for some years, but the prolonged illness of the latter made the conduct of both paper and printing business too much for one, and in July, 1970, the "Herald," a lively controversial and Nationalistic publication, "went into abeyance." The firm now concentrates on general printing, much of it for oil-related firms and developments, and is about to move, again because of road-widening, from one end of Friar's Street to the other.

Nineteenth century newspapers included the "Inverness Herald" (1836-46), founded by the Northern Protestant Association. Its first editor was the Rev. Alexander Clark of the West Church. It aimed to maintain Protestantism and refused to insert reports or advertisements about dances, concerts and other public entertainments, even when for a charity. Later a lay editor, Charles Bond, was appointed. His main claim to fame was that he edited in 1842 the extremely interesting little book called "Reminiscences of a Clachnacuddin Nonagenarian," the writer being John Maclean, who lived to be a centenarian and to see further editions of his work published.

After the "Journal" lapsed, it was felt that the "Courier"

must not be left in a monopolistic position, so on 19 June, 1849, the first issue of the "Inverness Advertiser" appeared, the proprietor being James McCosh, a young Dundonian of ability. The paper began well, but McCosh died on 10 January, 1850, at the age of 34. The paper was sold to Mr George France, of Silverwells, a former tenant of Wester Lovat farm, and an ardent Free Churchman. He secured as editor Thomas Mulock, the manner of whose departure, on 23 April, 1850, was unusual, for it took the form of a letter to his employer, which he had printed in the "Courier," furious at Mr France for having altered part of his (Mulock's) leading article. In 1855, the "Advertiser" passed to Ebenezer Forsyth, who brought to an end all the inter-paper bickerings, which made them a bit duller for their readers. Forsyth continued until his death in 1873. It was in the "Advertiser" that Charles Fraser Mackintosh's "Antiquarian Notes," and "Invernessiana" first appeared. Forsyth was succeeded by his son, W. B. Forsyth, who carried on the paper with decreasing profitability until 1885, when he was thankful to sell the copyright to the "Courier" — for £5!

Other 19th century papers included "The Scottish Highlander" (1885-98), edited by Alexander Mackenzie, well-known as "The Clach." It was in this paper that Charles Fraser Mackintosh's "Letters of Two Centuries" first appeared. "The Highlander" (1872-82) was a very popular paper conducted by John Murdoch, a retired supervisor of Inland Revenue, in which the Gaelic language and Land Reform were the principal topics.

"The Highland Times" ran from 1896 to 1926 in the Liberal cause, and others included "The Clachnacuddin Record" (1839-40), "The Inverness Times" (1855-59), "The Inverness Reformer" (1856-58), a satirical and frequently scurrilous paper, "The Inverness Frolic" (1882-82), the first attempt to produce a comic journal, which only had three monthly issues, and "The Northern Evangelist" (1896-1902), a monthly record of Christian work and thought, produced by Joseph T. Melven, of Melven Bros., booksellers.

There have been many attempts to establish magazines in Inverness, but, apart from the schools and the churches, no one has had much success. Of early periodicals, "The Celtic Magazine" (1875-88) was the most notable. Its first editor was Alexander Mackenzie, and later Alexander Macbain, headmaster of Raining's School, and in its pages first appeared in 1877, "Prophecies of the Brahan Seer."

Since the end of the Second World War, there have been attempts to produce "glossy" magazines, but neither "Inverness and Northern Counties Magazine," nor "Inverness Pictorial," both monthlies, published by one of the Eccles firms, lasted long. A more specialised monthly, "The Highland Tourist-maker," produced by the "Highland Herald," has been running for a few years for its particular market, the tourist industry.

Inverness figures largely in tourist guide gazetteers, Statistical Accounts and the like, but not many are published in the town. The first guide to be printed and published here was that which included George Cameron's "History" in 1847, and thereafter local firms and newspapers began to produce their own. The first "Courier" guide still in the firm's possession, and probably not their first, is undated, but, from the text, cannot be earlier than 1886, and from then on, apart from the years of two world wars, a new edition appeared each year, until 1953, when the Town Council began to sponsor one, and the "Highland News" got the contract. In earlier days, the "Inverness Advertiser" also produced guides, the earliest in 1872. In 1877, James Gornet, better known for many years thereafter for his time-tables, published "A Short Guide." Published in Edinburgh in 1832, with later editions up to 1863, were George and Peter Anderson's "Guides to the Highlands and Islands of Scotland," while in 1868, Peter Anderson pro-duced a "Guide to Inverness," also printed in Edinburgh. These two brothers were respectively the uncle and father of P. J. Anderson, of "Bibliography" repute, and of Harriet Anderson, whose books are mentioned later.

Directories began to appear in the mid-19th century, the first for Inverness burgh apparently being issued in 1855, stating in its preface that "The growing importance of Inverness . . . has suggested to the author of the present work (P. Grant, 30 High Street) that a directory exclusively of the town and neighbourhood, and full and complete in its information, was much called for." It is a slim booklet, listing householders, etc., alphabetically, and although it does not go through the town street by street, it has the following cry from the heart at the foot of one page, "The houses and shops on the East side of Inglis Street are all wrong numbered. The numbers are going forward in a backward direction." The "Advertiser" ran a series of directories from 1864-70, and in 1885 the first "Courier" one was published, to appear regularly, again apart from war years, up to 1960. Since then, the firm of Eccles have produced one or two.

Books which were published in the town included for many years the Transactions of both the Field Club and the Gaelic Society. In both are to be found papers covering every aspect of Highland life and culture; archaeology; the flora and fauna of the region; the language, and every conceivable subject which interested people at the time. After the death of James Barron, the last two volumes of the Field Club's Transactions, Vol. VIII (1912-18) and Vol. IX (1918-25) were edited by William Simpson, advertising manager of the "Courier," and in 1920, after giving his Presidential Address, he had the pleasure of introducing his boss, Evan Barron, as the next President. It is a great pity that since then, there has been neither the time nor the money available to contitnue the publication of these papers, but in 1971 the Field Club published, under the title, "The Dark Ages in the Highlands," the report of the special "Week" with which, in 1970, it celebrated its 95th birthday, and in 1972, printed by the University of Dundee, appeared the reports and findings of the preceding year's excavations of Craig Phadrig, which had been sponsored by the Club.

The Gaelic Society has been more fortunate with its Transactions, largely because of the foresight and acumen of its late secretary, A. N. Nicolson. That society's records appeared annually for years, and when the time came, after the Second World War, to re-start publication, Mr Nicolson managed to prevail on certain of the chiefs — those with most money! — to make a start by sponsoring *their* year's volume, leaving the others to be produced when funds permitted, so that by now there must be very few, if any, gaps in the series.

Although few books, other than those of purely local interest, have been published in Inverness, the town itself has figured in many books from Adamnan's "Life of St Columba" (c. 700 A.D.) to whatever is the latest traveller's tale of the Highlands, and in verse from Burns to McGonagle. Famous travellers, including Captain Burt (1754) and Pennant (1771), as well as Dr Johnson, have described the town and its environs. Its history at its most accurate appears in the "Courier" Guides, and in Evan M. Barron's "Inverness and the Macdonalds," written in 1930 to mark the conferring of the freedom of the burgh on three distinguished members of that clan, Ramsay Macdonald, Prime Minister; Sir Murdoch Macdonald, M.P. for Inverness; and Stanley Baldwin, whose mother was a Macdonald, and who preceded Ramsay Macdonald as Prime Minister.

Books issued in Inverness which are worthy of note, in addition to those mentioned, include David Nairne's "Memorable Highland Floods in the 19th Century" (1895), published by the "Northern Chronicle," and Alexander Macbain's "Personal names and surnames of the town of Inverness" (1895, Chronicle) and, from the "Courier," Major Duncan Warrand's five volumes of "More Culloden Papers," and his "Some Fraser

Pedigrees" and "Some Mackenzie Pedigrees;" Father Ninian Macdonald's admirable "Shinty;" Charles H. Ackroyd's "A Veteran Sportsman's Diary;" and a varied collection of pamphlets, several in its "Highland Handbook" series, which had just got under way by the outbreak of war in 1939.

Since that war there have been printed words by the thousand on a wide range of matters of Highland and Inverness interest, a great many dealing with the district's most famous "resident," the Loch Ness Monster. Most of the books and pamphlets have been printed elsewhere, but a recent "Monster" one, with excellent coloured photographs, was reissued in August, 1973, by the Inverness works of J. Arthur Dixon, whose headquarters are on the Isle of Wight.

An Comunn Gaidhealach has issued a series of attractive pamphlets on subjects ranging from "Highland Regiments" to "Plant Badges of the Clans," and from "Highland Cookery" to the Clearances. The indefatigable and versatile Frank Thompson has produced a series of "Highland Chapbooks," printed, as are the An Comunn pamphlets, by Eccleslitho. He also, as a lecturer in electrical engineering at Inverness Technical College, produces technical books, and, as a Lewisman, books on the Western Isles, to say nothing of Gaelic books as well. He is a moving spirit behind Club Leabhar, the Highland Book Club, which, helped by the Highlands and Islands Development Board and other bodies, aims to produce in paper-backs at least one English and one Gaelic book a year. The former are, on the whole, reprints of popular modern books, including novels, about the North, and the latter are also nearly all reprints of popular Gaelic works. Otherwise, such local writers as Allan Campbell Maclean, Eona K. Macnicol (née Fraser), Katharine Stewart, Janet Caird, Mollie Hunter, and others, have their works printed and published in the South, although many are inspired by local events or history. In this, they are but following a well-worn path, for some of the best-known old books on Inverness were published elsewhere.

One very old one is "Inverness Smugglers," the account of two trials before the judge of the High Court of Admiralty of Scotland, both at the instance of Duncan Forbes of Culloden, His Majesty's Advocate, in 1735, and published a year later for an Edinburgh bookseller. In 1885, appeared Harriet Anderson's "Inverness before the Railways," to be followed over the next ten years by several other reminiscent volumes, nearly all printed in Aberdeen. John Fraser, a chemist, published on his own behalf in 1905, "Reminiscences of Inverness Sixty Years Ago," not always accurate, but wholly entertaining, while

31. Common Seal

32. Badger

33. Long-eared Bat

34. Long-tailed Field Mouse

35. Missel Thrushes

36. Redshank

37. Cock Long-tailed Tit

39. Conjectural reconstruction of Urquhart Castle

38. Inverness Fire Brigade, 1900 (preceding page)

40. The Black Bridge from the east, between 1855 and 1860

41. The Old Stone Bridge (1685-1849) and the Steeple

42. Inverness Town Band, 19th century

43. The biggest roll-on/roll-off load — so far. March 1971. Weight 100 tons; value £140,000

44. 1975 — B.A.C. Super 111

an earlier recollection of memories is "Recollections of Inverness," by an Invernessian (Robert Munro), published locally in 1863. Thomas L. Mackintosh's "Musings by the Ness" and Alexander Penrose Hay's "Post-Office Recollections" were both books of 1855.

Inverness can lay some claim to the late Neil Gunn, one of the most highly regarded novelists in Scotland, who died in November, 1972, for though he was a Caithness man and had his books published in London, it was in Inverness, where he worked as an exciseman at a local distillery, that he first started to write and have published the books which brought him world renown.

Inverness, therefore, has had many words printed about and in it, and they grow no less, in spite of all the development of television and the cassette system of recorded sound. The pity is that so many of the older books mentioned are out of print, and are only available in public libraries. Nearly every daily and Sunday paper published in Scotland and London circulates in the town, and, with one bi-weekly, and one evening paper on Saturdays, Inverness continues to be well catered for by the Printed Word.

The Courier Trophy, designed in 1819 and used for many years as the headpiece of "The Inverness Courier."

X

EDUCATION

ALAN B. LAWSON

The Pre-1872 Period

The growth of schools in the Highlands was slow and not until the late 18th and early 19th centuries was there anything approximating to an educational system. The people were almost entirely Gaelic speaking, so that there was a language barrier between them and available books and teachers. The scattered population, the general poverty, the weakness of the church and the lack of concern on the part of the lairds, who, as heritors, should have provided parochial schools, all combined to suppress interest in education.

In "The New Road," Neil Munro makes Simon Fraser, Lord Lovat, speak disparagingly of schools. "What good are they to Gaeldom?" he asks. "So long as men of family can have their children tutored in what arts belong to their position, either in their homes or furth the country, the setting up of schools for all and sundry of the folk is contrar to the welfare of the State." The sentiment is a fair reflection of the views of the time. The lairds and their more substantial tenants made private arrangements for the education of their families: the rest of the population was largely illiterate. This dearth of schools, this illiteracy, would have been found in the country around Loch Ness.

The town of Inverness, however, was in a different position. From mediaeval times there had been a school here, and, as a centre of trade, justice and administration, the town had business which called for an educated merchant and professional class. Men of substance, whose interests were different from those of the country gentry, controlled the Burgh's affairs and saw to it that the town school — the Grammar School — was maintained. In the 18th century this was housed in the building known as Dunbar's Hospital, in Church Street, and hence the adjacent School Lane.

After the '45, the Northern Highlands were progressively opened up to trade and traffic with the South, and the para-military society was gradually changed to something more akin to that in the rest of the country. Parochial schools began to appear, or to have a more continuous existence. Voluntary agencies, particularly the Society in Scotland for Propagating Christian Knowledge, began to penetrate beyond the Grampians and to set up schools, so that by the time of the Statistical Account of Scotland (1792-95), the ministers who wrote of the twelve parishes of what may be called the Inverness area could, with a few exceptions, record the existence of a school or schools in the parish. Eight record a parochial school; four note also the school provided by the S.S.P.C.K.; Boleskine-and-Abertarff had an S.S.P.C.K. school, but no parochial school; Ardersier and Daviot-and-Dunlichty appeared to have no school of any kind.

The parish of Inverness, however, which included the Burgh, had no fewer than 11 schools. These included the newly established Inverness Academy (1792), which replaced the old Grammar School, and was maintained and managed, partly by private individuals or shareholders, partly by the Town Council. A Royal Charter of incorporation was granted in 1793. The Academy was built on New Street, later called Academy Street, where Cooper's Fine Fare shop now is, an extension for a girls' school being added in 1806. The main part of the present Academy was built on the Crown in 1895. It ceased to be an independent school in 1908, when it was taken over by the Burgh School Board, but it remained a fee-paying establishment until after the 1945 Education Act.

By the time of the New Statistical Account (1835-41), school provision had been considerably extended. Every parish had its parochial school — four, indeed, had more than one — and there was an increasing number of schools maintained by the S.S.P.C.K., the Assembly of the Church of Scotland and other voluntary bodies, including the Inverness Society for Educating the Poor in the Highlands. The ministers in some instances noted that there was a greater interest in education among the ordinary people. The Reverend James McLauchlan, minister of Moy-and-Dalarossie, waxed quite lyrical about the state of education in his locality. "There is perhaps not a parish in Scotland," he wrote, "where education is carried on to a greater extent than here. There is a school in almost every nook . . . Education is prized very highly." In addition to the parochial school, there were six "aid" schools provided by the societies, and a school for girls run by the S.S.P.C.K. But a further observation reveals weakness in the situation, ". . . it would be highly advantageous if one of the schools were permanent, i.e., kept up for the whole year, since the aid schools only continue six months, and sometimes not quite so much." A more realistic comment

was made in April, 1877, when Dalarossie School in Strathdearn was opened and H.M. Inspector of Schools, Mr William
Jolly, caused to be written in the log-book: —

> "This school was examined for the first time and is
> the first school that has been in the district for 30 years.
> The children . . . . made only a moderate appearance, but
> more could not be expected in the circumstances."

In fact, provision was nowhere satisfactory. The voluntary
schools were seldom housed in adequate premises and often
conducted by persons of doubtful competence. Nevertheless, the
mid-19th century saw a steady increase in schools, and a corresponding growth in the wish for education. In this, the
churches and associated bodies played a leading part. In particular, the fervour of the Free Church after the Disruption
of 1843, quickly led to the setting up of many Free Church
schools and to a wider availability of education in the
area.

For example, in 1848 the Trustees of the Free Church of
Stratherrick, having in the previous year obtained a feu-charter
from Fraser of Balnain for the ground on which he had permitted them to build a church, proceeded to grant themselves,
as Trustees for the Free Church school, Stratherrick, a Building
Sub-Tack, "for the erection of a School, School-house, Dwelling-
house for the teacher thereof . . . [which] shall in all time
coming be used for the purposes of educating the Children
of the Poor and working classes." Alas for the vanity of human
wishes! No trace of church, school or teacher's house remains
on the shores of Loch Farraline.

All this was part of a national trend, and as the demand
grew and the number of schools grew, it became more and
more clear that the parishes, the churches and the voluntary
societies could neither meet the demand, nor adequately sustain
the schools.

The Education Act of 1872 and the School Boards

The Education (Scotland) Act, 1872, made schooling compulsory between the ages of five and thirteen. Parish and Burgh
School Boards took over responsibility for education from the
heritors, the church and the town councils. The state, at last
and with reluctance, relieved the church of its educational
burden, empowering the Boards to impose rates for the erection
and maintenance of schools and giving them grants in addition.
For the first time, a modestly adequate coverage of schools was
given, and elementary education became available to all.

The administrative unit was still the parish and the burgh, so that in the Inverness area there were twelve Parish School Boards, and one for the Burgh of Inverness. The Boards, popularly elected, had either five or seven members, except that for Inverness Burgh, which had nine members. They tended to be dominated by the clerical members, who continued the tradition of church involvement in education. The finance at their disposal was limited, and, in their simple schools, could sustain only a rather bare curriculum of little more than the 3Rs. What would now be called secondary education was available only in the town of Inverness, and to some extent at Glenurquhart School, Drumnadrochit. In the rural parts, older pupils had to be content with what the local dominie could offer them, and the development of post-primary education was slow.

Inverness Academy had, from its inception, offered a good standard of secondary education. The subjects taught, according to the Old Statistical Account, included not only English, Classics, French and Gaelic, History, Geography and Science, but also "navigation with lunar observations, architecture, naval, civil and military, practical gunnery, fortifications, perspective and drawing." No doubt this wide-ranging curriculum was detailed in the prospectus, but one wonders how far it was implemented — and where the "practical gunnery" was conducted. Perhaps the subjects reflect the military background of many of the gentry among the original subscribers and directors. But the Academy did continue to offer a sound classical, literary and scientific education. It was, however, a fee-paying school, only marginally giving opportunity to those from humbler homes, whose high scholastic attainment earned them bursaries from endowments or, later, from public funds.

Good secondary instruction was, after some time, also provided at Inverness High School, which grew out of the Free Church School and, in 1894, became the School Board's Higher Grade School when it absorbed Raining's School. This latter school, part of which is still standing at the top of Raining's Stairs, was the principal S.S.P.C.K. school, built in 1757 with money gifted by John Raining, a Scotsman settled in Norwich. It, too, had a considerable secondary department. The High School continued until 1937 in what is today Crown Primary School.

There was also the Inverness College, an independent day and boarding school for boys, and Glenurquhart School, which had grown from an earlier parochial school, gained the status of a Higher Grade School in 1892 and so could present pupils for the Scottish Leaving Certificate. Thus, by the end of the 19th century, a thin pattern of secondary schooling had been established in the area, giving entrance to university or other higher education. Grants for secondary education were made from public funds and, to administer these, County Committees were formed in 1892, composed of representatives of the County Councils, the School Boards and Endowment Governors.

The Act of 1918 and the Education Authority

The County Committee for Secondary Education fore-shadowed future changes. By the Education Act of 1918, "ad hoc" County Education Authorities replaced the School Boards, being in their turn superseded by the Education Committees of the County Councils, under the Local Government Act of 1929. The County Council is still the Education Authority, and will remain so until the new Regional Authority takes over in 1975.

The "ad hoc" County Authority was able to secure more uniform standards than was possible under Boards with varying resources through rating available to them. It also obviated much petty local interference with the work of the schools. The Clerks to the Boards were part-time officials, not education-ists, but business managers, and in the schools guidance and criticism came from H.M. Inspectors. As grants from central government depended in part on the standard of attainment reached in individual schools, the visits of H.M.I. were crucial occasions for the teachers, and days of apprehension for their pupils. Most "ad hoc" Authorities, however, appointed pro-fessional Directors of Education to advise them on policy, to manage day-to-day business, and to guide and supervise the teachers. Inverness-shire's first Director (1919-37) was Mr Murdo Morrison, happily still very much alive, being 101 years of age on 19 November, 1973. Today the Authority has a whole corps of educational officers, reflecting the expansion and com-plexity of education in these times.

An interesting change came with the 1918 Act. The Act of 1872 had enabled voluntary bodies to transfer their schools to the Boards, on condition that they ceased to be denomina-tional in character. The Roman Catholic and Episcopal Churches were not prepared to accept this condition, but the 1918 Act permitted transfer without such condition, and the remaining church schools in the Inverness area passed to the management of the Education Authority.

The Education Act of 1945

Major changes came with the Education Act of 1945, which enunciated the principle that a child should be educated according to his age, aptitude and ability, and that adequate and appropriate primary, secondary and further education should be available to all who could benefit. The Qualifying Examination, taken at the end of the primary course, was replaced by the more sophisticated Promotion Examination, by which abler pupils were selected for full 6-year secondary courses, the remainder being placed in 3-year courses in junior secondary schools. With this went centralisation of post-primary education at a limited number of schools, which were given better facilities and more specialist staff.

In Inverness, traditional academic teaching was concentrated at the Royal Academy, which ceased to be a fee-paying and somewhat exclusive school. Inverness High School, which had transferred to its present site in 1937, was renamed the Inverness Technical High School, to emphasise that it offered full technical and commercial courses for selected pupils, as well as 3-year general courses. Some people still refer to it "The Tecky," although it reverted to its original name after a few years. In addition, the Burgh R.C. School kept a junior secondary department, but it did not have facilities for instruction in practical subjects, pupils having to go across to the High School for these. This was unsatisfactory, and contributed to the closure of the secondary department in 1969.

In the landward parts, Glenurquhart School continued as a full secondary school. Junior secondary departments were set up at Beauly, Fort Augustus, Tomnacross (Kiltarlity), Ardersier, Croy and Foyers, the last four being later discontinued in 1970, 1971, 1971 and 1964, respectively.

More recently, the acceptance of the idea of comprehensive secondary education led to further centralisation. In such a system pupils pass without selection to a district secondary school. Currently, in the Inverness area, only in the Fort Augustus district is there selection, abler pupils being allocated to Glenurquhart School, the less able attending Fort Augustus J.S. School. Elsewhere, schools are comprehensive in character.

On the East side of the River Ness all pupils, from both town and country, initially attend Millburn Secondary School, but may, at the end of two years, be selected for transfer to the Academy, which has no first or second year. On the West side, all pupils, from both town and adjacent landward areas, attend the High School. Abler pupils from Beauly School also attend there after two years in their local school.

Gaelic

It is difficult to assess the influence and place of the Gaelic language in the schools in the Inverness area. In the first Statistical Account, few references are made to Gaelic, but such as these are, they indicate that, except in the town, Gaelic was the daily speech of the ordinary people. In the New Statistical Account, however, frequent comment is made on the encroachment of English: e.g. Inverness — "Gaelic is fast wearing out:" Kilmorack — "The language of the inland part is Gaelic . . . All want their children to learn English:" "English is daily gaining ground."

The decline of Gaelic was hastened by the early School Board teachers, who found the language a hindrance to the teaching of the 3Rs, and either discouraged, or positively forbade, the use of the old tongue within the school. Not until the end of the century was there any active thought on the part of the Boards, that Gaelic needed some support; but by then the schools were set in their ways, and Gaelic became very much a peripheral interest in the classroom. This, combined with the attitude of the parents, many of whom had come to regard the speaking of Gaelic as a sign of lack of education, led to further contraction in its use. An attempt to support the language was made in the Act of 1918, which laid a duty on Education Authorities to make provision for the teaching of Gaelic in Gaelic-speaking areas. But by then, perhaps, the Inverness district was not regarded as a Gaelic-speaking area. At any rate, little was done. Older people in the rural parts commonly relate that, although their parents spoke Gaelic, they themselves did not, either at home or at school, come by any competence in the language. In the secondary schools, particularly in the Royal Academy, Gaelic was and is taught as a subject, but to a limited number of pupils.

Today, the Education Authority is doing more to encourage the study of Gaelic. Itinerant teachers visit many of the primary schools to give elementary instruction to interested pupils, and it is hoped that this may give at least some background of understanding of the Gaelic heritage of the Highlands, but it is almost certainly too late for this to lead to any real resurgence of the language in the area.

Private Schools

There has not been any great tradition of private schools in the district. In earlier times, there were a number of "dame" schools, and from time to time, in the burgh, "adventure," i.e., private, schools were started in competition with the Grammar

School, but the authorities commonly suppressed them. In more recent times, and again in the Burgh, there have been several private schools, but these have tended to have a short existence.

Inverness College, or Collegiate School, already referred to, was run for a time in Ardross Terrace and, from 1873, in Ardross Street. It is spoken of as being "conducted after the style of the English Public Schools and well-known for its success in training young gentlemen for the army and naval service." It seems to have been closed for a time at the beginning of this century, and to have succumbed finally during the 1914-18 war, when the building was occupied by the Admiralty.

Heatherley School started in 1913 as Inverness Ladies College in Glen Mhor on Ness Bank, moving to Heatherley two years later. It also had a period of difficulty after the First War, but continued as a day and boarding scool for girls until 1956, when Miss Bedale who, with her sisters, had conducted the school for many years, retired. The need for more sophisticated provision deterred others from carrying on the school. The building is now divided into flats and houses have been built in the grounds.

There was also a convent school, associated with the Roman Catholic Church on Huntly Street. Part of the building is still extant, but school and convent were replaced by a similar establishment housed in what is now Redwood Guest-house on Culduthel Road. Nuns of the Order of Notre Dame conducted this school, under the control of the Education Authority, until they were superseded by the Order of La Sagesse. They also taught in the Burgh R.C. School. The school was a fee-paying primary, mainly for girls, but did have a few little boys on its roll. It was discontinued in 1969.

Mention should also be made of the Abbey School, Fort Augustus. The Benedictine Order, which established the monastery on the site of the old Hanoverian fort, set up in 1875 a boarding school for boys, which still continues, but has included in recent years a few girls among its pupils.

None of these schools, nor others such as Elm Park or Craignish in Inverness, drew on more than a very small section of the child population, nor did they attain the place in public esteem held by the Royal Academy. They did not really establish themselves in the essentially egalitarian pattern of education in the Highlands.

Population Changes and School Provisions

In the post-war period, there has been a rapid expansion in Inverness. Between 1945 and 1972, the primary school population has increased from 2600 approx. to 4560 approx.; the secondary roll, from 1330 approx. to 3300. This latter increase, of course, is due not only to the general growth in population, but also to centralisation and the raising of the school leaving age. To match this increase of about 4000 pupils, the Education Authority has built a number of new schools in the town, both primary and secondary, or has added to existing schools.

The following is a list of the new schools: —

	Opened	Roll, 1972
Coronation Park Infant School	1950	96
Dalneigh Primary School	1954	421
Hilton Primary School	1957	400
Raigmore Primary School	1966	247
Lochardil Primary School	1964	471
Cauldeen Primary School	1968	606
Drakies Primary School	1971	252
Millburn Secondary School	1961	1109

There have also been extensions at the Academy and the High School.

In more or less the same period, some schools, mainly small, have ceased to function. These were: —

	Closed	Roll
*Farraline Park P. School	1937	—
The Cathedral Boys School	1943	8
†The Highland Orphanage School	1957	76
Culcabock P. School	1966	69
Convent R.C. School	1969	40

*Farraline Park, or Bell's School, was set up with funds left by Dr Bell, a Scottish educationist who developed in India the "Madras" or monitorial system of instruction, and left his considerable fortune to educational institutes in Scotland, £10,000 being bequeathed to the magistrates of Inverness to found a "charity" school. When the school closed, pupils transferred to the Crown P. School, but the building continued for a time as an annexe to that school. It now houses the Little Theatre and the Burgh Police Station—a not inappropriate mixture of the arts and discipline!

†This school, set beside the Orphanage, now converted into flats and known as Culduthel House, originally provided for Orphanage children only, but latterly other children attended

there as well. In 1957, it became simply an annexe of Hilton School.

In the landward parts, conversely, population has fallen, a common rural malaise, accentuated in the Highlands by the decay of crofting communities and a falling away in the establishments maintained on sporting estates. The improvement of roads has also made possible the conveyance of children to schools some little distance away, obviating the need to maintain small units in outlying places.

The following is a list of rural primary schools which have been closed in more recent times: —

	Closed	Roll
Abriachan School	1958	2
Bunachton School	1933	2
Bunloit School	1947	5
Bunchrubin School	1955	9
Culduthel School	1969	27
Culburnie School	1968	11
Dalarossie School	1956	5
Dunmaglass School	1947	3
Eskadale R.C. School	1968	7
Fort Augustus R.C. School	1972	12
Guisachan School	1946	5
Glenconvinth School	1963	12
Knockchoilum School*	1940	—
Marydale R.C. School	1969	6
Nairnside School	1948	9
Whitebridge R.C. School*	1915	10

*Knockchoilum P. School was destroyed by fire in 1940. For a few months, a schoolroom was set up in the Servants' Hall at Dell House — a novel arrangement which the pupils no doubt enjoyed. Later, the former R.C. School at Whitebridge was brought back into use, and in 1957 the name was changed to Whitebridge P. School.

All existing schools have had improvements of varying kinds made to the buildings, but only at Fort Augustus has a new school been built. As all these rural and village schools date from the 1872-80 era, there is much need for their replacement, but the Education Authority's resources have, of necessity, gone mainly to new schools in the Burgh of Inverness.

Boarded-out Children

A feature of many of the rural schools, particularly in the Aird district, between the two wars, and for a time after 1945, was the presence of children boarded-out by local authorities in other parts of Scotland, especially from the industrial West. These children, sometimes orphans, sometimes from broken or bad homes, found security and affection with foster-parents in humble cottages around the area. In some schools these children even formed a majority. How considerable an element they were can be seen from the following examples: —

	Total Roll 1948	Boarded-out Pupils
Abriachan P. School	28	23
Balnain P. School	77	35
Eskadale R.C. School	58	46
Glenconvinth School	53	37
Tomnacross School	136	73

It is easy to see what an influence this must have had on the character of the schools, and on the local children. The virtual cessation of boarding-out in the late 1950s led to a rapid drop in the rolls of the school most involved. It is pleasant to record that quite a number of these children stayed on as adults in their foster-homes and that some achieved scholastic distinction. All must have gained from a simple Highland up-bringing.

Transport and Hostels

Reference has already been made to school transport in relation to the closure of outlying primary schools. Even more important has been its part in the centralisation of secondary education, or to the secondary schools at Fort Augustus, Drumnadrochit (Glenurquhart S.S. School) and Beauly. These secondary pupils travel by public transport, or by buses or cars under contract to the Education Authority.

The homes of some children, however, are too far from a secondary school to permit of daily travel, and such children are accommodated in hostels in Inverness. These are used mainly by pupils from the Outer Islands who attend the Academy or the High School, but pupils from localities such as Stratherrick, Upper Strathglass, etc., are also housed in the hostels, going home at week-ends only.

Hostel provision developed gradually. Between the wars, there were hostels for both boys and girls attending the Academy.

Mr Robson, a teacher at the Academy, acquired the mansion of Hedgefield, Culduthel Road, to board boys. Girls were more formally provided for. In 1921, former pupils of the Academy raised funds to purchase the Inverness College building, to be a memorial to pupils who had fallen in the war and as a hostel for girls. The Education Authority shared in this purchase and accepted responsibility for the establishment, which was known as the Inverness Royal Academy War Memorial Hostel. In 1930, however, the County Council took over the Ardross Street building for administrative offices. Hedgefield then became the girls' hostel, and the mansion house of Drummond Park was bought to become a hostel for boys. Both houses have been extended and improved in recent years. Hedgefield now has places for 74 girls, while Drummond Park can house 46 boys. Pupils are boarded free of charge, and may attend not only the Academy, but also the High School and Millburn School. Each is in the care of a resident Warden, with domestic affairs in the hands of a Matron.

Further Education

While the Highland tradition has long encouraged scholastically able pupils to continue at school until they can proceed to some institution of higher education, only in recent years has there been sound arrangement for the further education of those who leave school from lower classes to enter employment. Between the wars, continuation classes were held in the evenings, in commercial and industrial subjects. There was some minor provision of day classes for apprentices and others, instruction being given in Inverness Technical School. This building, recently demolished, stood at the corner of Church Street and Friars' Lane. This system was greatly expanded after 1945, mainly in the Evening Institute conducted at the High School, where tuition was given for Royal Society of Arts, City and Guilds, Ordinary National Certificate, etc. examinations.

The need for more adequate education and training for apprentices and others, either in employment, or between school and employment, led to the building of Inverness Technical College in 1960, at first a modest establishment, about the future of which there was some head shaking. Happily, the Education Authority's faith was amply justified, and in 1970 a very large extension was opened. The College in 1972 had a roll of 445 full-time and almost 2,000 part-time students, in day release, block release and evening classes. It offers courses in Engineering, Commerce, Science, Agriculture and Forestry, Hairdressing,

Catering and General Education. Students, who are drawn from all over the Highlands, are prepared for a wide variety of national examinations. Apprentices attend one day a week, or by an equivalent block release arrangement. Associated with the College, there is a hostel for 80 male students at Millburn, and a similar hostel for female students is planned.

Apart from instruction for employment and career purposes, many classes are run in the evenings for those who wish tuition in subjects and activities of personal choice and interest. Such classes are run wherever there is demand, but naturally mainly where there is some concentration of population, particularly in the Burgh of Inverness. Classes cover subjects such as Art, Craft, C o o k e r y, Dressmaking, "Keep - Fit," Literature, Languages, etc.

Additionally, in association with the Extra-Mural Department of Aberdeen University, an extensive programme of lectures and lecture courses is maintained throughout the winter months in Inverness and in the larger villages, on scientific, historical and cultural topics.

As elsewhere in Scotland, it has been recognised that a broad view must be taken of what education is, and the Authority gives financial support or assistance to voluntary bodies and societies engaged in activities of an educational or recreational character, e.g., musical and dramatic organisations, certain sporting bodies, etc. Similar encouragement is given to youth organisations, while the Authority directly manages two youth clubs in Inverness.

Handicapped Children

Children who are handicapped by physical or mental defect present a problem in an area of scattered population. Where the handicap is of a special nature, they have to be sent away to schools which cater for a specific defect, such as the Royal Blind School, Edinburgh. Drummond School, Inverness, however, does provide for children whose ability to learn is much less than normal. Opened in 1963, it is a day and residential school for children who are educable, but not capable of coping with instruction as given in ordinary schools. For children of even less ability the Authority runs an Occupational Centre in the former Culduthel School, and, in association with Craig Phadrig Hospital, a similar centre for children who need hospital care.

Pre-School Children

The Education Authority has not, so far, set up nursery

schools in the Inverness area, but in recent years parents and others have organised playgroups, in which younger children have opportunity by playing with other children in a guided manner, to develop their mental and physical capacities and thus prepare for entry to school in due course.

School Meals Service

While some schools, particularly in the rural parts, had local arrangements for providing soup or hot drinks for pupils to supplement "pieces" brought from home, not until after the 1945 Act was a School Meals Service established. Now every school in the area offers meals, either on payment or free, according to family circumstances. Meals are cooked at the school, or at central points from which they are conveyed in insulated containers to outlying schools.

Libraries

The New Statistical Account records that "Inverness has . . . a valuable parochial library, under the direction of the kirk-session, several subscription and circulating libraries, two public reading-rooms." This was a not uncommon situation in a sizeable town. Inverness, under later Public Library Acts, set up a Burgh Library in Castle Wynd, but little was done in the landward areas. It was not until the Education Act of 1918 that Libraries were recognised as an integral part of the educational system. Prior to this, members of the Coats family of Paisley had gifted books and book-cases to rural schools in the Highlands. Some of these book-cases are still in use in the country schools, but filled with books from the County Library.

For a time, Town and County operated a Joint Library Service, but since 1961 have worked separately. The Burgh Library and Museum was replaced by new premises in 1966. The County Library has headquarters in the County Buildings. This is not a lending library, but a holding centre supplying branches at Ardersier, Beauly, Cannich, Drumnadrochit and Fort Augustus. A mobile library van makes regular visits to most other localities in the area. The two libraries make a very substantial contribution to education in the area.

Education has long been held in high esteem in the Highlands. This regard continues. The path to higher education is smoother and more walk it than ever before. It is to be hoped that those who reach the end of the road will not be forgetful of the simpler schools which nurtured their forerunners.

DEVELOPMENT AND CONSERVATION

FRANK SPAVEN

Development *or* conservation, as many see it, is surely a central issue of the modern scene in our time. That it should have become so in and around Inverness reflects the fact that here, as elsewhere, the pace of change in town and country has been quickening, its scale increasing, its character altering and the possibility of controlling it questioned. We may well have come to think of "development" as any self-sufficient economic, technological or commercial change which is imposed on us and has an adverse impact on our physical or social environment and habits. We even have development bodies on the one hand, and conservation bodies on the other, to point the contrast.

If, however, "development" is regarded rather as an unfolding and promotion of the use of the latent resources of a place and its people and "conservation" as a husbanding of these resources for sustained use, the two can be seen to be complementary processes and agencies for living, the one more active and the other more passive, each a necessary partner to the other. In this sense, this article looks at some contemporary changes to see how far they are making Inverness and its district a more habitable environment for living and working in.

Population and Employment Change

In the first place, 50,000 people in all, more than ever before, now finds this community worth settling in. Growth of the town itself is, of course, nothing new, for it expanded steadily during the last century, especially in 1861-81, after the coming of the Highland Railway, but it remained fairly static for some thirty years before 1931. There has been growth again since then, and the rate of increase in the decade 1961-71 (5,000 or 16%), most of which has been in the last five years, has been as fast as ever before, so that today the Burgh's population of 35,000 is double what it was in 1881 — and this is happening before the full impact of North Sea oil. The age structure is as balanced and the natural increase rate as high as the Scottish average, and for a long time the town has had a substantial gain by inwards migration from many sources in the South as well as the Highlands and Islands. All this, in a Highland context, is certainly a change for the better. Such a change, however, is hardly evident in the wide rural hinterland of Inverness. While its population remained fairly stable during last century at around 20,000, as many or more than in the Burgh, there has been depopulation since, reaching a fall of 12% in 1961-71 down to a level of 11,000, only 29% of the number in the Burgh and its parish. The population on farms, crofts and in local trades has fallen here as elsewhere in the country. There is not, however, a complete "drift to the town" and dependence on it, for most of the larger villages on the coast and in the Great Glen have maintained, if not increased, their size and their function as local centres for the services and the households which support the farms, forests, estates and the tourist industry. While the district as a whole now supports far more people, they are more concentrated in settlement in Inverness and in some of the villages; they are also more mobile and people in town and country are more inter-dependent.

The growth of Inverness has been mainly due to the expansion of its traditional role as a diverse service centre and "capital" for the greater part of the Highlands and Islands. The jobs which have been increasing most are in shops, offices (including some 1500 in central and local government), hospitals (over 1,000), transport, hotels and catering, building and contracting. Manufacturers are relatively much smaller, but have also been growing recently in the town and at Dalcross Airport, especially in electrical engineering and electronics, food processing, distilling and textiles.

On top of this have come the oil developments, mainly the making of production platforms east of Ardersier in this district, but more intensively on the Cromarty Firth. They have produced a sudden demand for male labour, which has led to a shortage in many existing service industries at, or based in, Inverness. There has been an accelerated influx of newcomers, limited however by a shortage of housing (despite the local authorities' previously good housing record) and there is an inflation of wages and of house and property prices. In the face of this, conservation means primarily attempts by central and local government and the developers to organise their resources, so as to plan for, and meet, these shortages and not disrupt the local commercial life on which further development depends. Compared with this problem, the physical impact of oil on the Inverness Coast has so far been very successfully dealt with;

there is, however, a shortage of suitable sites, and reclamation may become necessary, for example, in Longman Bay.

Tourism

This industry has been growing as fast as oil now is, but it is a traditional one, which has been here for a century, and it makes a seasonal impact on people and environment not only in the town and on the coast, but also on the whole Inverness, Loch Ness and Glen Affric district. This is indeed the focus of tourism in the Highlands and Islands — the focus of the routes and transport which bring in visitors and take them on tour, of the scenic and historic interests which attract them, and of the accommodation, shops and facilities provided for them, by which a large proportion of local people make or add to their livelihood.

The growth of tourism generally is, of course, a product of a higher standard of living, of holidays with pay, and of the wider ownership and use of cars. In recent years, the theme of "Escape to the Highlands and Islands" — with special reductions in early and late season — has been widely publicised and promoted by the Highlands and Islands Development Board, which has also financially assisted the expansion of hotel and other accommodation, the development of, for example, motor boat cruising on the Caledonian Canal, pony trekking, and the setting up of Area Tourist Organisations. The Forestry Commission, the Nature Conservancy, the National Trust for Scotland, some private landowners, the local highway and planning authorities and the Countryside Commission for Scotland, have all opened up more properties to visitors and provided roadside information and facilities. They have generally been able to do this to an acceptable standard, albeit with constant pressure on their staff and finance.

Colonel Hugh MacLean, Area Tourist Officer for the Inverness and Loch Ness Tourist Organisation, estimates that the number of visitors have doubled in the past ten years. They reached a peak this summer of 1973, when in Inverness itself up to 20,000 people were accommodated each night. About 11,000 of these were in bed and breakfast premises, 7,500 in camping and caravanning, both of which have increased greatly, and 1,500 in hotels, which have not increased in capacity in Inverness in the past twenty years. In the rest of the district, hotels have increased in numbers and size, and there have been large and increasing numbers in camping, caravanning, bed and breakfast, and furnished cottages and chalets. Colonel MacLean also notes a lengthening of the summer season, especially in

September/October, a widening of the classes and origins of visitors, especially from the Continent and overseas, and more use of rail and coach services. He considers the great majority are satisfied with their stay here, except that there is not enough to do, especially in poor weather, for families with children, and those staying more than the customary few nights.

The crucial question of development or conservation is whether this district of the Highlands has any more capacity to absorb such a great annual influx. The seeming summer chaos in the congested streets, and the packed places to stay and eat in Inverness and in other centres and along Loch Ness, suggests that it has not — without spoiling the scenic and cultural assets and the opportunities for recreation and relaxation which attract visitors. Yet there is still room enough for more people in the long off-season, and away from the main roads, towns and villages, in the vast wilderness of so much of the Highlands, particularly if cars are left behind. There are already signs of trends in these directions and of a willing acceptance of them by the visiting public. This gives hope for renewed policies based on the control and steering of tourism development in the interests of its own conservation. This will certainly make bigger demands on finance, staff and planning in the local authorities, the public transport operators and the government agencies concerned, as well as the private interests which benefit greatly from this industry.

Transport

Inverness has developed throughout its history on a focal site, where routes through the Great Glen and across the Grampians meet those along the coastal lowland of the Moray Firth from the East and the North West; and where also there is a crossing point of the River Ness and a short ferry to the Black Isle. Today, all modes of transport use these routes with increasing traffic flows, and they all converge on this town, most of them in, or not far from, its compact central area. This is, indeed, perhaps the most distinctive feature of the town.

Details of transport operations and traffic are given elsewhere in this book, and it will suffice to say here, that phenomenal increases in traffic have been occurring and are forecast to continue on the roads leading into Inverness, some of which are already the busiest in the Highlands, that £60 million is shortly to be spent on the new A9 north of Inverness and south to Perth; that Inverness is one of the most important railway centres in Scotland, handling some thirty-seven passenger and over thirty freight trains a day, with traffic increasing on both; that Dalcross Airport handles a relatively small, but fast-growing number of passengers; and that Inverness Harbour handles significant and growing numbers of cargo vessels and the Caledonian Canal carries ever more pleasure craft as well as fishing boats.

These rail and sea operations pose little or no problem of environmental impact or to conservation, nor does air, so far. They are confined to their own segregated tracks and/or terminals, which are often not used to capacity; they can easily handle bulk loads of goods and people. Their traffic volumes are related to development needs and they are run by a small corps of professionals, with high standards of safety and efficiency, using sophisticated guidance and control systems.

Road transport, on the other hand, uses tracks and terminals shared by the whole public; it handles both small loads on short trips, which it must do, and bulk loads on long hauls, which it need not. Its traffic volumes increase infinitely in proportion to road space and personal spending, and most of it is run by amateurs who like to make their own rules, in vehicles which are inherently both convenient and dangerous through complete flexibility. Its year-in, year-out, record of harassed, injured and killed victims, damage to property, disturbance through noise, fumes and visual omnipresence, and delays through congestion, must be counted the greatest failure in conservation today, here as elsewhere in the "developed" world. In this district, the problem is compounded by the seasonal imposition of heavy summer tourist traffic, by the sudden advent of part of the constructional and other traffic from the North Sea oil developments, by the funnelling of traffic into the centre of Inverness and into villages on main roads, and because it has received little attention until recently from authorities concerned with the traditional Highland problem of the open, sparsely-trafficked countryside.

The solution will have to be as many-sided and deep-seated as the problem itself. Will Government ensure that the national rail, sea and air alternatives to road for long hauls are properly financed, developed and used, or will this come about in any case and more drastically through the rising cost of oil fuel in an imminent world shortage? Will the new regional authorities have finance to reconstruct streets inside and by-passes outside towns and villages and tourist areas? Will they have the will, and the public support, to sort out and enforce priorities — for pedestrians over vehicles in shopping streets, for public transport over cars in town centres, and for small vans over outsize lorries for local deliveries?

Planning in Town and Country

With some significant exceptions, such as trunk road traffic, the impact of these growing activities on the ground, and its expression in buildings, is the statutory concern of the planning authorities of Inverness Town Council and Inverness County Council. They have the task of maintaining an acceptable balance of development and conservation, by controlling the siting and design of new structures within an overall town or county plan. Given the increasing complexity of this task in a diverse growth area, the uneven interest of many electors and elected in it, the limitations on their finances and the mounting pressures of urgent casework on their small (but now expanding) staff, it would be fair to say that the results are generally good, are certainly better than in countries without such a planning system, and could become even better under the new and stronger regional authorities.

In Inverness Burgh, a "mixter-maxter" of a town, with both good and bad in its architecture and amenity, the Council are wrestling to bring into statutory form acceptable to (but not financially assisted by) St Andrew's House, the comprehensive traffic and town plan for Eastgate and the central shopping and station area, which was mapped out for them by their consultants in 1971. Meanwhile this area suffers the worst of the road transport impact referred to, and has been well described as little better than a transport sewer. Comprehensive plans for housing, schools, light industry and open spaces have been made for continuing expansion on the south-east and west sides of the town. Conservation Areas have been designated along the riverside and lower Church Street, and proposals for their extension have been submitted by Inverness Civic Trust, which has also taken a hand in the preservation of the historical buildings of Bow Court and Balnain House in these Conservation Areas. The Trust is collaborating with the Town Planning Officer in looking into the parks and open space provision in the town.

In the experience of the Trust, since it was set up six years ago, in 1967, and no doubt in the opinion of most citizens, the new buildings which are most difficult to accept within the town are the dominating, often alien-looking premises of large companies and statutory undertakings. Perhaps it is inherently impossible to find an acceptable expression among small, riverside or suburban buildings for such massive functions as a telephone exchange, a gas-holder, a 200-strong bureaucracy, a 100-bedded hotel or a 500-patient hospital. They are, however, essential developments somewhere in this sort of town, and they will continue to present the greatest challenge to the best skills available to developers and planning authorities.

In the county area these urban problems are also present on a small scale in the villages and at points on Loch Ness and the Canal. Some good solutions have been found, or are in prospect, especially to meet the growing demands for tourist accommodation, caravanning, parking and recreation. In the open countryside, some less obtrusive routes for new pylon lines have been found. Large estate proprietors, farmers, the Forestry Commission and the Hydro-Electric and Water Board plan for their own purposes, and their work has made the developed rural landscape of the Highlands an integral and attractive part of the scenery. Often recently they have been making some provision for visitors' accommodation and access. Entry into, or through, these domains in the remoter glens is often restricted for car tourists, but seldom in practice for walkers or riders, and this may well be the best way to conserve them. There is great scope for extension and greater use of the many old cross-country tracks, as well as the newer forest trails.

The example of these landed developers suggests that the nearer planning for the environment is done to the "cutting edge" of development, the more effective it is likely to be. Some industrial, tourist and urban developers also show this, to their own and the public's benefit, by taking their proposals in principle to the planning officer at an early enough stage for him to suggest alternatives. Similarly, the Highlands and Islands Development Board, when approached by oil and other large firms for regional information and advice, has been able to indicate those sites suitable to the firm, which are likely to minimise disturbance to agriculture, habitations and wildlife, and in any case does not give financial assistance to any developer until after planning permission has been obtained from the local planning authority. It is also important for the plans of these authorities to be realistic, and the new "structure plans" they are to produce before making detailed local plans will take more account of basic economic and social trends, and of the intentions and needs of developers, as well as of the strategic policies for development of authorities such as the Highlands and Islands Development Board.

If developers and planners should get together early, so should conservers and planners, and conservers and developers. The Nature Conservancy, for example, is now doing this with particular reference to ecologically rare environments on the Moray Firth coast and on high mountains, which would be sensitive to disturbance by industry or organised recreation. Most of these are in Easter Ross. In this district, they include one site of 1st or 2nd Grade — the Tomnahurich/Torvaine esker, a line of sand and gravel hillocks of glacial origin, part of which is threatened by quarrying. The Kildrummie Kames, a somewhat similar ridge on the south side of the A96 to Nairn, are Grade 3. The upper Beauly Firth is also Grade 3 and is proposed as a Local Nature Reserve, and the inner Longman Bay is in Grade 4, both being wildfowl and wader wintering areas.

Voluntary bodies with an informed interest, and a positive concern, also need to formulate and submit their views at an early stage. They may not always be consulted, however, for all this liaison can put an impossible strain on the planning authority's staff time. The number of bodies with an interest in rural development and conservation in the Highlands is legion.

Recording and interpreting what, in fact, happens to the environment when large-scale industrial or other development takes place is also important. This is being done round the Moray Firth coast by Aberdeen University's Geography Department, sponsored by the County Councils and by the Highlands and Islands Development Board, which has itself carried out a comprehensive study of the effects of industrialisation on the agricultural industry.

Conclusion

It is suggested that development and conservation are not opposed but complementary aspects of growth in the Inverness district; that, when their promoters have worked together and with planners, there has been a successful outcome, especially in the countryside and in physical planning for industry; that the impact of road transport on towns and villages is a striking failure in this respect; that the buildings of large, urban institutions are also difficult to cope with; that the rapid pace of oil-related growth is creating shortages and inflations which are not yet under control; and that tourism is likely to move in the direction of more control and steering of development.

Nothing has been said here about the important, but intangible, question of conserving community life and values. Yet Inverness has always been a meeting place of Highland and Lowland people and ideas. It is well used to absorbing incomers, and it should be better able to continue doing so in conditions of oil and tourism boom than smaller more isolated communities farther to the west and north.

GENERAL

PEOPLE AND PLACES

RORY MACKAY

People and places. Highland people in Highland places. Gaelic speaking Gaels in the Gaidhealtachd. That was the state of the country until very recently. That it is otherwise today proves the success of the racialist policy which began in the 15th century with King James I. With the loss of language came the loss of song and music, story and tradition, but especially the loss of identity.

The Gaels, even of the recent past, had a vast knowledge of the poetry and music, the history and traditions of the race and the tribe. They also knew their country well and the legends associated with its places and features. When travelling they were not restricted, as we are, to main roads, but used hill roads and tracks which are forgotten today. Travelling on foot or on horseback, they could take in the countryside in a way that is not possible in a car. Putting up at houses or inns on the way, they would acquire information from their hosts and other travellers about the district through which they were passing. At home, the ceilidh houses were like schools where the oral literature, music and history of the Gael were learned. The knowledge was general and to be found in the homes, not only of the country folk, but in those of many of the nobility and most of the gentry until late in the 18th century. Then the rapid changes and pressures from outside drove some from the traditions and culture of more than a thousand years and encouraged others to forget them, so that the strong ropes that had bound them to the past began to fray into the mere threads that they are today.

The oldest literature in Gaelic is that of the Red Branch, alias the Ulster Cycle. Some say that its combination of prose and verse is the earliest form of literature known to the Indo-Europeans. The people and events recorded are thought to date from the century before the Birth of Christ, and, if so, the tales recall an older way of life than any vernacular literature in Western Europe. The best known of these tales is, perhaps, the story of Deirdre and the three sons of Uisneach. We can no longer appreciate the importance of these stories and of the tales of the later Feinne or Fingalians in the lives of Highland people, even of people round Inverness, so far from the west coast and Ireland.

Lochardil, long drained, is today an unimaginative housing scheme in Inverness. The Gaelic form and meaning of the name are now lost, but one writer in the last century claimed that it meant Deirdre's loch, Deardal being an alternative form to Deirdre. In the pass of Inverfarigaig is the precipitous hill called Dun Deardail, which unquestionably means Deirdre's Fort. Furthermore, the old people of this part associated the place with her and the three sons of Uisneach. Tomnahurich was believed to be the last resting place of Fingal and the Feinne. The story was that a boy herding cattle found a way into the interior of the hill. He saw before him sleeping warriors, and, hanging on the wall, a great horn, which he tried to blow. He had not the strength to blow it, but the slight sound which he made with it was enough to rouse the warriors, who raised themselves up on their elbows. The boy fled, leaving them in that position, in which they will remain until the horn, the "last trump," is properly and finally sounded. It does not matter that the associations of these people with these places is almost certainly fictitious. What it proves is the antiquity and continuity of Gaelic tradition.

Culduthel House, now part of the hospital, was once the home of the Frasers of Culduthel. Captain Fraser of Knockie, who lived in the first part of the last century, records in the notes to his collection of music, that the Culduthels of his youth and, indeed, other Frasers, were raconteurs of the poems about Fingal and the Feinne.

Near to Culduthel is Castle Heather, formerly Castle Leather, from *Lethoir* — an edge. Here, in the 18th century, lived Major James Fraser, a cadet of the Culduthel family. Major Fraser left two legacies that survive till today; a fine portrait of himself and his personal memoirs. The portrait was painted about 1714 and shows how a Highland gentleman of substance at that time was dressed and armed. It hangs in the entrance to the Inverness Town Hall and is one of the town's most precious possessions. Perhaps the most interesting part of the memoirs is the Major's description of his journey in 1714 to France to find and bring home the exiled Lord Lovat, the same one who was later to be beheaded in the Tower of London after the '45.

Fraser of Culduthel and other leading Frasers met and decided that Major James was the most suitable man for the task. The prospect of travelling such a distance on foot did not seem to daunt him, and his description of his leaving home is almost callous. "Upon the first day of May, be four of the clock of the morning, the Major took journey from his dwelling house with his habersack & left his wife and children spralling on the ground in tears." He records little of his journey south, only mentioning Newcastle and Shields, where he took ship for London. Of his stay there he only records an evening drinking punch with three other Highland people. Arriving at Calais, he called out to the crowd on the pier, enquiring if there were anyone present who could understand "his language." An Irishman answered, which suggests strongly that the Major called out in Gaelic. He makes it clear in his memoirs that he was bi-lingual. After many adventures and difficulties, the Major found Lovat and succeeded in bringing him home.

At the turn of the 18th century, Kenneth Mackenzie, a Gaelic poet, lived at Castle Leather. Except for one, his poems are not remarkable. The exception is of great interest because of the insight it gives as to how Highlanders felt about the Clearances, even if they themselves were not directly affected by them.

> " 'S chi mi dol a mach nan treudan,
> 'S loingeas bhreid gheal air a shuan,
> Chi mi Gaidheil 's iad nan éiginn,
> 'S iad ag éiridh suas bho 'n chuail,
> 'S chi me daoine gur sior thréigsinn,
> 'S nach 'eil spéis dhaibh 's an Taobh Tuath."
> " I see the departure of the heroes,
> Over the ocean in white-sailed ships,
> I see the Gael in travail
> Rising from their doors,
> I see the people leaving,
> For there is no love for them in the North."

Near to the Pass of Inverfarigaig, and lying to the north of the road to Errogie, is the small township of Allt na Goibhre, the Goat's Burn. Until recently it was occupied by Gaels, but now by incomers. Here in 1696 took place a small battle, the victor being Lord Lovat, the same Simon Fraser who was to be retrieved by Major Fraser from France in 1714. The background is very complicated but, briefly, there had been a dispute in the clan as to who should be chief. The Aberdeenshire Frasers favoured Lord Saltoun, while the Highland Frasers preferred Simon. The Marquis of Atholl, who was an enemy of Simon, sent against him a force led by his two sons. The invaders were encamped at Allt na Goibhre after a march from Inverness. Simon, with the Stratherrick Frasers and some of the Lochaber Macdonalds, came over the shoulder of Dun Deardail and attacked them, defeated them and captured Atholl's sons. The Marquis was on good terms with William of Orange, and succeeded in having Simon outlawed. In the end he had to go into exile, where he remained until brought home by Fraser of Castle Leather. It is fashionable to describe Lovat as a wicked man. While he was no saint, allowance is never made for the ill-treatment and injustice he suffered in his youth. Perhaps far more sinister and wicked was his contemporary, Norman Macleod of Dunvegan, but he and his doings do not concern us here.

A result, and perhaps also a symptom, of the loss of identity among Highlanders today, is the exaggerated importance now given to the Norse element in their history, as distinct always, of course, from the proper research. In fact, these invaders left remarkably little behind them in the true Highlands, other than place names. They feature but rarely in Highland tradition, and then usually as enemies in defeat. Loch Ashie, which supplies Inverness with water, is supposed to be called after Aisidh, a Norse warrior defeated in battle nearby. Overlooking the loch is Cather Fhinn, Fingal's Chair, suggesting that he might have been at the battle.

Inland from Drumnadrochit, a prominent feature is Craig Monie, Creag Mhonaidh, Monie's Rock. The tradition is again of the Norse in defeat. Having been brought to battle at this spot, Monie fled up Glen Urquhart, and was run down and killed at Coire Mhonaidh, now corrupted to Corriemony, where a stone marks the place of his death. In the summit of Craig Monie is a cleft called Leabaidh Nighean Righ Lochlainn, the Bed of the Daughter of the King of Denmark, Monie's sister. Here she hid, and was found after the battle.

Very little Highland history is taught, and much of what is, is full of omissions and distortions. Of the omissions, perhaps the most glaring is that of the Lordship of the Isles. This is one of the most interesting chapters in Scottish history, forming a bridge between the post-Dalriadic Gaels and those of the clan society on which we look back. At their greatest, the Lords of the Isles ruled the Hebrides, the whole of Ross-shire and the greater part of Inverness-shire. They were *de facto* kings, rather than chiefs, and their residences in the north were Dingwall Castle, Balconie (Baile Comhnaidh Mhic Dhomhaill, the township of Macdonald's residence), and Kinmylies near

Inverness. In the 15th century they came under attack from the King of Scots, who employed the Campbells, Gordons and the newly-emerged Mackenzies to do his work. Angus Og, the son of the Lord of the Isles of the time, came north to secure Ross and to meet the Royal Army, led by the Earl of Atholl. The battle took place at Lagaìdh Brìde (sometimes written Laga Braad), where Angus Og was victorious. Lagaìdh Brìde is now known as Logie Wester, a small disused cemetery near the river, in the policy woods of Conon House. The name Lagaìdh Brìde means the Place of Hollows of St. Bride, and there must once have been a chapel there dedicated to that Saint. Angus Og and his army came north again a few years later, about 1488, and camped at Inverness. During the night, Diarmad OCairbre, an Irish harper, murdered Angus by cutting his throat. It was believed that the harper had been incited to do this murder by Mackenzie of Kintail. A poem survives, censuring the murderer.

During the fearful century following the forfeiture of the land and titles of the Lords of the Isles, in 1494, the King of Scots encouraged strife, to keep the Gael from coalescing to restore the Lordship. Part of his policy was to grant or withold titles to land, thereby fragmenting society and creating the final clan society which died in 1746. During this period, the Earl of Moray summoned the Mackintoshes as his vassals to him at Tordarroch in Strathnairn, where he is said to have hanged some of them over the eaves of a barn, whose foundations can still be seen. The late Lachlan Mackintosh, while tenant of Tordarroch, claimed to have found a boot with foot and leg bones in it in a bog nearby. This outrage is supposed to have originated the saying "Chan ann a h-uile latha 'bhitheas mòd aig Mac an Toisich." "It is not every day that Mackintosh has a gathering."

During the 17th century the Highlands entered British politics and were to continue to do so, off and on, until 1746. Montrose's series of victories for King Charles is well known. One of his most famous exploits was the winter hill march which culminated in the victory at Inverlochy, over the Covenanting army and the Campbells. Montrose was in the course of marching his army up the Great Glen to deal with Seaforth, who was at Inverness, and had camped on the flat known as Leitir nan Lub, beside the Straight Mile between Fort Augustus and Abcrchaldei. Iain Lom Macdonald, the Lochaber poet, arrived hot foot with the news that the Campbells were in Lochaber burning and harrying. Alexander Macdonald, Alasdair MacCholla Chiotaich, Montrose's general, warned Iain

Lom that if his news were false, then he would hang. On 31 January, 1645, the army turned into the hills, passing Cullachy and the knoll there called Glùn Chuileachaidh, Culachy's Knee. Marching through that day and the following night, they reached Roy Bridge early on 1st February. They were still 13 miles from Inverlochy. At dawn on Candlemas Day, the King's forces, starving though they may have been, fell on their unsuspecting foes. Iain Lom, Cutting John, composed a fine poem to commemorate the march, the battle and the defeat of the Campbells. It is still sung.

At all times there were outlawed men living by the sword. These people are usually dismissed as broken men. While many must have been criminals, there were some who were unfortunates, victims of malicious people who had the ear of the King or his officers. One of these could have been Donald Macdonald of Bohuntine in Glen Roy, an outlaw and poet of the 17th century. He is still remembered as Domhnall Donn, Brown-haired Donald. Domhnall Donn made his living by rieving. One of the places where he used to hide was in the ravine at Allt Saighe on Loch Ness-side, near the Half Way House. The burn was the boundary between the lands of Glenmoriston and Grant of Seafield, the latter being an enemy of Domhnall Donn. Domhnall Donn, however, courted Mary Grant, Seafield's daughter. The legend is, that he was captured by a party of Grants and taken to Inverness and executed on the Castle Hill. As the head left the body, it was heard to say "Tog mo cheann, a Mhàiri." "Lift my head, Mary." Domhnall Donn, although he lived in the 17th century, is not quite forgotten for, apart from his poetry, the people of Bohuntine can point out the site of his home.

The travellers along Loch Ness-side will note the title on the loch-side, just north-east of Invermoriston, which was probably the first area planted by the Commission in the district. Their regrettable custom has been to call a forest by the name of its first plantation, which of course muddles up the place names of the countryside quite unnecessarily, not that this would concern the worthy southerners responsible. The name, which is taken from the Ordnance Survey, means the Rock of the Birds. According to the old Gaelic-speaking people of the place, however, the true name is Creag Iain, John's Rock. Unfortunately the Ordnance Survey has not always been accurate in its recording of place names. In the late 17th century, John Grant of Glenmoriston, because of his Jacobite activities, had on occasion to take to the hills and hide, and was nick-named Iain a'chreagain, John of the Rock. It could well be that this place was one of his refuges, for its shoulder is immediately above Invermoriston House.

Further up Glenmoriston is Blairie, a' Bhlaraidh, where lived Hugh Chisholm, one of the Seven Men of Glen Moriston who were hosts to Charles Edward in the cave of Coire Dho. More recently, Peter John Macdonald, a descendant of another of the Seven Men, lived at Blairie. He and his brother, another Peter, were full of history and stories of the Glen. Their old family home, now a ruin, was at Lagan Bàn, near Torgoil, where once there was an inn. There is a story associated with it which may well be a joke. After Culloden, a Highlander in hiding met a solitary English trooper, whom he killed. He wanted his long boots, but could not get them off, so he amputated the trooper's legs and wrapped them, boots and all, in his plaid. Coming to Torgoil, he asked for a night's shelter and was shown into the byre. During the night he extracted the severed legs from the boots and, departing very early in the morning, left the legs in the byre. When the inn-keeper came to the byre in the morning, he was horrified to see the cow with a pair of legs beside her, and no other sign of the guest. The animal was quickly slaughtered.

On Loch Ness-side, between Invermoriston and Inchnacardoch Hotel, there is a rock called Creag a Mhuirt, the Rock of the Murder, and to the west of it a burn called Allt an Eich, the Burn of the Horse. According to Mr Alexander Campbell, Fort Augustus, probably the best informed man in local history in the Great Glen, the story is as follows. An English officer, some time after 1746, was making his way along the lochside on horseback when a man on top of the rock shot at him, killing him. Dragging the corpse, the frightened horse bolted, but was itself shot and killed at the burn. The man found the saddle-bags full of money, which he took to be "Airgid Cinn," the "Head Money" for the Prince. He took one golden guinea as a souvenir.

The crannog in the loch near Inchnacardoch is properly called Eilean Mhuirich, Maurie's Island. Its English name, Cherry Island, was given to it by soldiers of Fort Augustus.

Strathglass is today tragically depopulated and the few people who live in it are not of the old native stock, indeed, many of them are not Gaels. Near Mauld Bridge is a pleasant-looking house which was once a school. The area round about it is called Innis nan Ceann, the Meadow of the Heads, because of a conflict there long ago. In its grounds is a tall pointed slab of stone, with the words Mo rùn geal òg, and the initials C.F. and W.C. and the date 1746 inscribed on it. It commemorates

Z

William Chisholm, the standard-bearer to the Chisholm, who died at Culloden and whose house was near-by. His wife, Christina Fergusson, composed an elegy for him which is still sung. It is perhaps one of the finest of the many poems of the '45, with a splendid tune. The refrain is Mo rùn geal òg, My fair young loved one.

In the western part of Glen Affric, beyond Ath nam Muileach, is an area called Còmhlan. This part of the glen was in the past occupied as grazings by Macraes from Kintail. One of them was a poet, John Macrae, still remembered as Iain Mac Mhurchaidh, John son of Murdoch. It is said that his father, Murdoch, was hanged by the Hanoverians outside the Town Hall in Inverness. Iain Mac Mhurchaidh lost his cattle at Còmhlan in an unexpected snow-storm, and he described in one of his songs how he saw their bones whitening on the hillside. This loss, and the rack-renting of Seaforth, persuaded him to emigrate with others to America, in 1770. Iain Mac Mhurchaidh never settled down and his homesickness is very evident in his songs, which are still sung. During the American War of Independence, he was a Loyalist and after the defeat of the British, he took to the woods and forests, where he perished. One of the emigrants, however, returned to Kintail, bringing with him the poems composed by Ian Mac Mhurchaidh in America. His descendants are in and around Dornie still. Iain Mac Mhurchaid's home in Kintail was on the farm of Lienassie, near to the River Connag, at a place called Dal an Eas, the Meadow of the Waterfall.

The grazing rights which the Macraes held in the Chisholm's Affric lands were given in return of wadsets (loans of money), and from time to time they gave rise to trouble with the Chisholm's own people. At the beginning of the 18th century Muireach Fial MacRath, Generous Maurice Macrae, was one of these wadsetters, and the story of his murder can still be heard in Kintail. Muireach Fial and his wife used to go to Inverness to sell dairy produce. One time when returning, they were met at Struy in Strathglass by a party of local men, who invited them to drink in the inn. Muireach Fial accepted the invitation, but his wife refused and continued on the road home, expecting her husband to catch her up. When he never came, she became anxious and pressed on for Kintail, where she raised a search party to return to Strathglass. The party searched for Muireach all over the strath, and made enquiries, but could not find him, so most of them returned home. One, however, remained behind and pretended to be an idiot. He wandered about, begging from door to door. One night, when lying at the door of a house, he heard a tapping on the window and a conversation between the man of the house and someone outside. Reference was made to the white-bellied salmon (bradan tarraghael) tied to a bush and hidden in a pool of the River Glass. The Kintail man went to investigate, and found the body of the murdered Muireach Fial, which he drew from the river and hid, before setting off for Kintail. A strong party left for Strathglass to bring back the corpse for burial in Kintail. As they were passing the cemetery of Clachan Comar, near Cannich, there was a funeral taking place and the mourners had a stone ready to erect. The Macraes took the stone from them, to provoke a fight, but the Strathglass people did not resist, so the party left with the body of Muireach Fial and the stone, which they placed over his grave in Clachan Duich. It is still there, at the south gable of the ruined church and is called Leac Chuileanach, the Puppy Stone. The explanation of the name is that the stone being in two pieces, one large and one small, it is like a bitch with her puppy.

It is said that the Macraes used ropes made from willow withies, "woodies" in Lallans, but "gad" in Gaelic, to carry the stone home, and that the marks made by the ropes can still be seen on the stone. Another version is, that they used a loban to transport it. A loban was a small cart used on steep ground. The body of the cart was a large creel or basket. Lobans were used in and around Glen Urquhart until quite recently.

The great story tellers are few now. Some idea of their accurate memories is given by tape recordings that were made in the Outer Isles. The tales lasted for 16 hours. Nine years later, the same story teller re-recorded the same tales. In the re-telling there were differences. They amounted to twelve words. One of the finest of the tellers of tales was Hugh Mackinnon of Eigg, who died in 1972. He and his kind had an immense knowledge of the history and traditions of their own districts and their people. They often knew much about other parts of the Highlands and, indeed, of national and world affairs. It was a wonderful privilege to know such people, the last of a kind which not long ago was commonplace. As long as they live, things which are of the past will not be forgotten.

Cha bhith an laithdean ann a rithist.

COUNTRY WAYS

KATHARINE STEWART

In a place only fifteen minutes by car from Inverness it is still possible to push open a neighbour's door without knocking, to go into a small, dark kitchen where there is the glow and flicker of peats on the hearth, to find faces warm with welcome, and to be greeted in the Gaelic tongue. The people there will be elderly, maybe, but there will be grandchildren in the style of the day coming in with an armful of sticks for the morning, cracking jokes in the current idiom, leaving a small present of shop cakes and the weekly paper, before they set off for their town home or their near-by farm. It was always so — a lingering contact between young and old, a sense of family, a sharing in the realities of living.

As we settle down with our neighbour for a "news" — an exchange of fact, comment and surmise on everything from the weather to the latest political gambit of the day — we know that it is not only the past we are seeing reflected in his features, but a signal to the future. He tells us, with quiet pride, that his youngest grandson lives for the days when he is free of school and can help with the croft work, that the tenancy of the holding is to be his, that it will not revert to bracken and the house a holiday home for strangers from the city. That there is a movement among young people to adopt a simpler way of living is undeniable and we rejoice with our neighbour that this is so. Given enough youngsters of like mind in a neighbourhood, perhaps some of the old communal pattern of living might yet be re-established.

Interdependence

Interdependence was always the keynote of Highland living. In the small, close-knit communities there were inevitable jealousies and feuds, but these were largely overcome when it was a question of giving timely help in a domestic crisis or of saving a neighbour's crops or beasts. Everyone was engaged in more or less the same kind of activities and was up against the same problems. One never had to ask for help. Every need was anticipated. Should one or other of an elderly couple die, the surviving partner would be visited daily and his or her immediate wants seen to. Should one's oat crop still be in the sheaf and a day of squally showers set in, then a neighbour would appear unbidden and start stooking his way down the field, only pausing for a greeting when within hailing distance. Without timely interventions of this kind, many a crop of oats, hay or potatoes would have rotted in the ground.

Of course, for many seasonal jobs, such as peat-cutting, sheep-dipping or clipping, threshing or potato-lifting, combined operations were planned in advance and turned into a social occasion, with shared meals and the exchange of news and gossip and much wise-cracking and mirth. The songs which used to lighten the load of heavy work have died out, but the high-heartedness, the mock rivalry, the sheer pleasure in companionship would bubble up and make the days pass too fast.

Self-Sufficiency

In older times, before the advent of easy communication by road, rail, air or telephone, communities were self-sufficient and included craftsmen of various kinds — a mason, a carpenter, a slater, a blacksmith, a miller, a weaver, a shoemaker or two, even a tailor. Often these crafts had been mastered to a state of real proficiency by a son who had gone away to serve an apprenticeship while waiting to take over the tenancy of the family croft, sometimes they were an acquired knack.

A hundred and fifty years ago a house for a couple of newly-weds could be put up in a day, when all the materials were to hand — stone for the walls, tree trunks to support the roof and sods and heather for thatching. Even with the coming of more sophisticated styles, the job did not take long when there was a mason on hand, a carpenter to make doors and window frames and a slater to fit the fine Ballachulish slates.

This self-sufficiency led to inventiveness, often of a really ingenious kind. One crofter in Abriachan, a community ten miles from Inverness, devised a system of underfloor heating by warm air convected from his peat fire which must have been years ahead of his time. His family subsequently emigrated to Canada and became builders of repute.

The crofter was always quick to appreciate and adopt those inventions he saw were of real help to his station, though I suspect he preferred those of his own devising. I have seen a rope-twister from a bicycle chain-wheel set in an old box with a door-knob for a handle which does the job to perfection.

The blacksmith, of course, was a key-man in any community, as he must have been from time immemorial. Iron, in the old legends, had a magical property. It was certainly costly and the shafts of working implements were made at home from wood. Rakes and harrows even had wooden teeth, which could easily be renewed, and boots and shoes, as well as dressers and chairs, were held together with wooden pegs. But ploughs and peat-knives, like horses, had to be shod with iron, and it was a sign of prosperity to possess a finely wrought chain, or a well-balanced "swee" — an iron arm on which iron pots would be slung at varying heights, that could be swung over the fire, or out into the room as required.

Women's Skills

The women took part in most of the outdoor work. Their special skills were handed on from mother to daughter and included the spinning and dyeing of wool and knitting, as well as butter and cheese-making, the salting of meat, cooking and baking, and the preparing of simple medicines and remedies from berries, roots and herbs. To make a pair of stockings from wool grown on the backs of one's own sheep and spun by one's own fingers, perhaps dyed in a brew of lichen gathered by the door, must have been a source of satisfaction. Equally satisfying must have been the making of porridge, brose or oatcakes from oats one had sown and harvested and seen ground at the mill down the road. Food was plain, but so fresh that it seldom palled. Potatoes and turnips would see the winter through, most years; milk and eggs were produced daily and cheese and butter in summertime. In autumn, two or three neighbours would band together to fetch barrels of salt herring from the West, the Abriachan crofters venturing to Loch Hourn. It was an exciting trip. Sometimes an early snow-storm would blow up, and then men and boys would be trapped in the carts if they were unlucky enough to be caught far from a welcome hostelry.

A pig or two might be fattened in a small sty and salted down for Christmas, and a cast ewe would give a taste of mutton. Otherwise meat was in short supply. In times of great need, the cattle would be bled and the blood mixed with oatmeal to make nourishing "black puddings."

People living in close contact with natural resources, however scant, soon find out to what uses they can be put. Lichens and roots produced the colours they craved for dyeing wool and cloth. Flowers and berries, they discovered, had medicinal properties against most forms of ill-health. The florets of camomile were made into an infusion which helped digestive troubles, sloe-jelly was taken to ward off winter coughs and primroses were an ingredient in healing ointments.

The Stills

A talent which the people in most parts of the Highlands developed during parts of the 18th and 19th centuries was that for distilling a good "dram." It was a skilled affair. It was also a ploy which intrigued the men like any game of chance and it had its economic necessity. Times were often hard, rents never got less and there was always a ready customer for an illicit brew. Many stories are told, with relish, of the means adopted to outwit the officers of the law when they came rampaging through the hills looking for the tell-tale rising of smoke from the smugglers' bothies. Casks of whisky were buried in the peat, and pots and "worms" (the coils of copper tubing used in distillation) were sometimes flung into lochans, to be retrieved later. Bottles were hidden in the thatch or under the women's voluminous skirts and tale-telling was taboo. Substantial bribes were offered for information which would lead to arrest, but these were seldom accepted, unless by arrangement, when they could be used to replenish equipment.

All in all, distilling was looked on as part of the pattern of life. Though sometimes abused, the custom of imbibing did little harm to people working hard out of doors in a cold, damp climate. Many a serious illness was no doubt warded off by the timely taking of a toddy — whisky with hot water sipped before bed on a winter's night.

Work

Though life was hard, it was healthy and had a completeness which kept every faculty in trim.

Before the introduction of sheep on a commercial scale (encouraged by Government subsidy after the world wars), hardy cattle were the mainstay of the crofts. Work revolved around the need to maintain these beasts and to provide subsistence at the best possible level for the family. The crops grown were, in earlier days, bere (a form of barley), and latterly oats, the straw being fed to the cattle in winter and the grain being used for domestic meal, as a feed for the horse and a scattering for poultry; hay for the horse and perhaps for a cherished house-cow; potatoes for the family and turnips for the wintered cattle and the home soup pot.

Springtime ploughing was often a long-drawn-out affair, with squalls of "cuckoo-snow" to hold things up. Even after the seed was sown, May-time downpours would wash it out of the earth and make a bog of the potato-ground. But eventually everything would be sown and planted and then, in early summer, neighbours would band together for an expedition to the peat-banks to cut a stock of winter fuel.

Peat-cutting

Peat-knives and baskets of food would be loaded on to the horses' backs and whole families would set set off together, as though for a holiday outing. The work was hard enough, but it was a happy occasion, for people would be meeting, perhaps for the first time for months, to compare notes on their winters, to exchange news and to plan futures. The men and boys would skim off the turf at the peat-banks and cut out the blocks of peat, the women and girls spreading them out to dry. Over a meal of bannock and cheese, with a drink of buttermilk or tea, brewed on a fire of heather roots, they would relax in happy mood and the easing of tension would bring out the humour in them, the teasing and the laughter of people who have weathered one winter and are preparing for the next. The larks would be singing and the peewits flashing and there would not be much wrong with their world.

A week or two after the first cutting expeditions, they would go back to arrange the peats in small stacks, so that the sun and wind would dry them, and in the late summer the men would cart them home and build them into large piles near the houses. The quality of the peat varied from region to region. The brown, fibrous kind was less favoured than the black, dense type, which more closely resembled coal. The peat harvest, like any other, depended on the weather for a satisfactory outcome. When thoroughly dry and hard, the peats gave a good, glowing heat. In some houses, in older times, the fire never went out. It was "smoored" in the evening, that is, covered over with ash and then blown into life in the morning. I have heard of a house in which the fire had not been out in two hundred years.

In the old houses, the roof-beams were black and shiny with peat-reek and the thatch, impregnated liked the beams, would be removed in spring and ploughed into a field as manure. With material immediately to hand, a new roof was quickly fashioned. With each making the building regulations which suited him, the houses had that fitness for their purpose and to their surroundings which came, perhaps, closest to perfection.

The Shielings

Up to the early years of this century, the practice of transhumance, more often known as the Shieling System, the survival of an age-old and widespread custom among hill-people, was common in the Highlands. Some time in May the cattle would be driven up to the high pastures, the women, girls and boys accompanying them in carts loaded with blankets, cooking pots, dairying utensils and perhaps a spinning-wheel. The men would return home to watch over the growing crops, now safe from marauding stock, and the women and young people would stay in the primitive shieling huts, looking after the cattle and making quantities of butter and cheese. The butter would be packed in wooden kegs and buried in the peat, which preserved it for an indefinite period. In August, when the pastures were eaten bare, the cattle would be driven down the hill again and all hands would be ready to take home the peat and then to get in the various harvests.

The shieling life was a carefree one, with a feel of holiday about it. The boys would fish and trap, in the intervals of herding; household chores would be reduced to a minimum and there was time to indulge in laughter and romance. Many Gaelic songs sprang out of the happiness of life at the shielings.

Harvest

This fortifying spell was much needed, for harvest was mostly a chancy business, being utterly dependent on the vagaries of the weather. Often the stooks of corn would be out in the fields till each was capped with snow, and hay would be hung, like washing, on the dykes and fences in a desperate attempt to dry it out before the winter set in. Potatoes would have to be dug laboriously by hand if the ground was too sodden to bear the weight of a horse-drawn implement. To over-winter the family and stock in some degree of comfort was the ultimate goal of all the year's work. There was much anxiety everywhere if stacks and barns were not filled to capacity, for no one could foresee how long and grim the coming winter might be and in what shape the life of the croft might survive it. The fatalism of the people, however, born of the survival of generations, came to their help even in the worst of harvest years, and the last sheaf would be put in place, even on a meagre, sodden stack, with a real sense of triumph.

The Ceilidhs

With the onset of winter began the season of indoor ploys. No matter how exhausted the people might be by the physical hardship and the anxiety of harvesting operations, their mental alertness and their powers of imagination were seldom dulled. The long, dark evenings were an invitation to the ceilidh, that is, the meeting of neighbours in a welcoming house to exchange news, to tell stories and to sing. Before the advent of radio and the easily procured newspaper, these exchanges were a vital release of mental and imaginative energy, and had real healing value. Sometimes the gatherings were quite small and informal, sometimes they were conducted with a certain amount of ceremony, when the master of the house, or Fear an Tigh, would start off the story-telling or singing and would then expect each person present to make his or her contribution. In older times, the exchanging of riddles and sayings was popular, and the people had a great gift for improvisation and for satire. Many an unpopular ground-officer or other symbol of authority was wittingly and pungently cut down to size in Gaelic metre. The women would often knit or spin during the ceilidhs and a light meal would be eaten before the company dispersed, often quite late, as rising was later in the winter days.

Sadly, little of the creative output of song and story of the ceilidhs has survived. It was an oral tradition, the stories being handed on and embellished in the process of repetition. Even the poems of the local bard, who had been an important member of the chief's followers, and who still emerged in many communities after the breakdown of the clan system, were mostly lost, though some were written down.

Winter Festivities

Hallowe'en, which coincides with the Celtic time of Samhain, marking the end of summer, was the first of the winter festivities, indulged in by the children and young people. As the eve of All Saint's Day was the time when witches and warlocks and all the hobgoblin tribe were loose about the world, it was quite in order for the youngsters to disguise themselves and to play pranks upon foe and friend. For weeks beforehand they would collect discarded clothes, make masks out of old stockings and carve turnip lanterns. The pranks were many and various — letting loose a styed pig being fattened for Christmas, blocking windows with sods so that the inmates of the house would sleep on in darkness till noon, or throwing peats down a chimney, so that the morning fire would not draw. In favoured houses, the gang would burst into the kitchen and sing for their hosts, failure to recognise them under their disguises bringing reward in the shape of apples, nuts or sweetmeats.

Divination rites were also performed at Hallowe'en, the girls quite seriously considering that their future husbands would appear, offering a drink, after they had eaten salt herring, or looking over their shoulder as they gazed into a mirror at midnight.

Christmas was the next festivity at which the children were indulged, though not on any great scale. Memories of pre-Christian festivals lingered in the instincts of the people and, after the Reformation, when such church-centred feasts were frowned on, they perhaps predominated.

It is certain that the New Year, the time when the daylight was perceptibly lengthening, was the cause of real, universal celebration. The house would be tidied, and the hearth swept, to ensure cleanliness throughout the coming year and, at midnight, guns would be fired to ward off evil spirits. Then the men would set off, armed with a bottle of whisky and a baking of bannocks, to be "first foot," first across the threshold, at their neighbours' houses.

At Christmas or New Year a great game of shinty would be played, the men and boys of a whole community taking part, with as many as fifty-a-side, and sometimes resulting in what resembled a battle. At any rate, it was a great and healthy releasing of energy.

In some places it was the custom, until recent times, to keep the "old" New Year, on January 12th, by which time, it was said, there was "an hour on the day." An extra hour's daylight meant a lot to people who had to work with oil lamps and lanterns, and to carry fodder to the byre and peats to the kitchen for the evening fire.

The midwinter festivities did a lot for morale. The endless round of feeding beasts, threshing out corn, repairing implements or making ropes in the barn and coping with weather conditions in the cold, short days, though not as exhausting as the field activities of summer, was certainly monotonous and there was often anxiety over illness and the sadness of bereavement.

Death

Early spring, when vitality was at the ebb, was often a time for death. As with all misfortune, the hard edge was softened by the rallying of the community. The sick person would have been visited throughout the period of illness, and when death came friends would be there to sit with the corpse, to help with the funeral arrangements, the making or procuring of the coffin, the summoning of the minister, the providing of food and drink for everyone. In older times, the men would carry the coffin on their shoulders, sometimes for miles, to its resting place in the family burying ground. Great importance was attached to the fitness of the place of burial, perhaps springing from a racial memory going back to the times of the great chambered cairns. In some parts the old funeral roads can still be traced, with the small cairns where the bearers stopped for rest and refreshment. The women stayed to comfort the bereaved and to prepare a meal for the men when they returned from the burying ground.

The Burnings

Though spring was often the most anxious time of the year, with fodder and food and sometimes fuel stocks running low, yet preparations for the growing season had to go ahead as best they could. One which the young men particularly enjoyed was the burning of the heather. The dead growth was destroyed so that the roots would spring afresh, and it was a release from the comparative inactivity to get out to the hill ground on an adventurous ploy. There was a symbolic side to it, too. It was as though the great purifying force of fire was laying the ghost of winter in the hills. Then, in spite of set-backs, confidence grew. There was the instinctive knowledge that nothing could stop the slow tilting of the earth towards the sun, and seed-time must inevitably follow once again.

Marriage

Early summer was a favoured time for weddings. The pattern of human life, with its times for gladness or for tears, its celebrations and its misgivings, its ritual and its surprises, was inextricably woven into the fabric of work for survival. This is what made it satisfying and complete. In the urban life of today, where people are cut off from their sources, there is a great lack of unifying force, so essential to health, or wholeness.

A wedding was again the signal for communal activity. Guests would contribute to the feast, fowls and great bakings of bannocks and bottles of whisky being produced on as liberal a scale as possible. A white cloth would be flown from the chimney-head of the bride's home and her party would walk in procession to the church, headed by a piper. After the ceremony, the celebrations would be held in the barn, which was swept and decorated for the occasion, with feasting and dancing to the fiddle or the accordion, which went on for days. The myth that gloom predominates among the Gaels should surely be dispelled. Traces of melancholy there are, perhaps, as is characteristic of a people sensitive to the chanciness of life in their surroundings. But this other facet shines very bright, this capacity for real enjoyment, for a healthy abandoning of care in song and dance, teasing and laughter.

Hand-fasting

In many parts of the Highlands, the custom of "hand-fasting" was prevalent. In Abriachan, hidden on the wooded slope rising from Loch Ness, is a "handfasting stone," bearing hollows capable of accommodating the hand in three different positions. The couple would join hands at this stone and declare themselves wed for a trial period of a year. If at the end of this time they found they were unsuited, or no child had been born, they were free to break the contract.

Birth

Still felt today is the eagerness with which good news is announced and received. Birth is, of course, the great sign of survival, and a boy is welcomed with the most genuine joy. A silver coin is pressed into the small hand. If the infant clasps it, he will prosper, so it is said. The old fears of a "changeling" being substituted for the real child by the fairy folk have been dispelled, though people still living can remember the time when women would put a drop of water from a "font" hidden deep in a wood into the baptismal bowl, to ensure protection against such a misfortune.

Fostering

The fostering of a chief's son by another member of the clan was common practice in older times. This is perhaps why, during the present century, the people easily adapted to the system of bringing up, along with their own family, children boarded-out by the authorities in the big cities. They received an allowance, of course, and the youngsters helped with the work of the croft. In most cases the arrangement worked out well. The orphans grew up healthy and many looked upon the croft as home, and would come back, sometimes from far overseas, to visit their foster-parents. Some orphans married into the fostering family, thus bringing it a healthy infusion of fresh blood. A favoured foster-son could carry on the tenancy of the croft, adapting easily to the rituals and traditions in which he had been brought up.

Religion

To people living in the closest possible touch with the forces of the universe, what is known as a "religious" outlook is quite simply part of their nature. To observe, to wonder, to venerate is a logical sequence. Then there is felt the need to placate. Folk memories are long and people of a sturdy breed do not take easily to the imposition of forms of worship. The pioneer missionaries of the early Celtic church realised this, and wisely grafted their teaching on to symbolism already understood. The notion of a Saviour bred in a hot land, where the cactus is beautiful, could mean little to the 6th century Highlander. A shepherd and a healer could be accepted readily. Yet still the old reliance on the observable facts remained. Fire and water were purifiers for all to acknowledge, and the rituals connected with them persisted. Springs were venerated as sources of life. Still, to this day, an old person in hospital relies on a drink of spring water brought in by a relative to replace that from the hygienic tap.

Yet the blood sacrifice of the Hebrew Saviour and the vision of an after-life of rest and peace had a strong appeal, and over the centuries the amalgam of faith and worship took a hold. When hard work and thrift are part of the necessary equipment for survival, the rigours of abstinence are easily borne and there was always room for the supranatural in Highland life. This was again part of the wholeness. Whoever has seen the northern lights play in the night sky in winter must have some inkling of paradise.

So the people turned gladly enough of a Sabbath from their daily chores to don fresh clothes and walk, perhaps for miles, to participate in communal worship. When the forms were rudely changed, at times of Reformation and Disruption, they must have wondered why, but still the basic pattern continued. Underlying it was the need to give form to life, to link it fore and aft to something that could be grasped by the mind and the heart. Again — a search for wholeness.

Education

Once the chance to acquire book-learning was offered, not only to the chief's sons in religious establishments, but to all children in community schools, it was accepted quite readily by the people. There were certain reservations. At times of seasonal activity on the land — at planting and harvest and peat-cutting, for instance — the children were kept at home to help. Initially, a certain amount of distress resulted from the fact that the authorities favoured the use of English as the medium of instruction. But, as time went on, and the acquiring of the English tongue meant the passport to the wider world of life and work in other parts, the people encouraged their children to abandon Gaelic. Only now is the loss of this great expressive language being sorely felt, and efforts are now made to revive it among the young.

Epidemics also caused alarm. Youngsters reared in pure air and unused to congregating in large numbers, built little immunity to infection. After an outbreak of disease, the parents would keep the children at home until the school premises had been fumigated.

The log books kept by schoolmasters since the Education Act of 1872 provide a fascinating record of school life. The fact emerges that the people had real faith in the value of education and from this stemmed their ability to cope with the increasing complexities of a rapidly developing world. Many of the ablest members of the profession today had the world of letters opened to them on a battered desk in a Highland schoolroom. Those who stayed on the crofts, or in the villages acquired confidence in themselves. Out of the age-old habit of communication with his peers at ceilidh-time, the crofter developed a power of self-expression which found its outlet in association and public debate. At no time has this been more necessary than at the present day, when the very existence of the small agriculturist is threatened.

The issue at the moment is whether the crofter should be entitled to become outright owner of his holding, and on this he is no longer afraid to speak his mind. With work on his door-step — in forestry, in fishing, in road-making, in hydro-electric schemes, in tourism and in the exploitation of oil — providing a wage to supplement his income and that of his family, he should be in a strong position to stand his ground. Accustomed as he is to decision-making within his own sphere of activity, he should be able to meet whatever challenges may loom. It is to be hoped that the newest developments will come at a pace and in a proportion suited to his needs, so that his way of living which, paradoxically, is the envy of many of those who appear to be engaged, perhaps unwittingly, in destroying it, may be enhanced, but not basically altered.

Since the Act of 1886, the crofter has had security of tenure in his holding. He has acquired, over the years, the benefit of agricultural subsidies and of grants for the improvement of his land and of his house. Now he may be able to buy himself into the system.

But what of his actual life, with its unique inheritance of tradition and outlook? A room may be lit by an electric bulb instead of an oil-lamp, but do the men and women living there still help their neighbours through a bad spell? Do they still feel the rhythm of the seasons, and find more satisfaction in getting a good crop of oats into the stack than in acquiring the means to buy gadgets and only have time to live life at second hand? In a further century's time, our grandchildren will know the answer.

Croft Museum

In Abriachan, a former crofting community 10 miles from Inverness (take the Fort William road, A82, by Loch Ness and turn right, up the steep hill, at the signpost marked "Abriachan 1½ miles"), there is a Croft Museum, initiated as part of a project carried out by Inverness High School under the "Highland Village 1970" scheme. Here is a 19th century croft house and steading, restored and equipped in the style of the period, and a comprehensive collection of crofting implements and household gear, illustrative of the way of living of a Highland community, once fiercely independent and only now disappearing.

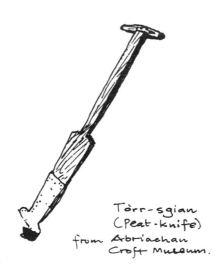

Tòrr-sgian
(Peat-knife)
from Abriachan
Croft Museum.

'MIDST HIGHLAND MALTS

IAIN CAMERON TAYLOR

The origins of whisky are, rightly and very properly, shrouded in the mists of antiquity. Some say, however, that the ancients of the East held that cereals and spirits were the secrets of long life and that the ingenious Celts simplified the recipe by merely combining the two in whisky. There are potent reasons, however, for the belief that the Celts, when they settled in Ireland, brought with them a knowledge of distillation. This knowledge was put into practice in their new homeland, and to good use. What could be more natural than that those Irish Gaels, or Scots as they came to be known, should, on their emigration north-east across the sea to the land of the Picts, carry the precious secret with them. There they eventually gave their own name to their new country and thenceforth the two races of arch-distillers, Scots and Irish, pursued their separate destinies, united only by language and an affinity of the spirit— although later the Irish were to spell theirs with an "e" — as whiskey.

In Scotland during the next millenium, as the new native Gaelic-speaking Scots withdrew northwards before the Anglo-Celtic and Anglo-Saxon incomers, who adopted the distiller's name but alas, not their language, the Highland fastnesses provided a sanctuary for the people and an eminently suitable laboratory for the perfection of "that malt spirit which commonly served both for victual and drink." Here the descendants of these old Celts used their ancient skills on the essential ingredients which Nature so liberally supplied — fresh mountain air, pure burn water "off granite through peat," locally-grown barley and rich, aromatic peat — and so Highland Malt Whisky was created, nurtured and respected. It is little wonder then, that the very word "whisky" is derived from the Gaelic "uisge-beatha," meaning "water of life."

The Scots' kingdom of Dalriada, approximating to modern Argyll (before the regional changes of 1975), was established in about 450-490 A.D. By 570, St Columba, who had founded a monastery on the Isle of Iona in 563 A.D., had journeyed on the mainland by the Great Glen from Lochaber to the Pictish royal seat near the River Ness. This route must have become very familiar to the Scots, through their raids on the Northern Picts and long before Kenneth MacAlpin, the Dalriadic king, succeeded to the throne of the Picts and eventually integrated Pictland with Gaeldom. The two ends of the Great Glen were to figure much in the intervening centuries of history before we bring the story of whisky in the district up to date.

Inverness-shire, from the point of view of whisky, can scarcely be considered a natural territorial division. It contains two groups of distilleries and several isolated ones. At either end of the Caledonian Canal (on the route St. Columba travelled) is a small whisky district; at the Lochaber end are the Fort William malt distilleries of Glenlochy, Ben Nevis and now, recently, a Nevis grain distillery. The two malt distillery products belong to a West Highland category, in which the fine Skye whisky, Talisker, and the new Tobermory one of Ledaig, are also to be numbered. Inverness at the north end of the canal has three distilleries of Glen Albyn, Millburn and Glen Mhor. The three Inverness whiskies they produce approach the Banff-shire type in character, but there are also the two isolated distilleries whose products are more difficult to classify. Tomatin, distilled near the River Findhorn, has a claim to be considered one of the inner core of Speyside Highland whiskies, while Buchanan's ("Black and White") Dalwhinnie, at the head of Loch Ericht, is styled a Strathspey whisky, although it is more than fifty miles from the nearest of its fellow Spey whiskies. Each of these eight has a story to tell and it wouldn't be stretch-ing the original boundary too far if we were to include one more — Royal Brackla, from just over the frontier.

If, however, we are to refine our remit to Inverness and District, we must plainly discard Fort William. A pity, for it was here that John MacDonald reigned unchallenged, whisky-wise, in the second quarter of last century. MacDonald, a great-hearted Keppoch Gael, was extremely tall and so acquired the nick-name of *Iain Fada,* or Long John. Although he died in 1856, his name still carries on and his whisky, which remained a single unit until 1909, is known today around the world as a blended whisky. Buchanan's lonely Dalwhinnie must also, and regretfully, be dropped. Although Sir Robert Bruce Lockhart tells a fine tale about it in his best-selling book "Scotch," Dalwhinnie at about 60 miles (96 km) south of the Highland capital is definitely out of our range. It has had a chequered story since its setting up by three Highlanders during the whisky boom of the 1890s, and has encountered half-a-dozen changes of ownership in its comparatively short existence. Its recent white painting and harling has rejuvenated its appearance and—

with luck its fortunes, too. It is certainly the nearest I know in the Highlands to a Swiss Hospice for snow-bound travellers!

Tomatin on the A9 main road is only 16 miles (25 km) south-east of Inverness. It is without doubt one of the biggest of the Highland malt distilleries and even by 1963 it was yielding a million proof gallons of spirit a year. Again, a fairly modern distillery, having been established in 1897, the present managing director, Peter Wright, who succeeded his father at Tomatin, has, by technological improvements and a major modernisation, now raised production over the two million gallon mark. Since World War II, the two pot-stills have become eleven, and a further sign of the enormous investment is that every one of Mr Wright's present 30 employees at the distillery is backed by £55,000 of capital. There are not many low labour-content Highland industries which can show this degree of capital intensity.

Although in recent years the Tomatin name has grown more familiar to the public, the main business is still the direct supply of malt whisky to Scotland's blending trade. Two Tomatin malts, however — the 5-year-old and the 10-year-old — are marketed as single malt whiskies and much appreciated by the knowledgeable. In 1966, a successful entry was also made into the field of blended brands. Tomatin's "Big T" blend is now selling in more than thirty overseas markets, principally in the U.S.A., but with a growing trade in continental Europe.

Not only are Dalwhinnie (1200 ft, 365 m) and Tomatin (1000 ft, 305 m), distilleries at considerable altitudes, but the loneliness and the isolation of their sites suggest that in earlier days, during "the heroic age of whisky," at the end of the 18th century, and indeed well into the 19th century, both perhaps had been known for their illicit stills. Although illicit whisky-making went on for many years (and still did in the writer's life-time, and to his knowledge!) the Act of 1823 encouraged the setting up of distilleries to produce good Highland whisky on a large scale. It was not just coincidence that the sites selected were in the areas where the illicit stills had flourished and in those parts which earlier had suffered much from the Jacobite defeat. Whisky and its long tradition had been saved, in the Highlands and by the descendants of those Gaels who had perfected it. The "smugglers" (who were very often the illicit distillers themselves) had, unsung, preserved the art and secret of true whisky distilling. What is remarkable in hindsight, is to realise the popularity and goodwill enjoyed by those Highlanders who fought the Government's attempts to control their traditional drink. Even the ministers were then mostly on the side of the local men, for they declined to support unjust man-made laws against the natural laws of Providence!

All the whisky-making areas of Scotland have an abundant folk-lore about smugglers, and the Inverness district is fortunate in having more than most. Perhaps the interplay of Gaelic and English may be responsible, for it is in those areas where the old tongue persisted longest that most of the tales can be uncovered. Little knowledge of Gaelic, however, is required now to bring to light the smuggling past of places like Abriachan, Glen Urquhart, Loch Ness-side, and Dores, Strathnairn and the Parish of Petty. The last-named is possibly unique in the district for being a noted centre of two-way smuggling, or a kind of early export/import entrepot.

From today's viewpoint, it is extremely unlikely that the law enforcement about whisky would have succeeded, in spite of the massive deployment of the military in support of an army of gaugers, spies and informers, had the people realised, that what started after Culloden as the London-inspired suppression of the last relic of Gaelic civilisation and the old Highland way of life, was to continue by subtler means, but with equal ferocity into the final quarter of the twentieth century. By slow and yet savage degrees, whisky has been taxed beyond the average Highlander's purse (or sporran) and his rightful heritage is in danger of becoming the preserve of the merely moneyed. On no other item in the U.K. has the English Government levied such a tax — more than 800%. Robert Burns' famous line "Freedom and whisky gang thegither" takes on a a new meaning. Writing of the future, in the post-war 1950s, Sir Robert Bruce Lockhart said that "most Scots are resolved that Scotland shall have a larger control of her own national affairs, and of these whisky is certainly one."

The digression above about smugglers and tax-gatherers has kept us from the delightful path we were following, in pursuit of the distilleries in the Inverness district. But at this point it would be quite fair to include another minor digression —a mile or two over the Nairn county boundary to Royal Brackla Distillery near Cawdor.

This distillery has at least two claims to distinction. Of only three out of some 130 distilleries — including all the Highland malt, Lowland malt, island and grain distilleries — Brackla was the first on which the honour was bestowed of using the Royal prefix in its title. This came about in 1835 and, surprisingly enough, from William, the Sailor King, who, to the best of the writer's knowledge, never even visited Scotland! In the same year, an advertisement in the London *Morning Chronicle* stated that Brackla had become "The King's Own Whisky." Macbeth, that earlier King of Scots and erstwhile Thane of Cawdor, could scarcely have done better. Queen Victoria, not to be outdone, confirmed the Royal Warrant on 15 November, 1838.

Brackla's second distinction is its age. It must be one of the oldest, if not *the* oldest Highland distillery of which definite records still exist. When the first of the present distillery buildings were erected in 1812 (a full eleven years before the distillery licensing Act of 1823) these were shown to be on the site of an even earlier distillery, which is marked on a map, dated 1773, in the Cawdor Castle Estate Office.

Captain Fraser's 1812 distillery was built on land leased from the Earl (and 23rd Thane) of Cawdor and remained more or less unchanged until 1967, although a substantial number of improvements were introduced in 1964. A superficial glance will note the disappearance of the distinctive malt kiln, with its pagoda-like roof. But this is in keeping with the modern distillery practice, now widely adopted, of using imported ready-made malt deliveries from vast new centralised maltings at Burghead, Inverness, Muir of Ord and elsewhere. This malt, incidentally, can be "peated" to the customer's desired degree.

Royal Brackla has long enjoyed the reputation of being among the dozen or so best whiskies in Scotland. By 1887, it was being produced to the tune of 70,000 proof gallons annually of Highland Malt Whisky. And if you were to doubt my use of the word Highland in relation to Brackla, then let me explain that the Highland Line on a whisky map of Scotland, in comparison with that shown on historical or clan maps, is kinder to Celtic susceptibilities and includes all the territory north of a straight line from Dundee to Greenock, then doubling round Arran, to take in Kintyre.

Even although production today is vastly increased over the 1887 figure above, unfortunately it is no longer bottled as a single unblended malt, although it was available as such up to the last war, as a few surviving labels can testify. The writer has reason to regret the present state of affairs, as he can remember its well-rounded mellowness and its subtle after-taste when he drank some eleven-year-old Royal Brackla at 105° proof. It was not just a drink — it was an experience! Nowadays the distillery product all goes for blending, with Haig and Johnnie Walker being but two of the better blended brands to include a measure of "the First of the Royals." The local witches from the Cawdor area whom Shakespeare features in

"Macbeth," didn't have a clue about what a cauldron (and worm) could really produce, in spite of all their

"Double, double, toil and trouble
Fire, burn; and, cauldron, bubble."

Now we come to the last trio in this pen-point analysis of the whiskies of Inverness and District. Taking them in chronological order, a start is made with Millburn. Although the oldest in Inverness, it is not as well known as the other two, or possibly it has not been so recently "in the news." The distillery stands beside the eastern access road, about a mile from the town centre and is situated under the brow of a steep hill, facing north towards the sea. It was first established in 1805, and then rebuilt on a larger and improved scale in 1876, when its annual output rose to some 60,000 proof gallons of Highland Malt Whisky. Later developments and expansion have increased this production figures enormously, but the cramped nature of the site has presented some difficulties. Indeed, it is difficult, when driving into the Highland capital, to realise that an entire modern distillery lies behind its stone boundary wall. Originally Millburn had its own cooperage, and even now the site still manages to include some employees' cottages.

Alas, however, the day is long past for the bottling of the distillery product as a single unblended Malt Whisky. Although now owned by the Distiller's Company Ltd., and operated by its subsidiary, Scottish Malt Distillers, today Millburn is leased to Macleay Duff (Distilleries) Ltd., as the licensee.

In 1846 (a hundred years after Culloden), when "the heroic age" was over and the Government had set aside armed force, replacing it with the exaction of a distilling licence fee and "a reasonable duty," the demand for whisky had begun to outstrip supply, and a number of new distilleries were being established. Glen Albyn Distillery in Inverness was one of them. It was established by the then Provost of the town on the bank of Thomas Telford's Caledonian Canal, near its northern end. As a further link over the preceding 100 years, it is said that the new distillery was built on the site of one of the many pre-Culloden maltings in and around Inverness which had been swept away during the Military Occupation.

Glen Albyn as a name is sometimes used for the whole of the geological fault-line of the Great Glen, whilst Albyn or Albainn is the old name for Scotland. Despite the ancient historical name, the distillery only lasted for twenty years before being converted into a flour mill. In 1884, it was rebuilt as a distillery by Messrs Gregory & Co., and soon after this it was producing 75,000 proof gallons per annum of Highland Malt Whisky. In recent years, none of the output has been bottled as a single or unblended malt whisky, but has found its way into many of the top brands of blended Scotch. Some idea of the improvement in distilling methods and efficiency may be gauged from the fact that today's output is at an annual rate of 320,000 gallons!

The new Glen Albyn was not to be on its own beside the Caledonian Canal for long. In 1892, the Birnie family, in the person of Provost Birnie of Inverness (how these civic dignitaries keep getting into the act!) built, and mis-spelled, Glen Mhor Distillery just to the south of the older distillery. They were later to be joined by Charles Mackinlay & Co. of Leith in the proprietorship of both the canal-side distilleries. Glen Mhor (pronounced "vore") was not long in acquiring a considerable reputation as a single malt whisky. It has been said that this was due in no small part to the care that the Birnies took from the beginning, over the preparation and full maturing of the spirit before selling.

The late Dr Neil Gunn, the well-known Highland novelist and for so long the doyen of writers on whisky, lived in his retirement on the other side of the Beauly Firth, almost within sight of the distillery where he spent so many earlier years as an exciseman. In a letter to the writer, he once said that he had Glen Mhor in mind when he wrote his now famous epigram that "until a man has had the luck to chance on a perfectly matured malt, he does not really know what whisky is."

The whisky industry today in Inverness and District, in the rest of the Highlands of Scotland and in its ramifications elsewhere, is now so capital-intensive that distillery ownership has become a complex matter, and consequently it has a tendency to attract take-over bids. Too much of it has unfortunately already passed into foreign or non-Scottish hands. The existence of the Distillers Company Limited one hopes will ensure that a sizeable part of the industry will remain under Scottish control, from a Company headquarters in Edinburgh. The D.C.L. is always on the look-out to strengthen its own position in the industry and especially on the malt whisky production side. Although D.C.L. had had a stake in the Glen Albyn/Glen Mhor Company of Mackinlays and Birnie Ltd., since 1960, it was only a minority one until July, 1972. In a deal concluded then, D.C.L. mopped up all the shares in the Company which it did not aready own or control — a dangerous 54% — which might have meant the controlling ownership being snapped up by a wide-awake English, American, Canadian, or even Japanese concern.

That success brings its own dangers with it, will be evident from the foregoing paragraph, and yet it must have been a very sad day for the late Mr William Birnie, the son of the Provost founder of Glen Mhor. Mr Birnie, then in his mid-eighties and who died earlier this year (1973), confirmed to the writer and to the local Press in Inverness that the deal, about which there had been so many rumours and reports in the town, had indeed gone through, and that Glen Albyn and Glen Mhor Distilleries had now been taken over by the Distillers Company Limited.

And what of the future? How long can D.C.L. remain Scottish? Its present chairman is a Scot by birth, education and domicile, but, nonetheless, there have been some ominous signs that Scottish control is slipping and that not only publicity and public relations, but also important policy decisions as well may be being taken at the London office, instead of at the Head Office in Edinburgh. Again, its size and strength are no longer a guarantee of safety against a take-over. After guarding whisky for a thousand years, through the persecutions of "the heroic age" and the injustice of the years of the locust tax-gatherers, surely Scots will not allow this great heritage to slip through their fingers now? We would then indeed be but serfs.

A Highland Malt Distillery

LOCAL FOLKLORE

DONALD ANDERSON

Any person who decides to make a study of the folklore of a region is very early beset by the necessity of making the decision — exactly what am I studying? At first it would appear that the subject is extremely wide. Hosts of tales are told by flickering firelight, appear in numerous books, fall from the lips of oldest inhabitants and surely all one must do is to collate and become acquainted with these or as many of these as one feels is necessary. Upon examination, however, it becomes apparent that there are varying degrees of merit in these stories and the reason is that throughout the ages true folklore has been invaded by superstitious belief, and the art of the student then becomes to separate them. It is doubtful if anyone really succeeds entirely in so doing, for, as has been said, decisions have to be made again and again. And what guide does one have in the making of them?

Folklore is of the country — deals with the life of its people, its flora and fauna, its history and its aspirations. Its medium in the early days was the spoken word, and herein lies much of the difficulty, for our forbears loved to talk just as much as we love to write. In truth, they were more clever than we, and their stories were well told to hold the interest of their hearers. Skill mounted upon skill, animals took upon themselves the power of speech, giants, dwarfs, witches, men with two thumbs, all appear, and perhaps the story-teller loses sight of his initial target in his desire to get his story across well. But careful study can help to restore the story, and it will be found to be about same facet of the country's life, warm with pride, alive with emotion.

So perhaps, and very briefly, that may give us a picture of what folklore is. Can we now try to find out what the interloper is like?

Science had not yet raised its omniscient head. The thunderstorm with its flashes of lightning was still a thing of horror. The darkness of the eclipse struck terror into the heart of man, and the fear of flood was ever with him. Comfort from these perils was needed if life were to be bearable. In every walk of life, in every age of human existence, there arises from the herd one who is greater, stronger, wiser or more shrewd or cunning than his fellow man. He is the one who is not quite overwhelmed by these phenomena which so sorely try his fellows. He has no more understanding of them than the others, but he is not so ready to be afraid, and his quick mind thinks out a reason, generally inaccurate, for present misfortunes, and if a reason can be given, so, with equal facility, can a cure be supplied. In their fear and misery, his friends are quick to seize upon the comforts offered them. So, by his imaginative explanations, this man becomes a power among his fellows, and, to keep this power, a steady stream of explanations, all based on ignorance, has to be maintained. This, then, is the tiny seed from which the strong branch of superstitious belief stems and twines itself around the tree of folklore.

A discerning eye, an imaginative mind, are prerequisites of the folklore student. It is said that the folktales all have a base of historical fact, or aim at pointing a moral, and it must, therefore, be the task of the student to use these tools to separate superstition from folklore, and this, we think, is the great pleasure of studying these old stories, evaluating their worth and, who knows? discerning their moral.

The thoughts, the customs, and the beliefs of a country are reflected in its folklore. In fact, one may go further, and sometimes be able to trace a country's origins by learning of similar folktales in other, often far-off, countries, known to be older in time. This might indicate an emigration from one country to another. It should, however, also be said that many cases arise where, quite inexplicably, there is evidence of striking similarity of tales from entirely unconnected countries. Perhaps one of the best illustrations of this is the popular Father Christmas story, which appears in Celtic, Teutonic and even Latin folklore.

The folktales of our country, like those of all nations, cover the various phases of man's life — and go beyond, too. The companions of his life time, the birds, the beasts, the flowers and the trees are all the subject of some of our delightful folk stories, and the seasons of the year too, play their part as will be illustrated in some stories which follow.

It is hoped, that what has been said points out the difference between sheer superstition and the more romantic folklore, to the advantage, it is hoped, of the latter. But who among us has not experienced the exquisite self-torture of an evening round the fireside, listening with prickling scalp to the weird superstitious tales of the past, and experiencing the feeling that indeed they must be true. Such a night is not complete without an incursion into the tales of second sight. Be it remembered that one may listen with interest, even with pleasure, to those beliefs, but let us not practise them. Black-magic and witchcraft are not yet dead, and it would be well to disassociate oneself from them.

Folklore had already sent down its roots into the life of the countryman, long before the days of compulsory education. Generations of country folk lived their lives, made their observations and accrued a fund of wisdom. The weather played a large part in their lives. When they should sow the seed? When should harvest begin? These are some of the governing factors of country life, and only native wit could supply the answers. It might be interesting to remember some of these, at this point.

Tomorrow's weather starts to be foretold the previous evening. The swallows fly high in their eternal search for insects, and good weather is expected. Dusk falls, and the grass becomes damp with dew. Then comes daybreak, and the cottar lights his fire and watches the smoke ascending high in the still air. These are some of the good-weather signs. On the other hand, the cattle bunch together in a corner of the field, and rain may be expected. Should they lie down, then more than a shower is foretold. Inclement weather is prevailing with cold, easterly gales, but improves when the wind backs north and then west. But the improvement will be of short duration until the wind backs in a southerly direction. Across the sky sweep the lights of Aurora Borealis (the Northern Lights or Merry Dancers), beautiful to behold, but foretellers of disturbed weather to come. Agreement of this comes when the new moon is seen "to have the old moon in her arms." The first balmy days of Spring arrive and the unwary relax, but the "lambing storms" are yet to come to renew the winter's icy grip when the shepherd least wants it.

Countless small indications like these form an integral part of the country-man's life, all based on common sense and observation. May we illustrate once more, but briefly, how ignorance and superstition creep in, even here. At one time the beautiful Kingfisher was eagerly sought after, killed, stuffed and hung outside the cottage door, not for its beautiful colouring, but because its beak always pointed to the North, or because it helped to keep thunder away!

It has been said that our folk tales bear a hidden moral. Right in the heart of our everyday life is one such tale — the Fiddlers of Tomnahurich (sometimes called the Hill of the Fairies, but, more accurately, the Hill of the Yew Tree). It concerns two itinerant fiddle players, Farquhar Grant and

Thomas Cumming, and is set in the days when the Ness was spanned by an old oak bridge. Their day had been spent with little reward for playing their fiddles in the streets of Inverness, and, as dusk fell, they dolefully made their way across the oak bridge to some cheap lodging. At mid-stream they were stopped by a small man in a red tam-o'-shanter and green jerkins and breeches. "Come, play at my party," he invited them, and eagerly the two followed him, leaving the town behind, untitl they came to a hill-side. Together the three ascended and near the top the guide stopped and opened a little door which neither Farquhar nor Thomas could ever remember having seen before. Through this, and along a narrow tunnel they went until it opened into a large warm hall. Here they were greeted by a number of people who regaled them and urged them to strike up their music. Soon the dance was in full swing; reel followed upon reel — drink and food were taken and all was merriment. The evening passed and dawn was near; their guide approached them and said, "Come, we must go." They followed him to the door and he gave them a large bag of gold. In the speech of the day they said, "In the name of God, we thank you," whereupon the man disappeared. Happily the two musicians wended their way back to town, but soon became conscious that they were a centre of attraction. Passers-by laughed and looked back over their shoulders. Puzzled, the two continued their way, and were further amazed. Unfamiliar sights were before their eyes. The old bridge was changed; passing the church-yard, they saw tombstones bearing familiar names. Thoroughly alarmed, they ran to the church door, where they could hear the minister taking a service; he would help them. They opened the door to run to him, but as they crossed the threshold, their bag of gold turned to brown leaves and they themselves dropped to the floor as two small heaps of dust. Thomas and Farquhar had been in concert with no ordinary people, but with the fairies, and not for one night, but for a hundred years!

A moral? Surely it must be a religious one, urging the people to have no dealings with the fairies. Or do you prefer it as a fairy tale?

The fairies play a large part in our folklore, but do not see them as dainty little winged creatures living in the pages of "Fairyland Tales." Our fairies are small, but endowed with considerable power. Unpredictable, full of mischief, quick to take offence, they can yet be kindly on occasion. They live underground mostly, sometimes emerging to dance in the moonlight, leaving a green fairy ring on the grass where their feet trod. Green is their colour and their homes can be seen as green hillocks; but do not disturb them. One of their most alarming characteristics is their love of beautiful human children, and the ways in which they steal them away. Because of this, the kind neighbour never comments on the beauty of a friend's baby, lest the fairies grow envious. It was common practice, not too long ago, to place a piece of iron in the bed of an expectant mother, for against this metal the fairies are helpless.

The tale is told of a baby theft. Both mother and babe were spirited away by fairies. Sad and lonely, the bereft father wandered by a loch-side when suddenly he was confronted by the wraith of his wife. Eagerly she told him that the coming night was the one on which the fairies would ride in procession through the land, and that they would pass by his house. "If you would have me and our baby back, you must rush out as they pass, and throw across my shoulders my wedding gown." But the husband was in fear, and he gathered round him all his neighbours, to sit with him for company. There came the sound of an approaching cavalcade of tiny horses. The time had come to act, but fear overcame the neighbours and, as the husband rose with the wedding gown in his arms, they threw themselves upon him, and held him powerless. The sound of the procession died away with the wailing of the wife, and never more was she or the baby seen.

If moral there be, surely the husband had failed to cherish his wife above all else, and allowed his fears to take the upper hand.

One feels that the many customs surrounding the main events, birth, marriage and death, must surely be superstitious. In the happy event of a multiple christening, it was important that the male children be christened first. Failure to do so could result in a mixing of characteristics, so that there could be boys with girlish build, or the converse. After baptism, the baby might be taken to a neighbour's house, but always in an upward direction. The mother must also move upwards, even if a stool was placed for her to mount on to do so. The neighbour would place salt on the child's tongue to protect him from the fairies.

"Marry in May, and you'll rue the day." The outcome of such a marriage could be a simple child, or perhaps a barren union. It is felt that the source of this belief is, that in the Roman calendar a feast was held to propitiate the ghosts of the dead, which they believed lived unseen around them, and part of the ritual was that no other ceremonies were held at that time. It appears that this part of the Roman calendar coincided with the Month of May in ours, so that a wedding ceremony would contravene this veto.

A further wedding custom was for the bride, as soon as she had settled down, to provide for herself and for her husband a winding sheet (often woven by herself) and to lay aside a sum of money sufficient to give them a decent burial. Good Scottish independence, one might say, but, inexplicably, the custom goes a further step, and at intervals these "deid claes" were laid out to air!

Probably Highland funeral customs are more prolific than those of any at other stages of man's life. However unexpected a death, a surprising number of folk would lay claim to having had forewarning — always after the event. "Deid bells" would have been heard ringing in the ears of the teller; a knock had come to the door; the deceased had appeared to some person. All these were told quite sincerely and in the grip of emotion. Such a story exists in our own neighbourhood — the story of the Kilmorack Disaster. A large black retriever dog howled piteously all night in the barn in which he was accustomed to sleep. The following day, a traction engine pulling a tender up Strath Glass fell into the ravine at Crask of Aigas, and all aboard were killed. Their bodies were laid out for coffining in the barn where the dog had been so ill at ease. Neighbours were convinced that the animal had had forewarning of this sad event.

Some of our place-names are also entwined with story. The origin of our lovely Loch Ness is a fine tale. In the neighbourhood there lived a Holy Man, who was blessed with the possession of a fine clear spring of water, and this was a thing of considerable value. True to his calling, he offered free use of it to all, and to keep it clean he constructed a wooden trapdoor over it, telling all to be sure to replace this lid after drawing water. There came a day when a woman arrived to draw water, carrying in her arms her baby son. Gently she placed him on the ground and lifted the lid off the spring. As her pitcher was filling, she looked round and saw an adder about to sting the boy. Frantically she swept him into her arms, and fled, leaving the trapdoor open — and the water rose and lipped over the well and trickled down the slopes and continued to do so until the loch was formed.

Years later, Nith, one of the sons of Uisneach, of Loch Etive, having lured away the sweetheart of his Irish cousin, sought out a quiet retreat, found this loch and named it after himself, and Loch Nith has become Loch Ness.

In Ross-shire, we find St Columba and his missionaries

coming across pagan wells, blessing away the pagan curse, and giving them their own names. In such a way did young St Mouri give his name to the beautiful Loch Maree.

In considering the place of the elements in folklore, it is found that water and fire are most frequently mentioned. Setting apart the more superstitious references to water as a guard against evil eye, we find that various wells figure in our lore. Of particular interest is St. Mary's Well, better known, through its votive uses, as The Clootie Well. St Mary lived in the Culloden area, probably at Chapelton, travelling throughout the countryside healing the sick and helping the poor. She carried with her a supply of water said to be taken from this well, and because of this, curative powers have been attributed to the water. With a very heavy iron content, it would doubtless be beneficial to those of strong enough will and stomach to drink it. The water springs up into a stone basin which is set among stone flags, and the whole is surrounded by a circular wall with an opening facing east. It is at this point that the older story is seen, for it must have been a votive well before St Mary used it, and strangely this story has survived her good works. Facing due east, the first rays of summer sun fall upon the water, and at this time the people flocked to it to drink of it and to rid themselves of their ills. The procedure was that the well was approached, silver was cast in, the water was sipped and cast around, and the supplicant repaired to the nearest tree, tore a shred from his clothing and tied this "cloot" to the tree, thus leaving his trouble behind him. Anyone removing such a "cloot" from the place where it hung, took also the ill which it represented.

Not far from this well, on the railway embankment, is the much less known Eppie's Well. She was a local cailleach and like St Mary did much to heal the sick, using the water from this well. This pattern is repeated throughout the area at various wells. One exists at the roadside between Kessock and Fortrose, and, further afield, in the island of Barra, whilst at Keith there is a cascade of water known as the Linn of Keith. An unusual well is that of St Mary at Tarradale, Ross-shire. The spring is known as Tober Voorie (Tobar Mhairie) and its qualities might perhaps be described as "peace giving," particularly to those about to die. The saying, "She asks for a drink of Tober Voorie," indicates that the lady is aware that her end is nigh.

The references to fire appear in the stories of the two main festivals of Scottish lore, Beltane and Hallowe'en. The latter festival is still observed locally, though apparently dying, and

Beltane has disappeared, at any rate from local lore. Beltane celebrated the "big sun," the brightness of the long summer days to come. It took the form of the lighting of bonfires by friction, the belief being that the flame came from heaven, purifying and protecting from evil, giving good luck and an increase in possessions. Before the lighting of the bonfires, all house-fires were extinguished and the hearths allowed to grow cold. Later, they were re-kindled with brands taken from the bonfire, these brands being whirled around while being carried to the house. They were called "the Brightness of God." On Beltane morning, the populace assembled on an eminence to watch the dance of "the new sun." It was said to whirl around three times on rising above the horizon. Faces were washed in the dew (present day references are still made to washing one's face in the May dew, but it is doubtful if the practice is carried out). Dancing took place round the fire, and to jump through the flame and smoke brought good luck. In like manner, the animals were driven through the flames to make them prosper, while the industrious housewife busied herself baking small cakes which were ceremoniously eaten, portions of them being cast into the fire.

At the other end of the year was the festival of Hallowe'en, or "the little sun" — the dark days ahead. The celebrations around the bonfire were much as in Beltane, but at this time, due to the darkness prevalent, there was a considerable amount of supernatural movement. The bolder people, probably the youngsters, arranged to protect the more nervous, dressing themselves in frightening attire, and this led to the custom of "guising" as we knew it in our day.

The folklore of our animals, birds and trees could fill many pages not presently available, but this review would be incomplete without some reference to them.

The Rowan tree is surrounded by many stories. An interesting one is that of a Rowan tree guarded by a monster in a pool. As its berries ripened, they fell into the pool and were eaten by the monster, giving us the beautiful red spotted salmon of our Scottish lochs and rivers. Other attributes of the Rowan are as a guard against witches (how many garden paths have a Rowan Tree at the gate?), and as a guardian of good luck. At Cromarty there was such a tree and before going climbing in the rocks, the boys would pitch stones at it. If the stones were deflected sideways, they cried "The danger goes past," and went about their climbing, but if they bounced back towards them, they sought some other safer pursuit for that day. Fishermen, too, looked to it for luck, and before setting out for their fishing grounds they deposited white pebbles in a hollow in its bole.

The red Rowan berries were used as a protection against evil, houses being decorated with clusters of them. It is thought probable that in winter, when they were no longer available, the red berries of the holly were used instead, giving rise to our present day custom of decorating with holly at Christmas time.

Thinking of flowers, one is surprised by the considerable number of these which are never brought into a house, for reasons generally unknown. Hawthorn, Broom, Whin, Foxglove, with others, suffer the same unpopularity.

Among our birds, the Robin is Scotland's favourite. It was said to have a drop of God's blood in its veins, and to have ministered to Christ as He hung on the Cross, gaining its bright red breast through His blood, and for both of these reasons, it was considered unlucky to harm it. In return it would repay any kindness done. Swallows, too, were lucky birds, and the houses on which they nested were considered favoured.

It was believed of the Kingfisher that it nested on the waters and reared its brood there, and was empowered to calm the waters, so that the young would survive. For this reason it was beloved of the sailors. An alternative name was the Halcyon, hence the term "Halcyon days," indicating days of peace and happiness.

One might pursue these ramblings in folklore at great length, through the fascinating subjects of second sight, ghost appearances, or fairy lore and other kindred subjects. They are rich in history, imagination and native wisdom, but also have roots in ignorant superstition, perhaps amusing in these days, but at one time very dangerous. The discerning mind should ever be present whilst studying them, so that the good, honest folk story be not strangled by the superstitious belief.

GLOSSARY OF SOME PLACE NAMES

JOHN MACPHERSON

Ever since I was a student of Celtic under Professor W. J. Watson, Professor of Celtic Languages and Literature at Edinburgh University, I have been interested in place-names. Before he went to Edinburgh he was the Rector of Inverness Academy. Later he himself produced a well-known work, entitled "History of the Celtic Place Names of Scotland," a copy of which should be in the hands of every student of place-names.

The Norsemen occupied the Western Isles and the Counties of Caithness and Sutherland for 470 years, but their rule came to an end in 1263, when they were defeated at Largs by Alexander III, King of Scots. They have left their imprint on many place-names in the North and West of Scotland and in the Western Isles, and on a few round here. Some place-names are of Pictish origin and these often begin with the letter "p" as in Petty, but I shall be mostly dealing with the names that are based on Gaelic words.

Place-names often describe the site. In the Parish of Kirkhill we find the name Ach na gairn *(Ach nan cárn)*, Field of the Cairns — the cairns are there. Other names speak to us of the saints who came to the Highlands long ago. St Cessoc, March 10, is probably the saint from whom *Port Cheiseig,* Kessock Ferry, takes its name.

My purpose in this chapter is not to deal with all the place names in the district, but only those near the main roads that will be of interest to natives and visitors alike, using Bartholomew's ¼ inch map, Moray Firth. I shall start with a brief list of the words from which most of the names are built, but it should always be remembered that few translations of a name can be definitive.

Aber — the mouth of a river, or a confluence. Pictish.

Ach, from *Achadh* — field.

Alt, Ault, from *Allt* — burn, stream.

Bal, from *Baile* — place, farmstead, *Scottice,* ferm-toon.

Beg, from *Beag* — small.

Ben, from *Beinn, beann* — mountain.
Cairn, from *Càrn* — heap of stones.
Clach, from *Clach* — stone.
Corrie, from *Coire* — cauldron, mountain glen.
Craig, from *Creag* — rock.
Dal, from *Dail* — field, plain.
Doch, Davoch, from *Dabhach* — a large measure of land.
Drum, from *Druim* — ridge, back, roof, keel.
Dun, from *Dùn* — fort.
Ess, from *Eas* — waterfall.
Inch, Insh, from *Innis, innse* — meadow, island, valley.
Inver, from *Inbhir* — mouth of a river, confluence.
Kil, from *Cill, ceall* — church, cell, grave.
Kin, from *Ceann* — head, end, top, chief.
Kyl, from *Coille* — wood, forest.
Loch, — lake.
Meal, from *Meall* — rounded hill, lump.
Mam, from *Màm* — round, steep hill.
More, Mhor, Vore, from *Mór* — large.
Tom — hillock.

INVERNESS TO NAIRN, A 96
Inverness — *(Inbhirnis)* mouth of the Ness.
Balloch — *(Baile an loch)* farm of the loch (which has been drained).
Allanfearn — *(An t-ailean fèarna)* Alder green.
Petty — *"Peit"* is a Pictish word that could mean "pit," or "land," or "homestead."
Balnabual — *(Baile na buaile)* farm of the fold.
Tornagrain — *(Torr nan gràn)* hill of the grain, *or* sunny fold.
Dalcross — *(Dealg an rois)* prickly point or wood.
Mid Coul — *(Cul =* a corner, hidden place) middle nook.
Ardersier — *(Aird nan saor)* headland of the carpenter.
Balnagowan — *(Baile nan gobhainn)* farm of the smiths.

INVERNESS TO CROY, B 9006 AND B 9091
Resaurie — *(An ruigh Samhraidh)* summer grazing.
Culloden — *(Cuil lodair)* nook of the marsh.
Balnuaran — *(Baile an fhuarain)* place of the spring of water.
Clava — perhaps from *Clach mhath,* good stone.
Cantray — a British word, probably meaning White Farm.
Cantraybruich — *(Bruach =* brae, slope) slope of the white farm.
Croy — *(Cruaidh)* hard place.
Kilravoch — place of the fort, *or (Cill abhach)* church of the stream-place.

Barevan — *(Barr Eibheinn)* high place of Aibhind, who was a holy maiden.

Kildrummie — *(Cill droma)* church of the ridge, *or (Coille droma)* wood of the ridge.

CULCABOCK TO SLOCHD, A 9

Culcabock — *(Cùil na càbaig)* nook of the cheese.

Inshes — meadows.

Balvonie — *(Baile a'mhonaidh)* moorland farm.

Muckovie — *(Mucomhaigh)* swine field.

Bogbain — *(Bog* = soft, wet place; *Bàn* = white) white bog, from the cotton plants.

Daviot — *(Deimidh)* probably a Pictish word, a strong place.

Craggie — rocky place.

Achnahillin — *(Ach na h-iodhlainn)* field of the stack-yard.

Meallmore — *(Meall mór)* large round hill.

Auchnagall — *(Ach nan Gall)* field of the strangers.

Moy — *(Moighe)* plain.

Dalmagarry — field of the thicket.

Tomatin — *(Tom aitinn)* juniper hillock.

Balnespick — *(Baile an easbuig)* Bishop's farm.

Croftdhu — *(Croit dhubh)* black croft.

Kyllachy — wood of cocks (moor cocks).

Slochd — pit, den, hollow.

DAVIOT TO DUNLICHTY, (un-numbered road)

Faillie — place on the edge of the slope.

Achlaschoille — field in the crook of the wood.

Dalveallan — *(Dail a'mheallain)* field of the hillock.

Gask — a tail-like point of land.

Achvaneran — (field of the sheep-fold).

Tordarroch — *(Torr darach)* hill of the oak trees.

Balloan — *(Baile lóin)* farm of the wet meadows.

Dunlichity — *(Dùn fhluich àite)* fort of the wet place.

Loch Duntelchaig — *(Loch Dun an t-sealachaig)* Loch of the snail mound.

DAVIOT TO BOLESKINE, B 851

Nairn (river) — Pictish word meaning stream.

Auchbain — *(Ach bàn)* white field.

Allt an fuar glaic — *(Allt an fhuar ghlaic)* burn of the cold hollow.

Inverernie — *(Inbhir fhearna)* mouth of the alder wood burn.

Drumlia — *(Drum liath)* grey ridge.

Flichity — *(Fluich àite)* wet place.

Tighanallan — *(Tigh an àilein)* house of the meadow.
Croachy — *(Cruach àite)* place of peaks.
Duchallow — *(Dubh thalamh)* black ground.
Aberarder — confluence of high water (spate).
Dunmaglass — fort of the sons of Glas, *or (Dùn magh glas)* fort of the grey field.
Garbh bheinn Mhór — big rough mountain.
Ruthven — *(Ruadh bheinn)* red mountain.
Gorthleck — *(Gort a'ghlaic)* field of the hollow.
Boleskine — *(Both fhleisginn)* farm of the withies/willows.

INVERNESS TO DRUMMOND, (un-numbered road)
Knocknagael — *(Cnoc nan Giall)* hillock of the hostages.
Torbreck — *(Torr breac)* dappled hill.
Essich — *(Easach)* place of waterfalls.
Drumashie — *(Druim athaisidh)* ridge of the bare meadow.
Lochan a Choin — little loch of the dogs.
Lochan nan Eun Ruadha — little loch of the Red Birds.
Drummond — ridge.

INVERNESS TO FORT AUGUSTUS, A 862
Scaniport — *(Sgàin phort)* cleft-ferry (ferry of the cleft).
Balnafroig — *(Baile na froig)* farm of the dismal hole.
Ballindarroch — *(Baile an daraich)* farm of the oak wood.
Aldourie — *(Dobhar = water)* burn of water.
Dores — This is a very difficult name. It could be *(Dubros) or (Dorus)* a door; *or (Dobhar + eas)* water + waterfall.
Kindrummond — head of the ridge.
Erchite — *(Airchoid)* a Pictish word, probably meaning On, or Near, the clearing. (See Urquhart in the next route)
Achnabat — *(Ach' nam bat')* field of the sticks.
Torness — *(Torr an eas)* hill of waterfalls.
Balnaglach — *(Baile nan clach)* farm of the stones.
Carnach — *(Càrnach)* place of the stones. cf. Carnac in Brittany.
Aultnagoire — *(Allt na goibhre)* goats burn.
Loch Conagleann — Loch of the wild glen.
Errogie — height of rushing.
Boleskine — *(Both fhleisginn)* farm of the withies/willows.
Foyers — *(Foithear)* slope, terraced declivity.
Loch Killin — *(Loch cill Fhionn)* loch of the church of St Fionn, *or* perhaps of the white church.
Knockcarroch — *(Cnoc carrach)* knoll of the uneven surface.

INVERNESS TO FORT AUGUSTUS, A 82
Dunain — *(Dùn an eoin)* fort of the bird. *(Eun* often means *the* bird, i.e. the eagle).

Dalreoch — *(Dail riabhach)* speckled field.

Dochgarroch — *(Doch garbhach)* davoch of rough land.

Dochnalurg — *(Doch na lurg)* davoch of the ridge running into the plain.

Cnoc na Gaoithe — hill of the winds.

Dochfour — davoch of good pasture.

Bona — *(Both an àth)* place of the ford.

Abriachan — mouth of the Briachan; *or (Obair fhitheachan)* mouth of the Fitheachan.

Carn an Leitire — *(Càrn an Leitire)* cairn with sloping sides.

Drumnadrochit — *(Druim na drochaid)* ridge of the bridge.

Borlum — the "bord-lands," lands for supplying the castle.

Strone — *(Sròn)* nose, nose of land, promontory.

Urquhart — *(Airchartdan)* near a copse, woodside. (See previous route).

Achnahannet — *(Ach na h-annaid)* field of the mother church.

Bunloit — lower part of the brae.

Meallfuarvonie — *(Meall fuar mhonaidh)* round hill of the cold moorland.

Alltsaigh — burn of the bitch.

Invermoriston — mouth of the River Moriston.

Inchnacardoch — *(Innis na ceardaich)* field of the smithy.

MILTON TO CANNICH, A 831

Gartally — lovely field, *or (Car Dalaidh)* Daly's circle.

Polmaily — Malie's pool. Malie was the saint of Kilmallie, and *Màli* is a by-form of *Màire*.

Badcaul — *(Bad calltainn)* Hazel clump.

Balnain — *(Beul an àth)* mouth of the ford; *or (Baile an athain)* place of commandment, instruction; *or (Baile an eadhain)* place or farm of the Ivy.

Loch Meikle — *(Miachlaidh)* probably Pictish, meaning unknown; but *(mi + achladh = un + fishing)* is a possibility.

Strathnacro — *(Strathan nan cno)* little strath of the nuts.

Glackchoile — *(Glac choile)* hollow of the wood.

Bearnoch — *(Bearnach)* little gap, or pass.

Corriemony — Monie's corrie. (See index).

Kerrow wood — *(Ceathramh)* wood of the quarter davoch of land

MILTON TO BALCHRAGGAN, A 83

Culnakirk — *(Cùl na circe)* back land of the hen.

Loch na Faoileag — *(Loch na faoileig)* seagull's loch.

Allt dearg — *(Dearg = trout, red deer, red)* red burn, burn of the trout, of the red deer.

Ardblair — *(Ard blàir)* top plain.
Bunblair — *(Bun blàir)* bottom plain.
Blairmore — *(Blàir mór)* big plain.
Convinth — *(Coinmeadh)* free quartering; but possibly similar to Conway, a pass.
Meall nan Caorach — round hill of the sheep.
Glaodhaich — place of shouting; or of rushing water.
Auchvaich — *(Ach a' mhoighich)* byre-field; or field of the hare.
Camault — *(Cam allt)* crooked burn.
Culmill — *(Cul mill)* back of a rounded hill.
Glackbea — *(Glac beithe)* Birch hollow.
Tomnacross — *(Tom na crois)* gallows hill.
Kiltarlity — church of St Talorcan.
Belladrum — *(Baile an droma)* farm on the ridge.
Cabrich — *(Cabraich)* place of antlers, or branches.
Balchraggan — *(Baile chreagan)* rocky farm.

Inverness to Beauly, A 9
Kessock Ferry — *(Port Cheseig)* St Cessoc's ferry.
Clachnaharry — *(Clach na h-aithrigh)* stone of repentance; or *(Clach na h-aire)* stone of the watch.
Brochnain — *(Bruach an eadhain)* Ivy bank.
Rhinduie — *(Rinn dubh)* dark point.
Groam — marsh place.
Clunes — *(Cluain)* meadow, green spot, ambush.
Aultnacardich — smithy burn.
Drumchardine — wooded ridge.
Bogroy — *(Bog ruadh)* red bog.
Moniack — perhaps *(Moin + ach)* field of the moss or bog.
Phoineas — *(Bho an eas)* below the waterfall.
Lovat — *(Loth àit')* rotten, putrefying place.
Beauly — *(Beau-lieu)* French words, beautiful place; or *(Beul ath)* mouth of the ford.

Lovat Bridge to Guisachan, A 831
Kilmorack — church of St Moroc.
Breackachy — *(Breac achaidh)* speckled field.
Teanassie — *(Tigh an fhasaidh)* house of the dwelling place.
Dun Fionn — Fort of Fingal.
Crask of Aigas — crossing by the waterfall.
Eskadale — *(Eskidalr)* ash-valley; or *(ösk-r dail)* roaring valley. Both are Norse words.
Bad a' Chlamhain — height of the buzzard.
Craigdu — *(Creag dhubh)* black stone.
Erchless — *(Air a'ghlass)* possibly, on the Glass.

Glass — possibly an old word meaning Stream, but *(Glas)* usually means grey, pale, and sometimes, green.

Struy — *(Na Struthan)* the streams.

Mauld — pleasant place, pasture land.

Creleven — *(Leamhan =* elm tree) place of elm trees.

Carn gorm — blue cairn.

Craoibhe-fearna — alder trees.

Cannich — *(Canach)* place of wild white cotton plants.

Comar — confluence of two rivers.

Fasnakyle — *(Fas na coille)* dwelling of the wood.

Tuill creagach — rocky hill with holes.

Mullach tarsuinn — top of the crossing.

Tomich — *(Tomach)* place of thickets or hillocks.

Guisachan — *(Guitheasachan)* place of fir trees.

Affric — *(Ath bhreac)* dappled ford.

BURGH OF INVERNESS

Inverness — *(Inbhirnis)* mouth of the River Ness.

Abban — *(Aban)* backwater of a river (a mouth of the Ness used to flow round here to the firth).

Ballifeary — *(Baile na faire)* place of watching.

Balloch Hill — *(Bealach =* a pass) at the top of Castle Street.

Balnafettach — *(Baile nam feadag)* farm of the plovers.

Broadstone Park — The Stone is now outside the Thistle Football ground; probably once a base for a flag-pole — 'bored' stone.

Bught — sheep pen.

Cameron Barracks — named after the Cameron Highlanders; the site was formerly Knockintinnel *(Cnoc an tionail),* the rallying hill.

Capel Inch — *(Capull innis)* horse meadow, the site of an old market.

Castlehill of Inches — *(Caisteal still)* castle of the Strip (of land). Castlehill is a corruption.

Castle Heather — originally *(Caisteal lethoir)* castle of the slope, and known as Castle Leather.

Clachnacuddin — *(Clach na Cudainn)* stone of the tubs; now the palladium of Inverness, it is outside the Town Hall.

Craig Phadrig — Patrick's Rock, not an ancient name for this old vitrified fort.

Culduthel — *(Cuil daothail)* nook of "duthel," but the meaning of "duthel" is obscure.

Dalneigh — *(Dal an eich)* horse field.

Diriebught — the poor's land; *or* the poor, barren land, or fold.

Haugh — *(An talchan)* flat land by the riverside.

Holm — *(An tuilm)* island in a river.

Kingsmills — In 1232, Alexander II mentions "our mill at Inverness."

Kinmylies — *(Cinn a' milidh)* warrior's head.

Leachkin — *(An Leacainn)* the hillside.

Lochardil — the name of an old barony.

Maggot — land between the Swimming Baths and the Black Bridge, from an early Chapel of St Margaret on the site.

Merkinch — *(Merk = a measure of land, the size of the island)* Horse Island, formerly a grazing ground for horses.

Porterfield — land belonging to the Porter of the Castle.

Raigmore — *(Rathaig mhor) Rath* is a fortified homestead, so this means a large, fortified farm; but the name came when Mackintosh of Raigmore (in Strathdearn) built his house there.

Scategate — the old name for Rose Street, probably because fish being brought into the town paid *scat,* or tax, there. The fish did not come in "scot-free."

Scorguie — *(Sgorr gaoithe)* windy point.

Tomnahurich — *(Tom na h-iubraich)* hillock of the yew trees.

Torvean — *(Torr Bhean)* hill of St. Bean.

Erchless Castle

APPENDIX

INVERNESS FIELD CLUB
Members, 1974-75
*Member of Council

Miss D. Aird, 10 Balloan Road, Inverness.
Mrs M. Alexander, 20 Montague Row, Inverness.
Mrs F. C. Anderson, 99 Culduthel Road, Inverness.
*Mr R. J. Ardern, 71 Drumossie Avenue, Inverness.
Miss R. K. Aspin, Broomhill House, Dulnain Bridge, Moray.

Miss J. Banks, c/o 1 Broadstone Park, Inverness.
Miss F. Barlow, 49 Old Edinburgh Road, Inverness.
Dr F. C. and Mrs Barlow, 49 Old Edinburgh Road, Inverness.
Mr J. Barr, 13 Broadstone Park, Inverness.
Mr and Mrs B. Barrett, 16 Glenurquhart Road, Inverness.
Miss E. Barron, Kilmeny, 3 Drummond Road, Inverness.
Mrs H. Barron, Charleston of Dunain, by Inverness.
*Mr J. Barron, Aultnaskiach Park, Inverness.
Miss V. H. Bell, 14 Douglas Row, Inverness.
Miss C. Bergamini, 60 Culduthel Road, Inverness.
Mr Q. Bone, 41 Grigor Drive, Inverness.
Mr J. S. Brennan, Dalcross Station, Inverness-shire.
*Dr J. Bruce, 13 Southside Place, Inverness.
Mrs Bulloch, Learag, Tomatin, Inverness-shire.
Miss G. Bush, 13 Warrand Road, Inverness.
Mrs S. W. Butler, 6 Oldtown Place, Inverness.

Mr and Mrs J. Caird, 1 Drummond Crescent, Inverness.
Miss V. Calder, Southcote, 41 Southside Road, Inverness.
Miss J. B. Cameron, 28 Ruthven Road, Inverness.
Miss J. Cameron, 12 Grigor Drive, Inverness.
Miss M. Cameron, 12 Grigor Drive, Inverness.
Miss M. Cameron, Balnakyle, Munlochy, Ross-shire.
Mrs A. F. H. Campbell, Ord House Cottage, Muir of Ord, Ross-shire.
Mr and Mrs J. Campbell, The Old Manse, Lochend, by Inverness.
Mrs Clark-Ayre, Beauly Firth Cottage, Charleston, North Kessock, Ross-shire.
*Mr and Mrs D. Coghill, Wester Lovat, Beauly, Inverness-shire.
Mr M. Constanduros, Druim Cottage, Aigas, Beauly, Inverness-shire.
Mr J. Cook, 2 Drumossie Avenue, Inverness.
Miss M. Corbett, 24 Midmills Road, Inverness.
Mr W. Cran, 16 Crown Street, Inverness.
Mrs G. F. Cumming, Currness, Culloden Road, Inverness.
Mr A. Currie, Balnabeen House, Duncanston, Conon Bridge, Ross-shire.

Mrs W. L. Dawson, 4 Dornie Place, Lochardil, Inverness.
Mrs D. Dow, 27 Daviot Drive, Inverness.
Mr J. Dymock, Duncanston, Conon Bridge, Ross-shire.

Mrs J. Eunson, Wayside, Beauly, Inverness-shire.

Mr G. Farquharson, 39 MacEwen Drive, Inverness.
Miss J. T. Ferguson, 45 Ross Avenue, Inverness.
Mrs W. Y. Fettes, Meru, Nairn Road, Ardersier, Inverness-shire.
Mrs A. D. Forbes, The Knoll, 2 Abertarff Road, Inverness.
Miss A. Fraser, 6 Queensgate, Inverness.
Mr and Mrs A. Fraser, Torran, Crown Circus, Inverness.
Miss C. Fraser, 9 Rangemore Road, Inverness.
Mr D. Fraser, Glebe Farm, Kiltarlity, Inverness-shire.
Mrs D. Fraser, Midmills Cottage, Midmills Road, Inverness.
Miss M. Fraser, Greenlea, Drumnadrochit, Inverness-shire.
Mrs M. R. Fraser, 23 Muirfield Road, Inverness.

Mrs C. A. S. Galloway, 10 Muirfield Road, Inverness.
*Mr G. Gill, 38 Braeside Park, Balloch, by Inverness.
Mr W. Glashan, 44 Glenburn Drive, Inverness.
Mrs Glynne-Percy, Tomatin House, Inverness-shire.
Miss A. M. Grant, 54 Culduthel Road, Inverness.
Mrs J. Grant, 19 St. Mungo Road, Inverness.
Miss Marjory Grant, 54 Culduthel Road, Inverness.
*Dr B. Gray, Tanera, Burn Road, Inverness.

Mr P. Harris, 50 Montrose Terrace, Edinburgh 8.
*Mr and Mrs R. Hastie, 9 Braeside Park, Balloch, by Inverness.
Mr and Mrs A. Hayman, 4 Bellfield Road, North Kessock, Ross-shire.
*Mr and Mrs J. Herrick, 52 Glenburn Drive, Inverness.
Miss A. Higginbottom, 12 Old Mill Road, Inverness.
Mr and Mrs D. Hughes, 36 Well Street, Inverness.
Miss E. M. Hutton, 15 Abban Street, Inverness.

Mrs E. S. Jacks, Braeview, Wester Galcantray, Cawdor, Nairn.
Miss V. James, Craig Dunain Hospital, by Inverness.
Mr and Mrs R. Jenkyns, Point Clair, Invermoriston, Inverness-shire.

Lt.-Colonel and Mrs L. J. E. Kewley, 11 Abertarff Road, Inverness.
Mrs King, 49 Old Edinburgh Road, Inverness.

Mr R. M. Laing, Shandon, Victoria Drive, Inverness.
*Mr and Mrs A. L. Lawson, Duhallow, Errogie, Inverness-shire.
Mrs Ledingham, Boyndie, Dores Road, Inverness.

Dr R. F. Macadam, 13 Heatherley Crescent, Inverness.
Mrs I. G. MacArthur, Caladail, Balloch, by Inverness.
Dr D. I. McCallum, 44 Braeside Park, Balloch, by Inverness.
Miss B. Macdiarmid, 1 Bellfield Road, North Kessock, Ross-shire.
The Revd. D. Macdiarmid, 1 Bellfield Road, North Kessock, Ross-shire.
Mr A. W. Macdonald, 29 Drumblair Crescent, Inverness.
Dr D. J. Macdonald, Craigdarroch, 22 Green Drive, Inverness.
Miss F. Macdonald, 91F Bruce Gardens, Inverness.
Mr and Mrs H. Macdonald, 34 Charles Street, Inverness.
Miss M. M. MacDonald, 76 Culduthel Road, Inverness.
Mr and Mrs N. A. Macdonald, Longford Villa, 5 Kenneth Street, Inverness.
Mr W. MacDonald, 60 Drumdevan Place, Inverness.
Mrs G. McHutchon, 16 Auldcastle Road, Inverness.
Mr I. R. Mackay, Netherwood, Inverness.
Miss J. M. Mackay, 189 Old Town Road, Hilton, Inverness.

Capt. W. Mackay, O.B.E., Upper Glassburn, Beauly, Inverness-shire.
Mrs W. T. Mackell, 3 Lodge Road, Inverness.
Miss C. A. Mackenzie, 34 Planefield Road, Inverness.
Miss R. T. Mackenzie, 3 Union Road, Inverness.
Mrs I. Mackinnon, 34 Culduthel Road, Inverness.
Mr J. Mackinnon, 25 Cameron Square, Inverness.
Mr L. M. Maclagan-Wedderburn, Pearsie, 52 Soutar Drive, Holm Mills, Inverness.
Mr A. Maclean, 10 Aldourie Road, Inverness.
Mr A. Maclean of Dochgarroch, yr., Seafield House, by Inverness.
Mr G. L. F. Maclean, Duart, 6 Ashie Road, Inverness.
*The Revd. D. A. L. and Mrs Maclean of Dochgarroch, Seafield House, by Inverness.
Miss I. Maclean, c/o Royal Academy, Inverness.
Miss C. M. Macleod, 42 Glenurquhart Road, Inverness.
Mr and Mrs J. Macleod, Bona Lodge, Aldourie, by Inverness.
Miss R. Macleod, Borlum Bridge, Lewiston, Drumnadrochit, Inverness-shire.
Miss E. Macmillan, 22 Montague Row, Inverness.
Mrs Macrae of Inverinate, Annat, Little Cullernie, Balloch, by Inverness.

Mr P. Malcolmson, Glencairn, Westhill, Culloden, by Inverness.
Miss E. B. Martin, Carlenrig, 27 Midmills Road, Inverness.
Miss A. J. Matheson, 24 Duncraig Street, Inverness.
Miss C. M. Matheson, 24 Duncraig Street, Inverness.
Mr H. A. Maxwell, O.B.E., and Mrs Maxwell, Greenacres, Culloden Road, Inverness.
Mr J. R. Mayne, Nessdale, Island Bank Road, Inverness.
*Mr and Mrs E. A. Meldrum, 22 Beaufort Road, Inverness.
Mr J. A. Menzies, Temple Pier, Drumnadrochit, Inverness-shire.
*Mr R. Milne, 4 St Fergus Drive, Inverness.
Mr and Mrs T. G. Mitchell, Swingle Tree, Balloch, Inverness-shire.
*Mrs J. Morrison, 83 Dochfour Drive, Inverness.
Miss M. Morrison, 4 Culduthel Gardens, Inverness.
Mr J. H. Mowat, 24 Southside Road, Inverness.
Miss E. Munro, 2 Hill Street, Inverness.
Dr J. G. and Mrs Munro, Glenoran, Beauly, Inverness-shire.
Mrs D. G. Murray, 27 Warrand Road, Inverness.
Mr and Mrs J. Musker, Mo Dhachaidh, Glenurquhart, Inverness-shire.

Mr A. G. Prentice, 68 Grigor Drive, Inverness.

Miss I. Rae, Dunlugas Cottage, 4 Wellington Road, Nairn.
Mr and Mrs M. Rasmussen, 219 Old Town Road, Hilton, Inverness.
*Mrs C. Richards, 65 Stratherrick Road, Inverness.
Miss F. E. Riddle, 4 Sunnybank Road, Inverness.
Sheriff and Mrs S. Scott Robinson, Flat 3, Drumallin, Drummond Road, Inverness.
Mr A. J. Ross, Ness Castle Gardens, Inverness.
Miss R. Ross, 6 Balloan Road, Inverness.
Miss E. I. S. Rowan, 27 Balnakyle Road, Inverness.

Mr L. F. Sarjeant, 2 Dores Avenue, Inverness.
Mrs E. M. Scott, Clonburn, Resaurie, Inverness.
Mr M. Scott, 25 Temple Crescent, Hilton, Inverness.
Miss K. Sinclair, Easter Daltullich, Culloden Moor, by Inverness.

Mr W. A. Sinclair, 4 Aultnaskiach House, Inverness.
Miss M. Skinner, 6 Auldcastle Road, Inverness.
Miss J. Skyrme, Jasmine Cottage, Knockfarrel, Dingwall, Ross-shire.
Mrs B. M. Smith, Glencoe, Ardersier, Inverness-shire.
Mr M. Smith, Glencoe, Ardersier, Inverness-shire.
Mr and Mrs J. Speirs, 41 Broom Drive, Inverness.
Mrs G. Spence, 2 Lochardil Place, Inverness.
Miss B. C. Stark, 13 Southside Road, Inverness.
Mr J. Steele, Schoolhouse, Culduthel, Inverness.
*Mrs K. Stewart, School House, Abriachan, by Inverness.

*Lt.-Col. and Mrs I. B. Cameron Taylor, Kilmoriebeg, 38 Muirfield Road,
Inverness.
Mr W. Taylor, Sun Court, Cromarty, Ross-shire.
Mrs Tedcastle, 63 Abertarff Road, Inverness.
Miss J. Thomson, 3 Ballifeary Road, Inverness.

Miss A. Urquhart, Rigfoot, 22 Southside Road, Inverness.
Miss E. Urquhart, Rigfoot, 22 Southside Road, Inverness.
Miss H. Urquhart, Muirton, Croyard Road, Beauly, Inverness-shire.

Mr I. G. Wallace, 44 Rowan Road, Dalneigh, Inverness.
Miss E. P. Watson, 3 Old Mill, Charleston, North Kessock, Ross-shire.
Mr A. White, Kinnaird, Drumnadrochit, Inverness-shire.
Miss M. F. Whyte, 39 Ballifeary Road, Inverness.
Miss C. Williams, Laggan View, Dores Road, Inverness.
Mr and Mrs D. Williams, Laggan View, Dores Road, Inverness.
Mr E. Williams, Laggan View, Dores Road, Inverness.
Mr W. H. A. Williamson, 7 Lovat Road, Inverness.

Dr E. I. Young, O.B.E., 36 Broadstone Park, Inverness.
Mrs L. A. Young, Galewood, Culloden Road, Inverness.
Mr R. M. D. Young, Langhouse, Nairn.
Mr R. M. Young, Langhouse, Nairn.

INDEX TO PEOPLE

CC

INDEX TO PLACES

Unless letters are given before a Map Reference, they should be read as NH.